Energy Choices in the Near Abroad

The Haves and Have-nots Face the Future

Energy Choices in the Near Abroad

The Haves and Have-nots Face the Future

AUTHOR

Robert E. Ebel

 THE CENTER FOR STRATEGIC & INTERNATIONAL STUDIES WASHINGTON, D.C.

About CSIS

The Center for Strategic and International Studies (CSIS), established in 1962, is a private, tax-exempt institution focusing on international public policy issues. Its research is nonpartisan and nonproprietary.

CSIS is dedicated to policy analysis and impact. It seeks to inform and shape selected policy decisions in government and the private sector to meet the increasingly complex and difficult global challenges that leaders will confront in the next century. It achieves this mission in three ways: by generating strategic analysis that is anticipatory and interdisciplinary, by convening policymakers and other influential parties to assess key issues, and by building structures for policy action.

CSIS does not take specific public policy positions. Accordingly, all views, positions, and conclusions expressed in this publication should be understood to be solely those of the author.

Library of Congress Cataloging-in-Publication Data

Ebel, Robert E.
    Energy choices in the Near Abroad : the haves and the have-nots /
Robert E. Ebel.
        p. cm. — (CSIS report)
    Includes bibliographical references.
    ISBN 0-89206-271-1
        1. Energy policy—Former Soviet republics. 2. Power resources—Former Soviet republics.
I. Title. II. Series.
HD9502.F672E24 1997   96-49937
333.79'0947—dc21   CIP

The Center for Strategic and International Studies
1800 K Street, N.W., Washington, D.C. 20006
Telephone: (202) 887-0200
Fax: (202) 775-3199
E-mail:books@csis.org
Web site: http://www.csis.org/

Contents

Pipeline Maps

About the Author

Robert E. Ebel is an internationally recognized expert on oil and energy issues. Formerly vice president for international affairs at Enserch Corporation, Ebel advised the corporation on global issues relevant to day-to-day operations. He has also held posts at the Central Intelligence Agency, the Department of the Interior, and the Federal Energy Office. He traveled to the Soviet Union in 1960 as a member of the first U.S. petroleum industry delegation, and in 1971 with the first group of Americans to visit oil fields in Western Siberia. Mr. Ebel presently is director, Energy and National Security, at the Center for Strategic and Internationl Studies. He holds and M.A. in international relations from the Maxwell School at Syracuse University and a B.S. in petroleum geology from Texas Tech. Mr. Ebel, author of two recent CSIS publications, *Energy Choices in Russia* (1994) and *Chernobyl and its Aftermath* (1994) was director on the project which produced the CSIS Panel Report *Nuclear Energy Safety Challenges in the Former Soviet Union* (1995).

CHAPTER 1

Introduction

The Soviet Union dissolved in December 1991 into 15 sovereign and independent nations, each with its own national interests and hopes for future prosperity and peace, but with conflicting interests that jeopardize those hopes.

During the Soviet era, Moscow had not permitted the individual Soviet republics to become sufficient in energy. Instead, each was specialized. For example, investment capital was directed to develop oil[1] and natural gas in Western Siberia, to the detriment of production elsewhere. Azerbaijan's oil-producing sector received very little capital, but its capacity to manufacture oil and gas field equipment was heavily emphasized. Ukraine and Lithuania became centers for nuclear power generation. Uzbekistan became the cotton-growing center of the former Soviet Union, but was kept dependent on Russian oil. Kazakstan and Turkmenistan were not allowed to develop their oil- and gas-producing potential. Any and all oil and natural gas exported beyond Soviet borders was transported by Russian pipelines.

When the Soviet Union broke up, the comparative fuel and energy advantage of such specialization among the republics was quickly transformed into a fuel and energy vulnerability. Would Russia now continue to supply the former republics with fuel in the amounts they required and at the favorable prices of the past? Or, would Russia sell to the former republics at arm's length—at world market prices and only for hard currency?

The energy-dependent former republics had little choice but to continue to look to Russia for oil and natural gas to meet their needs: acquiring supplies outside the former Soviet Union was not an option. First, paying for energy from non-Russian suppliers was impossible given the lack of hard currency. Second, the infrastructure inherited from the Soviet days was designed to handle supplies moving within the Near Abroad, not to facilitate imports from the outside.

The Republics of the Former Soviet Union

Russia remains the largest and most politically and economically powerful of the 15 republics. In Russia, the other 14 republics are often referred to as the "Near Abroad," a term also used in this report to refer to these 14 republics—Armenia, Azerbaijan, Belarus, Estonia, Georgia, Kazakstan, Kyrgyzstan, Latvia, Lithuania, Moldova, Tajikistan, Turkmenistan, Ukraine, and Uzbekistan. The term CIS (Commonwealth of Independent States) refers to 12 of the republics of the Near Abroad—excluding the three Baltic states of Estonia, Latvia, and Lithuania.

---

1.   Used in this report to refer to both crude oil and petroleum products.

Increasingly, however, the Baltics are being included by implication in what Russians refer to as the "Far Abroad," all nations outside the boundaries of the Near Abroad. For example, Russian statistical reporting agencies often allocate Russian oil exports between members of the CIS and the Far Abroad, which implicitly includes the Baltics in the latter group. Also, general statistical data provided by Moscow, such as inflation rates or gross domestic product (GDP), are usually reports for members of the CIS only.

The Haves and the Have-Nots

The republics of the Near Abroad are often grouped geographically. The Central Asia republics are Kazakstan, Kyrgyzstan, Tajikistan, Turkmenistan, and Uzbekistan. The Transcaucasus includes Armenia, Azerbaijan, and Georgia. The Baltics, as noted, comprises Estonia, Latvia, and Lithuania.

The natural resource endowments of the republics in each of these geographical groupings are similar to some extent, such as the overall terrain and climate, extent and type of mineral deposits, and access to water transport. However, the oil and natural gas resources of the republics diverge widely, often within a single region. Therefore, for the purposes of this report, the Near Abroad is divided into "Haves" and "Have-Nots" in terms of whether their indigenous fuel supplies are sufficient to meet their domestic energy needs.

The Haves—Azerbaijan, Kazakstan, Turkmenistan, and perhaps Uzbekistan—have the potential to be self-sufficient in energy and to become major exporters. The Have-Nots—the Baltics, Belarus, Armenia, Ukraine, Moldova, Georgia, Tajikistan, and Kyrgyzstan—are all dependent on Russia to supply oil and natural gas to meet their domestic demand. The Have-Nots must either develop their own resource bases, which are constrained by geology, or build mutually advantageous trading relationships with the Haves. Currently unable to pay for their oil and natural gas imports from Russia, even at concessionary prices, the Have-Nots cannot realistically consider exchanging dependence on Russia for dependence on Western energy suppliers, who would charge world market prices and would require payment in dollars.

The Haves

Azerbaijan, Kazakstan, Turkmenistan, and Uzbekistan have sufficient oil and/or natural gas reserves to satisfy domestic demand. Substantial oil discoveries had been made, but not developed, including the Azeri-Chirag-Gunashli grouping in the Caspian offshore Baku in Azerbaijan and the Tengiz and Karachaganak fields in Kazakstan. Turkmenistan has world-class natural gas resources. These three former republics have the potential to develop substantial exportable surpluses, to transform their economies using export-derived income and to secure their status as sovereign nations.

The fourth Have, Uzbekistan, has more limited energy resources and holds little current prospect of becoming a major exporter, but it can fairly easily meet its modest domestic demands. Uzbekistan is working to become self-sufficient in crude oil, a goal it reached in 1996, and has a relatively small exportable surplus in natural gas. Nevertheless, Uzbekistan must rely on pipelines through Russia to export natural gas to foreign customers. Its limited export potential does not justify construction of new pipelines outside its borders.

During the Soviet era, Moscow virtually ignored the potential for energy development outside Russia. The bulk of capital investment was directed toward the oil fields of Western Siberia and the natural gas fields of the Yamal Peninsula, which flourished. Planners in Moscow found it easier to seek the quicker and less labor-intensive returns on capital in these areas than to undertake the more challenging, time-consuming, costly, and risky task of developing discoveries in Azerbaijan, Kazakstan, and Turkmenistan. Instead, Moscow chose to take care of the energy needs of these three republics with supplies from other sources.

This forced dependency on Russia has worked to the ultimate benefit of Azerbaijan, Kazakstan, Turkmenistan, and even Uzbekistan. By not developing oil and natural gas production in these republics and leaving their resources relatively untouched, Moscow in effect has provided a guarantee for their financial—and political—independence.

Foreign investors bring capital and advanced technology to the table, while the Haves contribute their natural resource base. One advantage is worthless without the other. The investors and the Haves need each other if resource development is to proceed. But some of the Haves reject this mutual dependence. Just send money, they say, and we will do it ourselves, reflecting a spirit of nationalism unencumbered by reality. Foreign investors are not entrepreneurs in that sense. Rather, access to oil is the driving motivation. If access cannot be secured under acceptable commercial conditions, attention will turn elsewhere. Oil and natural gas resources may hold future promise for the Haves, but for the present, they are a heavy burden. If these former republics successfully exploit their energy potential and prudently invest the oil- and gas-derived income, they may join the ranks of developed nations. Conversely, significant delays in or failure of efforts to develop energy resources will bring economic stagnation and political grief. In truth, too much emphasis has been given in these countries to the potential future profits from oil and natural gas production, and this has raised expectations for greatly improved living standards that may be impossible to meet. These expectations will be particularly difficult to meet if the public objects to the arrangements and accommodations that will have to be made with Western investors to fully develop the energy resources.

In Azerbaijan, Kazakstan, and Turkmenistan, production levels had been declining at worrisome rates, not because oil and natural gas reserves have been depleted, but because the capability to put these reserves to work has been exhausted. Investment capital has been scarce, and the technology embodied in available oilfield equipment has not been up to the task. The recognition of this state of affairs led to an opening of the door to foreign investors, who responded eagerly. Nonetheless, despite their willingness to invest, foreigners have not always found the investment conditions acceptable.

Uzbekistan, in contrast, had been the only former republic where oil and natural gas production had risen since the Soviet breakup, although output levels remain comparatively small.

Virtually all the oil- and natural gas-related projects offered to foreign investors—whether joint ventures or production-sharing arrangements—involve deposits that have been confirmed and where production may have already begun. In effect, investors have traded the geological and technical risks normally associated with energy investments for the political risks associated with investing in these politically unstable countries.

All four Haves face political challenges that may compromise their ability to fully develop their energy potential. Strong and sometimes violent dissident and separatist movements have threatened political stability in Azerbaijan, for example. The governments in both Turkmenistan and Uzbekistan strongly resemble the authoritarian governments of the Soviet era. In Kazakstan, declining living standards hold the potential to ignite latent ethnic and regional tensions and cause political instability.

To date, foreign investors have reached agreement with the government of Azerbaijan to explore and develop a number of oil fields offshore in the Caspian Sea. The Azerbaijan International Operating Company (AIOC), a group of Western oil companies, is to develop the Azeri, Chirag, and deep-sea portion of the Gunashli oil fields. Another consortium is to develop the Karabakh oil field, and a third will develop the Shah Deniz oil field. One participant in all three consortia is LUKoil, Russia's largest vertically integrated oil company.

A fourth consortium, to develop the Dan Ulduzu and Ashrafi oil fields, to the north of the AIOC project, was approved in December 1996. The initial membership, which has Amoco in the lead at 30 percent, excludes LUKoil. Observers anticipate however that SOCAR, the State Oil Company of Azerbaijan, may eventually yield a portion of its 20 percent interest to LUKoil.

In Kazakstan, foreign investors are involved in three major projects: developing the giant Tengiz oil field, developing the Karachaganak gas condensate deposit, and searching for hydrocarbons in the northeast portion (the Kazak sector) of the Caspian Sea.

Western investment in Turkmenistan currently centers around developing proposed pipelines to transport oil and natural gas to markets to the south (Pakistan and India) and to transport natural gas to markets to the east (China and Japan) and the west (Europe).

The ability of Azerbaijan, Kazakstan, Turkmenistan, and Uzbekistan to fulfill their export potential and achieve political, financial, and energy independence from Russia depends largely upon the availability of pipelines to carry their exports to foreign markets. All now rely on the existing, Soviet-built pipeline infrastructure, which links them only with Russia and other states in the Near Abroad. Because of its dependence on earnings from oil and natural gas exports, Russia is very protective of its export pipelines. Access is granted to non-Russian producers only on a limited basis, after domestic transport needs have been met. Moreover, the current system has little spare carrying capacity. The four Haves will require new pipelines that circumvent Russia. At the same time, Russia's national interests will be best served by maintaining or restoring past linkages with producers in the Haves and with markets in both the Near Abroad and the Far Abroad. Pipeline access is often based on nothing more than politics, and the players in the game of pipeline politics include Russia and the Haves; the transit states of Armenia, Georgia, and Turkey; and the host governments of those oil companies that hope to develop oil and gas production in the Haves.

The Have-Nots

The remaining 10 republics of the Near Abroad historically have been almost completely dependent on Russia and the Haves to meet their fuel and energy needs. Before the breakup of the Soviet Union, these republics were insulated from the vagaries of world energy markets. Supplies were plentiful, and prices were heavily subsidized. Energy was regarded almost as a free good, and there was no reason to conserve or to invest in energy-efficient technology and equipment. As a result, energy consumption was profligate and energy intensity remains a multiple of the industrial West.

Some of the Have-Nots face greater problems than securing reliable and affordable energy supplies. Armenia, Georgia, Moldova and Tajikistan face civil war, dissident activities, and separatist movements. Belarus also faces significant political uncertainty with a president that is pushing for expanded personal powers and a return to the warm embrace of Mother Russia. Kyrgyzstan and Ukraine, although relatively quiescent politically, face severe fiscal constraints and declining living standards that could inflame latent ethnic and cultural tensions, particularly between Russian and non-Russian populations.

Russia's Steel Umbilical Cord

In the Soviet Union, a steel umbilical cord—a system of oil and gas pipelines—linked Mother Russia with the other republics, providing consumers with a steady and reliable flow of oil and natural gas at heavily subsidized prices. This network of pipelines largely withstood the trauma of Soviet disintegration and still provides nourishment to the Near Abroad, albeit at significantly reduced levels and much higher prices. Both the Haves and the Have-Nots have inherited a legacy of highly energy-intensive economies which can only be addressed by a complete makeover of the energy-consuming sector, including the pricing, billing, and collections systems.

Russian crude oil deliveries to the Near Abroad have declined by almost 2 million barrels per day (b/d) since 1990, which is basically equivalent to Russian crude oil exports to the Far Abroad during 1996. An overall decline in economic activity within the other republics has allowed Russia to continue to export oil and natural gas to markets outside the Near Abroad. These exports have been the leading earner of foreign exchange for Russia, absent which Moscow would have lost much of its ability to finance imports, service debts, and purchase equipment and technology from the West.

Further reductions in crude oil exports were planned for 1996, and preliminary reports show a decline in crude oil deliveries during the year of about 19 percent, to 479,000 b/d. Deliveries of Russian petroleum products to the Near Abroad were cut severely, by more than half. There has been an increase in so-called give-and-take arrangements, under which a refinery will process a given amount of crude oil for a fee or payment in kind (i.e., the refinery will keep some of the petroleum products). The petroleum products are then returned to the crude oil supplier. These kinds of arrangements serve crude oil producers that have no access to refining capacity but need products for marketing activities.

Russian natural gas exports to the Near Abroad—chiefly to Belarus, Moldova, and Ukraine—have held relatively constant over the past several years and continued to do so during 1996. Natural gas pipelines used to transport Russian exports to Europe must pass through these three countries, and it is therefore in Russia's interest to satisfy their natural gas requirements. Cutting off supplies to these three countries would jeopardize Russia's ability to fulfill its contracts with European buyers.

Pipeline Politics

The ability to develop oil and natural gas resources for export will be critical to the economic futures of all the Haves: Russia will continue to rely on oil and gas exports for hard currency, the Have-Nots will continue to depend upon regular energy supplies from Russia and are therefore dependent on Russia's ability to maintain its export capabilities. The Haves need to break their dependence on Russia's infrastructure. The political and economic futures of these countries therefore are closely bound to the construction of politically secure and financially viable pipelines to carry oil and natural gas to hard-currency export markets.

Because Azerbaijan, Kazakstan, Turkmenistan, and Uzbekistan are landlocked and physically isolated from potential markets in the Far Abroad, pipeline routes must be selected before field exploration and development can proceed. The financial viability of building certain of the proposed pipelines is questionable, primarily because of the great distances that separate centers of production and consumption. For example, proposed pipelines that would carry natural gas from Turkmenistan or oil from Kazakstan to consumers in China and Japan, although technically feasible, would be so costly that the delivered product likely would not be cost-competitive.

Yet the dominant concern is not economic—that is, how much crude oil and natural gas will be put into the market place, who are the likely buyers, and the impact these new supplies might have on prices. Instead, the dominant concern is largely political—what route any pipelines will take.

Several pipeline routes have been proposed to carry Azeri crude oil to world markets, all of which were technically feasible and would have imposed no unusual requirements on pipeline construction companies. Most were financially viable as well. But none could be characterized as politically secure—all pass through territories beset by civil war, dissident activities, or separatist movements. All parties involved understandably pursued some measure of influence and control over the final routes, which raised the political stakes.

A single route through Iran, which some partners in the AIOC considered best, could not be considered because of the U.S. policy of containment toward Iran, which prohibits U.S. firms from engaging in business arrangements that materially benefit Iran. Eventually, a two-pipeline option was selected: a western route from Baku to Supsa, Georgia, and a northern route from Baku to Novorossiisk, Russia.[2] In the end, politics rather than economics had prevailed. The two-pipeline policy was vigorously pursued by the United States because it offered added security to both producers and consumers and made winners out of all the players, avoiding the costly political dissension that opting for a single route would have caused. In fact, President Bill Clinton placed a telephone call to Azeri President Heydar Aliyev to stress the importance to have two exit routes for the early oil.[3]

What does a producer look for in the way of an export pipeline? First, if the risk of political insecurity is high, there should be multiple routes. Second, the tariffs charged must be reasonable, not punitive. Third, there must be no discrimination when allocating access to a pipeline's carrying capacity. Fourth, the rewards to the pipeline owner(s) must be proportionate to the risks involved. Finally, a pipeline should be built incrementally, in phases if possible, so that subsections can be put into operation as they are completed. This helps keep capital investment under control, reduces costs, and limits risk.

The importance of the eventual pipeline routings has not been lost on any of the players, especially Russia. According to the leading Russian newspaper *Izvestiya:*

> The struggle for future routings of crude oil from CIS countries to the world market is entering a decisive stage. The victor in this struggle will receive not only billions of dollars annually in the form of transit fees. The real gain will be control over pipelines, which will be the most important factor of geopolitical influence in the Transcaucasus and in Central Asia in the next century.[4]

Each prospective pipeline route faces political challenges. These local, regional, and international political challenges are of such long standing that there may be no feasible long-term solution. The conflicts of the region include:

❑ Abkhaz separatist movements in Georgia that occasionally erupt into violence. For example, Georgian president Eduard Shevardnadze narrowly escaped being killed by a bomb that exploded near his car in August 1995.

❑ Conflict between Armenia and Azerbaijan over Nagorno-Karabakh, a Christian-Armenian enclave created by the Soviet Union within the Mus-

---

2.   *Washington Post,* September 25, 1995. Washington's view on Caspian oil export pipelines was perhaps best expressed by Glen Rase, Director, International Energy Policy, U.S. Department of State, at a conference in London on February 23–24, 1995. His remarks had the enticing theme "Oil and Caviar in the Caspian." Among other things, he stressed the need for any pipeline "to make economic and commercial sense on its own merits." See *Middle East Economic Survey,* April 13, 1995.

3.   According to a White House spokesman, the president "expressed his support for commercially viable, early constructed, and multiple oil pipelines from the Caspian Sea region that would benefit the companies that were investing in oil development as well as all the countries of the region." UPI, October 2, 1995.

4.   *Izvestiya,* June 15, 1995.

lim-Turkic republic of Azerbaijan. When the Soviet Union began to disintegrate, the ethnic Armenians of Nagorno-Karabakh rose up to demand reunion with Armenia. There is now an uneasy cease-fire, but ethnic Armenian forces occupy up to 20 percent of Azerbaijan. Russia, which has two divisions stationed in Armenia to help enforce the cease-fire, hinted that it would end the cease-fire if Azerbaijan is not compliant to Russian wishes.[5]

❏ Struggles in Turkey between the government and Kurdish minorities.

❏ The Chechen rebellion against Russia, which threatens the security of pipelines from Azerbaijan.

❏ U.S. policy in the region, particularly its containment policy toward Iran which prohibits U.S. companies from activities that materially benefit Iran and has therefore slowed investment for construction of pipelines to transport Azeri and Kazak oil exports.

To some, the Caucasus remains the obvious route for transporting oil and gas from Central Asia to Mediterranean and European markets. The feasibility of using that route is affected by political tensions among and within the old nations and the new republics of the Caucasus and by regional rivalries that involve the major external players, notably Russia, the United States, and Iran.[6]

Within Russia, pipeline politics focuses on the narrower issue of access to the operating pipeline network. The matter of route selection for new export pipelines has yet to engender the publicity or the political gamesmanship that have attended the proposed pipeline routes for moving Azeri, Kazak, and Turkmen oil and natural gas to world markets.

One exception is the projected expansion of oil production in the Timan-Pechora, a very promising oil-bearing region in the Russian Northwest, which will demand new pipeline carrying capacity. The issue of where to locate this new pipeline capacity has pitted the Timan-Pechora Company (TPC)—the Western consortium seeking to develop oil in this region—against Transneft, the Russian joint stock company responsible for all oil pipelines in the country. The TPC prefers construction of a pipeline from the oil fields to a terminal on the Barents Sea. Transneft is designing a link between the producing areas and Primorsk, a terminal on the Baltic Sea, and on to Porvoo, Finland. The TPC is not prepared to invest unless and until a production-sharing law is enacted that will provide an acceptable level of risk protection.

---

5.   See "Oil and National Policy," Issue Brief (The Forum for International Policy), October 1995.

6.   John Roberts, "The Gate at the End of the World," *Geopolitics of Energy*, July 1, 1995. In this article, Mr. Roberts, editor of *Middle East Monitor*, recalls the Mamisson pass, known in classical days as the Gate at the End of the World: "Two thousand years ago, after subduing the Iberians of present day Georgia and the Albanians of present day Azerbaijan, the Roman general Pompey came to the Mamisson on his way home. Here, he decided, was Rome's natural frontier, the barrier that should not be breached. Pompey, it is said, locked the Gate. That gate is still locked today."

A Historical Perspective

The question of how to move crude oil from its place of production to refineries and then to move the finished products to the consumer has confronted the industry since the beginning. In the early days in the United States, crude oil was carried to the nearest railroad in wooden barrels, piled up in wagons drawn by horses. There the railroad took over. The cost of moving the crude by horse-drawn wagon to the nearest rail stop usually exceeded the cost of the much longer rail shipment. To break the monopoly held by the wagon drivers, wooden pipelines eventually were laid to connect the wells with nearby railroads.

By that point, John D. Rockefeller and his Standard Oil Company had strengthened his position within the U.S. oil industry, initially through the acquisition and expansion of refining capacity, and, by the early 1870s, Rockefeller had control over the largest refinery group in the world. Also at about this time, the supply of crude oil grew much faster than demand. Crude oil prices fell sharply, and Rockefeller used the opportunity to acquire assets at very low prices, coming to dominate not only refining capacity but also transportation.

One last effort was made by a group of independent producers to break Rockefeller's hold. These producers undertook construction of the U.S. first long-distance pipeline, 110 miles long. Four others shortly followed. The success of these pipelines forever changed the oil industry by allowing markets distant from sources of production to also benefit from this new form of energy. The successful challenge to Rockefeller and his Standard Oil was made possible by the creation of independent access to markets.

While Rockefeller was leading the way in the United States, an oil industry was being developed in Azerbaijan, led by the efforts of the Nobel Brothers, who put together a vertically integrated oil company in much the same way Rockefeller had. There were several important differences between the U.S. and Azerbaijan industries, however.

First, foreign capital played an extremely important role in financing the development of oil in Azerbaijan. The United Kingdom was by far the largest investor, the U.S. share was insignificant. Second, from the beginning, a comparatively large share of Baku production was exported—after all, that was why the foreign investors were there: to gain access to oil. In contrast, the U.S. market absorbed whatever could be produced.

Oil was exported from Baku only via the port of Batumi on the Black Sea. To facilitate exports, a pipeline was built between Baku and Batumi during 1897–1905. The Imperial Russian government did not utilize the pipeline to increase its own exports, but instead placed extremely high tariffs on oil transported through the pipeline as a way of increasing government income. These high tariffs strangled exports by virtually eliminating profits. Oil was diverted to consumers in the interior of Russia by river, to take advantage of lower shipping costs. The opportunity to considerably expand exports was lost because of Moscow's greed.

Return of the Foreign Investor

Azerbaijan, Kazakstan, and Turkmenistan stand today where the independent U.S. oil producers stood a century ago. Without pipelines to move the oil and natural gas to export markets, production cannot be expanded.

The attention of the world oil industry has turned to the former Soviet Union. Independent producers, large and small oil companies, oilfield equipment manufacturers and suppliers, service companies, and advisers of all kinds scramble to search out business opportunities. At the same time, the host governments have been almost overwhelmed by the responsibilities of trying to move peacefully and successfully from command economies to free markets, while simultaneously trying to provide a mutually advantageous investment climate.

Foreign oil investors have arrived in Russia, Azerbaijan, Kazakstan, and Turkmenistan for four quite compelling reasons:

❒ the attraction of something that has been denied in the past but that is now available;

❒ the world-class production potential of these countries;

❒ the need for international involvement in order for this production potential to be fulfilled within an acceptable time-frame;

❒ the fact that the oil and gas that will be developed will not be needed to meet domestic requirements but will be available for export.

Back to the Future

> It will be sad to see how the magnet of oil draws great armies to the Caucasus; it will be fascinating to examine how the oil companies mobilize their forces of diplomacy to fight their battles across green tables and behind the scenes...; it should be enlightening to study how far the foreign policies of nations, in the matter of recognition, of credits, etc., are influenced by that universal lubricant and irritant—oil....[7]

These words were written almost 70 years ago, but they come close to capturing what is taking place today. The multinational oil companies have returned to the Caucasus in search of oil. Battles are being fought over green tables and behind the scenes. Foreign policies have been adjusted to ensure that national interests are being served, in part through the oil companies.

The world, however, is far different today than it was in 1926. A trading interdependence among both exporter and importer nations now serves the security and well-being of both. Even so, there was considerable reluctance among the republics of the Near Abroad to allow foreign oil investors back in, for a variety of reasons:

❒ nationalism—why provide foreign capitalists, who not long ago were our

---

7.   Louis Fischer, *Oil Imperialism* (New York: International Publishers, 1926).

enemies, with access to our natural resources?;

❏ reluctance of government authorities to take responsibility for making decisions that would drastically alter their oil sectors;

❏ a complete absence of experience in negotiating at the world level;

❏ limited understanding of how a market economy worked.

All these factors, together with frequent changes in government, have combined to delay by several years the inflow of needed foreign investment. As a result, the energy sectors of the Haves continue to face the consequences of past mismanagement, obsolete oilfield technology, and a general shortage of investment capital.

The Export Potential of the Haves

How much oil and natural gas might be moving out of the Haves within the next decade? A number of factors will influence the answer.

❏ Will the necessary pipeline capacity be available?

❏ What will be the production capacity of Azerbaijan, Turkmenistan, and Kazakstan, and will world oil prices encourage full utilization of that capacity?

❏ Will regional conflicts hamper the development of oil and energy resources?

❏ Will there be changes in the Russian market that make it more profitable for the Haves to pursue Russian customers instead of those in the Far Abroad— for example, might Russia then pay world market prices and have a convertible ruble?

❏ Will Iran renounce its support of terrorism and thereby become an acceptable transit country for oil exports from the Near Abroad?

❏ What will the demand for oil and natural gas be in Armenia, Azerbaijan, Georgia, Kazakstan, and Moldova? What share of Azeri and Kazak production will be go to meet this demand, and how much will be available for export?

Oil-importing countries have searched for years for an acceptable alternative to Persian Gulf oil, for supplies that are more secure and less subject to political manipulation. The level of interest in how Caspian oil will be developed and moved to market indicates to some that Caspian oil may be that alternative. Not so.

In fact, at its peak, Caspian oil—defined to include production from Azerbaijan, the Kazak Caspian shelf, and offshore at Turkmenistan—may amount to about 3 percent of world supplies. Adding in Russian supplies, the capacity of the Near Abroad remains a small fraction of the Persian Gulf capacity. In addition, oil from the Near Abroad is not readily accessible to world markets and is more costly to produce. As shown in Table 1-1, the peak production of both Azerbaijan and Kazakstan (which will may between 2005 and 2010) may be on the order of 1.5–2 million b/d. In contrast, in 1995, daily world trade in oil averaged almost 70 million bbl. In addition, not all Azeri and Kazak production will be available for export, particularly to the Far Abroad.

Table 1-1
Azeri, Kazak, and Turkmen Peak Future Crude Oil Production

Source	Million b/d
Azerbaijan	
AIOC	0.7
Karabakh	0.25
Shah Deniz	0.2
Other	0.25
Subtotal	**1.4**
Kazakstan	
Tengiz	0.7
CaspiShelf	0.9
Karachaganak	0.3
Subtotal	**1.9**
Turkmenistan	0.3*
Total	**3.6**
*Offshore only	

OPEC: An Interested Observer

The potential discovery and development of new sources of oil in the Near Abroad carry significant implications for the Organization of Petroleum Exporting Countries (OPEC). Although OPEC has been careful not to react negatively to the attention being paid to the Near Abroad, clearly its members must consider how much world oil demand will be captured by new oil from this region. Much of the incremental growth in world demand during the past several years has been lost to non–OPEC producers which, in turn, has meant little growth in oil prices and no increase in OPEC production quotas since September 1993.[8]

OPEC estimates that new oil supplies from the Haves will average more than 1.8 million b/d by 2010 (Table 1-2). (Note that the data in this table are estimates of export volume, not total production, and therefore are not directly comparable to the production estimates given in Table 1-1.)

Table 1-2
OPEC Estimates of the Export Potential of Azerbaijan, Kazakstan, and Turkmenistan

Year	Export Potential (thousand b/d)			
	Total	Azerbaijan	Kazakstan	Turkmenistan
2000	625	167	398	60
2005	1,505	684	714	107
2010	1,823	819	791	213

Source: *OPEC Bulletin*, September 1995.

The Impact of U.S. Policy

Broad U.S. policy aims in the region are straightforward: to support the development of the former Soviet republics into independent, sovereign, and economically viable states that can become full members of the European family of nations. Specific U.S. policies have numerous implications—direct and indirect—for the future ability of the Haves to make this transformation. U.S. policy toward Iran is a particularly powerful influence.

The United States seeks to contain Iran as punishment for Iran's continuing support of terrorism and its continuing efforts to acquire nuclear weapons capabilities. Under U.S. policy, U.S. commercial firms are prohibited from engaging in actions or programs that would be of material comfort and aid to Iran. For example, Conoco was forced to relinquish a major oil-related business opportunity in Iran because the operation would yield significant benefits for Iran.

This very firm U.S. position has major implications for Azerbaijan, Kazakstan, and Turkmenistan, as it effectively precludes them from securing financing for any pipeline project that would transit Iran. The United States can be expected to exercise its full powers to attempt to dissuade any international lending institution or commercial lending facility from becoming involved in such a pipeline.

An argument can be made that one result of U.S. policy has been to deny competitive sources of supply to oil importers in Southeast Asia and East Asia, the areas of the world where demand is growing fastest. If and when Iran and the United States reach an accommodation—which is likely to be later rather than sooner—a pipeline through Iran to carry Azeri and Kazak exports to these markets will not be far behind.

---

8. *Platt's Oilgram News*, October 17, 1995.

Another result of U.S. policy toward Iran may be to negate overall U.S. policy to assist the former Soviet republics in moving toward democracy and a market economy. The future ability of the Haves to make this transition is tied to their ability to significantly increase their oil and gas production, which will be possible only with the involvement of Western—and largely U.S—oil companies. As noted, a side-effect of the U.S. sanctions has been to delay desperately needed financial infusions for developing oil and natural gas exports.

The delays that have been the unintended result of U.S. policy have played to the advantage of Russia, which has solidified its policies and has secured desired equity positions in major developmental projects.

One clear example of how Russia has exploited these delays is in Turkmenistan, which has a world-class natural gas resource base but is landlocked. Turkmenistan's only access to potential export markets is through the Russian pipeline network. A Turkmen-Iran-Turkey-Europe natural gas pipeline was proposed soon after the Soviet breakup, and it appeared to be technically, politically, and commercially feasible. Financing could not be secured, however, because of the tightening of U.S. sanctions on Iran, and the pipeline remains unbuilt. Other options have been proposed, but these have been less attractive and no less risky. With Western investment in developing Turkmen gas production stymied, Turkmenistan's only immediate option has been to make an accommodation with Gazprom, the Russian natural gas monopoly, in order to gain access to an export pipeline network.

The validity of U.S. policy toward Iran is unquestioned—the U.S. sanctions that have been imposed are fully supported by available intelligence on Iran's continued support for terrorism. The one glaring weakness of U.S. policy, however, is the absence of international support: U.S. sanctions against Iran are unilateral, and unilateral sanctions rarely work. In fact, some U.S. allies have been quick to exploit business opportunities in Iran that are presently denied U.S. companies. At the same time, the European policy of constructive dialogue with Iran has been no more successful than the U.S. containment policy in bringing about positive changes in Iran. That is not to say that Iran has not suffered from containment, but much of the financial pressure that Iran has experienced as a result of reduced oil revenues have been attributable less to U.S. sanctions than to a soft world oil market.

While U.S. foreign policy toward Iran has had a number of indirect consequences for the Haves, the effects of U.S. policy toward Azerbaijan have been significant and direct. Section 907 of the U.S. Freedom Support Act of 1992 prohibits the United States from providing any assistance to Azerbaijan, except for nonproliferation and disarmament matters. Assistance through nongovernmental organizations and by the U.S. government was allowed if the government of Azerbaijan were not involved. The legislation was a response to the Azeri blockade of Armenia that grew out of the ethnic conflict over Nagorno-Karabakh, an Armenian enclave in Azerbaijan, and was in part the result of heavy lobbying of Congress by Armenian groups. Section 907 reads, in part:

> United States assistance under this or any other act...may not be provided to the government of Azerbaijan until the President determines and so reports to Con-

gress, that the government of Azerbaijan is taking demonstrable steps to cease all blockades and other offensive uses of force against Armenia and Nagorno-Karabakh.

Congress granted some relief in early 1996, when it passed legislation that permits direct humanitarian assistance to Azerbaijan in the event that nongovernmental assistance is insufficient to meet the requirements of refugees and displaced persons, a determination to be made by the President.[9]

Foreign operations funding for fiscal year 1997 has relieved somewhat the burdensome language of Section 907. Now, assistance to Azerbaijan, including to Nagorno-Karabakh, by nongovernmental and international organizations shall not be precluded from using and repairing Azeri government facilities or services such as housing, warehouses, clinics, hospitals, and vehicles to effectively deliver humanitarian services and supplies to needy civilians. Previously, no Azeri government property of any form or type could be used, which placed ridiculous constraints on humanitarian assistance programs.

Nigerias of the Future?

In Azerbaijan, Kazakstan, and Turkmenistan, oil- and gas-derived revenues eventually will drive the economy. Will these revenues be spent wisely, or will they be wasted—as they have been in certain oil-exporting developing nations, such as Nigeria—on mega-projects for public show, subsidies for consumer goods and services, or lost through corruption?

In Azerbaijan, there are reports of growing public apathy and frustration about the pace of economic improvement. Recent parliamentary elections predictably (and suspiciously, to some) strengthened the hand of President Heydar Aliyev. Aliyev has brought a certain measure of stability to the country and was instrumental in the signing of the "contract of the century"—the agreement between the Azeri government and the Western-led AIOC to develop the offshore Azeri, Chirag, and Gunashli oil fields. Nonetheless, for the average Azeri, life remains unchanged, a struggle simply to make ends meet.

For Kazakstan, the initial failure of the Caspian Pipeline Consortium (CPC) to reach an agreement on construction of the Tengiz-Novorossiisk pipeline has been financially and politically costly. The original consortium has been replaced with a broader-based grouping, under terms and conditions that should allow construction to proceed. However, the delay gave Russia an opportunity to secure an equity position in the development of the Tengiz oil field and a dominant position in the Tengiz-Novorossiisk export pipeline.

In Kazakstan, which is struggling economically, tens of millions of dollars are being spent on palaces for President Nursultan Nazarbayev, on mosques for the public, and on vacant hotels for foreign business travelers. Water and electricity were once provided free of charge, although their availability is uncertain. If Turkmen natural gas exports continue to be channeled largely to countries of the Near Abroad, Turkmenistan will not be much different tomorrow than it is today. Gain-

---

9.   *FBIS-SOV*, February 2, 1996.

ing access to hard-currency markets for gas exports, without depending on the Russian gas pipeline infrastructure, is a prerequisite for any substantial economic growth. Unfortunately, all the proposed pipelines suffer from a combination of political and financial constraints that mean no early relief is in sight.

Russian Interests

Successfully developing the oil and gas potential of the Near Abroad will require finding compromises that serve the divergent interests of the parties involved. Such compromises will likely focus on building pipelines that simultaneously serve the needs of the Haves and offer transit states a vested interest in peaceful oil and gas development in these countries. Unfortunately, not all the interested parties may be willing to accept compromise.[10]

In practice, compromise has also meant giving Russia a seat at the table—and this translates into equity participation in pipeline construction and operation and in oil development projects. This has already proved to be the case for developing the oil fields offshore at Baku, developing the Tengiz field in Kazakstan, and building an export pipeline to Novorossiisk; it is also proving to be the case for the planned development of the Karachaganak gas condensate deposit and of Turkmen natural gas. There have been a number of not-so-subtle reminders that Russia will have the final say about how and when oil from Azerbaijan and Kazakstan and natural gas from Turkmenistan will flow to Western markets.

The designation of LUKoil as the sole coordinator of all Russian hydrocarbon exploration in the Caspian Basin clearly solidifies that company's primary role in forwarding Moscow's foreign interests. For example, when LUKoil secured a 32.5 percent equity in the Karabakh (Azerbaijan) oil field, Russian minister of fuels and energy Yuri Shafranik described it as a tremendous victory for the Russian oil industry and for Russian diplomacy.

One unresolved issue that is central to Russian interests is the legal status of the Caspian Sea—whether it is considered a sea or a lake under international law. Currently, each of the five littoral states—Azerbaijan, Iran, Kazakstan, Russia, and Turkmenistan—unilaterally is moving to develop its offshore resources. If the Caspian were designated a lake, all five littoral states would be required to reach joint agreements before offshore resources could be developed outside a 10–mile territorial zone.[11] In practice, this would mean the approval of all five states would be required for any development project outside territorial waters, which would jeopardize many current projects (unless there was a grandfather clause) and dissuade future foreign investment.

---

10.   Writing in the November 3, 1995, issue of *Prism,* Paul Goble proposes creation of a regional petroleum export authority. He cited three prerequisites: the construction of multiple pipelines through as many countries as possible, the division of transit fees among the countries regardless of the actual flow of oil, and a long-term commitment by Europe, the United States, and Japan to purchase oil and gas from these countries. As Goble points out, the politics of the issue raise serious doubts about the feasibility of actually creating such an authority.

11.   *Intercon's Daily,* May 17, 1995.

Two of the five littoral states—Azerbaijan and Kazakstan—have significant offshore oil and gas potential and naturally want the Caspian to be divided into national sectors, based on the median line principle (a position the United States finds legally compelling). Under the median line approach, the Russian and Iranian sectors would have less-than-promising energy reserves, although it is important to note that little or no exploration has taken place in these two sectors.[12]

Russia began to raise the question of the legal status of the Caspian Sea in January 1994, when the Russian foreign ministry used it as the basis for its objection to the Azeri's draft convention on the legal status of the Caspian, which appropriated the richest sites for Baku. Later that same month, Russia protested the actions by Turkmenistan to unilaterally define boundaries within the Caspian.[13]

The Russian government's position has not been entirely consistent. The Russian foreign ministry has been the champion of the legal position that the Caspian is a lake and has taken an unequivocal stand that it considers all agreements between the government of Azerbaijan and foreign investors to unilaterally develop oil in the Caspian Sea to be null and void unless and until the legal status of the Caspian has been resolved. This position has been questioned by Russia's Ministry of Fuels and Energy and by Prime Minister Viktor Chernomyrdin.

A declaration on the Caspian Sea was signed by Russian President Boris Yeltsin and Kazak President Nursultan Nazarbayev on April 27, 1996, in Almaty, Kazakhstan. The declaration calls for a consensus on the Caspian's legal status among the five littoral states. A key clause permits both Russia and Kazakstan to carry out their own exploration and production activities and allows for mutual cooperation in their waters, which, in effect is an opening for Russia to become involved in offshore oil activities in Kazakstan. If the other littoral states sign this declaration, Russia will have achieved a major policy aim—involvement, or at least the right of involvement, in the energy sectors of the other four Caspian states.

The foreign ministers of the five littoral states subsequently met in Ashgabat, Turkmenistan with the legal status of the Caspian as the key agenda item. Each country reportedly came to the meeting with their own proposal for an exclusive economic zone. Iran favored a 10-mile zone, Russia—20 miles, Turkmenistan—60 miles, and Kazakstan-80 miles, while Azerbaijan wanted the entire Caspian divided into national sectors.[14] Ultimate agreement was comparatively no closer but at least the process had begun.

❏ A Working Group was established to develop a convention on the status of the Caspian Sea.

❏ Russia was ready to recognize jurisdiction out to 45 miles. The central part of the Caspian would be held in a joint stock company by all Caspian nations on a parity basis, the Russian foreign minister said. (See Map 1.)

❏ Russia indicated it could recognize jurisdiction outside the exclusive eco-

---

12.   *Izvestiya,* October 26, 1995.
13.   *Russian Petroleum Investor,* June 1995.
14.   Open Media Research Institute, *Daily Report,* November 12, 1996.

M A P 1 .

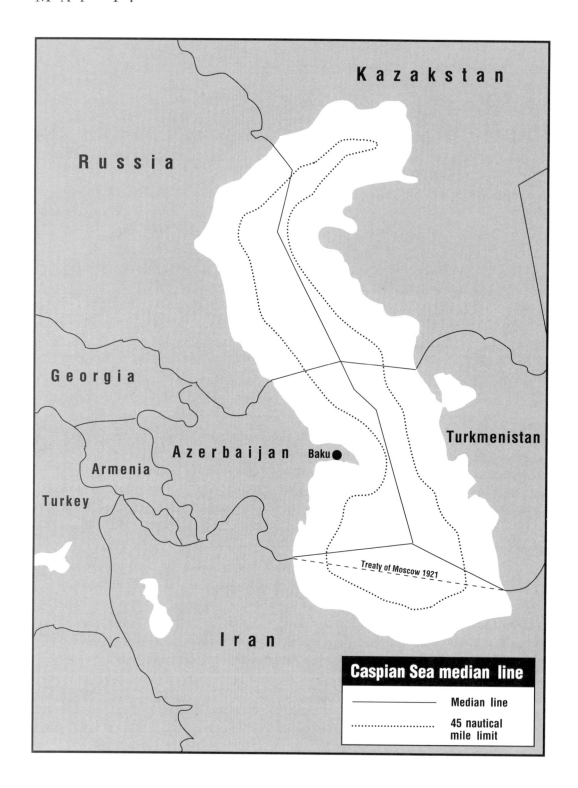

nomic zone, provided the fields were being, or about to be, developed.

The Russian approach would create the semblance of a hole in the center of the Caspian, and has become known to diplomats as the "doughnut" approach.

At the same time, and undoubtedly on purpose, Russia, Turkmenistan, and Iran signed a memorandum on cooperating in developing Caspian Sea oil resources. The other two states were invited to join in, but refused to do so.[15] The consortium to be formed would not operate outside the member-countries' national sectors.

Of more immediate concern than the legal status of the Caspian Sea, however, is the fact that its water level rose by 8.25 feet between 1978 and mid–1995. Caspian waters have moved on dry land in Kazakstan an average of 15–20 kilometers, flooding large areas of agricultural land and a number of oil fields.[16] The reasons for this dramatic rise remain unknown, and scientists do not know when the rise will stop, but it is expected to continue for at least 25 to 30 years. Within the next 15 years alone, up to 100 villages, 40 oil fields, and countless highways, railroads, water lines, and oil pipelines will be submerged. There is the prospect of severe environmental damage if shut-in oil wells are corroded by salt water.

Facing the Future

The easy division of the Near Abroad into Haves and Have-Nots masks the difficulties each of these nations faces as it either attempts to fully exploit its energy export potential (the Haves), develop an affordable and reliable supply of energy to guarantee future economic growth at an acceptable political cost (the Have-Nots), or continuing to play a critical role in the energy sectors of the Near Abroad while developing viable export markets in the Far Abroad (Russia).

None of these nations has a particularly clear idea of how best to tackle these future challenges, and none is self-sufficient enough to resolve them independently. The only certainty may be that Western participation and capital will be essential for each and every former Soviet republic. Russia and the Haves will require capital and technology from the West in order to fully exploit their energy export potential, and the Have-Nots will require Western financial assistance, investment capital, and know-how to make the transition to a market economy and to build the economic and human infrastructure necessary for long-term growth.

The economic challenges ahead will be a heavy burden for each of the former Soviet republics. Those republics with substantial oil and gas resources will face the added political challenge of reining in public expectations for future growth and prosperity, which, if unmet, may bring social and political crisis.

The Haves both need and want foreign investment, but they may not necessarily want it on the terms under which it is available. The Haves will find it necessary to accommodate the interests of Russia, Iran, Turkey, the United States, and other nations for which oil and gas is an economic and/or political commodity. They

---

15.   Open Media Research Institute, *Daily Report,* November 13, 1996.

16.   *Foreign Broadcast Information Service, Former Soviet Union* (hereafter, *FBIS-SOV*), July 14, 1995.

must balance the risks and potential benefits of moving closer to the West or staying closely aligned with Russia.

Azerbaijan, Kazakstan, and Turkmenistan are now poised to join the ranks of major crude oil and natural gas producers and exporters. But their political and economic futures will be closely bound to the success of efforts to build politically secure and financially viable pipelines to carry their oil and natural gas to hard-currency export markets.

The Have-Nots, for the most part, will remain dependent upon Russian energy supplies to meet the overwhelming portion of their needs because geology argues against the development of any meaningful local production. The governments of the Have-Nots therefore must contend with serious trade imbalances that will be corrected only by entering barter arrangements with Russia or, preferably, by developing a strong capacity to export goods and services that are competitive in world markets.

The decline in economic activity in the Near Abroad has allowed Russia to maintain its position as a major supplier of oil and natural gas to markets in the Far Abroad. These exports, in turn, have been the primary source of foreign exchange, absent which Russia would have lost much of its ability to finance imports, service debts, and purchase equipment and technology from the West.

Russia will seek to maintain control over existing export pipelines and will insist that new pipelines transit Russia and terminate at Russian ports. Other parties involved will find it necessary to accommodate Russia's interests or risk delaying or blocking development of the energy resources that are vital to the future economic and political health of the Near Abroad.

The remainder of this report is organized into three sections that reflect the natural division of the Near Abroad into Haves and Have-Nots. The first sector outlines the interests and prospects of the key player in the region's energy sector, Russia.

Section II surveys energy prospects of the Haves—Azerbaijan, Kazakstan, Turkmenistan, and Uzbekistan. This section describes the energy capacity of each of these former republics and explores the technical, political, and economic considerations factors that will affect their ability to become self-sufficient in energy.

Section III examines the energy prospects of the Have-Nots—Armenia, the Baltics, Belarus, Georgia, Kyrgyzstan, Moldova, Tajikistan, and Ukraine.

The final section offers a summary of key trends and developments and some broad recommendations for U.S. policy. The appendices provide statistical tables and supplementary data, a glossary of terms and abbreviations, and an index.

CHAPTER 2

Mother Russia's Steel Umbilical Cord

During the Soviet era, a steel umbilical cord—a system of oil and gas pipelines—linked Mother Russia with the other republics. This steel cord provided consumers with a steady and reliable flow of oil and natural gas at heavily subsidized prices. Indeed, consumers had come to regard these fuels as virtually free goods. Protected from the vagaries of price fluctuations, there was little incentive to conserve or to invest in more fuel-efficient technology and equipment. The cost of fuel could be safely ignored by the factory manager and the residential consumer alike.

This network of pipelines has largely withstood the trauma of Soviet disintegration and still provides nourishment, albeit at much reduced levels and at comparatively much higher prices. However, both the Haves and the Have-Nots have inherited highly energy-intensive economies that can be made more efficient only by a complete remake of the energy consuming sector, including the pricing, billing, and collections systems.

The decline in economic activity in the Near Abroad since the Soviet breakup has allowed Russia to maintain its position as a major supplier of crude oil and natural gas to markets outside the former Soviet Union. These exports in turn have been the leading earner of foreign exchange for the country. Absent these earnings, Russia would have lost much of its ability to finance imports, service its debts, and purchase equipment and technology from Western suppliers.

Russian crude oil deliveries to the Near Abroad have declined by more than 1.9 million b/d since 1990, which is basically equivalent to the 2 million b/d of Russian crude oil exports to the Far Abroad during 1996.[17] In other words, had the crude oil appetite of the Near Abroad not been so severely reduced, exportable surpluses available for delivery to the Far Abroad would have been eliminated completely.

---

17. Russia's capacity to export crude oil to the Far Abroad, considering pipeline and port limitations, is placed at about 2 million b/d. Design carrying capacity of the pipeline infrastructure reportedly falls between 2.2 to 2.4 million b/d. See *Neft i Kapital*, November 1996. Officials had planned for crude oil exports of 1.97 million b/d during 1996 but strains arise when allocating that export capacity. Who gets what? Joint ventures are given priority rights under certain government ordinances, with these rights totalling 80,000 b/d during 1996. But the Russian government has been appropriating more and more of the available oil export capacity as a way of securing funding for various activities. That in turn puts the squeeze on domestic producers who find themselves with reduced access to export pipelines and forced to sell in the lower-priced domestic market, rather than the more lucrative foreign market. See *Russian Petroleum Investor*, December 1996-January 1997.

Russian natural gas deliveries to the Near Abroad—chiefly to Belarus, Moldova, and Ukraine—have held relatively steady over the past several years. These three countries are important pipeline transit countries because they separate Russia from Europe. Russia is best served, therefore, by continuing to satisfy the natural gas requirements of these three former republics to ensure that there is no disruption in pipeline exports to European customers.

There is no hard evidence that Russia has played politics with its fuel deliveries. Cuts in Russian oil and natural gas exports to the Near Abroad have largely paralleled the decline in fuel requirements. To the contrary, deliveries have continued in the face of sizeable arrears on the part of the importing countries. Arrears had reached 15.2 trillion rubles by the end of April 1996, mostly for natural gas imports, but had been reduced to 8.3 trillion rubles by the beginning of November 1996. Various approaches are being employed to settle these debts, including among others, debt-equity swaps and converting arrears into long-term government debt.

Oil and Natural Gas Exports to the Near Abroad

Following the Soviet breakup, the Have-Nots had little choice but to continue to look to Russia for oil and natural gas supplies. The lack of hard currency made it impossible to look to suppliers outside the FSU, and the existing energy infrastructure had been designed to handle supplies moving within the FSU, not to facilitate imports from the outside.

Russian exports of crude oil, petroleum products, and natural gas to the Near Abroad in 1995 were barely one-quarter of the 1990 level (Table 2-1). The decline in deliveries of petroleum products appeared even more dramatic: only 73,200 b/d of petroleum products were made available by Russia to the Near Abroad—roughly one-half the amounts scheduled. Exportable surpluses of Russian petroleum products have been overwhelmingly directed to hard-currency markets.

Table 2-1
Russian Oil and Natural Gas Exports to Near Abroad,
1990–1996

Year	Crude Oil (million b/d)	Petroleum Products (million b/d)	Natural Gas (billion cubic meters)
1990	2.412	0.760	153.2
1991	2.348	0.540	155.8
1992	1.51	0.320	106.1
1993	0.952	0.240	78.8
1994	0.751	0.166	76.1
1995	0.622	0.066	73.2
1996 est.	0.479	0.031	71

Sources: OECD/IEA, *Energy Policies of the Russian Federation, 1995 Survey* (Paris: 1995); Supplement to *Delovyye Lyudi*, October 1994; Interfax, *Petroleum Information Agency*, Moscow, December 15, 1995; *Finansovyye Izvestiya*, January 18, 1996; British Broadcasting Corporation, *Summary of World Broadcasts, Part 1, Former USSR*, February 8, 1996 and May 2, 1996.; 1996 data from Tables 2-3 and 2-4.

Preliminary estimates indicate further cuts were made in oil and gas deliveries to the Near Abroad during 1996. Russian crude oil deliveries to the Near Abroad have fallen by more than 1.9 million b/d since 1990, while petroleum product deliveries have almost vanished, with 1996 deliveries equivalent to less than 3 percent of those volumes supplied during 1990. Exports of Russian natural gas to the Near Abroad have held up comparatively much better, having declined by roughly 54 percent. Contrary to some suggestions, Russia has not been playing politics with its exports of oil and natural gas to the Near Abroad. The sharp cuts in exports should be attributed to reduced requirements, together with a continuing inability or unwillingness to pay. Certainly no western supplier of oil or natural gas would have continued deliveries when confronted with such high arrears on the part of the importers.

The decline in Russian crude oil production from a peak of 11.4 million b/d during 1988 to around 6 million b/d in 1996 should not be linked to the dissolution of the Soviet Union. Past oil field mismanagement practices and the shortage of investment capital had already dictated a collapse, which indeed had set in three years prior to the political breakup. Had the Soviet Union held together, instead of falling apart, but faced with a troubled oil producing sector and declining output, what decision would Moscow have made: cut sales to buyers outside the Soviet Union, cut exports to the other 14 republics, or cut both proportionately? We will never know, but current oil deliveries to the Far Abroad almost perfectly match the volumetric cuts to the Near Abroad.

Reduced fuel requirements in the Near Abroad and Russia's need to maximize hard-currency earnings from its exportable surpluses of oil and natural gas have increased the relative importance of the Far Abroad as an export market (Table 2-2).

Table 2-2
Declining Role of Near Abroad in Russian Oil and Gas Exports

Percent of Total						
	Oil*			Natural Gas		
Year	Far Abroad	Near Abroad	Total	Far Abroad	Near Abroad	Total
1992	53	47	100	47	53	100
1994	76	24	100	57	43	100
1995	82	18	100	62	38	100
1996 est.	85.3	14.7	100	63.5	36.5	100

*Both crude oil and petroleum products.

Sources: Interfax, *Petroleum Information Agency*, Moscow, December 15, 1995; *FBIS-SOV*, February 20, 1996; *Interfax*, Moscow, February 13, 1996; British Broadcasting Corporation, *Summary of World Broadcasts, Part 1, Former USSR*, May 2, 1996; and Tables 2.1, 2-3, and 2-4; Interfax, *Petroleum Information Agency*, December 11, 17, and 27, 1996; *Neft i Kapital*, December 1996-January 1997.

However, not everybody is willing to accept the reported declines in industrial output in the Near Abroad at face value. A number of factors serve to distort official statistics, including widespread underreporting of output in order to avoid high taxes, overrepresentation of large state-owned industrial enterprises that are undergoing major retrenchment, and shortcomings of data collection in capturing ever-increasing private sector activities.

In an International Monetary Fund working paper, two economists, by relating electricity consumption levels, concluded that Russian GDP had not dropped as much as had been thought, perhaps by no more than 20 percent, that in part statistics had tended to overlook the growing shadow economy.

These World Bank economists considered electricity consumption to be a suitable proxy for guesstimating real output trends. On this basis, the output downturn in the individual countries of the former Soviet Union has been seriously overstated.[18] Employing this approach, the output downturn in the period 1989–1994 may have been inflated by more than twofold for Ukraine and by as much as threefold for Azerbaijan.

Now, doubt has been cast upon that approach. Recent Russian reports indicate that the energy intensity of the Russian economy had risen by 50 percent the past 5 years. Energy waste, high losses during transmission, an inefficient and aging capital equipment base—all contribute to high power consumption rates unrelated to economic activity.[19]

---

18.   World Bank, *Transition*, Volume 6, no. 9–10. Some skeptics argue that power consumption may not be a suitable proxy for economic activity in transition economies that are experiencing rapid and massive structural changes. Many argue that the increase in electricity consumption may reflect structural movement toward higher electricity intensity in GDP. (See Appendix Table A-1, Power Consumption and Gross Domestic Product (GDP) Trends, 1989–1994)

19.   Open Media Research Institute, *Daily Report*, November 12, 1996.

Oil

The bulk of the oil exports to the Near Abroad is delivered to just two importers—Ukraine and Belarus—which together accounted for 70 percent of all oil sold to the Near Abroad in 1994 and almost 79 percent in 1996 (Table 2-3). This oil export pattern is a carryover from the Soviet era. Large refining centers had been established in Ukraine and Belarus, in part because of the availability of crude oil via the Druzhba pipeline and in part because of high local demand. Most of the remaining republics were comparatively minor consumers and were supplied from regional refining centers.

Table 2-3
Russian Oil Exports to the Near Abroad,
by Importing Country, 1994 and 1996

Importing Country	Crude Oil (thousand b/d)		Petroleum Products (thousand b/d)	
	1994	1996	1994	1996
Ukraine	316.4	157	30.6	6.1
Belarus	207	221	11.8	6.3
Kazakstan	88.4	66	24.6	
Uzbekistan	61.8		0.1	
Turkmenistan	0.3			
Kyrgyzstan			3.5	
Tajikistan			1.8	
Georgia	2.0		0.2	
Armenia	2.7		2.3	
Moldova			10.2	
The Baltics	70.6	33	22.2	16.5
Total	749.1	479	110.2	30.8

Note: Totals may not add because of rounding.

Source: *Neft i Kapital*, September 1995: Interfax, *Petroleum Information Agency*, Moscow, December 16 and 17, 1996.

Natural Gas

Russian natural gas exports to the Near Abroad declined by about 54 percent during 1991–1994. At the same time, sales to the Far Abroad were increasing slightly, from 96 billion cubic meters (bcm) in 1990 to 105 bcm in 1994, and further to 123.6 bcm in 1996. Total Russian natural gas exports reached a reported 194.6 bcm in 1996[20], with the share allocated to the Near Abroad declining to 36.5 percent. Generally speaking, the negative trends attributable to the Russian gas industry—

declines in production and declines in deliveries to the Near Abroad—are almost wholly market-related; natural gas stays in the ground when there are no customers under contract.

The overwhelming portion—almost 87 percent—of Russian natural gas exports to the Near Abroad in 1996 was directed to Ukraine and Belarus (Table 2-4), which is a typical pattern. This concentration indicates low levels of demand for natural gas in the other importing countries.

Table 2-4
Russian Natural Gas Exports to the Near Abroad, 1994 and 1996

Importing Country	Billion cubic meters	
	1994	1996
Ukraine	55.0	48.5
Belarus	14.0	13.1
Moldova	3.2	3.2
Lithuania	1.6	4.1
Latvia	1.3	4.1
Estonia	0.5	4.1
Total	76.1	71
Note: Totals derived independently.		
Source: OECD\IEA, *Energy Policies of the Russian Federation, 1995 Survey* (Paris: 1995); Interfax, *Petroleum Information Agency*, Moscow, December 16 and 24, 1996.		

Energy-Related Indebtedness

There is little evidence to support the contention that Russia forced the reductions in oil and gas shipments to the Near Abroad, for example, to free up volumes for export to the Far Abroad or to exert political pressure upon the recipient country. To the contrary, Russian deliveries have continued despite mounting arrears on the part of these countries (Table 2-5). Physical shortages, where they have occurred, have come about because of an unwillingness or an inability on the part of the importer to pay for the fuels. Supplies have been available; funds have not.

The three Baltic states of Estonia, Latvia, and Lithuania—which are not members of the Commonwealth of Independent States and are increasingly considered part of the Far Abroad—today purchase oil and natural gas from Russia at world market prices. Other buyers in the Near Abroad continue to be favored with below-market prices, although these prices have been steadily rising. Payments, when made, are in the form of hard and local currencies, plus a variety of barter arrangements. More recently, arrears have been converted into long-term government debt.

20.   Interfax, *Petroleum Information Agency*, Moscow, December 24, 1996.

Table 2-5
Energy-Related Debts of the Near Abroad to Russia,
as of November 1996

Country	Trillion Rubles
Ukraine	3.69
Belarus	1.049
Moldova	2.156
Kazakstan	1.319
Baltics	0.123
Total	8.337

Source: Interfax, *Petroleum Information Agency*, Moscow, December 17, 1996.

The energy-related debt to Russia on part of the Near Abroad grew during 1995 and 1996, amounting to about $3.9 billion.[21] Ukraine is the biggest debtor and most of its unpaid bills relate to natural gas. Some 95 percent of Russian gas exports to Europe—a major source of hard-currency earnings—transits Ukraine by pipeline. Cutting off deliveries to Ukraine is impossible without consequently interrupting deliveries to Europe. As a result, Ukrainian arrears mount, at the expense of Gazprom, the Russian natural gas monopoly.

Two other transit countries are next in terms of arrears: Belarus, which is responsible for 12.6 percent of the total debt of the Near Abroad, mostly for natural gas, and Moldova, which is responsible for 26 percent of the total debt, all for gas. Russia has no viable means of cutting off deliveries to these pipeline transit countries, even with such high levels of nonpayment.

Debts were steadily paid down during 1996, to 12.5 trillion rubles by August and further to 8.3 trillion rubles by the beginning of November. Debts should again increase, however, with the onset of the winter months which translate into higher natural gas imports and delayed payments.

Russian sales of natural gas to Ukraine, Belarus, and Moldova serve as a form of foreign aid. Continued fuel supplies are vital to the political and economic stability of these importers, but these countries are not in a position to make little more than token cash payment for their imports.

---

21.   Interfax, *Petroleum Information Agency*, Moscow, January 10, 1996. These debts paled alongside arrears accumulated within Russia. For example, by May 1, 1996 electric power consumers owed a total of 67.6 trillion rubles ($13.3 billion). The power plants in turn owed 29.1 trillion rubles (about $5.8 billion) for fuel, largely natural gas. Despite all the negative implications deriving from consumer arrears—wages going unpaid, repairs and upgrading postponed or not performed at all, and shortages of fuel for lack of funds—there still is a strong reluctance to punish debtors by cutting off electricity and heat. See *Interfax*, Moscow, May 21, 1996.

Pipeline Politics

The Caspian Sea basin is of unquestioned and generally untouched oil and gas potential, but three of the littoral states—Azerbaijan, Kazakstan, and Turkmenistan—are landlocked. Pipeline routes therefore must be selected before field exploration and development can get under way. Broad-scale investments in these activities cannot be justified unless and until access to export markets has been secured. The importance of the eventual pipeline routes is clear to all the players, especially Russia.

At present, pipeline politics in Russia is fairly limited to gaining access to the operating pipeline network. The matter of route selection for new export pipelines has not yet generated the publicity or the political gamesmanship that has been evident in efforts to construct pipelines to move Azeri, Kazak, and Turkmen oil and natural gas to world markets.

One area where the issue has been joined is in the Timan-Pechora, a very promising oil-bearing region in the Russian Northwest. Developing these resources requires construction of new pipeline carrying capacity, and selecting a route for this pipeline is a source of tension between the Western consortium developing Timan-Pechora—the Timan-Pechora Company (TPC)—and Transneft, the Russian joint stock company responsible for all oil pipelines in the country. Specifically, the TPC prefers that the pipeline go from the oil fields to a terminal on the Barents Sea, while Transneft is working on a design to link the oil fields with Primorsk, a terminal on the Baltic Sea, and beyond to Porvoo, Finland. In the interim, the TPC is unwilling to invest unless and until a production-sharing law is in place to adequately protect its investment.

This tension is indicative of the future, although the pipeline politics of the Caspian Sea will be transcendent. Because it is inevitable that new oil and gas exports from Azerbaijan, Kazakstan, and Turkmenistan will compete with Russian exports for market share, it is also inevitable that Russia will seek to control export pipelines and to insist, to the extent possible, proposed pipelines transit Russia and terminate at Russian ports. Russia clearly will benefit from any delay in the arrival of Azeri, Kazak, and Turkmen energy supplies in foreign markets.

The stakes are high. Russia continues to be dependent on energy exports for much-needed foreign exchange, and the political and economic futures of the Haves are dependent on developing their energy export potential. For all these countries, then, access to politically secure and financially viable pipelines is essential. Existing pipelines are the means by which Russia will maintain or restore past linkages with producers in the Haves and with markets in both the Near Abroad and the Far Abroad. New pipelines are the means by which the Near Abroad will gain access to new supplies and new markets.

Russia seeks to ensure that all pipelines will transit Russia and terminate at Russian ports and that Russia gains an equity stake in pipeline construction and oil development projects. To date, Russia has been successful with regard to the latter, but less in terms of pipeline routings.

LUKoil, the company that coordinates all Russian hydrocarbon exploration in the Caspian Basin, succeeded in gaining an equity stake in the Azerbaijan International Operating Company (AIOC), the Western consortium developing fields offshore in the Caspian Sea. The importance of LUKoil's 10 percent equity share in the consortium was underscored by Russian Minister of Fuels and Energy Yuri Shafranik, who described it as a tremendous victory for the Russian oil industry and for Russian diplomacy.

In addition, it appears that the bulk of the early AIOC oil will move northward to the Russian Black Sea port of Novorossiisk. Russia helped ensure that Iran—Russia's most logical competitor as a transit country for Azeri oil—was effectively taken out of consideration by committing to complete for Iran the Bushehr nuclear power plant. This reinforced U.S. fears that Iran would develop nuclear capabilities and bolstered the case for continued U.S. sanctions against Iran.

Russia has two strong cards to play in the game of pipeline politics: control of access to the Volga-Don waterway and the legal status of the Caspian Sea.

The Volga-Don waterway is the route by which oilfield equipment and supplies will move into the Caspian Sea. Denial by Russia of access to that waterway would quite considerably raise the cost of developing Caspian Sea energy. Conflict between the littoral states concerning the Caspian legal status will not be easily nor readily resolved. Nonetheless, developmental plans offshore Azerbaijan and Kazakstan are moving ahead.

Legal Status of the Caspian Sea

One unresolved issue that is central to everyone's interests is the legal status of the Caspian Sea—whether it is considered a sea or a lake under international law. Using the median line approach would allows each of the five littoral states—Azerbaijan, Iran, Kazakstan, Russia, and Turkmenistan—to unilaterally develop its offshore resources. If the Caspian were designated a lake, all five littoral states would be required to reach joint agreements before offshore resources could be developed outside a 10-mile territorial zone.[22]

The Caspian Sea covers an area of more than 420,000 square kilometers, much larger than the whole of California. The water is the deepest in the central and southern part, where the depth exceeds 1,000 meters. The northern portion is comparatively shallow, but that also means the northern portion can stay frozen for up to 3 months during the winter. The Volga, the largest of the European rivers, empties into the landlocked Caspian Sea. Delivery of oil field equipment and supplies from the west to projects offshore in the Caspian can be made via the Volga-Don Canal, which links the Volga with the Don River, flowing eastward from Ukraine.

Russia bases its legal position on agreements between Russia and Iran dated February 25, 1921, and March 25, 1940, but neither of these agreements refer specifically to offshore oil and gas development. With the independence of the former Soviet littoral states, these agreements essentially lost their legal force.[23]

---

22.   *Intercon's Daily,* May 17, 1995.

23.   *FBIS-SOV,* July 14, 1995. Another source *(FBIS-SOV,* July 18, 1995) refers to the document signed on March 25, 1940, as the Treaty on Trade and Navigation. No agreements were signed pertaining to the division of the Caspian, and there are no international documents on this subject.

Two of the five littoral states—Azerbaijan and Kazakstan—have significant offshore oil and gas potential and naturally want the Caspian to be divided into national sectors, based on the median line principle (a position the United States finds legally compelling). Under the median line approach, the Russian and Iranian sectors would have less-than-promising energy reserves, although it is important to note that little or no exploration has taken place in these two sectors.[24]

Russia began to raise the question of the legal status of the Caspian Sea in January 1994, when the Russian Foreign Ministry used it as the basis to object to the Azeri's draft convention on the legal status of the Caspian, which appropriated the richest sites for Baku. Later that same month, Russia protested the actions by Turkmenistan to unilaterally define boundaries within the Caspian.[25]

The Russian government's position has not been entirely consistent. The Russian Foreign Ministry has championed the position that the Caspian is a lake and has taken an unequivocal stand that it considers all agreements between the government of Azerbaijan and foreign investors to unilaterally develop oil in the Caspian Sea to be null and void unless and until the legal status of the Caspian has been resolved. This position has been questioned by Russia's Ministry of Fuels and Energy and by Prime Minister Viktor Chernomyrdin.

Another illustration of the seeming divergence of views within the government is Russia's agreement to establish joint ventures with Iran to develop oil and gas fields in the Caspian Sea and to export oil from the region, an agreement to which Turkmenistan may become a third party.[26] This agreement appears to fly in the face of the Russian Foreign Ministry's position that the agreement of all five littoral states is required for such an arrangement. In fact, a joint Russian-Iranian statement issued at the conclusion of the visit by Russian Deputy Prime Minister Aleksei Bolshakov, during which the joint venture agreement was signed, questioned the legal right of the AIOC to develop the Caspian oil fields awarded to it. A senior Russian Foreign Ministry official declared:

> In keeping with the Caspian region's current status, the Caspian Sea does not belong to any of the coastal states, and the issue of the division of any object of joint use is always extremely painful, creating new problems in relations between these countries.[27]

He added that only Kazakstan and Azerbaijan insist on dividing the Caspian Sea, while Russia, Turkmenistan, and Iran "are ready to regard it as an object of joint use on a reliable international and legal footing."

Despite the fact that Russia's LUKoil has secured an equity stake in the AIOC, the Russian Foreign Ministry still declares that Caspian oil development requires the consent of all five littoral states. Aleksandr Khodakov, chief of the ministry's legal department, stated that Russia would not recognize any unilateral claims, unsupported by international accords, to any sectors or parts of the Caspian Sea.

---

24.   *Izvestiya,* October 26, 1995.
25.   *Russian Petroleum Investor,* June 1995.
26.   *FBIS-SOV,* October 31, 1995.
27.   *Interfax,* Moscow, November 2, 1995.

"At the same time," he said, "we do not deny the right of any of the adjacent countries to develop and extract natural and mineral resources in the Caspian Sea. The involvement of Russian companies in specific projects in the region does not contradict this stand, and we see no ground for hampering their activity."[28]

The Russian Foreign Ministry's position is legally weak. An opinion rendered to an oil company in 1994 concluded:

> Under international law the natural resources of the seabed and subsoil of the Caspian Sea are now owned in common. Those resources should be divided in accordance with equidistant lines, with some minor modifications to take into account historic rights, de facto boundaries and practical considerations.[29]

In other words, if the question of the legal status of the Caspian Sea were submitted to an international court or other tribunal, delimitation would be based on the median line principle.

A declaration on the Caspian Sea was signed by Russian President Boris Yeltsin and Kazak President Nursultan Nazarbayev on April 27, 1996, in Almaty, Kazakstan. The declaration calls for a consensus on the Caspian's legal status among the five littoral states. A key clause permits both Russia and Kazakstan to carry out their own exploration and production activities and allows for mutual cooperation in their waters, which, in effect is an opening for Russia to become involved in offshore oil activities in Kazakstan. If the other littoral states sign this declaration, Russia will have achieved a major policy aim—involvement, or at least the right of involvement, in the energy sectors of the other four Caspian states.

Russian Foreign Minister Yevgeniy Primakov issued an order on August 6, 1996 creating a special working group for the Caspian Sea within the Foreign Ministry, underscoring the importance of this issue. Among other things, this working group is to develop proposals on Russia's position on the status of the Caspian Sea.[30]

The foreign ministers of the five littoral states met in Ashgabat, Turkmenistan during November 12-13, 1996. Some softening of the Russian position could be noted, but Azerbaijan and Kazakstan continued to press for the definition of the Caspian as a sea, and employing the median line principle to define national sectors.

James Collins, a senior Department of State official, was in Baku at the time of the Ashgabat meeting. He presented a letter to Azeri president Aliyev from President Clinton, stating, among other things, that "the United States would back" agreements between all Caspian states on the division of the sea's resources and their intensive development—agreements which would "clearly define" ownership rights and allow unimpeded shipments in the Caspian region.[31]

---

28.   *ITAR-TASS,* Moscow, October 25, 1995.
29.   Bruce M. Clagett, "Ownership of Seabed and Subsoil Resources in the Caspian Sea under the Rules of International Law," *Caspian Crossroads,* Summer/Fall 1995.
30.   *Pipeline News*, no. 24, August 31, 1996.
31.   Interfax, *Petroleum Information Agency*, Baku, November 18, 1996.

The Caspian Sea legal card is still Russia's to play, backed apparently by Iran and perhaps Turkmenistan, who seems not quite sure just which side to support at this time. Nonetheless, it is clear, at least in Russian eyes, that responsibility for resolving the question at hand rests with the five littoral states, and no one else.

Of more immediate concern than the legal status of the Caspian Sea, however, may be the fact that its water level rose by 8.25 feet between 1978 and mid–1995. Caspian waters have moved onto dry land in Kazakstan by an average of 15–20 kilometers, flooding large areas of agricultural land and a number of oil fields.[32] The reasons for this dramatic rise remain unknown, and scientists do not know when the rise will stop, but it is expected to continue for at least 25 to 30 years. Within the next 15 years alone, up to 100 villages, 40 oil fields, and countless highways, railroads, water lines, and oil pipelines will be submerged. There is the prospect of severe environmental damage if shut-in oil wells are corroded by salt water.

Chechnya

One complication in Russia's efforts to secure access to and control over the pipeline network. is the rebellion in Chechnya. A quiescent Chechnya was important to Russia if oil produced by the AIOC was to flow through Russian enroute to world markets. Some observers have suggested that the decision by Moscow to send military forces into the breakaway republic of Chechnya was motivated by a desire to secure control over the Chechen oil industry. This is unlikely; production of crude oil in Chechnya in 1994 was only about 28,000 b/d—a production level too low to justify military intervention. In addition, the refineries in Grozny are seriously outdated and are therefore no prize.[33]

The recent war and ongoing tension threaten the security of that portion of the pipeline from Baku to Tikhoretsk. Pipelines and pumping stations may offer attractive targets for terrorist attacks by dissidents. The Russian government recently exempted oil exports from Chechnya to the Far Abroad from all duties and excise taxes, routed all Chechen oil exports through Novorossiisk and Tuapse, and earmarked oil export earnings for reconstruction of the damaged economy.[34] Although these exports will be insubstantial—averaging perhaps 30,000 b/d—this gives Chechen leaders a vested interest in ensuring the continued operation of the Grozny-Novorosiisk link of the northern route.

Exporting Chechen crude oil ostensibly would leave nothing for the Grozny refineries. To resolve that, then Russian Fuels and Energy Minister Yuri Shafranik has suggested that Kazak crude oil might be used to fill the gap. "After restoring their normal capacity, Chechen oil refineries will be capable of annually processing up to 5 million tons (100,000 b/d) of Kazak oil," he said.[35]

---

32.   *FBIS-SOV,* July 14, 1995.

33.   See Robert E. Ebel, "The History and Politics of Chechen Oil," *CSIS Post-Soviet Prospects,* January 1995.

34.   *FBIS–SOV*, October 25, 1995.

35.   Interfax, *Petroleum Information Agency,* Khanty-Mansiisk, December 10, 1995.

Conclusion

Russia is heavily dependent on the foreign exchange earned by its exports of oil and natural gas. Maintaining and expanding the ability to export oil and natural gas to hard-currency markets is therefore a vital Russian national interest. New oil and gas supplies from the Haves will inevitably compete with Russian exports in markets in both the Near Abroad and the Far Abroad. Russia therefore seeks to exert some control over these new sources of supply. Specifically, Russia seeks equity participation in the construction of any new pipelines and the development of any new oil and gas resources and it also seeks to ensure where it can that all new pipelines will transit Russia and will terminate at Russian ports.

Russia retains significant leverage over the Haves in the game of pipeline politics. The Haves will remain dependent upon the Soviet-era energy infrastructure until new pipelines are completed. Russia also wields political and economic influence that will make it imperative that the four Haves accommodate Russian interests or risk jeopardizing their energy future.

The Have-Nots will continue to be dependent upon Russia to supply their energy needs. In order to correct the trade imbalances and indebtedness that will be the result of this energy dependence, the Have-Nots will need to develop the potential to export goods and services that are competitive in markets in the Near Abroad and the Far Abroad. Russia will also need to find alternative ways to dispose of the high levels of energy debts owed it by the Have-Nots.

Source: States of the Former Soviet Union, CIA, 1992.

CHAPTER 3

Azerbaijan

Table 3-1
Azerbaijan at a Glance

Currency	Manat*
Rate of Exchange	4,371 manat/$1 (April 19, 1996)
Gross Domestic Product	
Inflation	84.6 percent (1995)
Population	7.79 million (1995 est.)
By Nationality	
Azeri	90 percent
Dagestani	3.2 percent
Russian	2.5 percent
Armenian	2.3 percent
Other	2 percent

*Introduced on 1 January 1994, with the official exchange rate set at 118 manat/$1.

Sources: *Finansovyye Izvestiya*, September 14, 1995; Central Intelligence Agency (CIA), *The World Factbook 1995* (Washington,D.C.: CIA, 1995); Interfax, *Financial Information Agency*, Moscow, January 18, 1996; Open Media Research Institute, *Daily Report*, April 26, 1996.

During the twentieth century, Azerbaijan has undergone a series of changes in its political status. In 1917, in the wake of the Russian revolution, Azerbaijan, Georgia, and Armenia were linked together as an independent Transcaucasian federation. This association failed quickly because of irreconcilable differences in national and religious beliefs. In May 1918 Azerbaijan declared its independence; it was briefly occupied by British troops at the end of World War I. In April 1920, following the British withdrawal, Russia invaded Azerbaijan, filling the power vacuum. Together with Armenia and Georgia, Azerbaijan formed the Transcaucasian Soviet Federative Socialist Republic at the very end of 1922. This association lasted until 1936, when these three countries became independent republics of the USSR.[36]

Azerbaijan once again declared its independence on August 30, 1991. Unfortunately, since then the country has been embroiled in an ethnic conflict over

Nagorno-Karabakh, an Armenian enclave in Azerbaijan. Nagorno-Karabakh was created by the Soviet Union in 1923 as an autonomous region within the Muslim-Turkic republic of Azerbaijan as a way of recognizing its sizeable Christian-Armenian population. In 1988, as the Soviet Union was disintegrating, Nagorno-Karabakh demanded union with Armenia, with the hope of eventual independence. Armenia responded positively to that request, and civil unrest ensued in both Armenia and Azerbaijan. Russia stepped in to take over direct control of the enclave in January 1989. Azerbaijan blockaded Armenia, and Moscow returned Nagorno-Karabakh control to Azerbaijan.

The ensuing conflict between ethnic Armenians and ethnic Azerbaijanis has ruined the economies of both countries, caused thousands of casualties, created over a million refugees and displaced persons, and produced considerable physical damage.[37] About 20–25 percent of Azeri territory is now occupied by Armenian forces. A cease-fire has been in effect since early 1994; it is fragile. A simple return of the occupied territory to Azerbaijan will not be sufficient to create a lasting peace.

It is difficult to precisely state why the issue of Nagorno-Karabakh brought Armenia and Azerbaijan to the point of armed conflict. The best explanation is probably that this is simply the most recent manifestation of a dislike between these peoples that is decades old, if not older.

The Azeri-Armenian conflict has negated many of the natural benefits Azerbaijan enjoys: huge oil and gas reserves, a good climate, fertile soil, and great natural beauty. The conflict has even colored Azerbaijan's relationship with the United States.

In particular, Section 907 of the U.S. Freedom Support Act of 1992 prohibits the United States from providing any assistance to Azerbaijan, except for nonproliferation and disarmament matters. Assistance through nongovernmental organizations and by the U.S. government is allowed if the government of Azerbaijan is not involved. The legislation was a response to the Azeri blockade of Armenia and was in part the result of heavy lobbying of Congress by Armenian groups.[38] Section 907 reads, in part:

> United States assistance under this or any other act...may not be provided to the government of Azerbaijan until the President determines and so reports to Congress, that the government of Azerbaijan is taking demonstrable steps to cease all blockades and other offensive uses of force against Armenia and Nagorno-Karabakh.

---

36.   See A. Seck, *Oil & Gas Investments in Azerbaijan, Part 1: Country Report* (Dundee, Scotland, UK: Centre for Petroleum and Mineral Law and Policy, University of Dundee, 1994).

37.   John Maresca, *War in the Caucasus: A Proposal for Settlement of the Conflict over Nagorno-Karabakh* (Washington, D. C.: United States Institute of Peace, no date).

38.   Credit for the passage of Section 907 should be given to the very strong and vocal Armenian diaspora within the United States. Groups such as the Armenian Assembly of America have become sophisticated lobbyists and have actively supported, financially and otherwise, election campaigns for members of Congress who support Armenia. These groups also have raised considerable sums of money to support Armenia's military actions against Azerbaijan.

Congress granted some relief in early 1996, when it passed legislation that permits direct humanitarian assistance to Azerbaijan

> ...if the President considers that assistance of nongovernmental organizations to Azerbaijan is not sufficient to meet the requirements of refugees and displaced persons.[39]

Azerbaijan has endeavored to counter the efforts of the Armenian diaspora to increase U.S. support for Armenia, but apparently with little success. Those oil companies hoping to do business in Azerbaijan, particularly Amoco and British Petroleum, have attempted to polish Azerbaijan's image to the extent possible. The U.S. government had been comparatively cool toward Azeri President Heydar Aliyev, because of his KGB past and his government's poor human rights record. There was a slight warming in U.S.–Azeri relations following a meeting between Vice President Albert Gore and President Aliyev in Cairo, Egypt, just prior to the signing the AIOC agreement in September 1994.

Azerbaijan will soon take on a new role, as an independent oil-producing nation, when the AIOC begins production of offshore oil fields in the Caspian. Adjusting to this new role will be difficult. The country must choose whether to link its future solidly with the West, to move further toward Moscow, or to find a neutral position in between. The country must also try to avoid squandering its substantial oil-derived income and, instead, to invest it wisely to help ensure longer-term economic growth and political stability.

Oil

The history of oil in Azerbaijan is long and rich. A Russian engineer is said to have drilled the world's first oil well, on the Apsheron Peninsula in 1848. At the turn of the century, the world's first offshore well was sunk at this same field. At that time, Baku accounted for almost one-half of the world crude oil production. In the years that followed, until the Russian Revolution, production held relatively constant (Table 3-2). Historically, development of Baku oil has been primarily in the hands of foreigners, European or Russian. Baku oil had been coveted by a succession of nations and rulers: Peter the Great, the Bolsheviks, and Germany.

The petroleum industry became the centerpiece of Baku trade in the 1870s and animated the economy of the entire region. Oil was moved by tanker, rail and, eventually, by pipeline to world markets first via the Volga and then across Caucasia to the Black Sea.[40]

Under centralized planning, Baku oil prospered until World War II. Access to Caucasus oil was a German objective during both world wars, but particularly during World War II:

> Germany is interested in creating a stable position in the entire Caucasus in

---

39.   *FBIS-SOV*, February 2, 1996.

40.   See Dr. Audrey L. Altstadt, "From White Oil to Black Caviar: Baku Commerce through the Ages," *Caspian Crossroads*, Spring 1995.

order to secure the safety of continental Europe, that is, to safeguard for herself the link with the Near East. It is only this link with the oil fields that can make Germany and the rest of Europe independent, in the future, of any coalition of maritime powers. The aim of German policy is to control the Caucasus and the adjoining lands to the south, both politically and militarily.... Economically, the German Reich must take all oil into its hands.[41]

Invading German forces caused Moscow to realize the geographic vulnerability of its oil fields. Exploration and developmental efforts were shifted eastward, which led to discovery of the Urals-Volga oil fields—commonly known as the Second Baku. These fields supplied the growing oil needs of the Soviet Union for the following quarter-century.[42] The task of satisfying future, higher domestic and export demands led geologists further eastward, in search of easy finds. Rather than concentrating on developing the Urals-Volga oil fields to their fullest, it seemed simpler and cheaper to look for new oil in unexplored regions, where there were better odds of finding easy-to-produce giant oil fields (that is, where recoverable reserves were at least 100 million barrels).

These efforts were rewarded with the discovery of oil in Western Siberia in the mid–1960s. The prolific oil fields of Western Siberia quickly displaced Urals-Volga and Baku oil, and investment funds were directed away from the older fields to these new discoveries. For the Urals-Volga and for Baku, the absence of investment capital meant that it was not possible even to maintain existing levels of output. The Baku fields in particular began quickly to show their age, and production began a decline that continues today.

---

41.   Robert Goralski and Russell W. Freeburg, *Oil & War* (New York: William Morrow and Company, Inc., 1987).

42.   The immensity of the Urals-Volga region and the extent to which these deposits could be exploited did not come as a total surprise. At the 18th Congress of the Communist Party in 1939, V. M. Molotov called for the creation of a new petroleum base—a second Baku—in the region between the Volga River and the Ural Mountains. See Robert E. Ebel, *The Petroleum Industry of the Soviet Union* (Washington: American Petroleum Institute, 1961).

Table 3-2
Baku Crude Oil Production, 1908–1916

Year	Thousand b/d
1908	151.4
1910	167.7
1911	152
1912	158.7
1913	153.6
1914	140.6
1915	149.0
1916	156.7

Note: Includes Baku and Cheleken Island output, so that the data can be compared with Azerbaijan of today. The contribution from Cheleken was very limited, and at its peak did not exceed 3 percent of total Azeri production.

Source: Heinrich Hassman, *Oil in the Soviet Union* (Princeton University Press: Princeton, 1953).

Crude oil production in Azerbaijan peaked in 1941 at 470,000 b/d, which was more than 71 percent of total Soviet output. Although there was some recovery following the end of World War II (Table 3-3), once the emphasis began to shift eastward to the Urals-Volga, production never returned to that peak level. It came closest in 1970, at 400,000 b/d, after which the oil sector entered a long, slow decline. (Table 3-4).

Table 3-3
Post–World War II Azeri Crude Oil Production

Year	Total	Thousand b/d Of Which, Off-shore
1948	230	21.6*
1950	296.4	31.4
1955	306.1	81.4
1959	356	112.8**

Source: Robert E. Ebel, *The Petroleum Industry of the Soviet Union* (Washington: American Petroleum Institute, 1961).

During the more than 150 years of Azeri oil, almost 9.7 billion bbl. of crude oil have been extracted, onshore and offshore.[43] The bulk of the cumulative produc-

43.   *FBIS-SOV*, September 21, 1994.

tion—roughly 6.75 billion bbl.—has originated at onshore fields. More recently, as onshore fields have played out, however, the contribution from offshore fields has dominated. The shallow-water portions of the Gunashli oil field currently provide the larger share—120,000 b/d—of Azeri offshore oil production. (See Map 2.)

The post–World War II Azeri contribution to Soviet oil supply was perhaps most notable in offshore production: virtually all Soviet offshore crude oil production was in fields offshore and adjacent to the Apsheron Peninsula of Azerbaijan. Commercial exploitation of these deposits began shortly after the end of World War II and soon became the basis for the growth of the Soviet oil sector.

The drop in Azeri crude oil production during 1975–1995 of some 162,000 b/d can be divided almost equally between onshore and offshore (Table 3-4), as both were equally affected by shortages of capital.

Table 3-4
Azeri Crude Oil Production, 1975–1996

			Thousand b/d
Year	Onshore	Offshore	Total*
1975	116.8	227.2	344
1980	99.3	194.7	294
1985	78.2	184.7	263
1990	51.6	198.7	250
1991	45.8	187.9	234
1992	40.2	181.5	222
1993	38.7	172.1	211
1994	34.8	155.45	191
1995	32.3	150.7	183
1996 est.	32	140	172

* Totals have been rounded.

Sources: Interfax, *Petroleum Information Agency*, Baku, November 3, 1995; *Post-Soviet Geography*, April 1992; *Platt's Oilgram News*, February 8, 1995; *FBIS-SOV*, January 27, 1995; Interfax, *Petroleum Report*, January 6-13, 1995; British Broadcasting Corporation, *Summary of World Broadcasts, Part 1, Former USSR*, January 10, 1996.

Domestic crude oil production in 1995 was just 69 percent of the 1985 level, and 53 percent of the 1975 level. Nearly 20 percent of all the wells in the country have been abandoned.[44] The inability to replace production volumes on a continuing basis has made further output declines inevitable.

Although new discoveries have been made offshore in the Caspian, there has been neither the funds nor the technology to development them. The Azeri, Chirag,

---

44.   Interfax, *Petroleum Report*, August 12-19, 1994.

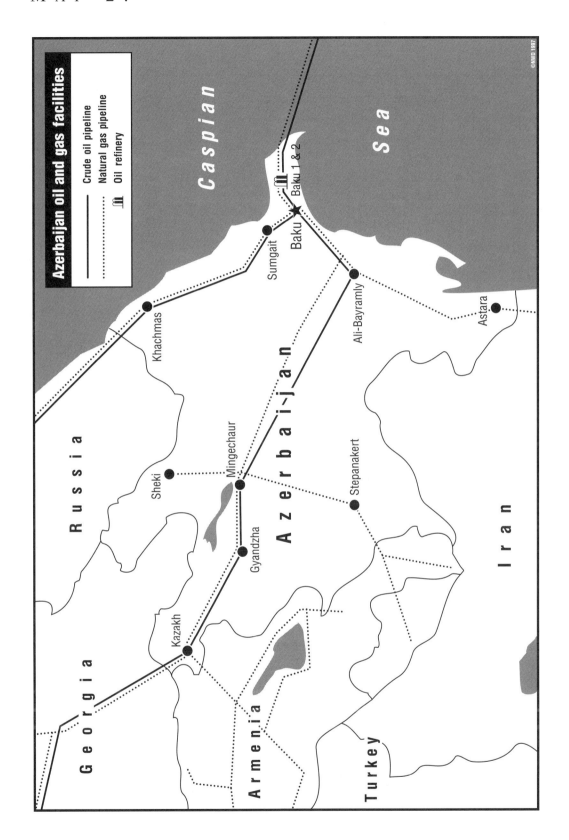

and deep-water portion of the Gunashli are just beginning to be developed by the AIOC.

In fact, the stark realization that Azerbaijan would face an oil crisis, and relatively soon, if foreign assistance could not be secured, undoubtedly strengthened the will of the Azeri government to reach an accommodation with the AIOC. The future was bleak; Azerbaijan simply could not go it alone.

Despite the steady decline in crude oil production, Azerbaijan still has been able to maintain its position as an oil exporter, because domestic needs, which average about 140,000 b/d, are still less than the supply. In 1994, 24,000 b/d of petroleum products were exported, [45] of which 20,000 b/d were sold to Iran; these exports provided Azerbaijan with 75 percent of its hard-currency earnings that year. Exports of petroleum products rose to 28,000 b/d during 1995. Plans for 1996 called for exports to reach about 40,000 b/d.[46]

Refining

Oil refining capacity in Azerbaijan is more than ample to handle all local production, as well as crude oil imported from Russia, Kazakstan, and Turkmenistan.[47] There are two refineries in Azerbaijan with a combined processing capacity of 406,000 b/d. The larger of the two refineries—Azerneftyag (formerly Baku)—has a 244,000 b/d capacity, with the Azerneftyanadzhakh refinery (formerly Novo-Baku) providing the difference of 162,000 b/d.[48]

Technologically, these two refineries are quite outdated. The yield of light products—gasoline, aviation fuels, diesel fuel, and lubricants—is only around 55 percent, far short of what is required to support a modern-day economy. A program has been drafted to upgrade and expand these two refineries and to boost throughput capacity to 480,000 to 500,000 b/d by 2005.[49] Oil consumption in Azerbaijan by 2005 is likely to be no more than 200,000 b/d, and the emphasis on exporting petroleum products is therefore likely to continue.

Natural Gas

The annual demand for natural gas in Azerbaijan is officially calculated at 16 bil-

---

45.   Azerbaijan has a reported petroleum product export capability of 40,000 b/d. See Interfax, *Petroleum Information Agency*, Baku, October 12, 1995.

46.   Interfax, *Petroleum Information Agency*, Baku, January 25, 1996. Iran takes most of the product exports, and diesel fuel is the key export product. A terminal is to be opened in the port of Poti for the shipment of diesel fuel to Georgia.

47.   Crude oil imports from Kazakstan averaged just 682 b/d during 1995 (see *Finansovyye izvestiya,* January 25, 1996). The joint stock company LUKoil-Baku has been purchasing crude oil from foreign companies and joint ventures to take advantage of the spare refining capacity available in Baku, although purchases to date have been quite small—averaging 608 b/d (see *FBIS-SOV*, January 19, 1996).

48.   See the country report, *Azerbaijan*, issued by the Energy Information Administration, U.S. Department of Energy, in October 1994.

49.   Interfax, *Petroleum Report*, August 26 to September 2, 1995.

lion cubic meters (bcm). Extraction in 1994 of 6.38 bcm and imports from Turkmenistan of 3 bcm provided the economy with just 9 bcm,[50] well short of requirements. Domestic production improved slightly in 1996 (Table 3-5), all from offshore sources.

Table 3-5
Natural Gas Extraction in Azerbaijan

Year	Billion cubic meters
1970	5.5
1975	9.9
1980	14.0
1985	14.1
1990	9.9
1991	8.6
1992	8.0
1993	6.8
1994	6.4
1995	6.6
1996 est.	7.0

Sources: *Post-Soviet Geography*, April 1992; Interfax, *Petroleum Information Agency*, November 3, 1995; Interfax, *Petroleum Report*, January 6-13, 1995; British Broadcasting Corporation, *Summary of World Broadcasts, Part!, USSR*, January 10, 1996; *East Bloc Energy*, April 1994; *Petroleum Information Agency*, Baku, December 7, 1995; *Interfax*, Baku, December 29, 1995; British Broadcasting Company, *Summary of World Broadcasts, Part 1, Former USSR*, January 10, 1996.

Natural gas imports have been an important element of supply in recent years (Table 3-6), although deliveries have been cut because of nonpayment and pipeline cutoffs.

---

50.   *East Bloc Energy*, July 1995.

Table 3-6
Azerbaijan Imports of Natural Gas

Year	Billion cubic meters
1990	7.3
1991	8
1992	4.3
1993	6
1994	2.5

Source: Habar Service Information Agency, *Oil and Gas Complex*, Baku, October 21–31, 1995.

Azerbaijan began buying natural gas from Turkmenistan in 1992, to supplement imports from Russia and to help offset the loss of Iranian natural gas and declining domestic production. Azerbaijan has rejected future imports of natural gas from Turkmenistan. Azerbaijan could no longer afford to import. Severe restrictions then had to be placed on gas consumption.[51]

Little natural gas is extracted onshore in Azerbaijan (Table 3-7), and in the context of current and likely future oil development projects, future increases in supply will also originate offshore. Short-term improvements in domestic natural gas extraction will be the result of a project to recover associated natural gas produced offshore in the Caspian Sea at the Neftyannye Kamni oil fields. Development of these fields began in 1949, and production peaked in 1967, at 168,000 b/d. Output has fallen gradually since and is currently just over 16,000 b/d.[52] Azerbaijan had never made the investments necessary to recover those amounts of natural gas produced in association with the crude oil at Neftyannye Kamni. These volumes had instead been vented into the atmosphere. Now, Pennzoil has done that for them, at a cost of about $150 million.[53]

Table 3-7
Offshore and Onshore Natural Gas in Azerbaijan

Year	Offshore	Onshore Billion cu. meters	Total
1993	6.571	0.238	6.81
1994	6.143	0.235	6.38
1995	6.41	0.23	6.64

Sources: Interfax, *Petroleum Information Agency*, November 3, 1995; Interfax, *Petroleum Report*, January 6-13, 1995; British Broadcasting Corporation, *Summary of World Broadcasts, Part 1, USSR*, January 10, 1996.

The associated gas is piped ashore and placed in the distribution network.

---

51.   *Finansovyye Izvestiya*, October 19, 1995.
52.   *Financial Times*, September 20, 1995.

Azerbaijan hopes that this program, in addition to cutting pollution, will replace expensive imports. However, the project has a design capacity of just 1.6 bcm annually, far short of the gap between current supply and demand. The level of gas recovered will increase as the Azeri sector of offshore Caspian Sea oil fields is developed and may eventually exceed local requirements.

Corruption

The oil sector of Azerbaijan is no less vulnerable to corruption than the oil sectors of other republics of the former Soviet Union. President Aliyev has pledged to root out corruption in the energy industry, stating that "(w)e have information that at the western borders of Azerbaijan, part of the oil and gas supplies are being resold to Armenia via Georgia."[54] The First Deputy Chairman of Goskomtekhnadzor (the state inspection agency) has claimed that the illegal production of crude oil in Azerbaijan amounts to 26,000 b/d. He noted that, according to official data, the onshore production associations transferred less than 20,000 b/d to the state in 1994, while refining almost 46,000 b/d at the oil refineries in Baku. The petroleum products refined from the undeclared crude oil were either illegally sold at filling stations or exported.[55] President Aliyev also expressed the belief that hard currency derived from the sale of oil abroad was being misappropriated,[56] and that a portion of the gas purchased from Turkmenistan was then being sold "on the side" even before it reached the borders of Azerbaijan.[57]

The higher prices created from shortages—including the shortages resulting from the Azeri embargo on Armenia—encourages the entrepreneur to find ways to fill the gap between supply and demand, dishonestly or not.

Electricity

Electricity-generating capacity in Azerbaijan is estimated to be about 5 million kilowatts, and production is estimated at 17.5 billion kilowatt hours (kwh). There are plans to more than double this level of output by the year 2005.[58] Other plans call for merging the electric power systems of Azerbaijan, Turkey, and Georgia.[59] A new power transmission line will be built to link Turkey with Nakhichevan and

---

53.   The Gas Utilization Project completed by Pennzoil consisted of erecting a gas compression and processing station offshore at Neftyannye Kamni and the laying of a 120-km underwater pipeline from Neftyanye Kamni to an onshore gas plant at Karadag. The project is designed to process and deliver 4.3 million cubic meters per day of natural gas from the Gunashli and Neft Dashlari fields. The initial Gas Utilization Project agreement between Pennzoil-Ramco and SOCAR was signed in October 1992. The first gas was delivered to Karadag in May 1994, and continuous operation began in September 1994.

54.   Open Media Research Institute, Inc., *Daily Report*, Part I, September 22, 1995.

55.   See *East Bloc Energy*, May 1995.

56.   *Interfax*, Baku, September 21, 1995.

57.   Interfax, *Petroleum Information Agency*, Baku, September 22, 1995.

58.   *FBIS-USR*, June 21, 1994.

59.   *Interfax*, Baku, December 8, 1995.

with additional electricity transmission facilities in Georgia, in conjunction with the decision to move a portion of the Azeri early oil through that country.

Power generation in Azerbaijan has held up reasonably well in recent years, particularly in light of the general decline in economic activity and the problems experienced with fuel supplies (Table 3-8).

Table 3-8
Electricity Generation in Azerbaijan

Year	Million Kwh
1985	20,702
1989	23,306
1990	23,152
1991	23.450
1992	19,770
1994	17,500

Source: A. Seck, *Oil & Gas Investments in Azerbaijan, Part 2: Economic & Legal Profile of the Energy Sector.* Dundee, Scotland: University of Dundee, Centre for Petroleum and Mineral Law and Policy, 1994.

Most of the generating capacity is found at thermal plants, with smaller shares provided by hydroelectric power stations and by combined heat and power facilities (Table 3-9). In the past, when the supply of natural gas was reliable, fuel for the thermal power plants was roughly divided between fuel oil and natural gas. Recent interruptions in natural gas supplies caused by the conflict with Armenia and Azerbaijan's inability to pay for imports from Turkmenistan has necessitated that fuel oil play a greater role. There are no nuclear power stations in Azerbaijan and no known plans to build any.

Table 3-9
Allocation of Electricity Generating Capacity

Type	Megawatts	Percent of Total
Thermal	3,600	71.6
Combined Heat & Power	616	12.3
Hydro	812	16.1
Total	5,028	100.0

Source: A. Seck, *Oil & Gas Investments in Azerbaijan, Part 2: Economic & Legal Profile of the Energy Sector.* Dundee, Scotland: University of Dundee, Centre for Petroleum and Mineral Law and Policy, 1994.

Azerbaijan had been a major supplier of electricity to the Caucasus, but it has lost markets in Georgia and Armenia for a variety of reasons, and exports sales have sharply declined. Spare generating capacity is available but likely will remain idle, given the absence of viable markets and, equally important, the inability to acquire fuels to fire this capacity. Moreover, as much as a quarter or more of the electricity-generating capacity is unavailable because of a lack of spare parts or insufficient funds for required maintenance. For similar reasons, a very high percentage of the power generated is lost in the distribution system.

The AIOC: "Contract of the Century"

The cycle is complete. World attention has again focused on Baku and the oil potential of the Caspian Sea. Foreign investors are again in the lead, as they were 100 years ago when the Nobel brothers of Sweden first developed Baku oil.

On September 20, 1994, the government of Azerbaijan and the AIOC signed an agreement to develop the Gunashli, Chirag, and Azeri oil fields in the Caspian Sea offshore at Baku. The contract contained three provisions: the first crude oil will be extracted within 18 months, full production will start in 48 months, and the export pipeline will be available no later than 54 months from the signing date.

Recoverable oil reserves at these three fields are estimated at about 4 billion bbl., distributed as follows: Azeri—1.825 billion bbl.; Chirag—1.132 billion bbl.; and Gunashli—694–803 million bbl.[60] As noted elsewhere, only the deepwater portions of Gunashli (below 200 meters) come under the authority of the AIOC; Russia's LUKoil is developing the shallow parts. Crude oil production over the lifetime of the project is expected to total 3.730 billion bbl. Aggregate peak production is expected at some 700,000 b/d. If the proper infrastructure is provided, some 55 bcm of associated natural gas and nearly 90 bcm of nonassociated natural gas will also be produced.

The negotiations leading to the agreement lasted several years and were impeded by corruption, political instability, the absence of legal and tax structures, and the undeclared war between Azerbaijan and Armenia.[61] An agreement had been reached in mid–1993, but it dissolved when the Azeri government, led by President Abulfax Elchibey, was replaced in a virtually bloodless coup that put Heydar Aliyev in the presidency. Political instability was perhaps the greatest hindrance: Azerbaijan has had five presidents since independence in 1991.

Initially, negotiations with interested foreign investors had been directed toward reserving the major oilfields for specific operators. For example, in June 1991, Amoco was given the right to negotiate an agreement to develop the Azeri oil field. The BP–Statoil alliance won Chirag in September 1992, and Pennzoil–Ramco won Gunashli in October 1992.[62] Then, in April 1993 Azerbaijan changed directions and began to work to create a consortium that would develop all three fields. The membership of the consortium was comprised of the earlier winners.

---

60.   The U.S. Department of Energy is somewhat more optimistic regarding the recoverable oil reserves at Azeri, Chirag, and Gunashli, and has put the total at 5 billion barrels. See *Platt's Oilgram News*, September 21, 1994.

61.   *The Washington Post*, September 20, 1994.

62.   *FBIS-SOV*, June 9, 1995.

(See Map 3.)

When LUKoil was assigned a 10 percent equity stake, the share owned by SOCAR was reduced to 20 percent. SOCAR subsequently sold a quarter of its share (equal to 5 percent equity in the project) to the Turkish Petroleum Company in order to raise capital. Azerbaijan intended to sell another quarter of its share to Iran, but U.S. opposition blocked that arrangement. This quarter share instead was sold to Exxon, much to the displeasure of Iran and the discomfort of Azerbaijan, who quite correctly feared a negative impact on Azeri-Iranian relations.[63] The AIOC, as it is now structured, heavily favors U.S. companies (Table 3-10).

---

63.   Indeed, a finalized agreement between Iran and Azerbaijan was presented to the other members of the AIOC, whereupon it was rejected. When application was made to transfer 5 percent from SOCAR to the Turkish Petroleum Company, approval was quick in coming. Iran was not alone in being kept out of the AIOC. A number of oil companies, including Shell, Mobil, Elf and Agip, also had sought to acquire an equity share, but were unsuccessful.

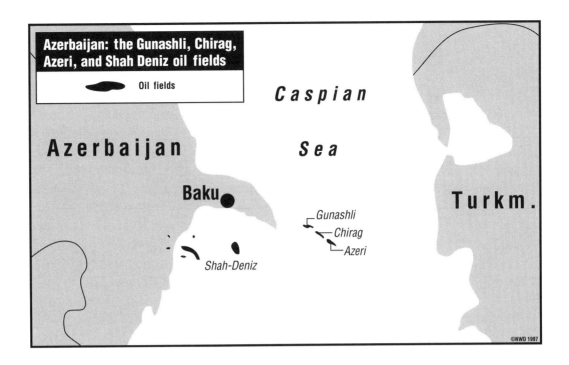

Azerbaijan: the Gunashli, Chirag, Azeri, and Shah Deniz oil fields

Oil fields

Azerbaijan

Caspian

Sea

Baku

Gunashli

Chirag

Azeri

Shah-Deniz

Turkm.

©NWD 1997

Table 3-10
Composition of the Azerbaijan
International Operating Company

Nationality\Company	Share of Equity (%)
United States	
Amoco	17.01
Pennzoil	4.8175
Unocal	9.52
Exxon	5.0
Total United States	36.3475
UK	
British Petroleum	17.1267
Ramco	2.0825
Total UK	19.2092
Azerbaijan	
State Oil Company of Azerbaijan	10.0
Russia	
LUKoil	10.0
Norway	
Statoil	8.5633
Japan	
Itochu	7.45
Turkey	
Turkish Petroleum Company	6.75
Saudi Arabia	
Delta-Nimir	1.68

Note: in March 1996 Itochu reached an agreement with McDermott to acquire the latter's 2.45 percent equity in the AIOC. In early April 1996 Itochu announced that it had acquired 5 percent of Pennzoil's stake, raising its equity position in the AIOC to 7.45 percent.

Sources: Interfax, *Petroleum Information Agency*, Baku, October 9, 1995; *Platt's Oilgram News*, March 13, 1996; *Wall Street Journal*, April 2, 1996.

The foreign investors in Azeri oil have found themselves in a somewhat dangerous neighborhood. Iran, Russia, and Turkey all have national interests in the region, apart from their national interests in the ethnic conflicts underway within Armenia, Georgia, and Azerbaijan. In addition, the participation of U.S. and British oil companies in the AIOC implicitly, if not explicitly, involves these two governments.

The hope that oil field development offshore in the Caspian Sea and the subsequent construction of export pipelines could proceed on purely a commercial basis has long since been abandoned. Although the partners may publicly state that decisions reflect only the economics of the project, political considerations will continue to carry the day. Far too much is at stake for politics not to intrude.

The Pipelines

Once the Azeri government had signed and ratified an agreement with the AIOC, it could begin a review of proposals for moving the new oil to world markets. There was no consideration of selling AIOC oil in the Azeri domestic market, because existing Azeri production was expected to be more than enough to meet local needs.

The several pipeline routes proposed were all technically feasible and would impose no unusual requirements on pipeline construction companies. Most of them were financially viable as well. But none could be characterized as politically secure. All would transit territories wracked by civil war, dissident activities, or separatist movements, and the operational safety of any of these routes, whether through Russia, Georgia, Armenia, or even Turkey, would be difficult to fully guarantee.[64]

The question of how the early oil would move to market was tracked breathlessly. Would the final decision be based strictly on economics, or would politics prevail over all other considerations?[65] Two working groups established by the AIOC compared the costs of moving the oil on a northern route, through Chechnya and onward to the Black Sea port of Novorossiisk, or on a western route, through Georgia to the port of Supsa on the Black Sea. The ground rules clearly had stated that the final decision would be based on economics, but that if the comparative transport costs were reasonably close, then politics would prevail.

Politics did prevail. The AIOC, after due deliberation, decided to move the early oil to market via two routes: a northern route, through Grozny to Novorossiisk, and a western route, through Georgia to the port of Supsa.[66] (See Map 4.) Both routes were shown to be technically feasible and commercially viable. The deci-

---

64.   The international oil industry has long dealt with pipeline sabotage. A major crude oil pipeline in Colombia is routinely blown up by guerrillas and Royal Dutch/Shell has been confronted with constant sabotage in Nigeria. See *Financial Times*, December 19, 1995.

Inasmuch as a pipeline cannot be guarded along its entire length (although protective forces can secure vital pumping and compressor stations), the multinational oil companies have become very adept at repairing damaged pipelines and returning them to service as quickly as possible.

65.   Early on, the AIOC had every intent of moving early oil to market via a swaps arrangement with Iran. Azeri oil would supply the Tabriz refinery in the north of Iran, and the AIOC would collect a comparable amount of oil from Iran at a port on the Gulf. According to the then president of BP Azerbaijan, "(t)he Iranian solution is going to be fairly central in the short term." See *Platt's Oilgram News*, August 26, 1994.

66.   The length of the northern route, Baku-Novorossiisk, is 1,346 kilometers. It has been stated that readying this pipeline to carry early oil would require 13 months, and an additional 4 months to fill it with oil. See *FBIS-SOV*, January 23, 1996.

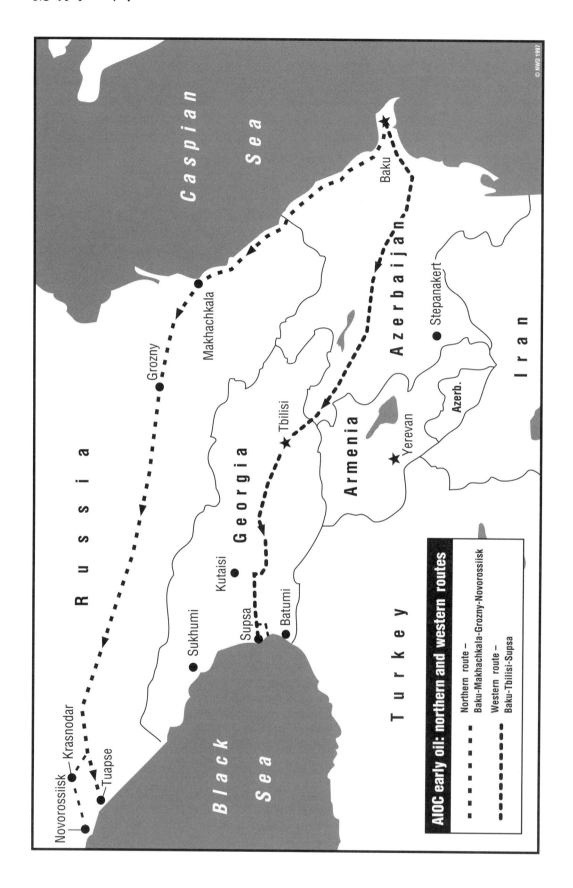

AIOC early oil: northern and western routes

Northern route –
Baku-Makhachkala-Grozny-Novorossiisk

Western route –
Baku-Tbilisi-Supsa

sion to split the early oil seemingly made winners out of all the players in this game—the AIOC, Georgia, Turkey, and Russia. The AIOC had gone to considerable lengths to ensure that the early oil decision in no way would prejudice selection of the route (or routes) for the later oil, but the decision was not an easy one for the AIOC. Some members publicly denounced the dual-line solution for the early oil, saying it would make no economic sense at all. It wouldn't be cost-effective to invest in multiple lines for initial exports.[67]

The government of Turkey worked diligently to make the case first for a western route for early oil and a pipeline through Turkey to the Mediterranean port of Ceyhan for later oil. The core of Turkey's position was that the Bosphorus Straits were to be avoided. A note circulated by Turkey's Washington, D.C.–based international communications counsel stressed that

> (t)he Bosphorus is one of the world's busiest waterways, and also one of the most difficult to navigate because it is so narrow, with fast currents and twelve abrupt turns. Under international treaty, it is open to all merchant ships of all nations, without cargo reporting or restrictions and without requiring pilots. And it flows through the middle of Istanbul, a city of 12 million people. All of this makes it a uniquely hazardous waterway, with 167 large scale accidents between 1983 and 1993. Significant increases in uncontrolled tanker traffic will raise the risk of collisions which could cause environmental damage and endanger the city's residents. If Caspian Sea oil is shipped through the Bosphorus, a major accident that closes the straits to traffic, as has happened with several recent collisions, will stop the flow of all Caspian Sea oil shipments to the West.[68]

Oil moving along the northern route will be delivered to the Black Sea port of Novorossiisk,[69] where presumably it will be placed in tankers serving European and other markets. For this route to work, however, LUKoil must reroute a portion of its Russian export oil away from the Tikhoretsk-Novorossiisk pipeline to make room for the early oil. The volumes arriving at Novorossiisk are scheduled to pass through the narrow Bosphorus Straits, likely bringing further tensions to Turkish-Russian relations.

Turkey indicated that it was willing to buy all the oil delivered to Supsa. From

---

67.   See *Platt's Oilgram News*, September 22, 1995. Then Deputy Secretary of Energy William White, during a visit to Azerbaijan in April 1995, stated that "(t)he United States comes out for shipment of the oil extracted in Azerbaijan to Europe through Georgia." See *FBIS-SOV*, April 24, 1995.

Renewed thought has been given to the shipment of some early oil to world markets via a swaps arrangement with Iran. But U.S. policy toward Iran, although not specifically rejecting this approach, nonetheless does not encourage it either. Those U.S. oil companies involved in the consortium have not been prepared to test the waters of public and private opinion.

68.   See *Transporting Caspian Sea Region Oil, The Early Oil Decision*, dated September 15, 1995 and distributed by Capitoline/MS&L, Washington, DC.

69.   The port of Novorossiisk has a capacity to handle 640,000 b/d of oil. In 1994 it handled 598,000 b/d. See *Neft i Kapital*, May 1995. Clearly, the port of Novorossiisk would have to be considerably expanded if it is to handle additional oil from Azerbaijan and Kazakstan in the future. But the port's vulnerability to weather effectively has closed that option.

Supsa, the oil would move by tanker to northern Turkish ports and then by rail tank car to markets in central Anatolia. Alternatively, the oil could be delivered to Romania and other East European countries for refining.

In retrospect, however, everyone may not be a winner. As details of the consortium arrangement emerged, the dominance of the northern route became evident. The northern route has a maximum throughput capacity of 340,000 b/d; the western line, 140,000 b/d. Both routes will use existing pipelines to the extent possible, but the expenditure needed to put the pipeline of the western route in operating condition will be far higher.[70] Moreover, Moscow's position of record is that it does not object to parallel transportation of early oil if the bulk is delivered by the Russian pipeline.[71] To that end, an agreement initialled in Moscow on January 18, 1996, by Russian Prime Minister Viktor Chernomyrdin and Azeri president Heydar Aliyev calls for sending about 70,000 b/d of the early to Novorossiisk.[72]

Nonetheless, the wording of the October 1995 AIOC statement itself appears deliberately vague about how the early oil would be divided between the two routes. Neither did it indicate whether export of the early oil would begin simultaneously through both lines. It simply stated that

> (f)rom the detailed work done...on two export variants currently available for usage, it was concluded that export via Azerbaijan pipelines onwards through Russia to the North and via Azerbaijan pipelines onwards through Georgia to the West, were both technically feasible and commercially viable.[73]

The cost of preparing the northern route to carry its share of early oil was placed at about $55 million. In essence, the direction of flow via the Tikhoretsk-Baku pipeline must be reversed, pumping stations reconstructed, and pipeline repairs made. The system should be ready when production from Chirag begins in mid–1997, building up to 80,000 b/d within 12 to 18 months (Table 3-11).[74] Vagit Alekperov, president of LUKoil, has indicated that the northern route is expected to deliver 28 million bbl. of Azeri oil in 1997 and 35 million bbl. in 1998, which implies an early crude oil production level in 1998 of almost 96,000 b/d, up from about 77,000 b/d average in 1997 and implies that all production would be placed into the northern pipeline.[75] The first or "early" oil was to be provided by the Chirag-1 platform, with production building to 80,000 b/d. Early production was to total 240 million bbl., over a period of seven years, until "later" oil would kick in. Production was initially expected to begin in mid–1996. However, indications are that production may not be so easy. For example, members of the BP Exploration

---

70.   See *Russian Petroleum Investor*, October 1995.

71.   *Sevodnya*, October 24, 1995.

72.   *Reuters*, Moscow, January 18, 1996. Some reports indicate that the Russian Foreign Ministry was able to insert a clause stipulating that the agreement would come into force only when both Azerbaijan and Russia had ratified the European Energy Charter Treaty, which has not yet happened.

73.   See *Platt's Oilgram News*, December 21, 1995.

74.   *Platt's Oilgram News*, February 20, 1996; *Platt's Oilgram News*, January 19, 1996.

75.   In view of the fact that production is now slated to begin by mid-1997, Mr. Alekperov is being overly optimistic. See *UPI*, Moscow, January 18, 1996.

team have noted that Chirag comes out higher on the scale of expected geological hazards than anything they have ever seen. There is a great deal of shallow gas, several mud volcanoes, and a number of unstable slopes. The site is geologically active, with more faults coming to the seabed than any members of the team could recall ever seeing.[76]

Expert opinion holds that reconstruction of the northern pipeline could be accomplished in five months or so, assuming no interference by Chechen rebel forces. The way for the early oil to move to Novorossiisk was cleared in mid-Feb-

Table 3-11
AIOC Initial Crude Oil Production Goals

Date	Thousand b/d
Mid-1997	80
2004	300
2010	700
Source: Terence Adams, "Offshore Azerbaijan: Emerging Issues and the Potential For the Coming Decade," presented to the 5th CGES (Centre For Global Energy Studies) Conference, London, April 10-11, 1995.	

ruary 1996, with the signing of a commercial agreement between the AIOC and Transneft, the operator of the Russian oil pipeline system.[77]

The western route will stretch for a total of 926 km, from Baku to the Black Sea port of Supsa (south of Poti), of which 446 km will pass through Georgia. A transit tariff has been fixed at 43 cents per barrel, with 26 cents going to Azerbaijan and 17 cents to Georgia.[78] Readying the western route for early oil will be much more complicated, which translates into higher costs—on the order of $238 million.[79] The early oil will come ashore at Sanchala, where a terminal will be built that will be linked to the Chirag platform by an underwater pipeline. A new 117 km pipeline must be built between Kazakh and the Georgian village of Gachiani, where a 350 km pipeline to Batumi begins.[80] The Gachiani-Batumi section must be rebuilt, and a 1.6 million barrel storage facility and terminal will be constructed at Supsa. The start-up date for operation of the western line has been continually pushed back, and is estimated for sometime in 1988.[81]

Some observers initially estimated that the western route would handle some Tengiz oil because 80,000–100,000 b/d of Azeri early oil would be insufficient to support both the western and northern routes. The AIOC clarified matters when it

76. *Oil and Gas Journal*, September 11, 1995.
77. *Platt's Oilgram News*, February 21, 1996.
78. *Interfax*, Tbilisi, March 9, 1996.
79. *FBIS-SOV*, November 13, 1995. This cost includes a 117-km section to be built within Azerbaijan and an oil terminal at the Georgian port of Supsa. A protected harbor is available at Supsa. The port of Batumi was not acceptable to the AIOC.
80. *Finansovyye Izvestiya*, November 23, 1995.
81. *Platt's Oilgram News*, June 17, 1996.

announced that a second drilling platform would be erected at Chirag.[82] The oil from this new platform would be handled by the western pipeline, which would still have room for crude oil from Kazakstan and Turkmenistan.

The question has arisen about how delivery of the early oil along the western route would be financed. Turkey has advanced several proposals: Turkey would finance construction of the pipeline through Georgia itself, or through a joint enterprise of the participating countries.[83] The AIOC indicated that Turkish financing would be helpful but not absolutely necessary.[84] Turkey subsequently declared that if it financed the western route, then it should have the right to build the pipeline, to purchase the oil at market prices, and to be given a commitment that the "main" oil would later move by pipeline through Turkey to the Mediterranean port of Ceyhan. In addition, Turkey requested that the Baku-Supsa pipeline capacity be capped at 120,000 b/d, which implied that a pipeline larger than that might render a pipeline through Turkey unnecessary.[85]

Clearly, the AIOC could not accept Turkey's requirement that later oil be exported through Turkey, which would not only be premature but would draw a very negative Russian reaction. Not surprisingly, the AIOC announced it would invest $250 million in preparing the western route, of which $130 million would be spent on rebuilding the 446 km section of the pipeline within Georgia and on constructing an oil terminal at Supsa.[86]

Financing the western route therefore remains the responsibility of the AIOC. Conversely, the cost of readying the northern route will be borne by Russia.

The carrying capacities of the northern and western routes will far exceed the amounts of early oil scheduled for production by the AIOC. The northern route alone after reconstruction will be able to handle 340,000 b/d. If these two routes are to be financially viable, additional throughput will have to be sought.[87] The most logical approach is to either increase the volume of early oil production, come to an agreement for moving Tengiz oil through the two routes, or both. The AIOC understandably is reluctant to discuss the prospect of raising early oil output much higher than the levels presently accepted, but Chirag could clearly support higher production if the market and the AIOC could accommodate it.

The Legal Status of the Caspian Sea

On the very day the government of Azerbaijan and the AIOC signed the "contract of the century," the Russian Foreign Ministry declared the agreement as illegal. The Foreign Ministry claims the Caspian Sea is a lake under international law,

---

82.   Interfax, *Petroleum Information Agency*, Baku, March 12, 1996.

Drilling of the first well, Chirag-1, was slated to commence August 1, 1996. This well, to cost $50 million, will be taken to a depth of 3,500 meters. The water depth at Chirag is 150 meters. See *Platt's Oilgram News*, May 22, 1996.

83.   *FBIS-SOV*, October 18, 1995.

84.   *Platt's Oilgram News*, November 9, 1995.

85.   *Platt's Oilgram News*, February 12, 1996.

86.   Interfax, *Petroleum Information Agency*, Tbilisi, April 8, 1996.

87.   *Platt's Oilgram News*, November 15, 1995.

classification that would require the agreement of all five littoral states—Azerbaijan, Iran, Kazakstan, Russia, and Turkmenistan—before any offshore resources could be developed. While the Russian position has been inconsistent on the legal status of the Caspian, with other parts of the government contradicting the Foreign Ministry's position, Moscow has been consistent in its determination that agreements between the government of Azerbaijan and any consortium for development of Caspian Sea oil will be null and void until the status of the Caspian has been resolved.

Once LUKoil secured an equity position in the AIOC, it was expected that the issue of the legal status of the Caspian would quietly disappear. That did not happen. The Russian position on the Caspian Sea is legally weak, and a recent legal opinion rendered to an oil company indicated that if the question of the legal status of the Caspian Sea were submitted to an international court or other tribunal, delimitation would be based on the median line principle, which would divide the Caspian among the five littoral states using equidistant lines.

Other Oil

Although the offshore Gunashli oil field is currently the center of attention, as the source for the early oil to be produced by the AIOC, development of production at other fields offshore in the Caspian Sea but outside the province of the AIOC will have their own say in determining future Azeri oil export levels[88] and export pipeline capacity requirements.

Karabakh Field

An agreement has been reached between SOCAR (the Azeri State oil company) and the Caspian International Oil Company (CIOC), a consortium that includes Pennzoil, LUKoil, and Agip, concerning development of the Karabakh oil field, located 120 km off the Baku coast in the northern part of the Azeri sector of the Caspian.[89] The participation of the consortium members is: SOCAR, 7.5 percent; LUK-Agip joint venture, 50 percent; LUKoil, 7.5 percent; Pennzoil, 30 percent, and Agip, 5 percent.[90]

With the combined shares of LUKoil, LUKagip, and AzeriLUKoil, LUKoil holds more than half the equity in Karabakh. For the first time, therefore, LUKoil will become a field operator outside Russia.

Recoverable oil reserves at Karabakh are estimated at between 500 and 600 million bbls. The deposit is 24-32 km offshore. Two wells have already been drilled, and future oil can be moved through the Baku-Novorossiisk pipeline. Com-

---

88.   Azerbaijan has indicated that the Kyapaz oil field may be offered for development, but foreign investment would not occur until lingering questions were resolved about whether Kyapaz actually lies in Turkmen waters.

89.   Interfax, *Petroleum Information Agency*, Baku, November 10, 1995. Russian Minister of Fuels and Energy Yuri Shafranik, present at the signing, observed that "(a) Russian company's active participation in implementing projects in Azerbaijan demonstrates Russia's strengthening position in the region."

mercial production is to begin in 2003,[91] and the maximum yield is expected to be 148,000 b/d.[92]

Shah Deniz Field

Azerbaijan made an offer to Iran to join in development of the Shah Deniz field in the Caspian Sea.[93] After some months, the offer was accepted in early May 1996. The Iranian National Oil Company will be represented by the Oil Industries, Engineering and Construction Company,[94] 60 percent of which is owned by private shareholders, and 40 percent of which is owned by the National Iranian Oil Company.[95]

Given the participation of Iran and the U.S. sanctions against Iran, no U.S. company is likely to participate in the development of Shah Deniz. While the United States expressed displeasure at Iran's participation, the British put an opposing spin on the agreement, declaring that it symbolized a new step in international relations that would help shape the 21st century.[96] It remains to be seen whether the participation of Iran will complicate the issue of whether Shah Deniz oil will gain access to the pipeline infrastructure built in part by U.S. companies.

The offer to Iran generally has been viewed as compensation for the refusal of the United States to permit Iran to assume a 5 percent share in the AIOC. Deputy Foreign Minister Mahmoud Vaezi had first stated that Iran had rejected the offer,[97] but in a later comment he noted that Iran was still undecided and would analyze the data which had been provided to them.[98]

Agreement to develop Shah Deniz was concluded with BP (25.5 percent), Statoil (25.5 percent), and the Turkish Petroleum Company (9 percent) in mid–1995. SOCAR took the remaining 40 percent.[99] LUKoil subsequently declared its intention to become a member of the consortium, and LUKoil president Vagit Ale-

---

90.   *Platt's Oilgram News*, March 4, 1996.

Sources say that part of the $135 million signing bonus put down by the participating firms will go to Pennzoil to offset SOCAR's $60 million debt to Pennzoil for its efforts in putting together the gas gathering project for the Gunashli and Neft Dashlari fields, where the natural gas previously had been vented into the atmosphere. See *Platt's Oilgram News*, November 15, 1995.

The Karabakh deposit lies just 15 to 20 km offshore. Its oil reserves are estimated at between 600 to 900 million barrels. Two wells have already been drilled at the deposit. Future crude oil production can be placed into the Baku-Novorossiisk pipeline.

91.   *FBIS-SOV*, November 13, 1995.

92.   *Finansovyye Izvestiya*, November 24, 1995.

93.   *Petroleum Information Agency*, Baku, October 17, 1995.

94.   Interfax, *Petroleum Information Agency*, Baku, May 8, 1996.

95.   *Platt's Oilgram News*, May 14, 1996.

96.   *Reuters*, Baku, June 4, 1996.

97.   Open Media Research Institute, *Daily Report*, December 11, 1995.

98.   *Interfax*, Baku, December 14, 1995.

99.   *Weekly Petroleum Argus*, July 17, 1995. There is no production at Shah Deniz and exploration has been limited. It lies in waters of up to 600 meters in depth. Negotiations actually had begun on Shah Deniz in 1989 but were postponed in favor of the AIOC project. The BP/Statoil alliance had been given sole negotiating rights to this field in 1992, and the Turkish Petroleum Company was brought into the deal in late 1993. Share allocations (Interfax, *Petroleum Information Agency*, February 16, 1996) are subject to further negotiations.

kperov indicated his expectation that LUKoil's stake would be between 20 percent and 40 percent and that it would come out of the SOCAR share. LUKoil was ultimately awarded a 10 percent share, and Elf Aquitaine was also given a 10 percent share. This reduced SOCAR's share to 20 percent.[100] LUKoil expressed a continued hope of acquiring a larger share, for example, by assuming Iran's 10 percent share if Iran turned away.[101] Moreover, LUKoil expressed a readiness to consider buying a portion of the BP-Statoil holdings.

The current membership of the CIOC is outlined in Table 3-12. British Petroleum will be the operator. The exploration phase is expected to require three years, with production flowing three years after that.

Table 3-12
Participation in the Caspian International Oil Company
to Develop Shah Deniz

British Petroleum	25.5 percent
Statoil (Norway)	25.5 percent
Iran	10.0 percent
Elf Aquitaine (France)	10.0 percent
SOCAR (Azerbaijan)	10.0 percent
LUKoil (Russia)	10.0 percent
Turkish Petroleum Co.	
(Turkey)	9.0 percent
Total	100.0 percent

Other Fields

❏ Umid, a promising site in the Caspian Sea, some 50 km south of Baku, is to be offered to Western investors. Umid may be largely gas-bearing.[102]

❏ SOCAR and United BMB Group, Inc., (a U.S. firm) have entered into an arrangement, financed by Citibank, to search for crude oil in the west of the Apsheron Peninsula and to develop crude oil already discovered in the northern wing of the Karadag structure and in the Kyrgyz oil field.[103]

❏ SOCAR and Petoil (Pet Holdings, of Turkey), under a joint venture arrangement (PetAzer), began production from the onshore Kemalettin oil field in mid–1994.

---

100.   Interfax, *Petroleum Information Agency*, Baku, April 4, 1996.

101.   *Platt's Oilgram News*, April 10, 1996.

102.   Occidental Petroleum is among those foreign oil companies interested in Umid. The resource base of Umid is placed at 300 billion cubic meters. See *Business Moskovskiye Novosti*, November 1, 1995.

103.   Interfax, *Petroleum Information Agency*, Baku, October 11, 1995.

❒ SOCAR established a joint venture—Anshad-Petrol—with the Turkish Atilla Dogan Petroleum Corporation to stabilize production at the Neftechala and Khylly oil fields and to explore the Babazanan and Durovdag regions.[104]

❒ Ponder Industries, a small Texas-based independent, entered into a joint venture with SOCAR to rehabilitate more than 2,000 wells and to undertake shallow infield drilling. Ponder was also to look into the feasibility of recovering oil from oil-soaked soils and water.[105]

❒ SOCAR is to enter into an agreement with Elf Aquitaine (France) to develop the Lenkoran-Deniz oilfield in the southern portion of the Azeri sector of the Caspian Sea,[106] but Elf was holding off until the tax regime is settled.

❒ SOCAR and Ramco (UK) are to jointly develop the onshore Muradkhanli oil field.[107] But Ramco appears to be holding off until Azerbaijan develops an onshore tax regime which compares favorably with conditions offshore.[108]

Both this agreement and the SOCAR-Elf agreement were to have been signed in mid-June 1996 but were postponed at the request of the Azeri government. Unresolved tax issues may *not* have been the stumbling block. There is conjecture that the Azeri government would like to see a greater role for international majors such as Exxon or Mobil, rather than smaller, European independents.[109] Azerbaijan needs corporate support in Washington as it attempts to correct the perceived inequities of legislation denying all but humanitarian aid.

Later Oil: The Real Prize

With the issue of how to transport the early oil now apparently settled, the AIOC will turn to selecting a route for the "later" oil, which may reach volumes 700,000 b/d or more at its peak. A final decision on the routing is expected by June 1, 1997. Indications are that the AIOC favors delivery through Georgia to the Turkish port of Ceyhan on the Mediterranean Sea.[110] (See Map 5.) Russia will continue to press

---

104.   Interfax, *Petroleum Report*, March 18-25, 1994.

105.   James P. Dorian and Farouk Mangera, *Oil and War: Impacts on Azerbaijan and Armenia* (Honolulu: East-West Center Working Paper no. 22, September 1995).

106.   *FBIS-SOV*, May 3, 1996.

107.   *Platt's Oilgram News*, June 3, 1996.

108.   *Platt's Oilgram News,* June 5, 1996.

109.   *Platt's Oilgram News*, June 12, 1996.

110.   The oil terminal at the port of Ceyhan has been idle since August 1990, when international economic sanctions were imposed on Iraq. The closure of the Iraqi-Turkish pipeline to Ceyhan has cost Turkey millions in terms of lost transit fees. Initially, Turkey had proposed a pipeline extending from Baku south across a minor portion of Iran, then back into the Nakhichevan area of Azerbaijan and then into Turkey where the pipeline would be extended southward, to join up with the closed Iraqi pipeline at Midyat.

M A P   5 .

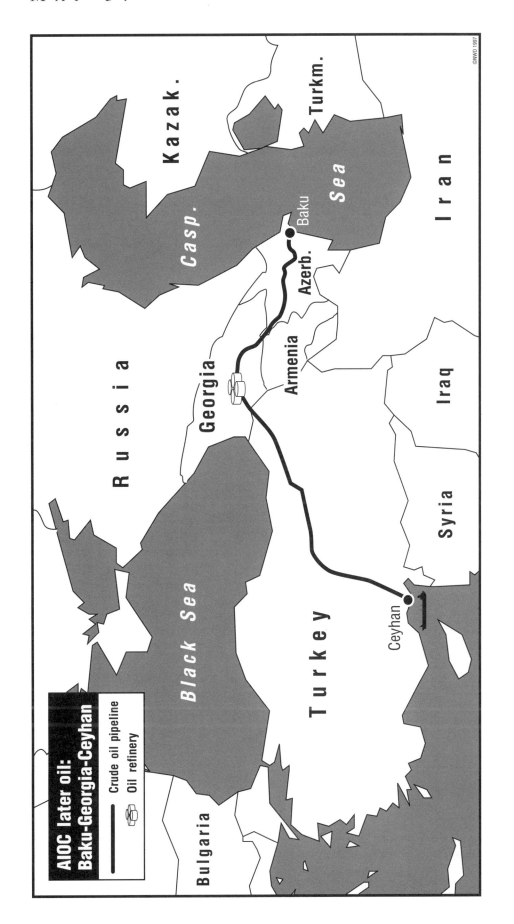

for the later oil to move northward to Novorossiisk. A third route was proposed in early June 1995 by Oil Capital Ltd., a U.S.–based company that indicated a readiness to build a 930-mile, 700,000 b/d pipeline between Baku and the Turkish Mediterranean port of Yumurtalik, which would transit Armenia.[111]

Under the terms of the contract between the AIOC and Azerbaijan, the pipeline moving later oil to market must be put into operation within 54 months of the date the contract is signed. The contract was signed in September 1994, and so an export route must be ready by March 1999.

Turkey hopes that successful operation of the early oil western pipeline will make the case for the later oil to be transported along the Baku-Georgia-Turkey route. Russia, which believes that most if not all of the early oil should flow along the northern route, believes this will set the stage for the later oil to follow.

Table 3-13 outlines a number of the options for moving the later Azeri crude oil to world markets that have been proposed. However, there are just two realistic possibilities: to Novorossiisk or to Turkey. Within Turkey, several export ports were considered, but Ceyhan was judged most viable.

Table 3-13
Pipeline Options for the "Later Oil"

Option	Length (km)	Diameter (in.)	Capacity (thousand b/d)	Cost ($million)
Baku-Ceyhan	2,170	40	800	4,140
(via Turkey)				
Baku-Ceyhan	2,070	40	800	3,929
(via Iran)				
Baku-Poti	1,040	40	800	2,107
Samsun-Ceyhan	890	40	800	2,049
	890	48	1,880	3.501
Baku-Novorossiisk	1,595	28/32/40	800	2,280

Source: Interfax, *Oil, Gas & Coal Report*, no. 43, October 27, 1995. These estimates were prepared by experts of Giprotruboprovod, a Russian scientific research institute specializing in matters relating to pipelines.

An early pipeline proposal had called for a portion of the line to be built across Iran. However, because current U.S. policy precludes any arrangement which might benefit Iran in some way, transiting Iran is not now a viable option.[112] Transiting Armenia cannot be considered as long as the Nagorno-Karabakh issue remains unresolved. By default then, Georgia becomes the choice as the transit

---

111.   An alternative to both the route to Novorossiisk and to Ceyhan was put forward in early June 1995. Oil Capital Ltd., a U.S.-based oil development and financing company, indicated it was prepared to construct a 930-mile, 700,000 b/d pipeline between Baku and the Turkish Mediterranean port of Yumurtalik, transiting Armenia enroute. See *Platt's Oilgram News*, June 6, 1995.

112.   An additional point to consider is that, according to the Iranian constitution, anything built in Iran is Iranian.

country between Azerbaijan and Turkey.

The Burgas-Alexandroupolis Bypass. Oil reaching the Mediterranean port of Ceyhan can be loaded into oceangoing tankers for direct delivery to world markets. Oil arriving at the port of Novorossiisk would naturally pass through the Bosphorus Straits, but the vehement opposition by Turkey to increased tanker traffic through the Bosphorus has encouraged a search for other options. A tanker must make 15 maneuvers as it passes through the Straits. At its narrowest point, the Straits are only 750 meters wide, and a tanker passes just 100 to 200 meters from shore. The nearby population totals 12 million.[113]

Russia has proposed a pipeline to bypass the treacherous Bosphorus Straits, running from the Black Sea port of Bourgas, Bulgaria, to the Aegean Sea port of Alexandroupolis, Greece[114] (Table 3-14). If nothing else, this proposal signals Russia's reluctance to challenge Turkey on the right of free passage of oil tankers through the Bosphorus Straits.[115] (See Map 6.)

Table 3-14
The Burgas-Alexandroupolis Pipeline

Origin	Terminus	Length (km)	Diameter (in.)	Capacity (thousand b/d)	Cost ($million)
Bourgas	Alexandroupo-lis	317	40	600	659-859
(Bulgaria)	(Greece)				
Note: The costs of storage tanks and port facilities may be excluded.					
Sources: Interfax, *Oil, Gas & Coal Report*, no. 43, October 27, 1995; Interfax, *Petroleum Information Agency*, Moscow, October 19, 1995 and March 20, 1996. See also *Middle East Economic Survey*, 18 September 1995, which notes the need to add tanker handling facilities and oil storage tanks both at Bourgas and at Alexandroupolis.					

The pipelines would be build by a Russian (50 percent)–Bulgarian (25 percent)–Greek (25 percent) company. Bulgaria initially sought the larger share of the construction project, to the consternation of both Russia and Greece.

The Burgas-Alexandroupolis pipeline could carry both Azeri crude oil and crude oil from the Tengiz field in Kazakstan. At the same time, its proposed carrying capacity would fall far short of handling all the oil likely to come onto the mar-

---

113.   See *FBIS-SOV*, December 1, 1995.

114.   Greek businessmen who saw an opportunity to expand their shipping interests were the driving force behind the idea of a pipeline bypassing the Bosphrous Straits. See *Cosmos*, Number 1, May 1995, a publication of the Institute of International Relations, Panteion University, Athens, Greece.

115.   Another pipeline, also to originate at Bourgas but with its terminal at the Albanian port of Vlore on the Adriatic Sea, was proposed in late 1994. The pipeline would have an initial capacity of 300,000 b/d, to be increased later to 800,000 b/d. Slovenia, Croatia, and Italy were viewed as potential markets for the crude the pipeline would handle. See *Platt's Oilgram News*, November 1, 1994.

ket from these sources. This indicates an implicit promise that some of the oil will be moved by pipeline to the Turkish port of Ceyhan, rather than to ports on the Black Sea.

The concept of a pipeline bypass of the Bosphorus may be politically viable, but its financial feasibility has been questioned. Gaining financing will require throughput guarantees, which have not been forthcoming. The oil would move by pipeline to Novorossiisk, be stored, loaded into tankers to transit the Black Sea to Bourgas, unloaded into storage tanks, and then pipelined to Alexandroupolis. There, it would be again put into storage, to be picked up by tanker for delivery to markets in Europe. Given the high handling costs associated with such a route, the oil is unlikely to be cost-competitive in European markets.[116] At the same time, some analysts conclude that the costs of unloading large amounts of oil in Bourgas would more than offset the cost of Turkish tolls and pilot fees in the Bosphorus.[117]

Burgas-Vlore Pipeline. The Balkan Pipeline Consortium has put forward another proposal for bypassing the Bosphorus Straits. This pipeline, promoted by AMBO (the Albanian, Macedonian, and Bulgarian Oil Corporation), would provide Azeri, Kazak, and Russian oil with direct access to the markets of southern and central Europe. It would also originate in Bourgas but would terminate at Vlore, Albania (Table 3-15).

Table 3-15
The Burgas-Vlore Pipeline

Origin	Terminus	Length (km)	Diameter (in.)	Capacity (thousand b/d)	Cost ($million)
Bourgas	Vlore	915	36	750	825
(Bulgaria)	(Albania)				
Source: Onnic Marashian, "A Survey of Petroleum Developments in the Caspian/Black Sea Region," 2nd Annual Black Sea/Central Asian Conference, Columbia University, February 8-9, 1996.					

This bypass proposal may be an element the great pipeline game. In the end, construction of the pipeline can be financed only if throughput guarantees are offered by an exporter. Russia could offer such guarantees to strengthen political relations with Bulgaria and Greece.

Nonetheless, the game of pipeline politics is not confined to the Caspian Sea, but also involves Kazakstan, Turkmenistan, and Uzbekistan, which like Azerbaijan must find acceptable ways of moving their oil and gas to export markets. A decision taken by one exporting country relative to the construction of export pipelines inevitably will impact on others.[118]

---

116. Vagit Alekperov, president of LUKoil, agrees. "The (Burgas-Alexandroupolis pipeline) is a very tricky project. At one time we considered it and decided not to take part in it. Calculations showed that shipping through three ports... would cost too much." See *FBIS-SOV*, July 19, 1995.

117. *Foreign Report*, June 30, 1994.

Total AIOC Crude Oil Production

A preliminary timetable had been laid out for developing oil production by the AIOC at the Azeri, Chirag, and Gunashli fields (Table 3-16); delays in completing all the necessary agreements has pushed the first appearance of the early oil to mid–1997 at the earliest. (See Map 7.)

Table 3-16
Future AIOC Crude Oil Production

Year	Thousand b/d
1997	30-40
1988	80
2004	300
2010	700

Source: Interfax, *Oil, Gas & Coal Report*, no. 43, October 27, 1995. Citing estimates prepared by Azerbaijani experts; AIOC estimates.

The estimate of 700,000 b/d coming from Gunashli, Chirag, and Azeri by 2010 may be below realistic peak production.[119] Yet, complications during exploration or development or continued softness of world oil prices may slow expansion and postpone peak production. It therefore may be premature to think in terms of peak production for the AIOC.

---

118. Valery Chernayev, president of Transneft, the Russian oil pipeline monopoly, puts little stock in statements about diversity of export routes. In his words, "(s)uch statements are prompted by politics. Most of the oil actually will be transported along the Russian route. The multiple-routes decision is just the AIOC's political courtesy to the United States and Turkey, which backed the Georgian route." See *Russian Petroleum Investor*, November 1995.

119. AIOC sources have talked in terms of 800,000 b/d by the year 2010.

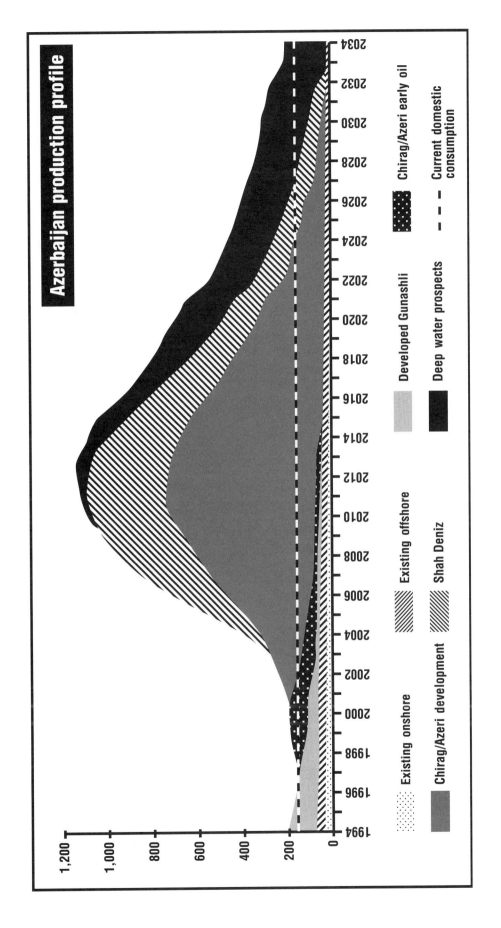

Source: States of the Former Soviet Union, CIA, 1992.

CHAPTER 4

Kazakstan

Table 4-1
Kazakstan at a Glance

Currency	Tenge (November, 1993)
Rate of Exchange	70.62 tenge/$1 (November 1, 1996)
Gross Domestic Product	$18 billion
Inflation	60 percent (1995)
Population	17.377 million (July 1995 est)
By Nationality	
Kazakh	41.9 percent
Russian	37 percent
Ukrainian	5.2 percent
German	4.7 percent
Uzbek	2.1 percent
Tatar	2 percent
Other	7.1 percent

Sources: Central Intelligence Agency (CIA), *The World Factbook 1995* (Washington, D.C.: CIA, 1995); *FBIS-SOV*, October 30, 1995; *Interfax*, Almaty, December 8, 1995; Ekonomika i zhuzn, no. 45, November 1996; World Bank data. *Finansovyye Izvestiya*, May 14, 1996; World Bank data.

Kazakstan was first organized as an autonomous republic of Russia in 1920 and was called the Kyrgyz Autonomous Soviet Socialist Republic (ASSR) until 1925, when the name was changed to the Kazakh ASSR. The Kazakh ASSR was raised to republic status in 1936.

Kazakstan declared its independence on December 16, 1991. Nursultan Nazarbayev, a former Communist party official who had assumed leadership of the country in 1989, was elected in the country's first presidential election. A new constitution was passed in August 1995, which greatly increased the power of president Nazarbayev and extended his term until 2000.

Kazakstan has a large population of both ethnic Russians, who were moved there during the Soviet era to run the economy, and Germans. During the years before and after independence, large numbers of Russians and Germans left the country in fear that they would become second-class citizens. This population shift cost Kazakstan almost 1.1 million people.[120]

Within the Soviet system, Kazakstan's economy centered around the output of raw materials, which were supplied to other republics, chiefly Russia. Kazakstan was and remains a major producer of grain; it is the only country among the former Soviet republics that has the ability to produce agricultural surpluses.

Although the crude oil and natural gas potential of Kazakstan was known to Moscow, a lack of capital and the physical complexities of developing the two key deposits—Tengiz and Karachaganak—effectively kept these resources locked in the ground.

Kazakstan has not made any notable progress in shifting to a market economy. In 1995, just 35 percent of the work force found employment in the private sector, while the private sector contributed only 25 percent to GDP.[121]

Crude Oil

Production of crude oil in Kazakstan had been declining in recent years (Table 4-2), falling more than 22 percent since 1991. A recovery in production was attained in 1996, although slightly below planned levels for that year. The future of the Kazak oil sector lies in development of the Tengiz oil field and the Kazak sector of the Caspian Sea; there are little or no funds for investment in other areas. Future production will continue to reflect until Tengiz gains, which cannot take place in a substantial way unless and until there is a way to transport it to markets in the Far Abroad.

---

120. *Financial Times*, May 23, 1996.
121. *Finansovyye Izvestiya*, May 14, 1996.

Table 4-2
Kazak Crude Oil Production

Year	Thousand b/d
1970	262
1980	374
1985	456
1988	510
1990	516
1991	532
1992	502
1993	459.4
1994	430.9
1995	
Original plan	452.0
Revised plan	432.8
Actual	412.6
1996	
Plan	466
Estimated	459
1997 Plan	530
Of which, joint ventures	162

Note: Includes production of natural gas liquids.

Sources: *Neft i Gaz Kazakhstana (Oil and Gas of Kazakhstan)*, a special supplement to *Neft i Kapital*, October 1995; Interfax, *Petroleum Report*, November 3-10, 1995; *Kazakhstan, An Economic Profile*, July 1993; British Broadcasting Corporation, *Summary of World Broadcasts, Part 1, Former USSR*, August 25, 1995; *East Bloc Energy*, July 1995; *Post-Soviet Geography*, April 1992; Interfax, *Petroleum Information Agency*, Almaty, December 15, 1995; *FBIS-SOV*, February 9, 1996; Interfax, Petroleum Information Agency, Almaty, December 1, 1996, and December 28, 1996.

Despite the fact that output at Tengiz has been comparatively frozen, Western oil-producing joint ventures are making notable progress in contributing to national oil production levels, comprising 37,100 b/d, or about 9.1 percent of total production in 1994. Joint venture production averaged 57,200 b/d during 1995, or about 13.9 percent of output (Table 4-3) and rising substantially to an estimated 107,000 b/d during 1996, to account for more than 23 percent of the national total (Table 4-4).[122]

Table 4-3
Joint Venture Production of Crude Oil Kazakstan, 1993-1995
Thousand b/d

Joint Venture	1993	1994	1995
Tengizchevroil	22.52	38.53	
Kazpromstavba	3,23	3.08.	
Embavedoil	-	0.12	n.a.
Gyural	0.09	0.11	
Svetlandoil	0.03	0.05	
Total	25.95	41.88	57.2
Share of national Total (percent)	5.6	9.1	13.9

Note: Totals have been derived separately and may not add.

Sources: *Neft i Kapital*, May 1995, and Table 4-2.

Table 4-4
Kazak Crude Oil Production: Actual versus Planned, 1995 and 1996
Thousand b/d

	1995	1995	1996
	Plan	Actual	Plan
Total (revised) Of which	432.8	412.6	480
Munaigaz	318.2	293.0	254
Kazakhgaz	58.5	49.2	69.4
Yutek	n.a.	n.a.	50
Joint ventures	56.1	57.2	106.6

Note: Of the actual total for 1995, 13,200 b/d has not been allocated by producer. This volume perhaps may be attributed to Yutek.

Sources: Interfax, *Petroleum Information Agency*, Almaty, January 18, 1996; British Broadcasting Corporation, *Summary of World Broadcasts, Part 1, Former USSR*, February 8, 1996; Interfax, *Petroleum Information Agency*, Almaty, April 2, 1996.

A successor company has been established to replace the national oil company Kazakhstanmunaigaz. This company, Munaigaz, is in effect the holding company for all the activities and assets of the Kazak oil and gas industry. There are eight oil extraction enterprises under Munaigaz, the largest of which are Mangystaumun-

---

122.   Interfax, *Petroleum Information Agency*, Almaty, January 18, 1996 and December 28, 1996.

aigaz, Uzenmunaigaz, and Embaneft (see Table 4-5). These organizations operate the Mangyshlak, Uzen, and Emba oil fields, respectively.

Table 4-5
Crude Oil Production Under Munaigaz, 1994

Producer	Thousand b/d
Mangystaumunaigaz	106.39
Uzenmunaigaz	66.68
Embaneft	32.84
Aktyubinskneft	53.49
Yuzhneftegaz	36.11
Tengizmunaigaz	17.72
Karazhanbasmunai	16.98
Munai	0.20
Total	330.41

Source: *Neft i gaz Kazakstana*, a special supplement to *Neft i Kapital*, October 1995.

Kazakstan's crude oil export pattern is quite different from Russia's, but not by choice. Kazakstan has depended upon access to the Russian pipeline network for much of deliveries to the Far Abroad, and that access is restricted. As a consequence, most crude oil exports have been delivered to the Near Abroad (Table 4-6). Within the Near Abroad, Russia imports the largest share (137,800 b/d), followed by Ukraine (36,200 b/d), the Baltics (13,000 b/d), and Azerbaijan (684 b/d).[123] Exports to Russia are part of the "swaps" arrangement, discussed below.

Kazakstan's quota for access to Russian pipelines leading to the port of Novorossiisk is just 76,000 b/d. Tengiz crude oil takes up the bulk of quota, about 66,000 b/d during 1996.[124] If Tengiz is to raise its output levels, then additional transport means must be identified. In recent months other routes to western markets, including swaps with Azerbaijan, swaps with Kazakstan, deliveries by rail and by inland waterway, have either come into play or soon will. These options have allowed crude oil exports to reach about 76,000 b/d during 1996, not much of an improvement over 1995, but implementation will be on a broader scale during 1997, permitting exports to reach roughly 140,000 b/d that year. Surprisingly, 40 percent of Tengiz crude oil production is now moved by means other than the pipeline to Samara, Russia.[125]

---

123.   Interfax, *Petroleum Information Agency*, Almaty, January 23, 1996.
124.   *Russian Petroleum Investor*, December 1996-January 1997.

Table 4-6
Kazak Crude Oil Exports, 1995, Thousand b/d

Production*	412.6
Exports	
To Near Abroad	137.8
To Far Abroad	74.2
Subtotal	212.0
Tengizchevroil	
To Near Abroad	10.0
To Far Abroad	44.4
Subtotal	54.4
Total to Near Abroad	147.8
Total to Far Abroad	118.6
Grand Total, Crude Oil Exports	266.4
*Includes joint venture output.	
Sources: British Broadcasting Corporation, *Summary of World Broadcasts, Part 1, Former USSR*, January 25, 1996; Interfax, *Petroleum Information Agency*, Almaty, January 23, 1996.	

Kazakstan increasingly has looked to oil exports as a source of government funds. Unfortunately, the tax authorities seem unaware of (or choose to ignore) the relationship between investors' willingness to invest and their prospects for attaining a return on investment. Joint ventures are exposed to a 20 percent value-added tax (VAT), a 15 percent withholding tax, a ban on consolidated taxes, an excess profits tax, and high tax rates on assets. Of these taxes, the excess profits tax, which is as high as 90 percent in some instances, is potentially the most damaging.

There is also an export tax of ECU23 per ton of crude oil (equivalent to about $3.78 per barrel) and ECU5 per ton of natural gas ($6 per 1,000 cubic meters). Most ventures that involve foreign investment have been able to secure exemptions from the export tax, and the 20 percent VAT on imports theoretically is refundable, but bureaucratic delays slow the process.[126]

Refineries: The Role of "Swaps"

There are three oil refineries in Kazakstan: Shymkent (formerly Chimkent), Pavlodar, and Atyrau (formerly Guryev) (Table 4-7).[127] Pavlodar and Shymkent are located in the eastern part of the country, far removed from the centers of oil production. These two refineries benefit from a swapping arrangement with Russia.

125.   *Platt's Oilgram News*, December 23, 1996.
126.   *Russian Petroleum Investor*, November 1995.
127.   See Interfax, *Petroleum Information Agency*, Moscow, September 19, 1995 for information on refinery limitations.

Under the swap arrangement, oil from western Kazakstan is delivered by pipeline for refining at Samara (formerly Kuybyshev) in Russia. (See Map 8.) In return, oil is delivered by pipeline from oil fields of Western Siberia for refining at Pavlodar and Shymkent.[128]

As a result of the swaps, just 30 percent of the oil charged to refining in Kazakstan is domestic in origin; the remainder is from Western Siberia. Atyrau is linked to oil supplies from Tengiz and other fields by a comparatively short pipeline.[129]

Table 4-7
Kazakstan's Three Refineries

Item	Atyrau	Pavlodar	Shymkent
Capacity (Thous. b/d)	100	150	130
Crude oil	Mixture of Martyshin and Mangyshlak crudes plus small amounts of Tengiz and Buzanchinsk crudes	West Siberian crudes	Mixture of West Siberian and Kumkol crudes plus Aktyubinsk crude & Uzbek condensate
Light product yield	54.9 percent	76 percent	58 percent
Capacity utilization			
Jan-Jun 1995	72.7 percent	30 percent	55.3 percent
1994	100.01 percent	44 percent	57 percent
Source: *Neft i Kapital*, No. 12, December 1995.			

Refinery capacity utilization in Kazakstan is very low, especially at Pavlodar which is wholly dependent on Western Siberian oil. The low utilization level for Atyrau is surprising, given that it handles only local crudes. The three refineries processed an average of 216,000 b/d during 1995 (Table 4-8), which was 8 percent less than in 1994.[130]

---

128.   A statement of intent has been signed between Kazakstan and YUKOS, one of Russia's largest vertically integrated oil companies, to set up a 240,000 b/d crude oil processing arrangement. As in the past, crude oil from Kazakstan will be delivered to refineries at Samara, Russia. YUKOS controls two refineries at Samara, with a combined processing capacity of 600,000 b/d. These refineries were constructed specifically to handle Kazak oil. See *Platt's Oilgram News*, May 20, 1996.

129.   The Atyrau refinery is scheduled for major reconstruction, to be carried out by a consortium led by Hydrocarbon Engineering (France) at a cost of about $650 million. The key unit to be added will be a liquid-phase catalytic cracker. Upon completion, Atyrau will be able to process 100,000 b/d of high sulfur crudes from Tengiz and Mangyshlak.

Table 4-8
Crude Oil Refined, 1995

Refinery	Thousand b/d
Pavlodar	60
Shymkent	72
Atyrau	84
Total	216
Source: *Petroleum Information Agency*, Almaty, January 19, 1996.	

The very low volumes of light products (essentially, motor gasoline, aviation gasoline, jet fuel, and diesel fuel, plus lubricants) at Atyrau and Shymkent are indicative of obsolescent technologies. Modern-day economies require much higher light product yields, particularly of gasoline. Gasoline yields at the Kazak refineries average 19.6 percent. In comparison, a modern Western refinery designed to maximize the production of gasoline would yield more than double that. All three Kazak refineries must be reconstructed, and a new refinery must be built at Mangystau to process heavy Buzachinsk oils.[131] The cost of carrying out these plans will be on the order of $3.5 billion.

The 1995 swaps arrangement between Kazakstan and Russia called for a substantial increase over the actual volume achieved during 1994. For a variety of reasons, the volume swapped actually fell during 1995 (Table 4-9).

Table 4-9
Russian and Kazak Oil Swaps

	Thousand b/d		
	1994 Actual	**1995 Plan**	**1995 Actual**
Kazak exports to Russia	102.6	196	88
Russian exports to Kazakstan	66.3	134.4	52.5*
*First 8 months 1995 average.			
Sources: *Interfax Oil, Gas & Coal Report*, no. 43, 27 October 1995; *Finansovyye Izvestiya*, January 25, 1996.			

Oil delivered from Western Siberia to the Shymkent and Pavlodar refineries

---

130.   *Petroleum Information Agency*, Almaty, January 19, 1996.

131.   The potential reserves of the highly viscous Buzachinsk oil-bearing region are placed at about 1 billion tons (7.3 billion barrels). Current extraction reaches about 120,000 b/d, and the market prices for such crude oil are comparatively low. To construct the Mangystau refinery, with a capacity of 60,000 b/d, would cost an estimated $1.575 billion. See *Neft i Kapital*, no. 12, December 1995.

moves via the Omsk-Pavlodar-Shymkent pipeline. (See Map 8.) This is not the best approach because the volumes are kept low, but there are no other viable options. Beginning in 1995, a second pipeline, from Aktyubinsk to Orsk, was used for the swaps between Russia and Kazakstan. This is a comparatively short pipeline which, in the past, delivered oil from the fields in the Aktyubinsk area of Kazakstan to a refinery across the border in Russia, at Orsk. A reported 70 percent of the product yield at Orsk was returned to Aktyubinsk. This arrangement suited no one: Kazakstan needed additional oil for its Pavlodar and Shymkent refineries, and Russia was short of petroleum products.

Under a swaps arrangement worked out for 1995, 32,000 b/d of Aktyubinsk oil would be supplied to Orsk, and ONAKO, one of the Russian vertically integrated oil companies, would provide a like amount to Pavlodar. After six months, Kazakstan had shipped an average of less than 5,250 b/d to Orsk. Swaps for the remainder of 1995 were revised, to half the original volume.

A Pipeline for Replacing Swaps

The proposed crude oil production schedule for Tengiz allows Kazakstan to plan construction of a pipeline running eastward across the country to link with the Pavlodar and Shymkent refineries. If and when that pipeline goes into operation, the need for oil swaps with Russia will have been obviated. Yet Tengiz oil will still be geographically close to Samara. If pipeline access can be maintained, Kazak oil could compete with Ural-Volga crudes.

Kazak crude oil has a higher sulfur content than Western Siberian crudes. Kazak experts believe it would be inefficient to attempt to refine Tengiz crude oil at Pavlodar and Shymkent because of the expensive equipment reconfigurations that would be required.[132] A better approach is to construct new refining capacities in the western part of Kazakstan, near the center of crude oil production, and to continue the swaps arrangement with Russia.

Give-and-Take

The three Kazak refineries also process some oil on a give-and-take basis: the refineries process the crude for a per ton fee, or can keep a portion of the petroleum products as payment. For example, Shymkent refined 2.25 million tons of crude oil on a give-and-take basis during the first eight months of 1995, under contracts with the crude suppliers at $13 to $17 per ton. On certain occasions, Shymkent takes payment in petroleum products.

LUKoil's Market Entry

None of the three refineries in Kazakstan produces motor oils. LUKoil is seeking to take advantage of this market opportunity to sell a portion of its output of lube oils to Kazakstan. Proceeds from the sales will be used to construct a lube oil facility at the Atyrau oil refinery. This facility, when completed, will produce about 1,000 b/d of lube oils, sufficient to cover about one-third of Kazakstan's daily requirements.[133]

---

132. *FBIS-SOV*, February 9, 1996.

M A P   8 .

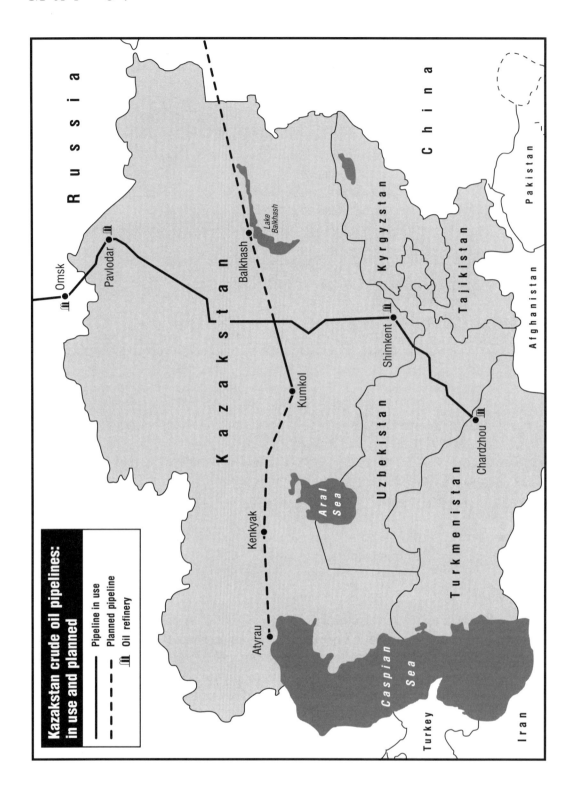

Kazakstan crude oil pipelines: in use and planned

Pipeline in use
Planned pipeline
Oil refinery

Oil Exports

The decline in crude oil production had been paralleled somewhat by a decline in oil consumption in Kazakstan. This has permitted oil exports to continue, albeit at considerably reduced levels (Table 4-10). Consumption hit a peak of 367,000 b/d in 1989, and has been slowly falling since.[134]

Table 4-10
Kazak Oil Exports, 1990–1995

Year	Thousand b/d
1990	64
1991	110
1992	162
1993	124
1994	82
1995	74.2

Note: These are *net* exports, and include both crude oil and petroleum products.

Sources: Various World Bank publications.

Kazakstan had never been a major contributor to the world oil market. During the Soviet era, about two-thirds of Kazak oil exports were directed to consumers in the Near Abroad. Kazakstan was just as dependent then on access to the Russian oil export pipeline network as it is now.

The present-day export potential of Kazakstan is determined largely by the volume of Kazak crude oil that Transneft, the Russian oil pipeline operator, is prepared to move through its pipeline network to buyers in the Near Abroad and Far Abroad. At one time, comparatively large amounts of oil, reaching 60,000 b/d, moved from Kazakstan by tanker across the Caspian Sea to ports in other republics. Currently, however, the volumes of Kazak oil handled by Caspian seagoing tanker are very limited. Shipment by rail is equally marginal.

Natural Gas

Kazakstan's natural gas sector is disadvantaged for several reasons:

❑ Most production is in the northwestern part of the country and, similar to oil, consumers are found in the east. No domestic pipelines link the two.

❑ Development of the huge Karachaganak natural gas and gas condensate

---

133.   Interfax, *Petroleum Information Agency*, Moscow, September 19, 1995.

134.   United States General Accounting office, *Kazakhstan Unlikely to Be Major Source of Oil for the United States*, GAO/GGD-94-74, March 1994.

field has been beyond Kazakstan's capability.

❑ Distortions in pricing—such as tariffs for the domestic sector that are lower than the price of imported gas and the cost of indigenous production—limit domestic extraction (Table 4-11) and artificially inflate demand.

Most of the natural gas consumed in Kazakstan today must be imported from Russia, Turkmenistan, and Uzbekistan. Southern Kazakstan, the location of major cities such as Almaty and others, is provided with natural gas from Uzbekistan.

Table 4-11
Natural Gas Extraction in Kazakstan

Year	Billion cubic meters
1970	2.1
1975	5.2
1980	4.3
1985	5.0
1988	6.6
1990	6.6
1991	7.9
1992	8.1
1993	6.7
1994	4.5
1995	5.4
1996 plan	6.3
1996 est.	4.2

Sources: *Kazakhstan Economic Survey*, Center for Economic Reform, Almaty, 1995: *Kazakhstan, An Economic Profile*, July 1993; *East Bloc Energy*, July 1995; *Post-Soviet Geography*, April 1992; Interfax, *Petroleum Information Agency*, Almaty, January 18, 1996; Interfax, *Petroleum Information Agency*, Almaty, April 2, 1996; *FBIS-SOV*, April 8, 1996; Interfax, *Petroleum Information Agency*, Almaty, December 1, 1996.

Natural gas extraction recovered somewhat during 1995, but still fell short of the 1993 level.[135] Output suffered considerably in 1996, falling to below 1980 output.

The geographic separation of natural gas producers and consumers will continue for some time, even after the Karachaganak field goes into production. Kazakstan therefore may continue to rely on imports, unless a very capital-intensive system for transporting natural gas within the country is built.

In 1995 for example, Kazakstan imported 2.5 bcm from Uzbekistan and about

135.   Interfax, *Petroleum Information Agency*, January 18, 1996.

3.2 bcm from Turkmenistan which, when added to domestic production, increased the volume of gas available to the economy to 11.1 bcm. The largest producer of natural gas in Kazakstan is the Karachaganak gas condensate field, which yielded 2.4 bcm during 1995, while Tengiz provided 0.9 bcm.[136]

Coal

Most of the expansion of coal extraction since 1970 has been provided by the Ekibastuz coal basin. Output rose from just under 23 million tons in 1970 to almost 90 million tons by 1988, the peak production year (Table 4-12). After 1988, production declined by about 27 percent (paralleling declines in other sectors of the economy). Nonetheless, Kazakstan remains a major producer of coal, with 1996 output to reach about 97 million tons.

Table 4-12
Coal Extraction in Kazakstan

Year	Million tons
1970	62
1975	92
1980	115
1985	131
1988	143
1990	131
1991	130
1994	104.6
1995	83.2
1996 plan	97.4

Sources: *Kazakhstan, An Economic Profile*, July 1993; *Post-Soviet Geography*, April 1992; *FBIS-SOV*, March 22, 1996.

Coal has historically provided the largest share of energy consumption, and continues to be the primary source of energy. For example, in 1991 the contribution of coal was greater than all other forms of primary energy (oil, natural gas, nuclear, and hydropower) combined.

As noted, the bulk of the electric power generated in Kazakstan originates at thermal power plants which in turn are 90 percent fueled by coal. Much of the coal is low grade, which means that environmental degradation is a serious problem in Almaty and elsewhere. Renovation of coal-burning plants is incredibly expensive, and for that reason Kazakstan is seriously considering embarking on a nuclear power program.

---

136. *Russian Petroleum Investor,* December 1996-January 1997.

Electricity

Kazak electricity users are no different than consumers elsewhere in the Near Abroad: they simply are not paying their bills. Even so, tariffs are too low and fall well short of covering generation costs. As a result, electricity generation and consumption have been less sensitive to declines in economic activity. Reduced electricity generation (Table 4-13) continues to be offset by favorable power imports from Russia. Electricity generating capacity totals 18.9 mw, of which thermal power stations account for almost 89 percent with hydropower making up the remainder.

Table 4-13
Electricity Generation in Kazakstan

Year	Billion kwh
1970	34.7
1975	52.5
1980	61.5
1985	81.3
1988	88.4
1990	87.4
1991	86.0
1992	81
1993	76.1
1994	67.9
1995	66.7
of which:	
Thermal	58.3
Hydro	8.3
Other	0.1

Sources: *Kazakhstan, An Economic Profile*, July 1993; *Kazakhstan Economic Survey*, Center for Economic Reform, Almaty, 1995; *Post-Soviet Geography*, April 1992; Central Intelligence Agency (CIA), *Handbook of International Economic Statistics 1995* (Washington, D. C.: CIA, September 1995); *FBIS-SOV*, March 22, 1996.

Consumers have taken advantage of the lack of Russian limits on electricity imports and had run up a massive $400 million debt by mid-1996, most of which had been accumulated in 1994. Russia imposed restrictions on electricity exports to Kazakstan, as did Uzbekistan and Kyrgyzstan for nonpayment. Kazakstan hoped to sharply reduce its consumption of Russian electricity from 23.5 billion kwh in 1992, to 15.9 billion kwh in 1994,[137] to 7.5 billion kwh in 1995, and to 4 billion kwh in 1996.[138]

Kazakstan balances its electricity imports from Russia with deliveries of about 40 million tons of Ekibastuz and Karaganda coal to power stations in the Urals and in Siberia.[139] Kazakstan also has been a traditional exporter of electricity to certain regions of Russia. Exports to these markets dropped from 16.7 billion kwh in 1992 to 10 billion kwh in 1994, largely because of a drop in power needs.[140]

Table 4-14
Kazak Electricity Supply and Demand, 1995

Domestic Generation	Billion Kwh
Thermal	58.3
Hydro	8.3
Other	0.1
Subtotal	66.7
Imports	19.5
Total Supply	86.2
Exports	12.7
Apparent Consumption	73.5
Source: *FBIS-SOV*, August 9, 1996.	

Kazakstan imported a total of 19.5 billion kwh during 1995 which, when added to local generation, provided the country with 86.2 billion kwh. Of that amount, about 73.5 billion kwh were consumed internally, and 12.7 billion kwh were exported, thus making Kazakstan a net importer of electric power.

Per capita consumption of electric power in Kazakstan has been declining in recent years, from 6,255 kwh/year in 1990 to 4,424 kwh in 1995, about one-third the U.S. average, roughly two-thirds the per capita electricity consumption in Russia, and slightly exceeding per capita usage in Ukraine. Effective domestic use of electric power is masked however by the high losses of power during transmission, exceeding 15 percent during 1995.

Nuclear Power

There is one small nuclear breeder reactor in Kazakstan, at Aqtau (formerly Shevchenko), where its main function has been to distill sea water.[141] The U.S. government has expressed some concern about this reactor, which began operations in 1972—concerns related both to the state of the reactor itself and to its proximity to

---

137.   *FBIS-SOV*, March 11, 1996.
138.   British Broadcasting Corporation, *Summary of World Broadcasts, Part 1, Former USSR*, February 8, 1996.
139.   *FBIS-SOV*, February 1, 1996.
140.   *FBIS-SOV*, March 11, 1996.

Iran. The Kazak government has disclosed its intention to operate the reactor beyond its intended life time, and that gives rise to the prospect of metal fatigue.[142] Border controls between Kazakstan and Iran are quite weak, and spent fuel is stored on site, which raises the prospect that, by various means, Iran might augment its nuclear weapons capability through its comparatively easy access to the reactor site.

Kazak officials are now working on a concept for developing the energy sector up to the year 2030. This concept envisages a role for nuclear electric power, with a nuclear power station to be built on the Semipalatinsk nuclear testing site.[143]

Privatization

Privatization of course is one approach to raising capital. Western observers doubted that much interest would be generated by the Shymkent refinery or the two oil enterprises, in part because of uncertainty surrounding the role of Russian oil companies in Kazakstan. Any interest in Aktyubinsk would center on the Zhanazhol oil field. Potential investors in the oil enterprises must consider the risk of oil reserve ownership.[144] Additionally, the oil ministry officials, obviously trying to protect their own interests, opposed any tender offering. Kazakstan plans to continue privatization of its crude oil, natural gas, and electricity sectors during 1997 but on a much broader scale, as a means of securing technology transfer and capital infusion, further enhancing the country's attraction to the foreign investor.

The heavy publicity surrounding development of the oil-producing sector and the multiple pipeline proposals for moving the oil and gas to foreign markets masks difficulties for other investors in the country. Bureaucratic entanglements at lower levels seem to be a key obstacle to getting anything done. Even at Tengiz and Karachaganak, progress is measured in inches, not miles.

Corruption is endemic. The Kazakstani State Property Committee has stated that more than $500 million earned from oil sales during the past several years was never received. Blame was placed on a corrupted system of trade.[145] The United States has taken its concern to Kazak president Nazarbayev. U.S. Ambassador-at-large Jim Collins, in bilateral talks with President Nazarbayev and other officials, emphasized that crime and corruption were impediments to western interests, and that Kazakstan must establish a rule of law.[146]

---

141.   The BN-350, a liquid-metal-cooled fast reactor has provided both electricity and heat for the production of drinking water. The BN-350 is still the only power reactor in the world being used to supply heat for industrial-scale desalination. See *IAEA Bulletin*, 2/1995.

142.   The BN-350 fast reactor went off-line in April 1995. A major refurbishment program followed and the reactor came back on-line January 5, 1996. See *Nucleonics Week*, February 15, 1996.

143.   *FBIS-SOV*, November 2, 1995.

144.   *Financial Times*, April 30, 1996.

145.   Open Media Research Institute, *Daily Report*, November 1, 1996.

146.   *Reuter,* Almaty, November 20, 1996.

Oil

The initial effort to privatize the oil sector of Kazakstan centered around the sale of the Shymkent refinery, with a processing capacity of 130,000 b/d, and the Yuzhneftegaz and Aktyubinskneft oil producing associations. Aktyubinskneft produced 52,900 b/d during 1994, while Yuzhneftegaz production was considerably lower, at 36,000 b/d. Both have substantial reserves, with those at Aktyubinskneft estimated at about 850 million barrels, and Yuzhneftegaz with slightly less than 600 million barrels.

Vitol SA won the tender for Shymkent, but the sale of Yuzhneftegaz is muddied, and there were no bidders for Aktyubinskneft. The Zhanazhol field is one of the more prospective sites of Aktyubinskneft, and several companies have held talks with Kazakstan regarding its development, not wanting to take all of Aktyubinskneft but hoping to split off Zhanazhol.

The Kumkol oil field is the centerpiece of Yuzhneftegaz, whose control ultimately was won by Hurricane Hydrocarbons (Canada). Earlier, Samson International (U.S.) had been declared the winner, but Samson also thought it should therefore be able to take over the LUKoil-Kumkol joint venture, involved in the northern portion of the Kumkol field. Kazak authorities said no; Samson stood firm and subsequently lost out to Hurricane which had improved upon its offer. In the end, Hurricane was able to acquire Yuzneftegaz's shares in all its joint ventures, including Kumkol.

LUKoil had signed a deal with Yuzhneftegaz in 1995 to develop the Kumkol field which feeds the Shymkent refinery but LUKoil has invested nothing to date at Kumkol. Kumkol will not be easy to develop. Kumkol has about 150 producing wells but the crude is very waxy and has to be mixed with Russian crude before delivery to the Shymkent refinery, leaving Yuzhneftegaz hostage to Moscow's whims. Far from any port, the Kumkol oil is limited to the Kazak market where it is sold for rates well below world market levels.[147]

Development began in 1990; output in 1996 should have averaged 50,000 b/d. Kumkol crude is free of hydrogen sulfide and has the added advantage of being located close to the Pavlodar-Shymkent pipeline.[148] But Hurricane recognizes difficult times lie ahead, and the reserves of Kumkol won't mean much unless the oil can be profitably pumped and transported to foreign buyers.[149]

Natural Gas

Kazakstan hopes to sell off its transit gas pipelines which carry natural gas from Uzbekistan, Russia, and Turkmenistan. Buyers would have management control and would earn transit fees, in return for investments and upkeep, which could be costly because these pipelines are in poor operating condition. Moreover, transit fees would have to be negotiated with Turkmenistan and Uzbekistan. But the key to successful operation would be securing access to the Gazprom pipeline network,

---

147. *Financial Times*, August 30, 1996.
148. *FBIS-SOV*, September 12, 1996.
149. *Pipeline News*, no. 27, August 1996.

as a way of moving gas to western markets.[150] Yet is it realistic to assume that foreign investors would be granted unrestricted access, when a member of the CIS is not? In addition, foreign investors likely might encounter higher transit fee demands from all transit countries.

The importance of Kazakstan as a transit country for natural gas almost rivals that of Ukraine. These transit flows are very substantial, having reached 80 bcm during 1993, then falling to about 46 bcm in 1995 but resurging again to an estimated 64 bcm during 1996.[151] Kazakstan generally takes natural gas in payment but unlike Ukraine, has avoided accusations of stealing gas from the pipelines in times of need. If foreign investors take over management of the transit pipelines, as the government hopes, would payment of transit fees in kind continue?

Electricity

Kazakstan has moved swiftly in its drive to privatize its electric power sector but this haste has been marked by corruption, with some companies literally being given away to select interests, and by deals that have fallen apart. Most sales have been accompanied by pledges to invest very substantial sums, but will that investment be forthcoming? Who will keep track of such commitments and how can these commitments be enforced?

There are two generating facilities to be privatized. Karagandinskaya Two is a coal-fired facility located near Karaganda with an annual generating capacity of 3 billion kwh although just 1.2 billion kwh were supplied in 1995. The second facility, Yermakovskaya, is a hydropower plant located near Pavlodar. It supplied 11.1 billion kwh during 1995, but has the capacity to produce 18.5 billion kwh. Both plants need updating.

Additionally, the national grid is to be tendered. The winner will have the right to operate the grid and to coordinate imports and exports of electricity, but must also make investments in the modernization and development of the grid.[152]

Agreements have been reached on the sale of four of Kazakstan's largest electric power stations: Ekibastuz, Almatyenergo, Dzhezkazgan and Pavlodar.

AES (U.S.) and Sun Tree Power Ltd. (Israel) have agreed to acquire the coal-fired Ekibastuz power plant, located in northeastern Kazakstan.[153] The facility is in very poor shape and in 1995 utilized just 20 percent of its capacity of 4,000 Mw. In the judgment of AES CEO Dennis Bakke, "it is not very safe, it is not very productive, not very clean." AES will charge Kazakstan about 3 cents per kwh, 25 percent less than it now pays Russia. AES holds a 70 percent stake in the joint venture and will operate the facility. Sun Tree, which is leading the government relations side of the development effort, holds the remaining 30 percent.[154]

---

150.   *Financial Times,* November 8, 1996.

151.   *Neft i Kapital,* December 1996.

152.   British Broadcasting Corporation, *Summary of World Broadcasts, Part 1, Former USSR,* October 18, 1996.

153.   In reporting on the sale of Ekibastuz, *Izvestiya* (August 16, 1996) perhaps reflected the true feeling towards what it once had but which has now been taken over by the Near Abroad. The headline to the story read: "Americans Buy One of the Largest Soviet Electric Power Stations."

154.   *Washington Post,* August 13, 1996 and *Intercon's Daily,* August 13, 1996.

AES pledged to raise output from 7.2 billion kwh to 22 billion kwh per year within 5 years, after which output is to be increased up to 27 billion kwh.[155] The commitment made by AES and Sun Tree is somewhat precarious, given the lower tariffs agreed to, and the willingness of Kazak consumers to forego payment.

Tractebel (Belgium) plans to buy the Almatyenergo regional power company for $340 million. The facility is comprised of 2 heating plants, several thermal and hydropower stations, and other plants providing Almaty with heating and electricity. Tractebel, in a move similar to that of the buyers of Ekibastuz, has pledged to raise the output of heat and power by 30 percent above the established capacity within 5 years and to repay the wage debts of the privatized companies.

In both instances, the buyers have committed to very substantial investments at the plants in question, running into hundreds of millions of dollars, for upgrading. Electricity rates for both privatized companies will be controlled by the State Committee on Antitrust and Price Policy.[156]

The Samsung Corporation (South Korea) has won the tender to purchase the Dzhezkazgan heat and power station, and Whiteswan Ltd. (U.K.) has won the tender to buy the Pavlodar heat and power station.[157]

Looking Ahead

Development of Tengiz and Karachaganak will be paralleled by a considerable remake of the Kazak energy sector. A number of priority projects have been defined which, if completed, will form the basis for a major transformation and rejuvenation of energy supply and distribution: [158]

❑ reconstruction of the Atyrau oil refinery

❑ reconstruction of the Shymkent oil refinery

❑ construction of the Mangystau oil refinery

❑ construction of the Novozhanazhol gas processing plant

❑ renovation of the Uzen oil field

❑ utilization of associated natural gas from the Kumkol oil field

❑ construction of the Tengiz-Novorossiisk oil pipeline

❑ construction of the Tengiz-Mediterranean Sea oil pipeline

❑ construction of the Karachaganak-Atyrau oil pipeline

❑ construction of the Atyrau-Kenkiyak-Kumkol oil pipeline

---

155. *Interfax*, Almaty, August 15, 1996.

156. *Interfax*, Almaty, August 15, 1996) If so, profitable operations may be wishful thinking.

157. British Broadcasting Corporation, *Summary of World Broadcasts, Part 1, Former USSR*, August 23, 1996.

158. Remarks by Kazak First Deputy Minister of Oil and Gas Marat Salamatov, to a United States-Kazakh Council Symposium on Investment in Kazakhstan, Washington, D. C., October 5- 6, 1995.

❏ construction of the Aksai-Kr.Oktyabr and Kustanay-Kokchetau-Akmola gas pipelines

❏ construction of the Chelkar-Shymkent gas pipeline.

Each of these projects can easily be justified on the basis of need but few if any are likely to go forward to completion without the substantial involvement of Western partners and Western capital.

Crude Oil

Kazakstan's political and economic future is of course closely linked to the development of its oil sector. Kazak analysts foresee a steady growth in crude oil production in the coming years and, along with this growth, an economic resurgence and recognition of Kazakstan as a nation of influence. But these are not likely to be tranquil years. If Tengiz is developed as originally hoped for—390,000 b/d by the year 2000, rising to 520,000 b/d by 2005 and further to 780,000 b/d by 2010[159]— then Kazakstan's future would seem secure (Table 4-15).

Table 4-15
Kazakstan's Oil Future

Year	Million b/d
2000	1.0
2005	1.2
2010	1.4
Source: Interfax, *Petroleum Report*, September 1-8, 1995.	

At the moment, the goal for 2000 appears very optimistic in view of the delays in providing an outlet for that volume of Tengiz oil. By 2010, more than one-half the indicated national output is to come from so-called mixed enterprises, that is, joint ventures and production-sharing agreements. Domestic firms will be led by Munaigaz with a projected 340,000 b/d by the year 2010 and by Kazakhgaz (a holding company) with 260,000 b/d.[160]

Just as oil exports await pipeline availability, the movement of oil within Kazakstan is also dependent upon pipeline availability (Table 4-16). The early availability of a west-to-east trunk oil pipeline would allow further expansion in crude oil production and would eliminate the need to import oil from Russia, if politics were the determining factor—that is, if elimination of dependence on Russian oil for its refineries were the primary goal.

---

159.   *East Bloc Energy*, July 1995.
160.   Interfax, *Petroleum Information Agency*, Almaty, November 17, 1995.

Table 4-16
Pipelines for the Future

Origin	Intermediate Points	Terminus	Commodity
W. Kazakhstan	Kumkol, Pavlodar	Shymkent	Crude oil
Karachaganak		Krasnyy Oktyabr	Natural gas
Pavlodar	Semipalatinsk	Ust-Kamenogorsk	Products
Pavlodar	Akmola Karaganda Shymkent	Almaty	Products
Kazakstan		China's Pacific coast	Crude oil
Source: *FBIS-SOV*, August 18, 1995.			

The key internal pipeline is the crude oil link from Tengiz to the Pavlodar and Shymkent refineries. Work on the first phase, from the Kenkiyak oil field to Kumkol, a distance of 750 km, was to have begun early in 1996, for completion in mid–1997. The second phase, from Atyrau to Kenkiyak, was to be completed in mid–1998. The entire system will be 1,200 km in length and will be capable of handling 460,000 b/d.[161] But financing for this pipeline will be difficult to arrange in advance of Tengiz development, and the project is on hold.

Natural Gas

Kazakstan is not now a major producer of natural gas, and future expansion will be based on successful development of the Karachaganak gas condensate deposit and utilization of any natural gas produced in association with Tengiz crude oil or by the Caspian Sea Consortium (CSC). Kazakstan will not likely be a major consumer of natural gas in the future; gas usage is to increase by barely 18 bcm during 1995–2010 (Table 4-17).

Table 4-17
Future Gas Consumption in Kazakstan

Year	Billion cubic meters
2000	30.3
2005	35.3
2010	36.4
Source: OECD/IEA, *The IEA Natural Gas Security Study* (Paris: OECD, 1995). Quoting data provided by Kazakhgaz.	

---

161.   Interfax, *Petroleum Report*, June 16-23, 1995.

Even these comparatively modest forecasts of gas consumption in Kazakstan may be too high. The reserve base is not the limiting factor, it is more than adequate. Rather, building a broad natural gas transmission network and distribution system, supported by adequate storage facilities, and equipping a gas consuming sector may be beyond the country's anticipated financial capability.

Refining

Published data surprisingly imply that the larger share of crude oil production in 2000 and beyond will be refined domestically (Table 4-18). Projected crude oil charge to refining for the year 2010, compared to the anticipated crude oil production level of 1.4 million b/d, will yield an exportable crude oil surplus slightly less than half of domestic production.[162]

Table 4-18
Projected Charge to Refining, 2000 and 2010

Year	Thousand b/d
2000	686
2010	750

Note: Based on a product yield of 92 percent of the refinery charge. The product yield has been projected to be 630,000 b/d by the year 2000 and 690,000 b/d by the year 2010.

Source: Interfax, *Petroleum Information Agency*, Almaty, November 17, 1995.

Currently, there are no plans for new refinery construction, except for Mangystau although considerable effort is to be made to upgrade and expand capacities at Atyrau, Pavlodar, and Shymkent. The projected charges to refining seem considerably overstated, given these upgrades. The probability is that crude oil production for 2000 has been overestimated, given the current refining capacity of about 380,000 b/d. That, in turn, implies that larger amounts will be available for export than anticipated by planners, which creates the need for greater export pipeline carrying capacities.

Defining the Oil Export Future

Tengiz

The Tengiz oil field, located in northwestern Kazakhstan, just inland from the Caspian Sea, is generally regarded as the largest oil discovery in the world during the past quarter-century, with a production potential matching that of the Prudhoe Bay of Alaska. Commercial production was initiated at Tengiz in 1991, but the breakup of the Soviet Union and the lack of capital soon put further development on hold.

The potential of Tengiz awaits the availability of an export pipeline (or pipe-

---

162.   However, these projections apparently do not take into account future production of gas condensates at Karachaganak nor possible future production from KazakhstanCaspii Shelf.

lines). In the interim, the volume of crude oil production at Tengiz largely has been determined by the pipeline access granted by Russia.

The world-class potential of Tengiz was spotted by Chevron, which initiated negotiations for rights to develop this field as early as 1987.[163] The dissolution of the Soviet Union and Kazak independence meant that the process had to begin all over. It was not until April 1993 that a mutually satisfactory agreement could be reached. A 50–50 joint venture, designated as Tengizchevroil, was finalized.

Tengizchevroil planned to utilize the Russian oil pipeline network to move Tengiz crude oil to market, and an arrangement to that effect was worked out with the Russian government in September 1993. Tengiz crude oil, under this arrangement, would be delivered to the Black Sea port of Novorossiisk. Complications arose, however, in the form of the Caspian Pipeline Consortium (CPC), described in more detail below. These complications prevented the early construction of an export pipeline to accommodate Tengiz production.

Tengizchevroil, the Chevron-Kazak joint venture, had the capacity to produce 120,000 b/d,[164] but limited pipeline access effectively capped actual output at a lower level.[165] Tengizchevroil had set 1995 export (i.e., production) targets at 60,000 b/d[166] but fell short of that level (Table 4-19). Frustrated by an inability to gain greater access to export pipelines, Chevron sharply reduced its 1995 investment budget for Tengiz and served notice that it would spend only the amount earned from oil exports—about $50 million.

Production fluctuated somewhat during 1996, averaging 83,000 b/d during the first quarter and around 90,000 b/d during July, down slightly from 100-110,000 b/d during June, but officials hoped Tengiz would be averaging between 130-140,000 b/d by year's end. Goals of 150,000 b/d and 160,000 b/d have been set for 1997 and 1998, respectively. Given the availability of additional desulfurization facilities and the means to move the crude oil to market, production may increase to 200,000 b/d by the year 2000.[167]

How can the hoped-for incremental crude be delivered to markets, in advance of improved pipeline access? New outlets include shipments to Finland by rail, increased sales on the domestic market, and purchases of extra Russian pipeline capacity from LUKoil. But these approaches accommodate only limited volumes. Permission for U.S. companies to engage in swaps with Iran might be granted, but the negative political fall-out might more than offset any financial gain. Rail shipments through the Transcaucasus corridor to ports on the Black Sea appear to be the best remaining option.

This latter approach would involve complex arrangements between Tengiz,

---

163. A review of the history of Chevron and Tengiz can be found in the Appendix, Tengiz—A Look Back.

164. *Platt's Oilgram News*, October 3, 1995.

165. Limits originally had been placed on access for Tengiz crude oil to the Russian pipeline network because of its high mercaptan (sulfur impurities) content. Tengizchevroil then spent some $102 million on facilities to remove these impurities, with the expectation that greater access would be allowed. See *Platt's Oilgram News*, August 1, 1995.

166. *Platt's Oilgram News*, September 6, 1995.

167. *U.S.-Kazakstan Monitor*, May-June 1996.

Azerbaijan, and Georgia. At Aqtau, Kazakstan Tengiz crude would be mixed with crude from the Buzachi oil field, a scheme Munaigaz has been using for several months to move some Tengiz crude to Bulgaria.[168] From Aqtau the crude oil would be loaded onto tankers for delivery across the Caspian to the port of Dubendi, in Azerbaijan. From Dubendi the crude would be moved by pipeline to an onshore storage facility at Ali-Bairamly, near Baku, and then to the Azerneftyanadzhad oil refinery.[169]

Azerbaijan would then provide an equivalent amount of crude oil to be shipped by rail car from Ali-Bairamly to the Black Sea port of Batumi. In reality then, the scheme is a swap with Azerbaijan, with both parties benefiting.

A trial delivery began in mid-October when a tanker, loaded with about 50,000 barrels of oil, departed the port of Aqtau. Eventually Chevron planned to ship up to 40,000 b/d annually through Batumi if the test shipments are regarded as successful.[170] Shipments to Azerbaijan were halted soon thereafter because of necessary repairs to the terminal at the Azeri port of Dubendi. A total of about 55,000 barrels of crude had been delivered before the terminal was closed. If this approach is viewed as successful, then deliveries will begin on a regular basis, to average at least 20,000 b/d.[171]

Table 4-19
Tengiz Crude Oil Production, 1993–1996

Year	Thousand b/d
1993	29.84
1994	38
1995 est.	49
1996 plan	87.2
Sources: Interfax, *Petroleum Report*, November 3-10, 1995; *FBIS-SOV*, September 26, 1995 and July 21, 1995; *Platt's Oilgram News*, February 29, 1996; Interfax, *Petroleum Information Agency*, Almaty, April 2, 1996.	

The possibility has been considered of working out a swaps arrangement with Iran, under which crude oil would be delivered to northern Iran and an equivalent volume exported from an Iranian port on the Persian Gulf. For Chevron, however, engaging in a swaps arrangement with Iran would be politically risky. In May 1995, President Clinton signed an executive order banning all trade and investment between Iran and the United States. Although U.S. companies were given a limited exemption to enter into an oil swap with Tehran, the punitive mood of Congress toward Iran warned against seeking such exemptions.

There was a strong logic for swaps for Tengiz crude oil, given the limited

---

168.   Interfax, *Petroleum Information Agency,* Almaty, August 12, 1996.

169.   *Platt's Oilgram News*, August 1, 1996; *Platt's Oilgram News*, August 20, 1996; and *Neft i Kapital*, November 1996.

170.   *Interfax*, Batumi, October 18, 1996.

171.   Interfax, *Petroleum Information Agency*, Tbilisi, December 11, 1996.

access to the Russian pipeline network and the fact that Russian pipelines are operating near capacity. Thus, the swaps agreement between Iran and Kazakstan, reached in early May 1996, was not totally unexpected. If Tengiz crude oil production was to expand over the near term, it was imperative to find additional means of getting it out of Kazakstan. Initially the swaps involve 40,000 b/d, with the prospect of increasing it to as much as 120,000 b/d in ten years. [172]

In the beginning, the Kazak crude oil involved in the swaps will be a blend of crudes from the Uzen, Mangystau, and Buzachi fields.[173] Tengiz crude may be involved later, but only that portion that is clearly non-U.S. owned.

The blended crude would move by rail to the Caspian port of Aqtau and then by barge to the Iranian Caspian port of Neka,[174] for delivery by pipeline to Tehran and Tabriz for refining. There are no Iranian crude oil lines terminating on the Caspian Sea. However, petroleum product pipelines connect the Tehran and Tabriz refineries to the ports of Bandar Anzali and Neka.[175] These pipelines can be made over to handle crude. Some small volumes could be delivered by rail to Tehran, but eventually pipeline delivery is the more sensible option.

Iran will also have to expand its Caspian terminals if it is to swap 40,000 b/d of crude oil with Kazakstan, with the prospect that the quantities of oil involved could be raised to 120,000 b/d in a decade. The Kazak crude would be delivered to refineries at Tehran and Tabriz in northern Iran and a comparable volume of Iranian oil would be made available at Persian Gulf ports. Moreover, as noted it may have to consider building a pipeline to link these terminals with the refineries.   But the question of who will pay for the costs of refitting Iranian infrastructure to handle Kazak crude oil is another point of contention. The question of who will be responsible for the costs of transporting the crude from the port of Aqtau to Iran has also complicated discussions.[176]

Iranian refineries are not equipped to process Kazak crude which is high in sulfur compared with Iranian crudes. Considerable new investment would be required in the construction of desulfurizing units. Considering all these constraints, swaps of Kazak crude with Iran in any meaningful way is questionable.

Kazakstan was to have begun exporting 40,000 b/d to world markets through Iran, beginning in November, 1996 but start-up was postponed to January 1997, still a tenuous date.

Restructuring Tengizchevroil. Restructuring Tengizchevroil would be necessary if there were to be further development of producing capacity at Tengiz, greater access to the Russian pipeline system, and timely construction of the Tengiz-Novorossiisk export pipeline.

By late March to early April 1996, the long and sometimes unavoidably contentious discussions began to pay off. Chevron reportedly would transfer to LUKoil a small portion of its 50 percent equity in the Tengizchevroil joint ven-

---

172. *Reuters*, Dubai, May 13, 1996.
173. *Platt's Oilgram News*, May 24, 1996.
174. *Middle East Economic Survey*, June 24, 1996.
175. *Middle East Economic Survey*, June 3, 1996.
176. *Platt's Oilgram News*, August 15, 1996.

ture.[177] In turn, LUKoil would transfer part of its access to the Atyrau-Samara crude oil pipeline to Tengizchevroil, allowing the joint venture to increase production and export to world markets. In April 1996, Kazakstan transferred half its 50 percent equity in Tengizchevroil to Mobil Oil, at a reported price of $1.1 billion.[178]

If the Chevron-LUKoil transfer were executed, Chevron would hold 45 percent of the equity in Tengizchevroil, Mobil 25 percent, LUKoil 5 percent, and Tengizmunaigaz (the government-owned Kazak partner), 25 percent. Russia increased the pipeline access of Tengiz crude oil to 90,000 b/d, and on that basis the joint venture hoped to be able to further raise output by the end of 1996 to a level approaching current production capacity.

LUKoil also wanted a 5 percent equity share from the Kazak government. Several times its president, Vagit Alekperov, indicated these acquisitions had been completed or were close to completion. Discussions ranged back and forth, with Alekperov admitting at the end of August 1996 that LUKoil was "not close" to finalizing a deal with Chevron or the government of Kazakstan on acquiring a 10 percent stake in the Tengizchevroil joint venture. LUKoil "can't agree on a price for either share of equity in TCO (Tengizchevroil)," he complained. Alekperov earlier said LUKoil would be prepared to pay Chevron just $30 million for 5 percent of TCO. Mobil paid $1.1 billion for a 25 percent stake, purchased from Kazakstan earlier in 1996. A pro rata price would put the cost to LUKoil at closer to $300 million.[179]

Nonetheless, Chevron Overseas president Richard Matzke subsequently was quoted as saying that a deal between LUKoil and Chevron on the sale of 10 percent of Chevron's 50 percent share was not imminent, but was in the cards and was not a long way away.[180]

Karachaganak Deposit

The Tengiz oil field has a rival in the Karachaganak deposit, described by Kazak sources as the world's largest oil and gas condensate deposit.[181] Karachaganak literally straddles the international boundary between Kazakstan and Russia.

The history of development of Karachaganak has mirrored the breakup of the Soviet Union, with a rupturing of economic contacts, nonfulfillment of contract obligations, collapse of credit and financial systems, and the insolvency of the economy.[182] Discovered in 1979 and put into operation in 1984, production capacity at Karachaganak expanded slowly because of the technical challenges. Production has steadily fallen after a peak in 1991, when there were 140 producing wells (Table 4-20). In 1995, only 21 wells were operating, and this is reflected in the sharp reductions in production levels.

---

177.   Interfax, *Petroleum Information Agency*, April 18, 1996.
178.   *Financial Times*, April 18, 1996 and *Platt's Oilgram News*, May 17, 1996.
179.   *Platt's Oilgram News*, August 30, 1995.
180.   *Platt's Oilgram News*, October 4, 1996.
181.   *FBIS-SOV*, July 21, 1995.
182.   *FBIS-SOV*, 31 October 31, 1995.

Table 4-20
Declining Production of Karachaganak, 1991–1994

Year	Crude oil and gas condensate (Thous. b/d)	Natural gas (Billion cu. meters)
1991	85	4.5
1994	32.5	1.68

Source: *FBIS-SOV*, October 31. 1995.

There had been some improvement by mid–1995, when extraction of crude oil and condensate averaged 42,000 b/d and gas extraction averaged 6 million cubic meters (annually, 2.19 billion cubic meters).[183] These levels were still considerably short of production capacity. Karachaganak natural gas is delivered to a gas processing plant at Orenburg, Russia. By mid-July 1996 it was thought that up to 90,000 b/d of liquids and four bcm of natural gas might be produced that year.

A British Gas (U.K.)/Agip (Italy) alliance had won an international tender in 1992 giving them an exclusive right to negotiate an agreement with the Kazak government to develop the Karachaganak gas condensate field. British Gas/Agip won the right to develop Karachaganak in competition with a group comprising BP, Statoil (Norway), and Grynberg Production (U.S.). Production at Karachaganak in 1991 was put at 450 mmcfd of gas (4.5 bcm/yr) and 85,000 b/d of liquids. At the time of the award, British Gas thought the gas flow could be increased to 2 bcfd (20 bcm/year) and liquids to 200,000 b/d.[184]

Karachaganak is world-class by almost any measure. Reserves are placed at 1.3 trillion cubic meters for gas, 654 million tons of condensate, and 189 million tons of crude oil, for a combined liquids total of roughly 6.2 billion barrels.

Karachaganak is located near the city of Uralsk, about 25 km south of the border with Russia. This gas condensate deposit has the advantage of being just 100 km from Orenburg, where a large gas processing facility is available. Orenburg is also the starting point for the Soyuz natural gas export pipeline system of Russia.

Karachaganak does not yield its wealth easily nor cheaply. Among other complications, Karachaganak natural gas is high in sulfur. Reportedly, more than 3,400 tons of harmful substances are emitted into the atmosphere annually. Blame has been placed on equipment shortages and the poor operational state of the infrastructure. Expanding production at Karachaganak will lead to the recovery of very large amounts of sulfur. The economics of the joint venture will, to a degree, be affected by the need to dispose of this by-product.

The gas is also high in carbon dioxide and paraffins (up to 4 percent in the gas condensate). There is the additional, larger problem of maintaining formation pressure at a level which would ensure the maximum recovery of liquid hydrocarbons. To do that most of the dry gas may have to be reinjected.[185]

---

183. *Platt's Oilgram News*, July 28, 1995.
184. *Oil & Gas Journal*, July 13, 1992.
185. *Gazovaya Promyshlennost*, November 1991.

Developers also were confronted with the possibility that Karachaganak had been contaminated by underground nuclear explosions carried out in the area between 1962 and 1987. Testing actually took place at Semipalatinsk, some 600 miles away, and the devices were not weapons but smaller devices designed for peaceful purposes. Initial studies carried out by BG and Agip showed no contamination.[186]

Talks were held during 1993-94 between Gazprom and Kazakstan, with Gazprom seeking the right to participate in this project. Gazprom and the Kazak Oil and Gas Ministry signed an agreement in December 1994, which provided for Gazprom's participation equally with British Gas/Agip. Beyond that, there had been little or no movement regarding Karachaganak in subsequent months. In mid-1996 Gazprom declared its intention to withdraw. Reportedly, failure of Kazakstan and BG/Agip to recognize Gazprom's previous investment at Karachaganak led to that decision.[187] Other sources speculated that Gazprom was now preoccupied with other projects and had not paid its share of maintenance costs.[188]

Gazprom chairman Rem Vyakhirev later attributed the withdrawal from Karachaganak to the political situation in Kazakstan and to frictions with the project partner BG/Agip.[189]

The withdrawal is not yet a done deal, and Gazprom ultimately might keep a share, if its requirements could be met. Russia regards Karachaganak, where maximum output might reach 25 bcm, as a direct competitor to its Yamal-Europe gas pipeline project, under any scenario.[190] If so, then there would be no sense of urgency on the part of Gazprom to move this project forward, but rather every reason to see it delayed. Delay, after all, is the deadliest form of denial.

If Gazprom withdraws or at least reduces its share, who might take its place? LUKoil quite naturally indicated that it might be interested, but had not yet made up its mind. LUKoil would have to seek membership through its arrangement with Arco (U.S.), under which Arco finances LUKoil-initiated participation in development projects. At the same time, British Gas is seeking to reduce its stake, which could open the door for Mobil and Texaco who have also been attracted to Karachaganak's potential. British Gas is having problems with its UK operations and would like to reduce its exposure at Karachaganak, but nonetheless wishes to retain a presence in Central Asia.[191]

For Karachaganak, as for Tengiz, the key to development will be found in the availability of export pipelines. The gas condensate probably will find its way into the pipeline carrying Tengiz crude oil to market. Karachaganak natural gas logically would be placed into the Russian gas pipeline system.

---

186. *Financial Times*, August 20, 1996.
187. Interfax, *Petroleum Information Agency*, August 20, 1996.
188.   *Financial Times*, July 1, 1996.
189. Interfax, *Petroleum Information Agency*, Moscow, July 11, 1996.
190. *Neft i Kapital*, July-August 1996.
191. *Financial Times*, September 6, 1996.

The Caspian Sea Consortium

The Caspian Sea Consortium (CSC) is the international consortium set up between Kazakstan and six multinational oil companies to conduct geographical and seismic sweeps of the northeastern portion of the Caspian Sea (Table 4-21). The consortium was established on December 3, 1993; geophysical research began September 10, 1994; and this first stage was scheduled to be completed in 1997.[192] However, because of favorable weather, the surveying was completed in August 1996. The responsibilities of the CSC will end in May 1997 and the CSC will be liquidated. Exploration blocs will be put up for bid and the members of the CSC will be given first refusal, but the future consortium must include Russian companies.

Table 4-21
Membership in the Caspian Sea Consortium

Kazakstan	KazakhstanCaspiiShelf
Italy	Agip
UK	British Gas
Norway	British Petroleum-Statoil
France	Total
United States	Mobil
UK/Netherlands	Royal Dutch/Shell

Note: KazakhstanCaspiiShelf was formed by the Kazak government prior to the formation of the consortium. British Gas has indicted it would like to divest itself of one-half of its share in the consortium.

In late June 1996, a spokesman for KazakhstanCaspiiShelf stated that a seismic survey had shown the area under study (100,000 km^2) held crude oil reserves of 73 billion bbl. and natural gas reserves of 2 trillion cubic meters.[193] Western partners in the consortium downplayed these estimates, cautioning that no drilling had been carried out as yet. (Drilling is to begin sometime between mid-1997 and early 1998 and, on that basis, first production might be expected by 2003.) Consortium members have been working on the assumption that crude oil reserves may be on the order of roughly 30 billion barrels—still a massive crude oil source. The consortium is now negotiating a production sharing agreement and will be awarded just 6 percent (6,000 km^2) of the area being surveyed. The remaining 94,000 km^2 will be

192.   Preliminary estimated reserves have been put at 25.6 billion barrels of crude oil and more than 2 trillion cubic meters of natural gas. See British Broadcasting Corporation, *Summary of World Broadcasts, Part 1, Former USSR*, October 6, 1995.

As part of the cost of doing business in Kazakstan, the CSC has already provided the neighboring community with a water bottling plant, a kidney machine, water distillation equipment, and helped make possible the reconstruction of a runway at the Aqtau airport. See *FBIS-SOV*, December 7, 1995.

193.   *Reuters*, Almaty, June 26, 1996.

made available to other investors.

Experts advise that development of the northeastern shelf of the Caspian will likely be more complicated than development of Tengiz, the major difference being that exploration and production will take place offshore which will bring environmental sensitivity into play. The need to protect the environment, in particular, the sturgeon, will be fervently championed by Russia. The producing horizons will likely be deep-seated, formation pressures and temperatures quite high, and there is also the prospect of the presence of mercaptans. While available technology can meet these challenges, costs of production will necessarily be influenced.[194]

Meeting any early production goals will be difficult, for a variety of reasons.[195] The northern Caspian freezes over during the winter months, there is no supporting coastal infrastructure, it will have to be created; there is no pool of experienced offshore personnel; meeting strict environmental requirements can be expected to delay work; and operations will have to cope with the rising waters of the Caspian. In sum, it would be extremely difficult to reach a production level of 100,000 b/d by the year 2004.

Finally, development of the northern Caspian will not be undertaken in isolation. Tengiz geographically is close by, and to the south exploration offshore Turkmenistan will have begun as well. These combined activities could well overburden the region to a breaking point. The head of KazakhstanCaspiiShelf, Baltabek Kuandykov, earlier believed that production from the offshore areas being surveyed should reach 1.2–1.3 million b/d by the year 2020—double Tengiz peak production.[196]

CSC has not yet publicly addressed the question of how future crude oil production from those offshore areas will be delivered to world markets. A number of options should be available, two of which involve pipelines that should be in place by the time production begins, and the possibility remains that Iran might be a viable transit route in the future.

Some of the crude oil could be marketed in Russia. CSC's area of operation is favorably situated with respect to Russian refining and industrial centers, and its crude oil should be able to compete with more distant Russian producers.

Other Fields

There are other oil and gas opportunities for foreign investors:

❏ A joint venture set up between Carey Energy Company (U.S.) and the Karazhanbas Oil Company has suspended activities. Established in 1992, it was to raise annual output at the Karazhanbas oilfield to about 11,500 b/d.[197] Problems were encountered in supplying equipment and in financing.

---

194.   *Russian Petroleum Investor*, November 1996.

195.   *FBIS-SOV*, October 31, 1996.

196.   British Broadcasting Corporation, *Summary of World Broadcasts, Part 1, Former USSR*, April 18, 1996.

197.   *Russian Petroleum Investor*, October 1995.

❐ Exxon will prospect on the Mertvyi Kultuk block south of Tengiz, through a joint venture with Oryx Kazakhstan Energy Company.[198] Oryx also has a joint venture to develop the Arman oil field, in the Mangystau region of western Kazakstan.

❐ Canadian Occidental had negotiated a contract to develop oil production in the Turgai Basin. Output was projected at 35,000 b/d, all of which was to be delivered to the Pavlodar and Shymkent refineries.[199] But this license has been withdrawn for reasons of nonperformance.

❐ Chaparral Resources Inc. (U.S.) has signed an agreement to develop the Karakuduk field.[200]

❐ Another Russian vertically integrated oil company, ONAKO, has formed a joint venture with Aktyubinskneft, an oil-producing enterprise under Munaigaz.[201] Aktyubinskneft is not a major producer; its output was 52,400 b/d in 1993; 52,900 b/d in 1994; and 52,000 b/d (planned) for 1995.

Mobil holds a 50 percent share of the Tulpar oil field, in the northwestern part of the country.[202] Mobil then set out to reduce its holdings, selling a 12.5 percent stake to Shell Tulpar Development, a subsidiary of Royal Dutch/Shell, and an additional 12.5 percent stake to Japan Petroleum Exploration Company Ltd. and Sumitomo (Japan). Mobil's share now stands at 25 percent. Three Kazak companies hold the remaining 50 percent: Aktyubinskneft Joint Stock Company (25 percent), Aktyubmunaigazgeologiya (12.5 percent), and Uralskneftegazgeologiya (12.5 percent).[203]

No matter how attractive these projects appear to foreign investors, pipeline access remains the key to success. Some feasibility studies may cool a prospective investor's ardor, and some investors may have made commitments beyond their abilities. For example, a contract between Bidermann International (U.S.) and the Atyrau regional administration to develop the Kinbayevskoye oil field was broken because Bidermann failed to invest as stipulated.[204]

Additionally, high tax rates erode investor profits and limit the attractiveness of the oil and gas sector unless and until relief can be provided.

The Legal Status of the Caspian Sea

When Russian president Boris Yeltsin stopped off in Almaty in late April 1996, on his return from China, a number of protocols were signed between the governments of Russia and Kazakstan. One of these protocols called for cooperation on the use of the Caspian Sea, including the exploitation of Caspian mineral

---

198. Interfax, *Petroleum Information Agency*, Almaty, October 11, 1995.
199. *Platt's Oilgram News*, October 2, 1995.
200. *Petroleum Intelligence Weekly*, September 18, 1995.
201. Interfax, *Petroleum Information Agency*, Orenburg, December 8, 1995.
202. Open Media Research Institute, *Daily Report*, May 6, 1996.
203. See *Platt's Oilgram News*, August 13, 1996.
204. Interfax, *Petroleum Report*, September 8-15, 1995.

resources.[205] A key point of the declaration reads that

> (t)he parties are convinced that it is in the interests of both to participate jointly in the exploitation of the natural resources of the Caspian Sea. They recognize each other's right to carry out work to exploit the mineral and biological resources of the Caspian Sea.[206]

The document relieves the prospect of a Russian protest against the work of the CSC, while making it possible for Russia to become involved in exploration and exploitation of the Kazak sector of the Caspian Sea. Kazakhstan and Azerbaijan share a common view of the legal status of the Caspian Sea, that is, development of its oil resources at least should be based on the median line principle. Neither is Kazakhstan likely to join in the consortium formed by Russia, Turkmenistan, and Iran to explore for and develop Caspian oil. Nonetheless, President Nazarbayev is constantly mindful of his neighbor to the north, and political realities conceivably could cause him to be more accommodating of the Russian position.

Rising Caspian Waters

There is an issue of more immediacy regarding the Caspian. The rising Caspian Sea is causing a growing number of oil fields to be flooded, causing hundreds of wells to be abandoned or shut in. These wells are not designed to withstand a lengthy exposure to sea water. Seals on the wellhead may fail, posing the threat of an environmental catastrophe.[207] Of particular concern, segments of the Tengiz-Atyrau pipeline are being exposed to sea tides. The Atyrau-Tengiz electric power transmission line is also being exposed to the corrosive effects of sea water.

Since 1978 the level of the Caspian Sea has risen by almost 8 feet, and in some places the sea has advanced up to 70 km.[208] Eventually, up to 1,000 wells will be flooded out.

Moving the Oil

Kazak crude oil has been moving across its borders in three different ways, for three different purposes:

❑ swaps with Russia

❑ via the Transneft oil pipeline system for export[209]

❑ via the Atyrau-Samara pipeline, specifically for Tengiz crude oil for a limited time

At the present time Tengiz crude oil has been granted limited access to the Atyrau-Samara (Russia) pipeline.[210] (See Map 9.) This pipeline has a carrying

---

205.   *UPI*, Moscow, April 27, 1996.
206.   *FBIS-SOV*, May 13, 1996.
207.   *FBIS-SOV*, November 2, 1995.
208.   *FBIS-SOV*, June 26, 1995.

Samara ●

R u s s i a

Kulsary
Atyrau ●

K a z a k s t a n

Tengiz

Aral
Sea

Georgia

Caspian

Sea

A z e r b .

U z b e k i s t a n

T u r k m e n i s t a n

Tengiz-Samara crude oil pipeline

——— Oil pipeline   Refinery

I r a n

© NWD 1997

capacity of about 200,000 b/d, allocated as follows for 1995: 70,000 b/d for export of Kazak crude oil to the Near Abroad; 70,000 b/d for export of Kazak crude oil to the Far Abroad; and 48,000 b/d for delivery of Kazak crude oil to Samara (formerly Kuybyshev) for refining, in exchange for 44,800 b/d of Western Siberian crude to be delivered to the Shymkent and Pavlodar refineries in eastern Kazakstan.[211]

The export quota of 70,000 b/d to the Far Abroad is allocated at the discretion of the Russian Ministry of Fuels and Energy. Formally, the quota is available to all joint ventures and to all oil-producing enterprises in Kazakstan, but the overwhelming share—60,000 b/d—has been given to the key joint venture in the country—Tengizchevroil.[212]

If oil refining capacities are to be utilized to the fullest extent, Kazakstan must deliver for swaps a minimum of 100,000 b/d of crude oil (these volumes, as indicated, are outside the export quota) and if the export quota itself is to be enlarged, the Atyrau-Samara pipeline must be modernized. Current plans would yield to an increase in carrying capacity to 220,000–240,000 b/d, or by 20-40 percent,[213] not sufficient to both enlarge the swapping arrangements and to allow an increase in the export quota.

Kazakstan has just one major port, Aqtau, on the Caspian Sea, which is endangered by the rising water level. Some of the port's utilities have already been damaged. Funds are to be secured from the European Bank for Reconstruction and Development (EBRD) to erect protection against the rising waters and to upgrade the port so that it can handle Tengiz oil moving inland.[214]

The Caspian Pipeline Consortium

The Caspian Pipeline Consortium (CPC) was established on June 17, 1992, by the

---

209.   During 1995 a total of 3.656 million tons (73,120 b/d) of Kazak oil had transited Russia enroute to buyers in the Far Abroad. See *Neft i Kapital*, no. 2, February 1996.

Kazakstan wants greater access to the Russian export pipeline network and a 1996 transit quota of 6 million tons or 120,000 b/d had been requested by Kazak president Nursultan Nazarbayev, according to Interfax, *Petroleum Information Agency*, Almaty, September 27, 1995. Making room for more Kazak oil would have to come at the expense of Russian producers or joint ventures seeking pipeline access. Kazakstan also indicated it was prepared to purchase unused export quotas of Russian producers.

Each month Kazakstan is allocated a quota for oil exports to the Far Abroad. For the first 8 months of 1995 the quota had been averaging almost 80,000 b/d but was cut for September 1995 to just 33,000 b/d. See *Platt's Oilgram News*, September 6, 1995.

210.   *Neft i Gaz Kazakhstana* (Oil and Gas of Kazakhstan), a special supplement to *Neft i Kapital*, October 1995.

211.   The slight difference of 3,200 b/d in this exchange, in favor of Russia, reflects the higher quality of the Russian crudes provided to Kazakstan.

212.   The allocation of the remaining export quota of 10,000 b/d is held confidential so as to avoid any problems between rival exporters.

213.   It is planned to reconstruct the pumping stations and to replace 150 km of pipe, at a cost of between $10 to 15 million. See *Neft i Gaz Kazakhstana* (Oil and Gas of Kazakhstan), a special supplement to *Neft i Kapital*, October 1995.

214.   *Platt's Oilgram Service*, April 26, 1996. The EBRD is to make $54 million available for these purposes, contingent upon a Kazak commitment of $20 million of its own funds.

governments of Kazakstan and Oman to build and operate a crude oil export pipeline linking the Tengiz oil field with the port of Novorossiisk on the Black Sea. Moscow signed a protocol on joining the CPC in July 1992, and the agreement was ratified by the Russian parliament on July 30, 1993.[215] Oman was represented by the Oman Oil Company (OOC) (not the government of Oman).[216] Azerbaijan had early indicated its intention to join, but later pulled out.

Russia and Kazakstan were to contribute manpower, materials, equipment, existing pipelines, and land to the CPC. Oman was to pay for project planning and the feasibility study and to arrange for financing.[217] If outside financing could not be secured, then Oman was obligated to step in.

Responsibility for development of the Tengiz oil field is a completely separate undertaking and rests with the Tengizchevroil joint venture. This joint venture was set up in April 1993, with the Kazak government and Chevron each holding 50 percent of the stock, for the purpose of developing the Tengiz oil field.[218] For the CPC pipeline project to go forward, a throughput agreement was needed from the joint venture, and Chevron was not prepared to offer that in the absence of an equity position in the pipeline.

Overtures for membership in the CPC consistently had been rejected by Chevron on the basis that the equity position and in turn the profit share due to Oman would be far out of proportion with the latter's financial contribution to the project. Chevron, for its part, had offered to pay one-half the cost of the Tengiz-Novorossiisk pipeline, in exchange for 25 percent of the shares in the CPC. This offer was refused. The partners in the CPC wanted Chevron instead to ante up 50 percent in return for becoming a minority shareholder with no voting rights.

Chevron held to the position that all parties involved in the CPC have equity in proportion to their financial commitment. The financial commitment of the Oman Oil Company, some $70 million by late 1995, in the judgment of Chevron was far short of qualification for a 25 percent equity in the proposed pipeline. The failure of the CPC to reach accommodation with Chevron was costly to Kazakstan and to

---

215. Interfax, *Petroleum Information Agency*, Almaty, February 6, 1996.

216. The original ownership in the Caspian Pipeline Consortium was as follows. The Oman Sultanate, Russia and Kazakstan each had 25 percent (all Class A, voting shares). The remaining 25 percent was in the hands of the Oman Oil Company, but these were Class B (nonvoting shares) tentatively assigned to Oman in return for possible future financing. See *Russian Petroleum Investor*, October 1995.

Although it is generally presumed that the pipeline carrying Tengiz crude oil to the Black Sea will terminate at the port of Novorossiisk, that is not quite correct. The port of Novorossiisk will not be the terminus. It was not acceptable to the CPC because the harbor is unprotected and often has to shut down because of storms.

Rather, a new loading facility—Novorossiisk-2, a 300,000 b/d single-point mooring system 3-4 km offshore—will be built at Yuzhnaya Ozeryeevka, 20 km to the west of Novorossiisk. An oil storage base will be built 7-8 km north of Yuzhnaya Ozeryeevka. See *Neft i Kapital*, July-August 1995.

217. *FBIS-SOV*, February 20, 1996.

218. The Tengizchevroil joint venture also has obtained rights to develop the Korolev oil field, which has initial recoverable reserves of about 400 million barrels. See *FBIS-SOV*, July 21, 1995.

all the parties, because it put development of the Tengiz oil field on hold.

The CPC initially had hoped to take advantage of existing pipelines to move Tengiz crude oil to Western markets. The plan to utilize a pipeline that would have moved Tengiz crude around the Caspian Sea to Grozny, the capital of Chechnya, where it would have entered the Grozny-Tikhoretsk-Novorossiisk pipeline, had to be abandoned when fighting broke out between Chechnya and Russia.

The CPC then restructured the proposed pipeline routing. The crude oil would move through an existing 40 in./28 in. pipeline between Tengiz and Komsomolsk, as before. A new 42 in. pipeline would be built from Komsomolsk to Kropotkin, some 50 km south of Tikhoretsk. The pipeline would be extended to the Black Sea port of Novorossiisk (Table 4-22). A new loading facility, deemed Novorossiisk-2, would be constructed.

This revised routing appears logical and provides the most direct route to a port of export. This route is perhaps distinct from other routes proposed for Kazak and Azeri crude oils in that its transit territory is presently free of political strife.

Table 4-22
The CPC Tengiz-Novorossiisk Crude Oil Pipeline

Length:	1,580 kilometers
Diameter:	42 inches
Carrying capacity:	1.34 million b/d
Cost:	$2 billion
Sources: *FBIS-SOV*, September 15, 1995; *Executive Summary, The Crude Oil Pipeline System of the Caspian Pipeline Consortium*, June 1994.	

The cost of completing the pipeline and the new loading terminal (Novorossiisk-2), would be just under $2 billion.

Anxious to start on the pipeline, the CPC decided to launch construction of Phase 1 by January 1996. Phase 1 was to be built backwards, from Novorossiisk to Kropotkin. The total cost of Phase 1 was to be in the $350-400 million range.

The availability of Phase 1 also would be essential to the flow of early crude oil from Baku along the northern route to Novorossiisk. The Tikhoretsk-Novorossiisk segment, to which the pipeline from Baku would link, has little or no spare capacity. Unless new capacity is made available—and Phase 1 of the Tengiz-Novorossiisk line would accomplish just that—Russian oil would have to be displaced to make room for Azeri oil, and that would be politically unacceptable to Russia.

Phase 2 of the Tengiz-Novorossiisk pipeline would stretch 1,250 km from the Tengiz oil field to Kropotkin and would be able to handle more than 1.34 million b/d. Phase 2 would incorporate the 770-km Tengiz-Komsomolsk section of the existing Tengiz-Grozny crude oil pipeline, completed in 1990 but never used because of the failure to develop Tengiz.[219]

---

219.   *Ekonomika i zhizn*, no. 25, June 1995. The portion transiting Kazakstan is 438 km in length. The diameter of the pipeline is 1,020 mm (40 inches), except for a 720 mm (28-inch) section between the 116-204 km posts.

The Oman Oil Company was given the task of arranging financing for Phase 1 by October 1, 1995. It was unable to do so. The Oman Oil Company claimed the fault was not theirs: Russia was to have made throughput guarantees of 180,000 b/d, and Kazakstan was to have made guarantees of 90,000 b/d, both by May 1, 1995. These guarantees were not forthcoming, and financing was impossible to attain without them.

Caspian Pipeline Consortium, Version 2

Rumors began in autumn 1995 that changes were afoot that finally would allow construction of the pipeline from Tengiz to Novorossiisk. One of the changes was a recognition that little if anything would be accomplished until Russia secured an equity position both in the Tengizchevroil joint venture and in the proposed pipeline. Moreover, terms for participation in the CPC would have to be altered in a way acceptable to Chevron. Stated simply, the pipeline link between Tengiz and Kropotkin could not be financed in the absence of a throughput agreement on the part of Chevron. Chevron, in turn, would not provide such a guarantee as long as it was not a member of the CPC, and, given the original terms of the invitation to join, membership seemed improbable.

A new consortium would have to emerge, with an expanded membership perhaps to include LUKoil, Chevron, Mobil, British Gas, Agip, and Kazakstan.[220] An expanded membership also would ease the burden of project financing. Oman could take part in the pipeline construction, it was emphasized, but its equity share would be directly proportional to its financial commitment,[221] just as it would be for all participants.

The share holdings of Kazakstan and Russia would be based on those material assets, valued at $215 million and $310 million respectively, which they have contributed to the pipeline project. Oman emphasized that its investment had reached $100 million by the end of March 1996 which would qualify for at least an 8 percent equity share.

Creating a new consortium was seen as the only way out of the current standoff, but doing so would set back the promise of Tengiz oil by at least two years. First, a number of very sticky legal points surrounding the agreements already entered into by the members of the CPC would need to be resolved.[222] Moreover, the OOC would not quietly give up its position in the CPC and would remind Kazakstan, when and where appropriate, that Oman had come to its aid with a $100 million loan when the country had struggled in the aftermath of independence from the former Soviet Union[223]

---

220. Inclusion of British Gas and Agip, who are involved in developing the Karachaganak gas condensate deposit, strongly implies that liquids produced at Karachaganak will be placed into the Tengiz-Novorossiisk export pipeline. Indeed, those priority projects identified for the Kazak oil and gas sector include an oil pipeline from Karachaganak to Atyrau.

Undoubtedly the decision in October 1995 by the AIOC to move its early oil to markets via two separate pipelines helped concentrate the efforts of the interested parties toward finding a way out of the impasse. It would reflect badly on Kazakstan and on the CPC to have Azeri oil coming onto the market well in advance of Kazak crude.

221. *Reuters*, October 31, 1995.

For the original CPC to dissolve, the OOC had to acquiesce. Its failure to secure financing for Phase 1 pipeline construction, together with the following events, signalled that the newly constituted CPC was not far away:

- ❏ the death in the autumn 1995 of Omani Finance Minister Qais al-Zawawi, a key backer of the OOC[224]

- ❏ resignation of OOC Chairman John Deuss[225]

- ❏ delegation by OOC of senior officials to the CPC Board of Directors[226]

- ❏ resignation of Omani minister of Petroleum and Mines from the board[227]

Kazak Minister of Oil and Gas Nurlan Balgimbayev, in announcing (prematurely) in October 1995 that agreement on a new consortium had been reached, stated that Russia and Kazakstan would each have a 25 percent share in the consortium, with the remaining 50 percent to be distributed among Chevron, Mobil, LUKoil, British Gas, and Agip.[228] These five companies would be responsible for 100 percent financing of the pipeline construction.[229]

In March 1996, the first positive step since the departure of Deuss occurred, when Russia, Kazakstan, and Oman agreed to reduce their holdings in the CPC

---

222.   Kazak prime minister Akezhan Kazhegeldin brushed aside these concerns during a press conference in London. He saw "no serious problems whatsoever" in annulling the CPC. See *Journal of Commerce*, November 27, 1995.

Nonetheless, Yevgeniy Davydov, general director of Oman Oil Company Services (the Oman Oil Company's subsidiary in Russia), stated that the position of the OOC was protected by an intergovernmental agreement between Russia and Oman, signed in 1992 and ratified by the then Supreme Soviet of the Russian Federation. See *FBIS-SOV*, November 20, 1995.

223.   The first indication that the Oman Oil Company might be willing to accept a buy-out was given in late November 1995 by Mr. Ed Smith, a representative of the Oman Oil Company and a director of the CPC. "At the right price, I think that is a possibility," he said. See *Financial Times*, November 25, 1995. The Oman Oil Company could accept a buy-out and walk away, or turn around and use the funds to acquire an equity position in the new consortium, if so desired.

224.   *Petroleum Intelligence Weekly*, February 5, 1996.

225.   A press release issued by the Oman Oil Company in Houston on January 19, 1996 offered the following information.

"Oman Oil Company Limited was formed in 1992 as a vehicle to make strategic investments in the energy industry outside Oman and to assist in the establishment of a broadly diversified energy-based industry in Oman.... (P)rojects include oil pipelines in Russia and Kazakhstan via the Caspian Pipeline Consortium.... Since inception, the day-to-day activities of Oman Oil have been managed by Transworld Oil Limited and Oman Oil's first President Mr. John Chr. M.A.N. Deuss.... The Government of Oman and Transworld have mutually agreed that in early 1996, Oman Oil will increase the level of involvement and management responsibilities for Omani nationals. In order to implement the direct involvement of Omani nationals, John Deuss has handed over his responsibility as President and Director of Oman Oil and his executive and director positions with Caspian Pipeline Consortium Limited...."

226.   British Broadcasting Corporation, *Summary of World Broadcasts, Part 1, Former USSR*, February 15, 1996.

227.   *Platt's Oilgram News*, February 13, 1996.

228.   *Interfax*, October 31, 1995.

229.   Balgimbayev later was rebuked by the government of Oman for getting ahead of the game with his public announcements.

from 75 percent to 50 percent.[230] That was followed in mid-April by an announcement by LUKoil President Vagit Alekperov that Chevron had agreed to transfer to his company a 10 percent share in Tengizchevroil.[231] Russia now had the seat at the table that it sought.

Additional impetus for breaking the CPC impasse undoubtedly was provided by the agreement of the AIOC to move its early Azeri oil through two pipelines, both terminating on the Black Sea. If a Tengiz-Novorossiisk pipeline had not been in the making, then Tengizchevroil most probably would try to bypass Russia by moving its oil through the Baku-Georgia corridor to the Black Sea or through Turkey to the Mediterranean.

The composition of the new CPC was clarified by late April (Table 4-23), and a protocol reallocating shares in the consortium was signed by the CPC board of directors on April 27, 1996. Russia made out quite well in the reallocation: not only did Russia's equity in the pipeline total 44 percent, which gave it a dominant position, but Transneft (which is responsible for all Russian oil pipelines) was designated as operator of the Tengiz-Novorossiisk export pipeline. The government of Kazakstan retained 19 percent, and Oman received 7 percent. The possibility remained that Oman might leave the CPC in the near future, ceding its 7 percent interest to other participants.[232]

---

230. *Platt's Oilgram News*, March 28, 1996.
231. Interfax, *Petroleum Information Agency*, Moscow, April 16, 1996.

Table 4-23
The New Caspian Pipeline Consortium

Government/Company	Equity Share (percent)
Russia	24
Kazakstan	19
Oman	7
Subtotal	**50**
Chevron (United States)	15.0
LUKoil (Russia/U.S.)	12.5
Rosneft (Russia) - Shell Caspian Ventures (U.K.)	7.5
Mobil (United States)	7.5
British Gas (UK)	2.0
AGIP (Italy)	2.0
Kazakmunaigaz (Kazakstan)	1.75
Oryx (United States)	1.75
Subtotal	**50.00**
Total	100.0
Source: *Reuters*, Almaty, April 28, 1996.	

There are new faces at the table—two Russian groups (LUKoil and Rosneft) as well as Mobil, Oryx, British Gas, Agip, and Kazakmunaigaz. British Gas and AGIP anticipate that natural gas condensate will be available from nearby Karachaganak at a level of about 120,000 b/d. Oryx needs pipeline access because it plans to raise output from its oil field on the Caspian shore from 4,000 to 10,000 b/d, although not until the next decade.[233]

Kazakmunaigaz would find it difficult to finance its 1.75% equity share, which translates into a commitment of some $70 million. Amoco has indicated it is interested in financing all or part of Munaigaz's share, and to that end a 50/50 joint venture between Amoco and Munaigaz may be formed.[234]

In retrospect, the foreign investors accepted rather stiff terms which could lead to complications in the coming months. First, there is the mandatory selection of a Russian general director. The use of domestic equipment must be maximized and foreign bidders for construction contracts must have Russian or Kazak partners. These requirements are in addition to Transneft serving as CPC operator and all of the funding being provided by the western partners.

---

232. *Interfax,* Almaty, April 27, 1996.
233. *Financial Times*, April 27, 1996.
234. *Platt's Oilgram News,* December 20, 1996.

The protocol on the allocation of shares within the new CPC does not clear the way for construction. To start, formal agreement by the companies to commit to the new CPC must take place. Tariffs must be negotiated, taxes agreed upon, and financing arranged. The Duma also will have to ratify Russian participation, and that is not necessarily a given. The final allocation of shares has yet to be determined. A restructuring deadline (of three to five months) was set for the eight companies to reach a final decision.[235]

The proposed Tengiz-Novorossiisk pipeline has been the center of attention the past several years, as interested parties sought to find an acceptable way to move Tengiz crude oil to market. However, ensuing complications held the door open for a variety of other proposals to be brought forward for consideration. But the combination of politics and economics have ruled out many of these proposals, at least for the present. Despite all its inherent difficulties, the Tengiz-Novorossiisk route continued to remain the center of attention.

The three participating governments and the ten oil companies ultimately reached agreement on December 6, 1996 for the new structure of the CPC. Under this agreement, the governments of Kazakstan, Russia, and Oman will hold 50 percent, and the 10 oil companies will hold the other 50 percent but importantly will be responsible for all of the project financing.

Transneft, which has responsibility for the Russian oil pipeline network, will be the CPC operator. Transneft lobbied vigorously for an equity share in the CPC but was not successful. The prospect of a conflict of interest between being the operator and as well a shareholder was disturbing to the western partners. Nonetheless, Transneft next sought the privilege of managing the Russian government's 24 percent share, but then so did Rosneft and LUKoil.

Other important features of the agreement follow:

❑ The pipeline is to be constructed as a single project, and not in phases as had once been conjectured.

❑ If schedules are met, the pipeline should be ready for operation by 1999.

❑ The project cost has been placed at about $2 billion.

❑ Shareholders have the right to reassign their equity, but the proportion between the governments and the companies, that is, 50-50, will not change. For example, if Oman wished to reassign part or all of its 7 percent holding, Russia and Kazakstan have preferential rights.

❑ Carrying capacity during the first stage will be 560,000 b/d, with eventual expansion to 1.34 million b/d.

❑ The combined 30 percent equity held by U.S. oil companies protects them against double taxation, permitting the deduction of taxes paid in Russia.[236]

The companies holding 50 percent of the equity will be responsible for cover-

---

235. *Platt's Oilgram News,* May 16, 1996.
236. *Platt's Oilgram News,* December 6-10, 1996; *Reuter,* Moscow, December 6, 1996

ing the full cost of building the pipeline to Novorossiisk. The larger question remained whether LUKoil and Rosneft could arrange financing in amounts commensurate with their holdings. Because the companies will foot the entire construction bill, LUKoil with its 12.5 percent share would become responsible for 25 percent of the total cost. Similarly, Rosneft, with a 7.5 percent share, would have to come up with cash to cover 15 percent of the cost.

Both LUKoil and Rosneft would have difficulty meeting cash calls if left to their own resources. Both instead arranged financial backing with major oil companies. Arco will fund LUKoil's share of the CPC cost and will acquire a 49 percent interest in LUKoil's 12.5 percent share.[237] Rosneft signed a letter of intent with Shell Exploration B.V. (U.K.) to establish a joint venture. Rosneft will own 51 percent and Shell 49 percent, and the joint venture will be used to finance both parties' equity shares in the CPC.[238] For both Rosneft and LUKoil, their equity shares will be transferred to the respective joint ventures, which guarantees them a seat at the table.[239]

Valery Chernayev, president of Transneft, the Russian oil transport company which will operate the Tengiz-Novorossiisk pipeline,[240] has voiced confidence that the first section, from Kropotkin to Novorossiisk, will be ready for operation sometime in late 1997 or early 1998.[241] The second stage, to be constructed eastward from Kropotkin to Komsomolsk, would be put into operation between 2001-2002. (See Map 10.)

Financing Phase 1 and Phase 2 of the pipeline will be separate undertakings. The producer companies will put up the necessary cash for Phase 1, between $400 to $500 million. To finance the second phase, from Komsomolsk to Kropotkin, the companies will seek the participation of international lending institutions.

The carrying capacity of the CPC appears to be basically committed, meaning that additional pipeline carrying capacity will be required if production elsewhere in Kazakstan and Turkmenistan seeks access to foreign markets. A second major export pipeline would appear to be in order, not only if the dual pipeline option applied by the United States to AIOC early oil is equally applied to Kazakstan. A restructuring protocol dated April 27, 1996 made allowances for Tengiz, Karachaganak, and other sources. The "Other" category clearly would not be adequate, however, to handle production originating with the Caspian Sea Consortium.

---

237.   *Middle East Economic Survey,* March 25, 1996. It will be recalled that in March 1996 LUKoil and Arco set up a joint venture—LUKArco, with Arco holding a 46 percent interest. Arco is expected to fund the bulk of the joint venture's undertakings.

238.   Interfax, *Petroleum Information Agency,* Moscow, June 14, 1996.

239.   *Platt's Oilgram News,* June 17, 1996.

240.   Although Transneft has not been successful in securing an equity share in the new CPC, it has been assigned two important roles. Transneft will serve as coordinator during the pipeline designing and construction phases and later will act as pipeline operator, but it will not be responsible for setting tariffs. The partners will do that. See *Petroleum Intelligence Weekly,* May 6, 1996.

241.   *Izvestiya,* May 5, 1996.

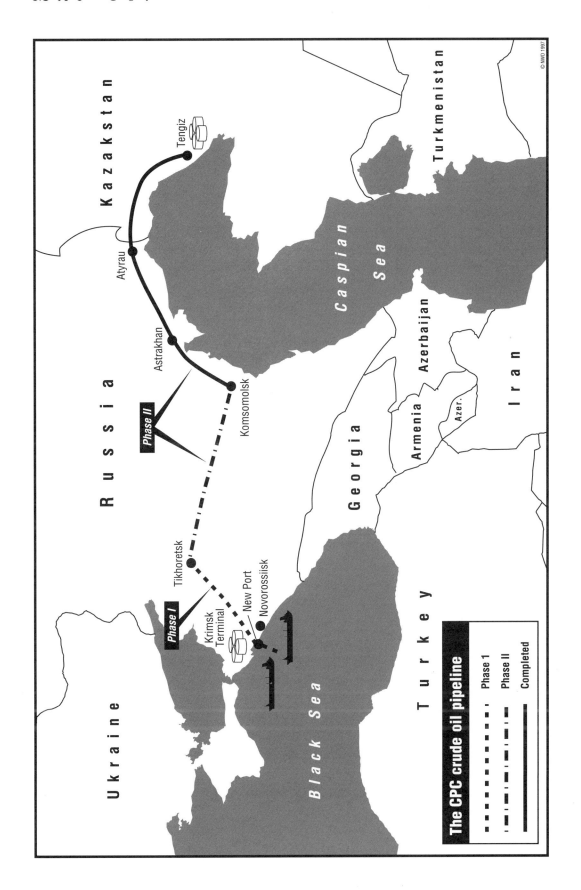

The CPC crude oil pipeline

· · · · · Phase 1
· — · — Phase II
———— Completed

Table 4-24
Allocating CPC Carrying Capacity

Year	Thousand b/d	Tengiz	Karachaganak	Other
1998	480	280	60	140
2000	564	300	110	154
2002	760	440	120	200
2006	960	600	120	240
2010	1,170	780	120	270
2014	1,440	900	120	420
Source: *Russian Petroleum Investor*, September 1996.				

Clearly, there is a considerable give in these allocations, beginning with the delay in building the Tengiz-Novorossisk pipeline which now is not scheduled to be ready for operation until late 1999. These allocations should not be taken as precise indicators of future crude oil production levels but nonetheless carry the message that one pipeline by itself will likely not be sufficient to cover future needs.

Tengiz-Baku-Ceyhan and Other Outlets

If Kazak oil lives up to its promise, then the carrying capacity of the Tengiz-Novorossiisk crude oil pipeline will have to be supplemented by another pipeline. It alone will not be sufficient; moreover, it would be risky for Tengiz to depend on just one outlet. Prospective routes for the movement of Kazak oil to Western markets are limited in choice. Several options stand out among all others.

❏ construction of a pipeline from Tengiz across the Caspian Sea to Baku, and then onward to the Turkish port of Ceyhan on the Mediterranean

❏ construction of a pipeline linking Kazakstan with northern Iran.

The prospect of building a pipeline eastward to a terminus in China has been raised, but the length of such a pipeline is reason enough to question its viability. Construction would not present any unusual technical challenges, and clearly Kazakstan would benefit from access to the growing market not only in China but in the Far East as a whole. Regardless, it is a project for the next decade, if then.

Iran is particularly attractive as a transit country for Kazak oil moving to Southeast Asia and beyond. Unfortunately, as discussed elsewhere, current U.S. policy toward Iran complicates matters.

Finally, Kazak President Nursultan Nazarbayev has raised the possibility of a pipeline through Afghanistan to the Pakistani port of Karachi.[242] He was referencing a subsequent proposal by Unocal (U.S.), which envisages the construction of an oil pipeline from Turkmenistan to a port on the Arabian Sea. Tengiz could be linked to this export line.

---

242. Interfax, *Petroleum Information Agency*, Moscow, May 16, 1996.

Gold

Kazakstan's riches extend beyond crude oil and natural gas to include significant gold deposits. Kazakstan produced about 12 tons of gold in 1994,[1] which put it third among the CIS. Like oil, further production will depend on the availability of foreign capital and foreign investors. Indeed, the number of planned joint venture projects in gold mining in Kazakstan with foreign investors is comparable to the number of oil-related joint ventures.

Unfortunately, Kazakstan's partnerships with foreign investors in gold mining ventures have been unsuccessful.[2] To illustrate, Placer Dome, Inc., a Canadian firm, reached agreement with the government of Kazakstan to exploit the very large Vasilkovskoye gold deposit. At that time, its known reserves were estimated to contain an average gold content of 5 grams per ton of ore. The appropriate documents were signed in April 1995, at which time Placer paid a bonus of $35 million to the Kazak government. During the course of the feasibility study, Placer Dome found that the gold content averaged just 2.6 grams per ton and the nature of the rock bed was such that developmental expenditures would be much higher than originally projected. In short, the venture would not be profitable; Placer asked that the signing bonus be returned[3] and did not sign the contract. Kazakstan delayed returning the deposit, and the EBRD indicated that there will be no funding for Vasilkovskoye until the repayment has been made.

Subsequently, a consortium of three Western companies—the TECK Corporation (Canada), Bakyrchik Gold (U.K.), and First Dynasty Mines (U.S.)—won a tender for the right to develop the Vasilkovskoye gold field. The road to development of the Vasilkovskoye gold deposit, one of the largest in the world, continues to twist and turn. Recently, Lonro (U.K.) appears to have gained the upper hand, after negotiations with a consortium led by Teck (Canada) failed to reach any agreement.[4]

---

1. *Finansovyye Izvestiya*, September 29, 1995.

2. Kazakstan badly mishandled the joint venture set up to develop the Vasilkovskoye deposit, reportedly one of the three largest gold deposits in the world. An Australian company, Dominion Mining, thought it had exclusive negotiating rights and spent a considerable sum on exploring and proving reserves at the deposit. Then Kazakstan put the project out to open tender where Dominion had to compete with others. Several months later, however, Kazakstan struck a direct deal with Placer Dome, brought in by Consolidated Mines of Kazakhstan, a private company with Russian and Kazak shareholders. See *Financial Times*, August 9, 1995.

International lending institutions, particularly the European Bank for Reconstruction and Development, deplored Kazakstan's actions and indicated they would not assist in financing development of this particular gold deposit.

3. *FBIS-SOV*, October 30, 1995.

4. *Financial Times*, August 20, 1996. If the contract had not been signed by July 1, then the Kazak government could approach any of the losers of the tender. See *Interfax*, June 4, 1996.

Tengiz—A Look Back

Background

The Soviet oil philosophy had been simple: find and develop the giant fields where investment requirements would be minimal and where production levels could be raised quickly. First came Romashkino (1948), the Urals-Volga giant. Then, moving eastward into Western Siberia came Samotlor (1965) and Urengoy (1996), a huge natural gas deposit. Explorers in 1979 next came up with Tengiz, within the Caspian Sea basin, in northwestern Kazakstan. The oil sector then seemed set for another decade or so, but the demands of Tengiz proved to be beyond Soviet capabilities.

The Soviet Union had neither the expertise, the technology, nor the capital to develop Tengiz. The producing strata are deep-seated and sub-salt, the reservoir pressure is high (about 12,500 psi), the geology is complex, and the sulfur content of the associated natural gas can reach as high as 25 percent. Tengiz crude oil itself is of very high quality (46 deg. API) and a low sulfur content (0.7 percent). Soviet geologists in 1990 estimated 25 billion barrels of oil in place and 46 trillion cubic feet of natural gas in place, defining Tengiz as one of the world's largest discoveries.

The combination of high formation pressures and high sulfur content in the associated natural gas could prove lethal not only for the immediate work force but for the surrounding community. Complex protective measures must be in place in the event of an accident releasing the sulfurous gases. There was a well blowout in 1985 which burned for 14 months before being extinguished with U.S. help. Western technology, western equipment, and western know-how were absolutely essential to the future of Tengiz. Without these advantages, Tengiz would be bypassed in favor of continued emphasis on Western Siberia.

How It All Began

With the status of the Caspian Pipeline Consortium (CPC) and the improved prospects for developing Tengiz having dominated the scene for the past months, observers may have forgotten that Chevron's original joint venture proposal in Kazakstan related to the Korolev field, with reserves in the one billion barrel category. An agreement to conduct a feasibility study of Korolev had been signed in late 1988, two years after its discovery. Korolev was much smaller than Tengiz but developing this field would get Chevron's foot in the door where inside the real prize, Tengiz, awaited.

Chevron had first visited Tengiz in November 1988. But even before that Tengiz had attracted international attention.

An international consortium which included Occidental (U.S.) had signed a protocol of intent in early 1988 to build and operate a petrochemicals complex using Tengiz natural gas.

Hungary had become interested in Tengiz in 1985 and by early 1990 some 5,400 Hungarian workers reportedly were engaged in construction there.[243]

Tengiz, with recoverable reserves equal to Alaska's Prudhoe Bay (the largest oil field in the U.S.), was a prize worth going after, regardless of the frustrations to come. To participate in the development of Tengiz was the opportunity of a lifetime and although Chevron had to be prepared to walk away at any time, the magnitude of Tengiz firmed the resolve of the company.

A "protocol of intentions" was signed between Chevron and Soviet oil officials in early June 1990 during President Mikhail Gorbachev's visit to the U.S., the path having been smoothed by James Giffen, an entrepreneur who had convinced President Gorbachev to support the proposed joint venture. The geographic proximity of Korolev and Tengiz made it reasonable to develop both simultaneously, so Chevron stated at that time. Chevron indicated that about 60 wells had been drilled at Tengiz but none were in commercial production. Tengiz investment to date then totalled $850 million.

Chevron at the time of the signing of the protocol of intentions was a member of the American Trade Consortium (ATC), which had been formed early in 1988 to pursue joint ventures with Soviet partners. Other members were Archer Daniels Midland, Eastman Kodak, Johnson & Johnson, RJR Nabisco, Chevron, Ford Motor Company, and the Mercator Corp. The thinking of this consortium was that a wide variety of projects would be undertaken, reflecting the varied business interests of its members. Oil exports from Tengiz would allow the companies to repatriate profits.

As negotiations progressed, the Chevron deal emerged separately and no longer related to the other planned investments of the original consortium. The ATC eventually collapsed in late 1991 as the remaining members decided to go their own ways and as the Soviet Union disintegrated. Ford Motor Company and Kodak had left earlier. It is interesting to note that James Giffen, president of Mercator and head of the ATC, is now advising Kazakstan on Karachaganak development.

The Forgotten Role of Sulfur

Little has been said of the high sulfur content of the Tengiz associated natural gas. The first of two trains of an oil and gas processing plant destined to handle high pressure corrosive well streams from Tengiz was scheduled for start-up in late 1990. The two trains when in operation would produce 60,000 b/d of stabilized oil and 77 mcm/d of dry gas. A Chevron official estimated that for every barrel of Tengiz crude oil produced, 30 pounds of sulfur will be recovered.[244] When Tengiz reaches its peak of around 700,000 b/d, that means the recovery of 21,000,000 pounds or 10,500 *tons* of sulfur every day or 3,832,500 (short) tons every year. It

---

243.   *Report on the USSR,* June 20, 1990.
244.   *Oil and Gas Journal,* August 5, 1991.

has been estimated that over the life of the project 92 million tons of sulfur would be produced. Chevron in time will likely become the world's largest producer of sulfur.

The gas/oil ratio at Tengiz is 1 ton/500 cubic meters or about 2,400 cubic feet of associated natural gas recovered for every barrel of crude oil lifted to the surface. The processed natural gas would be made available to the domestic market for about the first 10 years, after which it will be reinjected to maintain formation pressure. The desulfured crude oil was to be refined in Grozny after shipment through the Tengiz-Grozny pipeline, constructed in 1987. An equal value in crude oil would be exported from western Siberian and Urals-Volga fields until an export pipeline serving Tengiz could be put into operation.

Questions Arise

Sniping at the Chevron/Tengiz project in the Soviet press began in May 1991 with a letter from an independent expert panel directed to Soviet President Mikhail Gorbachev. This letter, printed in the weekly *Moscow News*, demanded that the project be scrapped, describing it as a scheme for "plundering the USSR with impunity." Of particular interest, the Chairman of this commission of experts was Ye. T. Gaidar (subsequently Russia's first vice-premier).

In essence, the critics had concluded that far too much revenue would flow to Chevron. The arrangement with Chevron was heavily weighted in its favor and should not go forward.

Earlier, in March 1991, at Kazak President Nursultan Nazarbayev's request, a commission had been appointed by the USSR cabinet of ministers to look into the agreement with Chevron. The draft agreement was approved with only minor comment.

Chevron responded quickly and emphatically to the *Moscow News* article, releasing the following statement.

"Clearly, someone in the Soviet Union is trying to undermine our proposed joint venture, which has already been negotiated in tentative form. While this is unfortunate, we're not surprised, in light of the volatile political atmosphere in the Soviet Union. We can say, however, that the *Moscow News* article is irresponsible and contains inaccurate, confused and distorted interpretations of our tentative joint venture agreement..."[245]

Keep in mind that while all this finger-pointing was taking place, crude oil production in the USSR was falling dramatically. A coming crude oil shortage was in the thoughts of some reporters. Tengiz crude oil should stay at home and should not be used to enrich foreign oil companies.

Why the public outcry at that time? Kazakstan and Moscow were engaged in a struggle for control over the oil. The USSR in the summer of 1991 had been attempting to create a new union treaty and to redefine power sharing between the republics and the central government. Kazakstan had taken the position that all natural resources on its territory belong to the republic alone, while Moscow

---

245.   *Moscow News*, no. 25, 1991.

believed the oil was the property of the "center."

The failed coup of August 1991 further complicated Chevron effort's to jump-start Tengiz. These were undoubtedly the darkest days for Chevron, who envisaged Tengiz being lost forever. Kazakstan by then had become quite assertive in its efforts to remove themselves from Soviet control. Kazakstan nationalized its natural resources in August 1991. Negotiations between Kazakstan and Chevron continued, but at the republic level where the local expertise and experience could not match that of Moscow. The dissolution of the Soviet Union in December 1991 effectively took Moscow out of the picture although for all practical matters that had already happened.

A Joint Venture Signed

Chevron's prospects were not revived until May 1992 when Richard H. Matzke, president of Chevron Overseas Petroleum, travelled to Almaty with John Deuss to hear President Nazarbayev's "final offer." When the difficult and often contentious discussions ended, agreement to set up a joint venture had been hammered out. But any relief was tempered by the recognition that the December 1991 breakup also meant Chevron and Kazakstan would now have to negotiate with Russia over access to export pipelines, to ports, and to refineries.

President Nazarbayev, hoping to avoid domestic opposition and criticism of an agreement with foreign investors over Tengiz development, had sought and received advice and opinions from a variety of consultants and advisers (primarily the investment bank J. P. Morgan and the British law firm Slaughter & May). He rightly had feared Kazakstan might be seen as accepting unfavorable terms. The 1991 media debacle was easily recalled and Kazak authorities had become overly cautious regarding Tengiz.

Both sides later would agree that this decision to seek independent, outside review was a turning point. John Deuss was also providing informal "technical assistance" to Kazakstan through the Oman Oil Company (OOC) which he headed. Indeed, his may have been a critical role as Kazakstan in early 1992 had asked the Sultanate of Oman to conduct detailed consultations on its behalf with Chevron, although the full impact of Oman's involvement is subject to differing opinion.

A protocol leading to a joint venture agreement between Chevron and Kazakstan to develop Tengiz was finally signed in Almaty in early May 1992. The agreement also included the Korolev oil field and an exploration area covering about 4,000 square kilometers. The joint venture agreement itself was signed on May 18, 1992 on the occasion of President Nazarbayev's first visit to Washington. Terms were now much more favorable, and acceptable, to Kazakstan. Equity would be shared 50/50 between Tengizneftegaz and Chevron, and cash flow after reinvestment would average about 80 percent to Kazakstan and 20 percent to Chevron. At that time Tengiz was producing about 60,000 b/d. Korolev was not yet in production and start-up had not been scheduled until 1999.

One month later, with the ink barely dry on the Chevron-Kazak joint venture, Oman and Kazakstan signed an agreement to set up a consortium (the CPC) to design, finance, construct, and operate a crude oil pipeline to link Tengiz and other oil fields in western Kazakstan to export terminals. At that time as many as 8 prospective pipeline routings had been identified. Chevron soon thereafter signed a memorandum of understanding (MOU) to participate in the consortium. But this MOU only expressed Chevron's interest in participating in the consortium *once the pipeline was built.* That is, Chevron sought priority access to the pipeline for its 50 percent share of Tengiz and Korolev crude oils.

Azerbaijan signed onto the CPC in early July, for reasons of geography and pipeline access, followed by Russia later on in the month.   Oman would arrange for financing construction of the pipeline and the OOC would act as project manager. By the end of 1992 Chevron was discussing equity participation in the pipeline. Additionally, all the fine details of the joint venture Tengizchevroil had been worked out to both parties' satisfaction, with the joint venture expected to begin operations April 1, 1993.

Meanwhile, the CPC in late October 1992 had signed a contract with Bechtel (U.S.) for the construction of a new 500-mile, 42-inch pipeline extending from Grozny through Tikhoretsk to Novorossiisk. At Grozny, the new pipeline would be linked with an existing pipeline running between Tengiz and Grozny. The initial installed capacity of the new pipeline system would be 300,000 b/d, to be incrementally expanded as needed.

The subsequent outbreak of fighting in Chechnya would lead the CPC to abandon this routing and instead to agree upon a new pipeline further to the north, bypassing Chechnya altogether.

Act II: Pipeline Construction and Pipeline Access

As 1992 came to a close, Act I, "the Tengiz Adventure" seemed over and the curtain on Act II, "Pipeline Construction and Pipeline Access," had been raised. In terms of time and in terms of frustration, Act II would more than match the opener. Chevron, a key player because of its 50 percent equity in Tengizchevroil joint venture, had laid out very clearly those conditions which would have to be satisfied if Chevron were to acquire an equity position in the CPC.

❒ Ownership of the pipeline must be represented by a single class of stock issued to investors in proportion to their investment.

❒ With this ownership must come shared risks and shared rewards, and sharing must be in proportion to the equity interests of the owners.

❒ Shippers must have nondiscriminatory access to the pipeline and nondiscriminatory tariffs.

❒ Tariffs should provide a reasonable return on equity, yet should be low enough to encourage resource development.

❒ Investors must be protected against political risks resulting from action—or inaction—of the republics and their subdivisions.

These principles, in the judgment of Chevron, would apply to any successful pipeline proposal in the former Soviet Union. The pipeline routing chosen for Tengiz crude would be the proposal that best fit these five general principles.

Unfortunately, so Chevron concluded, the CPC proposal did not meet any of the principles. Absent a Chevron equity position in the pipeline, there could be no throughput agreement. Absent a throughput agreement, financing the proposed pipeline would be extremely difficult if not impossible. There matters rested for months to come, until the deadlock was broken and steps were taken to realign and revitalize the CPC.

Source: States of the Former Soviet Union, CIA, 1992.

CHAPTER 5

Turkmenistan

Table 5-1
Turkmenistan at a Glance

Currency	Manat (November 1, 1993)
Rate of Exchange	3,000 manat/$1
Gross Domestic Product	$4.4 billion (1994)
Inflation	1,400 percent (1995)
Population	4.075 million (July 1995 est.)
By Nationality	
Turkmen	73.3 percent
Russian	9.8 percent
Uzbek	9 percent
Kazakh	2 percent
Other	5.9 percent

Sources: Central Intelligence Agency (CIA), *The World Factbook 1995* (Washington, D.C.: CIA, 1995); Open Media Research Institute, *Daily Report*, April 26, 1996, World Bank data.

Turkmenistan declared its independence on October 27, 1991, two months before the Soviet Union's disintegration. Saparmurad Niyazov, who had been head of the Communist Party in Turkmenistan since 1985, became president when the post was created for him in October 1990. He was formally elected president in June 1992, when he ran unopposed, and in January 1994 a popular referendum extended his term in office to the year 2002. Niyazov has created something of a personality cult, defining himself as "Turkmenbashi," or leader of all Turkmens. The only political party permitted in Turkmenistan is the Democratic Party of Turkmenistan.

Turkmenistan has consciously taken a very slow approach to economic reform and to the privatization of industry and agriculture. In large part, this is a reflection of the thinking of those former Communists who are now in positions of authority.

Turkmenistan's economy revolves around two key sectors: agriculture (chiefly cotton) and energy (natural gas). Exports of these two commodities kept the economy alive following the Soviet breakup. Subsequently, however, the economy has suffered from sharp reductions in natural gas sales and extremely high inflation.

The Turkmen economy is not particularly energy-intensive. Natural gas consumption peaked in 1989 at around 15.6 bcm, and by 1994, consumption had fallen to 10.5 bcm. Even so, natural gas remains the primary fuel. Electric power and water had been provided free of charge until mid-1996, although these were often unavailable.[246] When water is available, which is usually only at night, it is generally unfit for drinking without purification.[247] Most food staples are rationed—including meat, sugar, butter, rice, and tea.

Resource Potential

The resource potential of Turkmenistan is great, even when compared against the more highly publicized potentials of Azerbaijan and Kazakstan. One Western expert noted,

> when you compare even conservative resource estimates for Turkmenistan with those of other oil and gas provinces around the world, (Turkmenistan's) oil and gas potential is huge. For example, the oil and gas in place in Turkmenistan is likely to be larger than that in the U.S. part of the Gulf of Mexico, larger than that of the North Sea, or as large as a sizeable fraction of Saudi Arabia.[248]

Estimates of natural gas reserves range between 10 and 14 trillion cubic meters, and oil reserves may be as high as 6 billion bbl. In comparison, proven U.S. natural gas reserves are estimated to be just under 4.6 trillion cubic meters and proven crude oil reserves at 23 billion bbl. Bridas, an Argentine energy company long active in Turkmenistan, estimates proven reserves to be 4.3 trillion cubic meters, compared to 49.3 trillion for Russia and 1.8 trillion cubic meters for Kazakstan.

Turkmen experts, who use a liberal evaluation scale, estimate natural gas reserves to be 20 trillion cubic meters—which would rank Turkmenistan fourth in the world—and crude oil reserves at 46 billion bbl.[249] Half of the proven reserves of Turkmen natural gas are concentrated at the Dauletabad-Donmezskoye field, which also accounts for 45 percent of all natural gas extracted in the country.[250]

The Turkmen sector of the Caspian seabed is generally agreed to be the most promising oil and gas region in the country, but it is virtually untouched. That will change; seismic surveys are now being taken as a precursor to discussions with potential investors.[251] By the time pipelines are in place to carry Azeri crude oil to market, the offshore area of Turkmenistan should be ready for exploration.

The coal industry is of no economic significance and Turkmenistan must import what it consumes.

---

246.   *FBIS-SOV*, August 21, 1995.

247.   *Prism*, September 8, 1995.

248.   Robert B. O'Connor, Jr., Senior Vice-President, WaveTech Geophysical, Inc., letter to the editor, *Russian Petroleum Investor*, October 1995.

249.   Interfax, *West*, Minsk, October 23, 1995. Turkmen spokesmen have a tendency to use "resources" and "proven" and "recoverable" reserves interchangeably, and some probably do not know the difference.

250.   *FBIS-SOV*, January 23, 1995.

251.   Interfax, *Petroleum Information Agency*, Ashgabat, March 13, 1996.

Optimistic Production Goals

In 1993, a plan "On the Development of the Oil Industry in Turkmenistan to the Year 2020" was submitted to Russian reviewers for comment. The plan set extremely optimistic goals for crude oil and natural gas production (see Table 5-2).

Table 5-2
Turkmenistan: Goals for Oil and Natural Gas Production, 1998–2020

Year	Crude Oil (thousand b/d)	Natural Gas (bcm)
1998	320	110
2000	560	130
2010-2020	1,600	230
Source: Interfax, *Petroleum Report*, June 10-17, 1994.		

The Russian reviewers quickly disabused Turkmenistan of the practicality of using these goals as the basis for developing the oil and gas complex. The plan showed little or no understanding of the costs of development projects, of project financing, or of the likely market effects of the high production projections. Moreover, the Russian experts found the estimates of potential oil and natural gas reserves, as developed by Turkmenistan, to be far too high, although it is unknown whether their judgments were colored by politics.

President Niyazov was perhaps being more realistic when he predicted in late 1996 that within five years natural gas extraction would reach 100 bcm and crude oil would average 200,000 b/d.[252] Even these levels would appear doubtful unless export pipeline construction is expedited.

Discouraged Foreign Investors

The lack of understanding in Turkmenistan of how market economies operate and what motivates foreign investors has noticeably slowed foreign investment. The successful investors, and there are very few, have learned, often at their own expense, that the best approach to success is to work through the power elite in the country. Even that route to success, however, may be only temporary. Investment arrangements with the power elite are tenuous as best, because they can quickly come to an end when there are changes at the top. Even so, transparency and predictability are scarce commodities in Turkmenistan, and the lack of a reliable legal or banking system makes personal contacts the only concrete local currency.[253]

Turkmenistan's support for joint ventures has been somewhat spotty and not very successful. For example, International Petroleum Corporation, a Canadian firm, withdrew from a joint venture offshore Turkmenistan, complaining that it had received no cooperation from the government, citing in particular the government's

---

252. Open Media Research Institute, *Daily Report*, October 2, 1996.
253. *Financial Times*, January 3, 1995.

refusal to approve the assignment of its interest in the joint venture, the government's refusal to renew the joint venture's license to export oil, and the government's effort to renegotiate the financial terms of the joint venture.[254]

International Petroleum Corporation's 30 percent stake was sold to Lamarg Energy (Netherlands), which already held 20 percent of the concession.[255] Lamarg's relationship with the Turkmenistan government has steadily deteriorated, as governmental demands have escalated while Larmag has been unable to meet the investment timetable specified at the establishment of the joint venture in January 1993.[256] Production of the joint venture has averaged under 10,000 b/d.

The Bridas Corporation (Argentina) is by far the largest foreign investor in Turkmenistan. It has spent some $255 million to develop the Keimir crude oil deposit and $140 million to develop the Yashlar natural gas deposit during the past four years.[257] Bridas has every intention of increasing its investment to as much as $3 billion, but its relations with the government have been precarious. Bridas's right to export oil from Keimir had been revoked,[258] ostensibly for failure to invest as promised, but also because Turkmen officials believed that the joint venture agreements favored Bridas.[259]

Reorganization

The Turkmen Ministry of Oil and Gas was abolished at the beginning of July 1996 and replaced by the Ministry of Oil and Gas Industry and Mineral Raw Materials. Three state concerns and two state corporations were formed. The state concern Turkmenneft was formed on the basis of the Balkanneftegazsenagat and all of the gas-producing enterprises were transferred to Turkmenneft. All oil and gas construction organizations are now under the state concern Turkmenneftegazstroy. The state corporate Turkmengeologiya Production Association for Geological Exploration now also includes the geology and geophysics enterprises of the Ministry of Oil and Gas. Production of petroleum products and gas processing, supplying of natural gas and petroleum products to the population, and all foreign contacts are assigned to the state trading corporation Turkmenneftegaz.[260]

254.   Open Materials Research Institute, *Daily Report*, October 5, 1995.

255.   *Platt's Oilgram News*, October 3, 1995.

256.   The experience of Larmag Energy NV (a Dutch company) should be studied by all potential investors in Turkmenistan. It faced export restrictions in 1994 and again in 1995 and was forced to renegotiate the terms of its original contract. See *Russian Petroleum Investor*, October 1995.

257.   Interfax, *Petroleum Information Agency*, Ashgabat, March 15, 1996.

258.   Oil Daily *Nefte Compass*, March 14, 1996.

259.   Bridas has taken its grievance to the World Court, where it will attempt to make the case that Turkmenistan has broken its exploration contract with Bridas for Keimir. See *Platt's Oilgram News*, June 25, 1996.

260.   *FBIS-SOV*, August 22, 1996.

Crude Oil

Crude oil production in Turkmenistan peaked in 1975 at 316,000 b/d, and then entered a long, slow decline, with output in 1995 at no more than 70,000 b/d (Table 5-3). The plan for 1995 had been set at 120,000 b/d, the 1985 level, but it was an unreachable goal, although there was a gain in output.

Table 5-3
Turkmenistan Oil and Gas Production, 1970–1996

Year	Crude Oil (thousand b/d)	Natural Gas (bcm)
1970	290	13.1
1975	316	51.8
1980	160	70.5
1985	120	83.2
1990	112	87.8
1991	108	84.3
1993	78	65.21
1994	76	35.63
1995	70	32.3
1996 plan	100	48

Sources: *FBIS-SOV*, August 19, 1995; *FBIS-SOV*, August 21, 1995; Interfax, *Petroleum Information Agency*, September 26, 1995; Interfax, *West*, Minsk, October 23, 1995; *Post-Soviet Geography*, April 1992; *Turkmenistan, An Economic Profile*, December 1993; *Platt's Oilgram News*, December 28, 1995; *FBIS-SOV*, March 4, 1996; *FBIS-SOV*, April 8, 1996; Interfax, *Petroleum Information Agency*, Ashgabat, November 6. 1996.

There were just two crude oil joint ventures operating in Turkmenistan in 1994: the Larmag-Cheleken venture to develop oil offshore in the Caspian Sea noted above, and Keimir, the joint venture with Bridas to develop two oilfields in southwestern Turkmenistan.[261] Production in 1994 at these two joint ventures averaged just 14,400 b/d, against a plan of 18,600 b/d.

U.S.-based Oil Capital Ltd. has gained the right to develop two major oil and gas fields in Turkmenistan—the Gubkin-Livanov offshore gas condensate and crude oil field designated as Bloc One, and the Kotor-Tepe onshore oil field designated as Bloc Two. These fields are ready for development but lack the infrastructure to move production to paying customers.

Turkmenistan and the Malaysian national oil company Petronas have signed the first agreement on the development of three oil fields—Gubkin, Barinov, and Livanov—on the Caspian Sea shelf under a production sharing agreement, where it is hoped to have oil flowing within two years. At present there is only one foreign

261. Interfax, *Petroleum Report*, January 27 to February 3, 1995.

company—Larmag Energy—developing the Turkmen section of the shelf.[262] A consortium of Occidental, Oil Capital and Lapis Holdings had won a tender in 1993 to develop the Gubkin and Livanov fields, but backed out of the deal in 1994.[263]

Monument Oil & Gas (U.K.) has signed an exploration and production agreement covering four existing fields: the Burun, Nebit Dag, and Kum Dag oil fields, and the Kyzl Kum gas condensate field. Burun today is producing at around 4,500 b/d but how to get the crude to market is a key question for this investor, as it is for others. For Nebit Dag and Kum Dag, the Monument deal covers just the unproduced deep portions. For Kyzl Kum, Monument will have access initially just to the deep areas, and access to the shallow areas after 5 years.[264]

Finally, Mobil and Monument Oil & Gas will jointly rehabilitate more than 2,000 idle wells in western Turkmenistan, boosting crude output from about 80,000 b/d at present to 280,000 b/d by the year 2000.[265] A successful rehabilitation program, even approaching the very optimistic goal for the year 2000, would provide a tremendous boost to the Turkmen oil sector. Given all the political and economic complexities of offshore development, the near term future of Turkmen oil will be defined by what happens onshore.

Refining

There are two refineries in Turkmenistan—Turkmenbashi (formerly Krasnovodsk) and Chardzhou. Both are obsolete and will need to be reconstructed to modern specifications. Turkmenbashi, built during World War II, has a refining capacity of 110,000 b/d. The Chardzhou refinery is slightly larger, with a capacity of 120,000 b/d. The combined refining capacity considerably exceeds domestic crude oil production.

The Turkmenbashi refinery processes only domestic crude oil, whereas Chardzhou was built to refine crude oil from the West Siberian oilfields of Russia.[266] Chardzhou has fallen on hard times, as deliveries of West Siberian crude oil have dried up. In 1994 for example, Chardzhou processed just 3,240 b/d of natural gas condensate.

The Turkmenbashi refinery, the only source of motor gasoline, produced just 14,700 b/d in 1994, far short of needs.[267] Production of diesel at both facilities averaged just 31,820 b/d.

Prices of gasoline, diesel fuel, and kerosine have been steadily increasing,

262.   Interfax, *Petroleum Information Agency*, Ashgabat, July 8, 1996.

263.   *Middle East Economic Summary*, July 22, 1996.

264.   *Platt's Oilgram News*, August 15, 1996.

265.   *Platt's Oilgram News*, November 27, 1996.

266.   British Broadcasting Corporation, *Summary of World Broadcasts, Part 1, Former USSR*, January 3, 1996.

267.   *Petroleum Information Agency*, Ashgabat, November 9, 1995. High-octane gasoline was selling for the equivalent of just 12.5 cents per liter at state-owned filling stations, but 10 to 15 times higher at commercial stations. See *Interfax*, Ashgabat, November 8, 1995. Letting prices at government-controlled facilities rise to market-clearing levels undoubtedly would better align demand and supply.

largely because these products and others are being illegally exported. Turkmenistan has approximately 250,000 privately-owned automobiles. On the average, each consumed approximately 63 liters per month. A quota of 100 liters of gasoline per month has been established, at a price of 200 manats per liter. The price will be the same both for state-owned vehicles and private vehicles. Currently the population owns about 6,000 trucks. For both private trucks owned by rural commodity producers and for state-owned trucks, gasoline and diesel fuel will be released at a rate of 1,200 liters/month at 200 manats per liter.

Finally, Turkmenistan has in operation 10 stations for refueling motor vehicles with natural gas. The president has stated he is requiring all state-owned trucks to be converted to natural gas within 1 year, a decidedly unrealistic goal.[268]

Turkmenistan needs about 1,200 b/d of liquefied petroleum gas, which is used largely as a cooking fuel. The Turkmenbashi refinery can supply 360 b/d. The remainder is purchased from Russia. To help fill the gap between domestic supply and demand, a Turkmen-Russia joint venture has been established in the city of Turkmenbashi to process natural gas currently being burned off at the local heating and power plant. The processing facility will provide 200 to 240 b/d of liquefied petroleum gas.[269]

Natural Gas

In the past, Turkmen natural gas was placed in the Central Asia-Center gas pipeline system or in pipelines carrying natural gas to Europe. This access was taken away in 1993, when Russia proposed that Turkmenistan market its natural gas to buyers in Ukraine and the Transcaucasus. This shift has had a negative impact on the Turkmen natural gas industry.

Turkmen natural gas extraction peaked in 1990 and has fallen dramatically since, not because of problems in the producing fields, but because buyers have not been paying for deliveries (Table 5-4). Buyer insolvency and reduced demand on the part of the traditional importers have sharply cut into Turkmen natural gas trade. The decline in production was most severe in 1994, when extraction fell by almost 45 percent, caused by the unwillingness or inability of customers outside Turkmenistan to pay; the accumulated indebtedness forced Turkmenistan to halt further sales.[270] This loss in sales created a major cash flow problem for the government. The increase planned for natural gas extraction during 1996 very much depended upon buyer solvency.

Ukraine, Georgia, Armenia, Tajikistan, and Uzbekistan all are heavily in debt

---

268.   *FBIS—SOV*, September 6, 1996.

269.   *FBIS—SOV*, October 3, 1995.

270.   Turkmenistan has just commissioned its first gauging center to measure the volumes of natural gas exported. This gauging center, located on the Turkmen-Uzbek border, measures the basic volumes of natural gas exported by Turkmenistan through the Central Asia-Russia and Bukhara-Urals pipelines. In the past, export volumes were measured by gauging centers in those republics of the former Soviet Union that received the Turkmen gas. Naturally, this often led to disputes between producers and buyers over the amounts involved. See British Broadcasting Corporation, *Summary of World Broadcasts, Part 1, Former Soviet Union*, October 20, 1995.

to Turkmenistan, with these debts reaching $1.3 billion or more by the beginning of 1996.[271] Arguments over higher fees charged by transit countries as well as periodic pipeline ruptures also contributed negatively to gas export levels.

Ukraine has been the leading importer of natural gas from Turkmenistan. In 1993, for example, Turkmenistan sold 41.6 bcm of natural gas to the Near Abroad, of which Ukraine took 25.5 bcm, Kazakstan 6.2 bcm, and Georgia 3.7 bcm. Roughly half the drop in 1994 natural gas exports can be attributable to cuts in deliveries to Ukraine made because of mounting arrears. At year's end, deliveries totalled just 11.5 bcm.[272]

Table 5-4
Turkmen Exports of Natural Gas

Year	Gas Exports (bcm)
1989	74.3
1991	74.9
1992	46.9
1993	55.7
1994	24.7
1995 est.	22
1996 plan	45
1996 est.	24
1997 plan	40

Sources: Interfax, *Petroleum Information Agency*, Ashgabat, October 17, 1995; DEIK Bulletin, *Turkmenistan*, April 1993; OECD/IEA *The IEA Natural Gas Security Study* (Paris: OECD, 1995); *Platt's Oilgram News*, Decembers 28, 1995; Interfax, *Petroleum Information Agency*, Ashgabat, November 6, 1996.

As noted, Turkmenistan consumes very little natural gas and, for that matter, very little energy. In 1991, for example, Turkmen consumers took just 11 percent of domestic gas production; the remaining 89 percent was exported.[273] The bulk (about 84 percent) of Turkmen natural gas exports were directed to other republics of the former Soviet Union. Turkmenistan does not import natural gas.

Despite the severe contraction in natural gas production in 1994, which has continued, exports still represent roughly 70 percent of supply.

Before the breakup of the Soviet Union, pipeline access for Turkmen natural gas was a given. Following the breakup, however, Russia viewed Turkmenistan as

271.   *FBIS-SOV*, November 2, 1995. The bulk of this debt—almost $1.1 billion—is for natural gas delivered but not paid for. As of mid-1995 Ukraine had incurred a natural gas-related debt in excess of $300 million, Georgia owed almost $450 million, and Armenia $200 million.

272.   Interfax, *Petroleum Report*, January 20–27, 1996.

273.   This relatively small volume of natural gas, less than 10 bcm, still accounted for 55 percent of all energy consumed in Turkmenistan in 1991.

a competitor and access became severely restricted.[274] In 1993 Russia cut the Turkmenistan quota for natural gas exports to Europe via the Russian pipeline network to 11.3 bcm and further to 8.2 bcm in 1994.

Turkmen authorities quickly realized that alternative pipeline routes were an absolute necessity and that it was advisable to seek markets in Asia rather than in Europe. Uzbekistan covered gas markets in Tajikistan, Kyrgyzstan, and in southern Kazakstan. Natural gas markets in Belarus, the Baltic states, and Moldova were Russia's. Nothing was left for Turkmenistan, other than the Transcaucasus and a portion of the market in Ukraine.

Turkmenistan is not expected to halt exports of natural gas to the Near Abroad, although unpaid bills continue to accumulate. Turkmenistan is heavily reliant on gas exports and likely to remain so. If Russia continues to cut back on natural gas deliveries to the Near Abroad, Turkmenistan could find itself as the main supplier. Importers may see a clear advantage in diversifying supply and in reducing their dependence on Russia. Indeed, the very optimistic plans for future growth in natural gas production have been based largely on prospective natural gas sales outside Turkmenistan. Sales to the Far Abroad will depend on the availability of new gas pipelines that circumvent Russia, without which Turkmenistan's potential gas exports will remain severely constrained.

Natural gas export volumes are to markedly increase during 1997. Turkmenistan is to supply Ukraine with 15 to 20 bcm, compared with 15 bcm in 1996.[275] Further, in agreement with Gazprom, 20 bcm will be exported to Europe. Turkmenistan is wholly dependent today on access to the Russian gas pipeline network for its exports of natural gas both to the Near Abroad and the Far Abroad. President Niyazov believes that access should now be forthcoming, particularly to Europe, now that Russia has been given permission by Turkmenistan to participate in the development of oil and gas on the Turkmen continental shelf.[276]

Electric Power

There are five electric power generating stations in Turkmenistan, and the generating capacity is relatively small, at just 2.48 Mw (17 billion kwh per year). Neighboring Tajikistan and Kyrgyzstan possess considerably more generating capacity. Nearly all of the electric power stations burn natural gas, which accounts for at least half of the domestic natural gas consumption.

The Bezmein thermal power plant, the key Turkmen power generating facility located on the outskirts of Ashgabat, is to be doubled in capacity. A $43 million loan from Citibank will finance the upgrade, and the work will be carried out by General Electric.[277]

---

274. The cost of extracting Turkmen natural gas reportedly is cheaper, by $1 to $2 per 1,000 cubic meters, than for gas produced in Western Siberia. Natural gas can be delivered from Turkmenistan to the border with Ukraine, even paying full transit fees, at a cost not more than one-half the world price. See *Neft i Kapital*, March 1996.

275. *Interfax-Ukraine*, Kiev, December 11, 1996.

276. *Russian Petroleum Investor*, December 1996-January 1997.

Table 5-5
Electric Power Generation in Turkmenistan

Year	Billion kwh
1970	1.8
1975	4.5
1980	6.7
1985	11.0
1990	14.6
1991	14.9
1994	13

Sources: *Post-Soviet Geography*, April 1992; Central Intelligence Agency, *The World Factbook 1995* (Washington: CIA, 1995); British Broadcasting Corporation, *Summary of World Broadcasts, Part 1, Former USSR*, January 3, 1996.

Despite its comparatively small generating capacity, Turkmenistan has been able to maintain a position as a net exporter of electricity to other Central Asian republics. Turkmenistan has a current export capacity of 12 billion kwh,[278] assuming that all idle capacity is utilized. Construction has begun on a 321 km power line to Armenia, envisaged as part of a future system to export electricity to Europe via Turkey. The link to Armenia, via Iran, is to supply 2 billion kwh to Armenia beginning in 1997.

Not all regions are now included in the national power grid. Northeastern Turkmenistan, for example, had been heavily dependent on imports of electricity from neighboring Uzbekistan. This dependence has been relieved upon completion of a high voltage power line fed from domestic sources, but some electricity still must be imported.[279]

Prospective Pipelines

Turkmenistan's very optimistic estimates of future oil and natural gas production appear unrealistic. For example, natural gas production is more likely to be at 110-130 bcm by 2010 than at the 230 bcm projected. Nevertheless, Turkmenistan is and will remain dependent on oil and gas exports, regardless of production levels. Given Turkmenistan's relative remoteness from the natural gas growth markets in Europe, Southeast Asia, and the Far East and the high degree of competition expected for exports to these markets, Turkmenistan must build large-diameter, long-distance export pipelines that circumvent Russia. All the proposed export

277.   British Broadcasting Corporation, *Summary of World Broadcasts, Part 1, Former USSR*, October 26, 1995.

278.   British Broadcasting Corporation, *Summary of World Broadcasts, Part 1, Former USSR*, April 18, 1996.

279.   *FBIS-SOV*, February 2, 1995.

routes involve substantial political and financial risks, which are now being carefully examined. For the near future, however, Turkmenistan will remain dependent on access to the Russian gas pipeline grid.

On November 15, 1995, the presidents of Russia and Turkmenistan signed an agreement on cooperation, which established the Turkmen-Russia joint stock company, *Turkmenrosgaz*. The Turkmen government holds the controlling interest in Turkmenrosgaz, with 51 percent of the stock. Gazprom holds 44 percent, and ITERA (International Trading Energy and Resources Association, a U.S. company) has 5 percent.[280]

Turkmenrosgaz has pledged to buy all of the natural gas to be exported from Turkmenistan and will pay $42 per 1,000 cubic meters at the Turkmen/Uzbek border. It will be responsible beyond that point for transporting and selling Turkmen gas to customers outside Turkmenistan. Gazprom, for its part, will guarantee the delivery (that is, pipeline access) of up to 30 bcm of gas to Ukraine and to the Transcaucasus.[281] In itself, that guaranteed pipeline access does not improve the financial position of Turkmenistan, because customers in Ukraine and the Transcaucasus can be expected to remain heavily indebted to Turkmenistan for gas deliveries. Also, it is unknown whether the agreement grants any substantial access to the Russian pipeline grid for Turkmen gas exports to the Far Abroad.

The Turkmenrosgaz joint venture also has the right to explore for natural gas within Turkmenistan. In its own way, this gives Gazprom access to the rich natural gas resource base of that country. Turkmen president Saparmurad Niyazov, in his remarks about the agreement on Turkmenrosgaz, noted that this new company would focus, among other areas, on the Caspian shelf.[282] Gazprom thus becomes a potentially major player in the Caspian, strengthening Russia's grip on this vital area and further clouding the legal status of the Caspian.

If Turkmenistan is unable to expand natural gas exports to hard currency markets, it will lack capital for growth capital. A lack of growth, particularly relative to neighboring Kazakstan and Azerbaijan, surely will result in internal rumblings, perhaps not deep enough to challenge president Niyazov, but sufficient to cause concern, especially among prospective investors.

Turkmenistan can locate markets for its natural gas no matter which direction it looks. To the north, for markets in the Near and Far Abroad; to the south, for markets in Pakistan; to the east, for markets in China and Japan; and to the west, for markets in Turkey and Europe. With the exception of the Near Abroad, all potential markets are geographically distant and serving them would require construction of very expensive long-distance gas pipelines, which today are not feasible politically or financially. Russia is likely to continue to serve as a transit country.

---

280. *Russian Petroleum Investor*, December 1995/January 1996.

281. *FBIS-SOV*, November 20, 1995. A transit fee across Russia of $1.50/1,000 cubic meters/100 kilometers was also set by the agreement. Turkmen natural gas can be delivered by pipeline to Georgia, Armenia, and Azerbaijan. But to reach these markets it must transit Uzbekistan, Kazakstan, and Russia.

282. *Interfax*, Ashgabat, November 15, 1995.

Natural Gas

South to Pakistan. An agreement was signed in October 1995 between Turkmenistan, Delta Oil Company, and Unocal which gave these Western companies the right to buy natural gas from Turkmenistan at its border with Afghanistan, from which point the gas would be pipelined to Sui in Pakistan and marketed internally.[283] Of the various pipeline proposals put forward, this appeared to be the most feasible. Unocal and Delta were to build a 1,271 km pipeline to transport Turkmen natural gas to Pakistan via Afghanistan.[284] (See Map 11.) This pipeline would be built to the Sui gas fields located in Pakistan's southwestern province of Baluchistan. The cost of construction was placed at about $3 billion. Marketing outlets would be developed in Pakistan, including gas-fired thermal power generating facilities.[285]

Turkmenistan, for its part, was to dedicate to the proposed pipeline the production of the Dauletabad natural gas field, which is located about 160 km from the Afghan border and which holds about 1.3 trillion cubic meters of reserves.[286] Unocal/Delta will not be involved in production of the natural gas to be carried by the pipeline.

A Turkmen-Pakistan pipeline would cross politically insecure territory, like the proposed pipelines to carry Azeri crude oil to Western markets. Its route would cross lands held by the opposition Taliban Islamic militia in Afghanistan. Kabul authorities welcomed the prospect of a gas pipeline, viewing it as serving the interests of the region as a whole.[287]

Although major factions contesting for control in Afghanistan have provided written support for proposed pipelines from Turkmenistan through Afghanistan to Pakistan, political instability remains a problem. Despite the assurances given and despite the fact that these pipelines are financially viable projects, they cannot be financed because there is no effective central authority.[288]

The Turkmen natural gas potential is too rich for Gazprom to ignore, and the acquisition by Gazprom of a position in the Unocal/Delta partnership was probably inevitable. An agreement was reached in principle in March 1996.

Turkmenistan, Gazprom, Unocal, and Delta Petroleum signed a Memorandum

---

283.   That Afghanistan was not represented at the signing ceremony underscores the political tenuousness of the project.

284.   *Reuters*, Islamabad, January 17, 1996.

285.   Unocal has made an offer to help develop oil production offshore in the Turkmen sector of the Caspian Sea. See *FBIS-SOV*, November 6, 1995.

286.   *Reuters*, Islamabad, January 17, 1996. See also *Middle East Economic Survey*, October 23, 1995. The Delta Oil Company is a wholly owned subsidiary of Delta International which in turn is a privately owned Saudi Arabian company. The venture in Turkmenistan is being carried out by Unocal and Delta under the Unocal-Delta Alliance, a recently formed joint venture.

Unocal and Delta recognize that other plans have been put forward regarding the export of Turkmen natural gas to Pakistan, as well as projects which proposed supplying gas to Pakistan from Qatar and Iran. See *Platt's Oilgram News*, October 23, 1995.

287.   *Reuters*, Ashgabat, May 13, 1996.

288.   Chris Taggart, Executive Vice President, Unocal Turkmenistan, at a CSIS conference on Central Asia, September 18, 1996.

MAP 11.

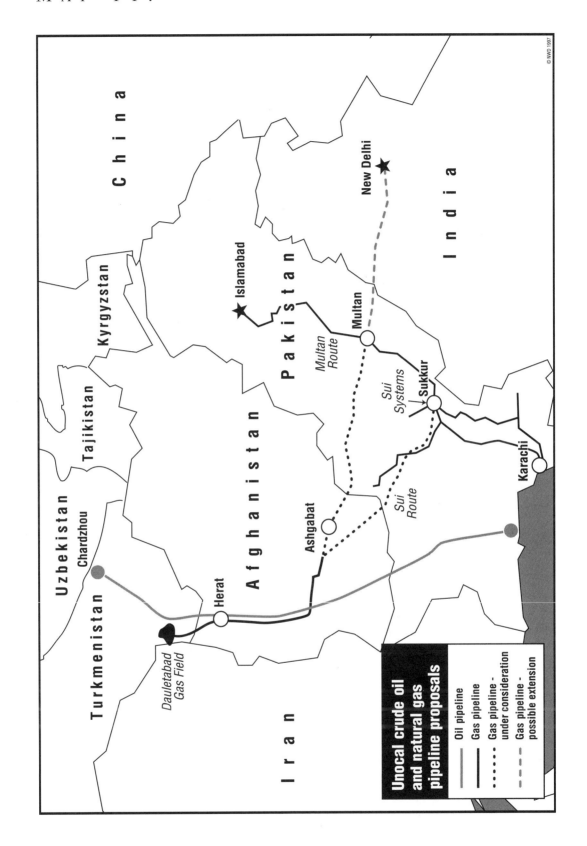

of Understanding for the construction of a gas pipeline from Turkmenistan through Afghanistan to Pakistan. By 1999 Turkmenistan plans to supply up to 20 bcm to Pakistan via this pipeline, and up to 40 bcm annually by the year 2002,[289] a goal not reachable.

Gazprom will hold a 10 percent share in the planned Turkmenistan-Afghanistan-Pakistan gas pipeline. Partners Unocal and Delta Oil will hold 85 percent, and Turkmenrosgaz will hold 5 percent. Dauletabad currently produces about 20.7 bcm per year. Geographically the field lies between the Serakhs and Murgab rivers near the border with Afghanistan. Commercial production began in 1982.[290]

The proposed gas pipeline will pass through Herat, Kandahar and Geneshk, crossing the Pakistani border near Quetta. The terminus selected will reflect market dynamics. For example, the line could continue on beyond Kandahar through Multan (Multan is already integrated into Pakistan's gas grid) to New Delhi, India. Or the line could be directed southeast, before Kandahar to the gas fields at Sui. The total length of the pipeline to the Sui gas field in Pakistan is 872 miles, including 105 miles in Turkmenistan, 519 miles in Afghanistan, and 248 miles in Pakistan.

A Turkmen-Pakistan export gas pipeline is important to Turkmenistan because it:

❑ represents a key element in Turkmenistan's desire to reduce its dependence on Russian pipelines.

❑ is thought that the willingness of Unocal to commit to the project would help create a more attractive investment climate.

Bridas Corporation (Argentina) had developed its own proposal for an Afghanistan-Pakistan pipeline for exporting Turkmen natural gas, which would tap into the Yashlar gas deposit. Relations between Bridas and Turkmenistan have been somewhat stormy, however, and Amangeldy Esenov, minister of oil and gas, has snubbed Bridas by supporting the Delta/Unocal proposal.[291]

Although exporting Turkmen natural gas to Pakistan can be presumed to be technically and financially viable, it is not risk-free. The continuing civil war in Afghanistan poses the greatest threat to the project, although Pakistan is also highly risky. The key question remains how the diverse interests of the warring factions in Afghanistan can be met in a way that would guarantee the security of the proposed pipeline.

Westward to Europe. Present-day plans for moving Turkmen natural gas ultimately to markets in Europe envisage construction of a pipeline which would transit Iran, Turkey, and the Balkan peninsula.[292] The proposed line would have a throughput of 28 bcm/year and would cost an estimated $3.5 billion.[293] But U.S. policy prohibits any actions or programs that would benefit Iran, and this effectively precludes financing for the Iranian portion of the pipeline.

---

289.   Interfax, *Petroleum Information Agency*, Moscow, August 8, 1996.
290.   *World Gas Intelligence*, November 1991.
291.   *Financial Times*, April 3, 1996.

The first leg of the Turkmenistan-Europe gas pipeline would target Turkey as a major customer, with deliveries to customers in that country reaching 15 bcm by the time period 2010–2020. Deliveries would begin in 1988, at 2 bcm per year, rising to 5 bcm by 1999–2004, and to 10 bcm by 2005–2010—a schedule that is obviously unrealistic.[294]

Considerable publicity has been given to the initiation of construction on a gas pipeline to move Turkmen natural gas to Iran. An agreement was signed in September 1995, which called for building a pipeline to link the Korpedzhe natural gas deposit in southwestern Turkmenistan with the northern Iranian village of Kurt-Kyi.[295]

Construction reportedly has begun on a 200 km gas pipeline (140 km of which will lie in Turkmenistan) from the Korpedzhe gas field in Western Turkmenistan to Kurt-Kyi in northern Iran. (See Map 12.) This $190 million project, the bulk of which is to be financed by Iran, is scheduled for completion by the end of 1997. President Niyazov views this project as the first step in delivering Iranian natural gas to buyers in Turkey and Europe. Delivery through the line to Kurt-Kyi is to reach 8 bcm by the year 2000.[296]

Iran is to build the pipeline on a turnkey basis and will finance 80 percent of the project. Turkmenistan, for its part, has pledged to cover the construction costs from natural gas deliveries during the first three years of the pipeline's operation.[297]

---

292.   The concept of a natural gas pipeline from Turkmenistan through Iran and Turkey to markets in Europe was first proposed in November 1993. Impetus came from a U.S. company, U.S.-CIS Ventures, Inc., in which former U.S. Secretary of State Alexander Haig was a principal. No progress could be made because financing could not be secured. The Turkmen government took over as sponsor and owner at the close of 1994.

A ceremonial welding of two segments of a projected pipeline to carry Turkmen natural gas via Iran and Turkey to Europe was attended on October 27, 1994, by the presidents of Turkmenistan, Azerbaijan, Turkey, and Iran. But then, financing realities again took over.

In January 1995 a so-called "Turkmenistan Transcontinental Gas Pipeline" (TTP) organization was set up and charged with securing financing for the project. A new set of problems arose. Setting aside the issue of financing, who would actually own the pipeline? A multinational structure could not, for example, because anything built on Iranian territory would become the property of Iran. See *Neft i Kapital*, March 1995.

U.S.-CIS Ventures, through its subsidiary, U.S.-CIS International, Inc., were given exclusive authority by the TTP to manage the development of the Turkmenistan-Europe gas pipeline. See *Platt's Oilgram News*, January 30, 1995. However, the stepped-up sanctions by the United States. against Iran has meant that this pipeline project is impossible and the Alexander Haig-led consultancy basically withdrew.

293.   Interfax, *Petroleum Information Agency*, September 26, 1995.

294.   *Neft i Kapital*, March 1995.

295.   British Broadcasting Corporation, *Summary of World Broadcasts, Part 1, Former USSR*, October 20, 1995. This pipeline has been described in the local press as the official launching of the Turkmenistan-Iran-Turkey-Europe transcontinental gas pipeline. It is far from that, simply because project financing could not be procured from outside sources. Inasmuch as the proposed gas pipeline to Europe could not be self-financed, any immediate extension beyond this initial portion is unlikely.

It is equally regarded, and perhaps more correctly, as the first step in relieving the dependence of Turkmenistan upon the pipeline system of its northern neighbor. See *Izvestiya*, July 7, 1995.

296.   *Reuters,* Almaty, October 11, 1996.

M A P 1 2 .

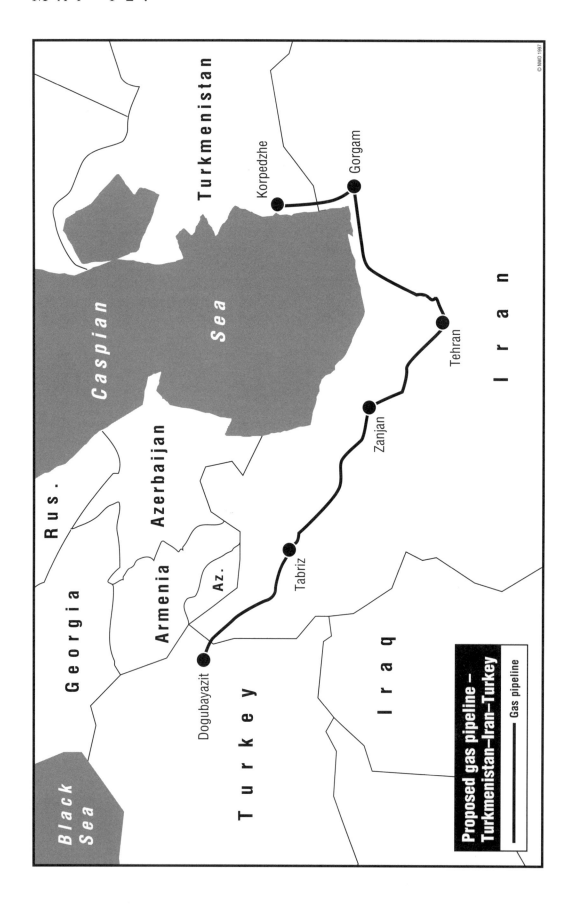

© NWD 1997

Proposed gas pipeline —
Turkmenistan–Iran–Turkey

Gas pipeline

It is unlikely that this pipeline will soon be extended across Iran to Turkey, not least because Iran has little reason to facilitate the export of Turkmen natural gas to markets that it covets.

A gas pipeline from Turkmenistan to Europe could circumvent Iran, by using a shorter, more direct route from Turkmenbashi across the Caspian to Baku, where it could then follow the track of the proposed crude oil pipeline from Baku.[298] A proposal to do just that has been put forward by Oil Capital Limited, Inc., a U.S.-based company.[299] This pipeline would extend from western Turkmenistan across the Caspian Sea to Baku, at which point it would parallel a Baku-Yumurtalik crude oil pipeline, also proposed by Oil Capital, Ltd. The proposed gas pipeline would be built of 56-inch pipe and would carry 3 billion cubic feet daily (about 11 bcm/year).

An Argentine company, BOTAS, has put forward a somewhat comparable proposal. It envisages construction of a gas pipeline from Krasnovodsk, across the Caspian Sea to Baku, and on to Turkey via either Georgia or Armenia.

Building a linkage with the Russian pipeline network would seem to be a cheaper option, although it carries substantial political risk. In the end, Russia is not prepared to make room for any substantial volumes of Turkmen gas destined for buyers in Europe, which would displace Russian gas. However, when and if a system of pipelines is operating to carry natural gas from the Yamal Peninsula to markets in Europe, Russia might accommodate some volumes of Turkmen gas.

Eastward to China and Japan. Of all the export options under consideration, exporting eastward to buyers in China and Japan, southern Korea, and Taiwan would appear least feasible. (See Map 13.) The proposed pipeline would parallel the existing Chardzhou-Tashkent-Shymkent-Bishkek-Almaty natural gas pipeline and would be the longest in the world. Commercial operation would begin between 2005 and 2010.

Though technically feasible and politically desirable, this proposed 56-inch pipeline would be some 8,000 km long and would probably cost $12 to 13 billion to construct. Delivery of the natural gas to Japan would require either laying a pipeline on the bottom of the East China Sea to the Japanese island of Kyushu, a distance of at least 900 km, or delivering the gas to Japan in liquefied form. Natural gas liquefaction projects are very capital-intensive, and the landed cost most likely would not be competitive with other fuels.

There are no major points of consumption along the way that would allow the gas pipeline to be built in stages or that would make financing considerably easier. For China, however, the pipeline is important because it would link exploitable gas deposits in the Tarim and Turfan-Khamiinsk basins with consumers along the coast, while stimulating industrial development of China's western and central regions.

Moreover, there are tremendous undeveloped natural gas resources awaiting

---

297. *Petroleum Information Agency*, Ashgabat, October 17, 1995.

298. *Platt's Oilgram News*, May 9, 1995.

299. Presentation by Martin G. Pranga, Executive Vice President, Oil Capital Limited, Inc., at the 3rd Kazakhstan International Oil & Gas Projects Conference, Almaty, October 2-3, 1995.

MAP 13.

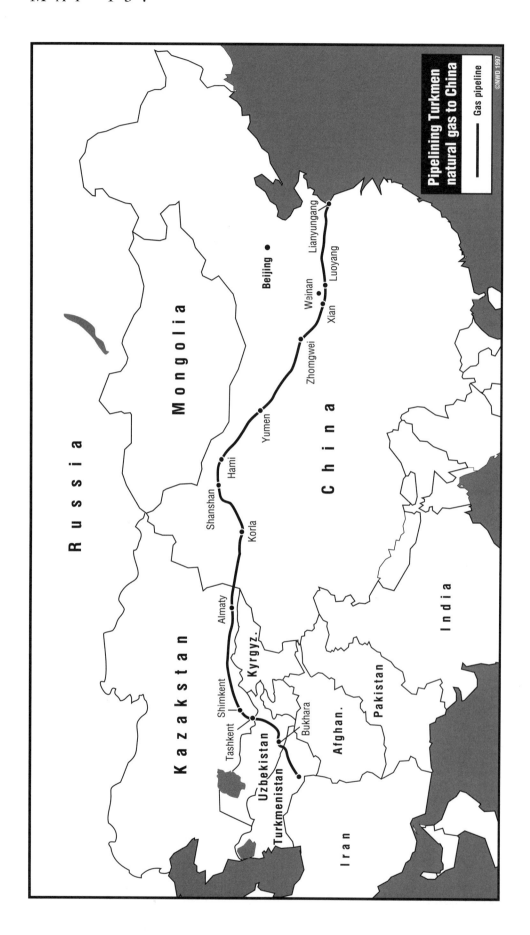

exploitation in Eastern Siberia, in the republic of Sakha (formerly Yakutiya). Projects to develop these reserves have been considered periodically over at least the past quarter-century.[300] These gas resources are attracting renewed interest. President Boris Yeltsin, during a visit to China in late April 1996, signed an agreement on the construction of a gas pipeline from Eastern Siberia through Mongolia and China to the Yellow Sea coast.[301](See Map 14.) This proposed pipeline would be some 4,000 km long and would have an initial carrying capacity of 15 bcm, with the possibility of being subsequently expanded to 30-40 bcm. Two-thirds of the natural gas would be delivered to buyers in Mongolia, southern Korea, and China.

Natural gas for the pipeline would originate at the Kovyktinskoye gas field, located 350 km north of the city of Irkutsk. Recoverable reserves at this gas field total a minimum of 870 bcm. Production in 1998 would reach 3.3 bcm, and by 2005 would reach 32 bcm.

The cost of developing this field, which holds an estimated 1.5 trillion cu. meters of reserves, and building a 4,500-km pipeline to South Korea is estimated at $5-7 billion. China reportedly has guaranteed to import 10 bcm, a step towards beginning construction of a Siberia-Mongolia-China-South Korea gas pipeline but for the project to be profitable, and to secure financing, exports must total at least 20 bcm.

The license to develop Kovyktinsk is held by RUSIA Petroleum, a subsidiary of Sidanko, one of Russia's vertically integrated oil companies. The Hanbo Group (South Korea) acquired a 27.5 percent stake in RUSIA in June 1996 and at the end of October the administration of the Irkutsk region, where the deposit is located, announced its intention to sell 18.6 percent of RUSIA Petroleum to China, through the China National Gas Corporation.[302]

Crude Oil

Oil Pipeline to Arabian Sea (Pakistan). Unocal has proposed the construction of a crude oil pipeline (The Central Asian Oil Pipeline Project—CAOPP), to originate at Chardzhou (Turkmenistan) and to extend through Afghanistan to a Pakistani port on the Arabian Sea. The proposed line would be 1,667 km in length and would be 42 inches in diameter, and could handle 1 million b/d. Of that length, 458 km would be within Turkmenistan, 697 km within Afghanistan and 512 km within Pakistan. Several Pakistani ports are under consideration: Gwadar, Pasni and Omara, among others. The cost, including single point mooring systems for the loading of tankers, is put at $2.7 billion.

A large-diameter pipeline moving crude oil from the West Siberian fields to two refineries in Kazakstan—Pavlodar and Shymkent—and continuing on to the Chardzhou refinery in Turkmenistan is in place and has been operational for some time. This system however is considerably underutilized:

---

300. See Robert E. Ebel, *Communist Trade in Oil and Gas* (New York: Praeger, 1970).
301. *Finansovyye Izvestiya,* May 21, 1996.
302. *FBIS-SOV,* November 5, 1996.

MAP 14.

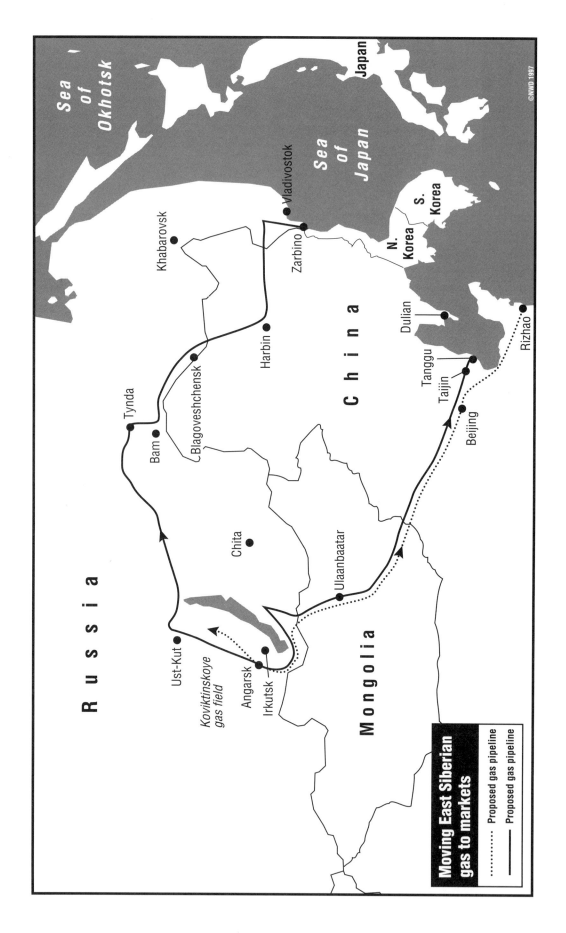

Sea of Okhotsk

Japan

Vladivostok

Sea of Japan

S. Korea

Zarbino

N. Korea

Khabarovsk

Dulian

©NWD 1997

Harbin

Tanggu

Rizhao

Blagoveshchensk

Taijin

Tynda

Beijing

Bam

C h i n a

Ust-Kut

Chita

Ulaanbaatar

Koviktinskoye gas field

Angarsk

Irkutsk

R u s s i a

M o n g o l i a

Moving East Siberian gas to markets

.... Proposed gas pipeline
———— Proposed gas pipeline

Table 5-6
Underutilized Kazak Oil Pipelines

Segment	Length	Diameter	Capacity	1995 Actual
	(miles)	(in.)	(million b/d)	(million b/d)
Surgut-Omsk-Pavlodar	860	40	1.0	0.5
Pavlodar-Shymkent	1,045	32	0.5	0.02
Shymkent-Chardzhou	431	24	0.2	idle

The Tengiz deposit is located some 880 miles to the northwest of Chardzhou, while the three oil fields—Azeri, Chirag, and Gunashli—offshore in the Caspian and being developed by the AIOC lie some 960 km to the northwest. Both projects could be tied into the CAOPP with little technical difficulty, although linking up with the AIOC fields would require laying approximately 200 miles of pipe under the Caspian Sea.

Finally, there is an operating pipeline that links the Kumkol oil field in south-central Kazakstan to the Pavlodar-Shymkent pipeline. If a line were build westward from Kumkol to Kenkiyak, a distance of 471 miles, crude oil from the Urals-Volga fields could be fed into the CAOPP.

The proposed CAOPP has much to offer. It offers diversity to both producer and consumer, a desirable advantage when dealing with oil, an easily politicized commodity and it fits into the multiple pipeline policy of the U.S, among other things. More importantly, however, it would provide the crude oils of Russia, Kazakstan, and the Caspian Sea with an outlet on the Arabian Sea from which these crudes could easily be moved to the growing markets of Southeast Asia and the Far East. (See Map 15.) Conversely, Russia not surprisingly downplays both the crude oil and natural gas pipelines, as Russian energy minister Pyotr Rodionov said that they might not be feasible because of the high costs of construction through the mountainous terrain.[303]

Neither the proposed natural gas pipeline nor the proposed crude oil line will be able to be financed unless and until a strong central authority is in place in Afghanistan. By the summer of 1996 the Taliban had established control over 70 percent of Afghan territory, but not yet enough, and certainly not recognized by the international community as governing Afghanistan. The Taliban movement was formed by "Islamic scholars," Afghan students attending Islamic schools while living in Pakistan. The movement is intent on building an autonomous state based on Islamic morality. The Taliban is provided with military aid by Pakistan.[304]

---

303. *Platt's Oilgram News*, December 13, 1996.
304. *Russian Petroleum Investor*, November 1996.

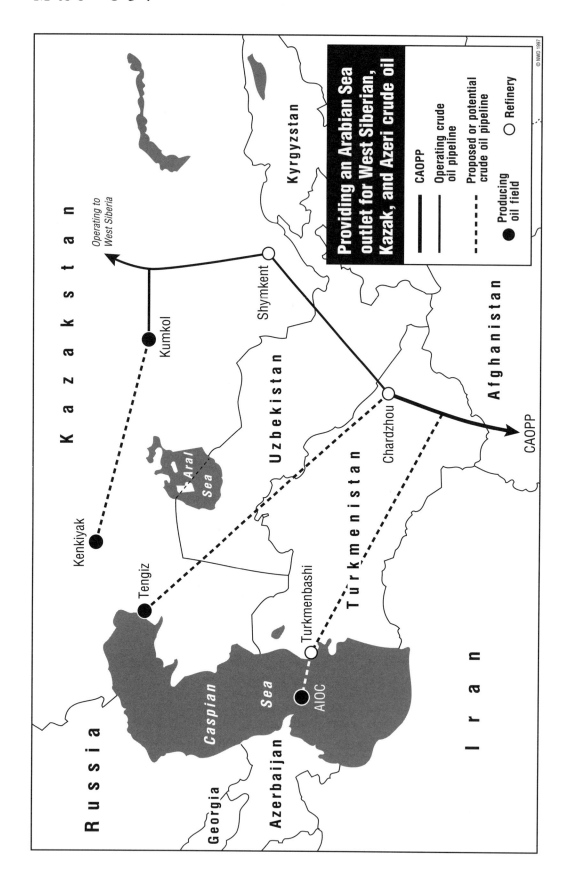

Providing an Arabian Sea outlet for West Siberian, Kazak, and Azeri crude oil

Stand on Caspian Sea Legal Issue

Turkmenistan had been somewhat cautious about taking sides in the dispute over the legal status of the Caspian Sea as it sometimes was seen to support Kazakstan and Azerbaijan but on other occasions seemed to line up with Iran and Russia. In general it had been careful not to come in conflict with Russia on this very contentious issue. Then, Turkmenistan clearly tilted away from Kazakstan and Azerbaijan when together with Russia and Iran it signed on November 13, 1996 a Memorandum on Cooperation on the Development of Mineral Resources of the Caspian Sea. This memorandum laid the foundation for a joint company to explore for and develop oil and gas on the coastal zones of the three signatories. Kazakstan and Azerbaijan were invited to join the proposed company but refused.

The joint company furthers Moscow's ambition to participate in Caspian Sea oil and gas development projects and it also complicates matters because Iran for all practical purposes is out-of-bounds for U.S. investors.[305]

At the same time, Russia, Iran, and Turkmenistan lack the financial capabilities to explore and develop the Caspian on their own, which means that foreign investors somehow will have to be brought in.

---

305. *Neft i Kapital*, December 1996-January 1997.

Source: States of the Former Soviet Union, CIA, 1992.

CHAPTER 6

Uzbekistan

Table 6-1
Uzbekistan at a Glance

Currency	Sum*
Rate of Exchange	55 sum/$1 (December 4, 1996)
Gross Domestic Product	$19.1 billion (1994)
Inflation	+40 percent (1996)
Population	22.2 million (1994)
By Nationality	
Uzbek	71.4 percent
Russian and other European	8.3 percent
Tajik	4.7 percent
Kazak	4.1 percent
Tatar	2.4 percent
Karakalpak	2.1 percent
Other	7.0 percent

*Introduced as official currency July 1, 1994, at an established rate of $1=7 sum.

Sources: Central Intelligence Agency (CIA), *The World Factbook 1995* (Washington, D. C.: CIA, 1995); Interfax, *Financial Information Agency,* Tashkent, February 15, 1995; Interfax, *Financial Information Agency,* Tashkent, March 1, 1996; Open Media Research Institute, *Daily Report,* April 26, 1996; World Bank data.

Uzbekistan is the most populous of the Central Asian states, and Tashkent, the capital, is recognized as the commercial center of the region. Almost all the great historic cities are in Uzbekistan. These three attributes, and the fact that the country has a very strong president, Islam Karimov, make Uzbekistan a regional force to be reckoned with.[306]

Following the prescription laid down by Moscow for specialization among the republics of the former Soviet Union, Uzbekistan became the land of cotton.

---

306.   Graham E. Fuller, "Central Asia's Geopolitical Future," *Post-Soviet Prospects,* October 1994.

Uzbekistan had tillable soil, water could be made available, and the climate was right. The growing of cotton flourished, while the development of basic industries was neglected. As a result, Uzbekistan is among the least industrialized of the former Soviet republics.[307]

"White gold," as cotton is called, has been a source of wealth and the cause of shocking environmental degradation. The heavy use of pesticides and fertilizers[308] to support planners' demands for increasingly higher yields has poisoned the land and water of Uzbekistan, perhaps beyond repair.[309]

Uzbekistan and Kazakstan share the Aral Sea, once the fourth-largest lake in the world. Beginning in the early 1960s the lake began to shrink dramatically because waters from the AmuDarya and SyrDarya Rivers were diverted to irrigate cotton and rice in the region. The surface area of the Aral has shrunk from 68,000 sq. km to about 37,000 sq. km (as of 1992) because of this diversion.

Some experts believe that Aral Sea may completely evaporate within three decades. In the interim, the increased salinity of the irrigation water has severely diminished crop yields, while salt and dust blown from the seabed have severely retarded plant growth.[310] The shrinkage of the sea has resulted in the loss of its fishing industry, the destruction of the ecosystem of the sea and the deltas, and the depression of the economy of those areas close by.[311]

Uzbekistan has emerged as the leading power in Central Asia. President Islam Karimov repeatedly emphasizes Uzbekistan's geographic centrality and political stability as justification for this role.[312] U.S. policy toward Uzbekistan has somewhat reversed itself during the past few years, from being critical of Uzbekistan's human rights record, to recognizing the potentially key role of Uzbekistan in the region. Yet, concerns remain that Ubekistan abrogates human rights.

Natural Resources

Uzbekistan is comparatively rich in natural resources: crude oil, natural gas, coal, uranium, and gold, plus a variety of other precious metals. Uzbekistan can make one claim that no other republic of the former Soviet Union can make: production of crude oil and natural gas in Uzbekistan has been increasing since the breakup of

---

307.   U.S. government, *Uzbekistan: An Economic Profile,* October 1993.

308.   About 62 kilograms per hectare, while international norms set the limit at seven kilograms per hectare. See Interfax, *Nukus,* September 19, 1995.

309.   The combination of extremely heavy use of pesticides and the gradual drying-up of the Aral Sea has proven deadly to the health of those living in the area of the Aral Sea (Karakalpakstan). According to the Uzbek Health Ministry and the World Health Organization, 90 percent of the women in this area suffer from anemia. Infant mortality now stands at 60 deaths per 1,000 births, the highest in the former Soviet Union. Some 120 women per 100,000 die when giving birth. Life expectancy in the area is 20 years less than the CIS average. See Interfax, *Nukus* (Uzbekistan), September 19, 1995.

310.   U.S. Government, *Uzbekistan: An Economic Profile,* October 1993.

311.   *U.S.-Kazakhstan Monitor,* July-August 1995.

312.   Roger D. Kangas, "Taking the Lead in Central Asian Security," *Transition,* May 3, 1996.

the Soviet Union. Uzbekistan became independent in fuel during 1996. Fuel independence means considerable savings because the country will no longer need to import crude oil from Russia and also means a considerable degree of political independence.

Uzbekistan falls between the Haves and Have-Nots—it is a Have because it is self-sufficient in energy, but it is also a Have-Not because its known oil and gas reserves are not large enough to make Uzbekistan a meaningful contributor to world markets. At the same time, Uzbekistan has no immediate access to these markets. Like the other Haves, Uzbekistan's fuel and energy sector requires a considerable cash transfusion, on the order of $1 billion, over the next several years. This cash transfusion cannot come from within; if it is to occur, the funds will have to originate with international lending institutions, foreign investors, and international vendors.

The energy sector wish list is long, but the key projects include:

❏ developing the Kokdumalak oil field,

❏ modernizing the Fergana (now known as Uzneftepererabotka) oil refinery,

❏ the construction of an oil refinery in the Bukhara region, and

❏ building a petrochemical complex in Shurtan.

The Kokdumalak crude oil and gas condensate field, located in the northwest Kashkadarya region, is particularly attractive, with crude and condensate reserves of some 1.4 billion bbls.[313] Table 6-2 outlines the cost of these projects.[314]

Table 6-2
The Cost of Key Projects in Uzbekistan's Energy Sector

Project	Cost in $Million
Kokdumalak oil field	170
Shurgan gas field	120
Mubarek oil fields	60
Mingbulak oil field	40
Bukhara refinery	160
SyrDarya electric power station	112

Note: Kokdumalak straddles the Turkmen-Uzbek border. Turkmenistan is upset because Uzbekistan began producing from Kokdumalak while Turkmenistan was still engaged in prospecting from its side.

Sources: Interfax, *Petroleum Report,* March 3-10, 1995; *FBIS-SOV,* May 11, 1995; *Moscow News,* December 1-7, 1995.

Uzbekistan is moving to privatize its fuel and energy complex, including oil

---

313. *Russian Petroleum Investor,* November 1995.
314. *FBIS-SOV,* May 11, 1995.

and gas producers and oil and gas transport facilities.[315] Privatization has become a popular approach for raising capital and has been heavily promoted by the West.

The demand for fuels and electric power has held up quite well in Uzbekistan, largely because there has been comparatively little drop-off in industrial activity. Industrial production actually increased by 1.8 percent in 1991, then declined by 6.7 percent in 1992, but gained 3.6 percent in 1993 and 1 percent in 1994. In comparison, industrial production for the CIS as a whole dropped 23 percent in 1994.[316] Moreover, industrial production in the CIS that year stood at just 56 percent of the 1991 level, whereas industrial production in Uzbekistan had declined just 2 percent during this same period.

Uzbekistan was only one of two CIS member-countries (Armenia was the other) where industrial output actually grew during 1995. Although this growth was relatively minor, at 0.2 percent, it nonetheless compared favorably with that of the CIS as a whole, where industrial output was off 6 percent.[317]

Uzbekistan is moving toward becoming a remarkably self-reliant nation. Some mistakes have been made in this transformation, and some citizens and government officials can be quite arrogant about what has accomplished and what the future holds. At the same time, Uzbekistan will never be a democracy in the Western sense, and any attempt to emulate the West in this regard would likely fail.

The obstacles to investment in Uzbekistan mirror those encountered elsewhere in the former Soviet Union. It is difficult to ascertain who is in charge; tax codes are constantly changing; laws and regulations are conflicting and there is no system for adjudication or enforcement; the country is protective, nationalistic, and secretive. Finally, Uzbekistanis are fearful of being taken advantage of, which often makes pursuing business opportunities difficult, time-consuming, and sometimes impossible. Once commitments have been made, however, Uzbekistan generally follows through. There is some measure of corruption, bribery, and kickbacks, but not an unreasonable amount.

Coal

Coal is a minor but locally important source of energy for Uzbekistan (Table 6-3). Very small amounts are exported to neighboring countries. In 1993 exports totalled just 138,000 tons, with slightly more than half sold to Turkmenistan. Most of the remainder was delivered to Kazakstan.

Uzbekistan also imports coal—405,000 tons in 1993—with 80 percent originating in Russia. Coals mined in Uzbekistan are primarily lower-quality brown coals; the country must therefore import sizeable amounts of hard coal, some of which is reexported. On balance, however, Uzbekistan remains a net importer of coal.

---

315.   Interfax, *Petroleum Information Agency,* Tashkent, September 14, 1995.

316.   *Ekonomika i zhizn,* no. 17, April 1995 and *FBIS-SOV,* March 22, 1995.

317.   *Finansovyye Izvestiya,* February 20, 1996.

Table 6-3
Coal Production in Uzbekistan, 1980–1994

Year	Million tons
1980	5.7
1990	6.4
1991	5.9
1992	6.5
1993	3.76
1994	3.8
1996 est.	3.8
2000 plan	5.9

Sources: Interfax, *Petroleum Report,* February 24 to March 3, 1995; Central Intelligence Agency (CIA), *Handbook of International Economic Statistics 1994* (Washington, D. C.: CIA, September 1994); IEA/NMC(92)9, June 10, 1992; U.S. government, *Uzbekistan: An Economic Profile,* October 1993; Interfax, Tashkent, July 30, 1996.

Some growth in coal extraction has been scheduled through the year 2000, with the goal for that year set at 5.9 million tons. At the same time, domestic demand for coal is to increase only modestly, to 4 million tons, thus leaving an exportable surplus of 1.9 million tons for sale to its Central Asian neighbors.[318]

Nonetheless, the need to import hard coals will still remain.

Crude Oil

Crude oil was first discovered at Shorsu in the Fergana basin in 1880, and production there was the mainstay for the oil industry for a number of years. Nonetheless, domestic crude oil supply always fell short of requirements, making it necessary to import crude oil. Estimates of Uzbek crude oil reserves vary widely, ranging from the 300 million bbl noted in Table 8-1 to between 1.75 and 5.1 billion bbl often attributed to Uzneftegaz.[319]

The expansion of crude oil production (Table 6-4) following the breakup of the Soviet Union has allowed a concomitant reduction in crude oil imports from Russia (Table 6-5). Reduced imports from Russia have been beneficial not only to Uzbekistan but also to Russia, which has been able to maintain oil exports to hard currency buyers even as Russian crude oil production has declined rather severely.

---

318. *Interfax*, Tashkent, July 30, 1996
319. Interfax, *Petroleum Information Agency,* Tashkent, September 22, 1995.

Table 6-4
Uzbekistan: Crude Oil Production, 1980–2010

Year	Thousand b/d
1980	26
1990	57
1991	57
1992	66
1993	80
1994	111
1995 est.	150
1996 plan	160
2000-2010 plan	180

Sources: Interfax, *Petroleum Report,* March 17-24, 1995 and July 7-14, 1995; Interfax, Tashkent, June 16, 1995; *Interfax,* Tashkent, February 21, 1995; FBIS-SOV, July 28,1995; Interfax, *Petroleum Information Agency,* Tashkent, September 22, 1995; U.S. government, *Uzbekistan: An Economic Profile,* October 1993; *Petroleum Intelligence Weekly,* February 26, 1996.

The crude oil production goal of just 180,000 b/d within the next decade is surprisingly modest.[320] Other former Soviet republics often set long-term production goals that are overly optimistic; Uzbekistan's goals, in contrast, are realistic. Near-term growth in crude oil production will be based largely on expansion of the Kokdumalak oilfield, where output is to jump from 40,000 b/d in 1994, to 130,000 b/d by 2000, using funding from the U.S. and Japanese export-import banks.[321] Half the field is located in Uzbekistan, and half is in Turkmenistan, at the border south of Bukhara. Turkmenistan reportedly has ceded full field development rights to Uzbekneftegaz.[322]

---

320.   The Kantor consortium, made up of representatives from London Economics, Arthur D. Little and the London Business School, plus the leader of the group, Kantor of Greece, recently completed a full audit of the oil and gas industry of Uzbekistan. Its views of future oil production levels in Uzbekistan correspond with those levels projected by the government. See *FBIS-SOV,* October 10, 1995.

321.   *Petroleum Intelligence Weekly,* February 26, 1996.

Table 6-5
Uzbekistan: Crude Oil Imports From Russia

Year	Thousand b/d
1991	90
1993	80
1994	60
1995 est.	15

Sources: Interfax, *Petroleum Information Agency,* Tashkent, September 7, 1995; Interfax, *Petroleum Report,* August 25 to September 1, 1995; *FBIS-SOV,* September 12, 1995.

As noted, the supply of crude oil and gas condensate in Uzbekistan is reduced somewhat by export of small volumes to a wide variety of countries (Table 6-6). In 1994, Uzbekistan exported the equivalent of 13,600 b/d, or about 8.4 percent of supply (production plus imports).

Table 6-6
Crude Oil and Gas Condensate Exports from Uzbekistan, 1994

Destination	Barrels per day
Kazakhstan	5,420
Turkmenistan	700
Belarus	3,680
Ukraine	440
Russia	1,420
Lithuania	546*
Luxembourg	656*
Malaysia	480*
Great Britain	200*
Finland	69*

*Gas condensate only.

Source: Interfax, Petroleum Report, February 24 to March 3, 1995.

The largest recent discovery of crude oil was at Mingbulak, near the SyrDarya River. The discovery well blew out in March 1992, and oil flowed at a reported 35,000 to 62,000 b/d. Flames reached a height of 330 feet, and it took two months to bring the well under control.[323]

There are two crude oil refineries in Uzbekistan. Uzneftepererabotka, (for-

---

322. *Oil & Gas Journal,* January 30, 1995.

merly known as the Fergana refinery), which can process 108,000 b/d, and Alt-yaryk, which can process 66,000 b/d.[324] As the stream of crude shifts from Russian supplies to local supplies, the Uzbekneftepererabotka refinery must be modernized. Local crudes—that is, those crude oils produced in the Fergana valley—have higher sulfur contents than imported Russian crude, and the light product yield is lower.

The Uzbekneftepererabotka refinery has a somewhat higher light product yield—76.7 percent— than the average for Russian refineries (about 63 percent). This means Uzbekistan is better able to meet domestic demand for gasoline and diesel fuel.

Table 6-7
Crude Oil Refining in Uzbekistan, 1992-1994
Thousand b/d

	1992	1993	1994
Charge to refining	134	148	146
Product yield*	123.7	138.7	134.8
Of which:			
Gasoline	30	32	28
Diesel fuel	40	46	46
Heating oil	28	38	44
*Estimated, except for 1994, which was reported.			
Source: Interfax, *Petroleum Report,* March 17-24, 1995.			

Virtually all supplies of refined products are directed to the domestic market. Petroleum product exports in 1993 represented little more than 1 percent of the yield from refining. Petroleum product imports have been an important part of total supply in the past, but that is likely to change over the coming years. Uzbekistan imported an average of 208,000 b/d in 1989, declining to 130,000 b/d in 1992, and further to 62,000 b/d in 1994.[325]

The Karaulbazar refinery, now under construction in the Bukhara region and slated for completion by the end of 1996,[326] will process condensate from the Kok-

---

323.   Joseph P. Riva, Jr., *Petroleum in the Muslim Republics of the Commonwealth of Independent States: More Oil for OPEC?* (Library of Congress: Congressional Research Service, September 1, 1992).

324.   The larger refinery is comparatively obsolete by Western standards. For example, Uzneftepererabotka has not been able to produce enough aviation kerosine to cover domestic needs. As a result, Uzbekistan was to buy an average of 3,000 b/d of aviation kerosine from Turkmenistan during 1995. The costs of these imports were to be offset by transit fees collected for movement of Turkmen natural gas across Uzbekistan enroute to Ukraine. See Interfax, *Petroleum Report,* March 17-24, 1995.

325.   *East Bloc Energy,* July 1995.

326.   Interfax, *Petroleum Information Agency,* Tashkent, January 9, 1996.

dumalak field. This refinery will have an initial capacity of 50,000 b/d, to be increased to 100,000 b/d at a later date. It will be linked to Kokdumalak by a 94 km pipeline.[327] Bringing the Karaulbazar refinery into operation should complete the Uzbek drive for energy independence, because domestic production of petroleum products should then obviate the need for product imports. Karaulbazar was reported to be 50 percent complete as of late August 1996, placing its original completion date in jeopardy.

Generally speaking, most Western investors seek access to oil and gas for export purposes. Uzbekistan does not hold the same geologic promise as Turkmenistan or Kazakstan. Current oil and gas production is basically for the domestic economy or, if for export, for the Near Abroad. The exportable surpluses of these fuels would not now nor in the near term support the construction of a pipeline to carry crude oil or natural gas to the Far Abroad.[328]

That should not be taken to mean Uzbekistan will never be a player in world energy. As exploration for oil and gas expands and as Mingbulak, Kokdumalak, and other finds are developed, the prospects for increasingly large exportable surpluses are good. Domestic requirements should not make a major claim on future production.

The first major breakthrough relative to Western investment came in late June 1996, when the Overseas Private Investment Corporation (OPIC) announced that it would provide funding and insurance guarantees for an Uzbek-U.S. joint venture with Enron Oil and Gas Company. Enron, together with its Uzbek partner Uzbekneftegaz, is to undertake development of the country's natural gas reserves.[329]

Another company, ExproFuels (United States), simultaneously announced that it will sign two joint venture agreements to convert Uzbekistan's fleet of cars, trucks, and buses from imported gasoline to natural gas.[330] The project is to help Uzbekistan convert 200,000 gasoline and diesel vehicles to natural gas. A joint venture, Gasmotors, was to be formed with Uzbek partners Uzminvodhos and - Uzavtotrans Corporation. At a cost of between $1,500-$2,000 per vehicle, conversion is quite expensive and well beyond the means of most owners. The project presumably is based on comparative fuel costs. Gasoline costs an average of $1.54 per gallon, against 85 cents for an equivalent amount of compressed natural gas.[331]

Finally, it was announced that Texaco planned to use OPIC financing to manufacture and market lubricants throughout Central Asia in a joint venture with Uzbekneftegaz.

Uzbekistan at the moment remains outside the highly contentious pipeline

---

327. Interfax, *Petroleum Report,* July 15-22, 1994 and September 8-15, 1995.

328. The Kantor Group, in making a full audit of the Uzbek oil and gas sector, concluded that Uzbek oil exports could increase by 4 to 5 million tons (80 to 100,000 b/d) by the end of the 1990s. It was proposed to export the oil by rail. Upon completion of the Bukhara oil refinery, crude oil exports should be replaced by the export of petroleum products. See *FBIS-SOV,* October 10, 1995.

329. *UPI,* Washington, June 24, 1996.

330. *Platt's Oilgram News,* June 25, 1996.

331. *Journal of Commerce,* July 2, 1996.

routings issue of the day. There is, of course, the prospect of access to the Russian pipeline network, or of Uzbekistan oil and gas being sold to Europe by means of swaps with Russia. But neither the foreign investor nor the Uzbek oil and gas sector would necessarily want to develop any such dependence on Russia. Perhaps the best option is to piggyback on the pipelines proposed for moving Turkmen crude oil and natural gas to foreign markets. To that end, Uzbekistan and Unocal have signed an agreement to determine the feasibility of tying part of Uzbekistan's pipeline network into Unocal's proposed Turkmenistan-Pakistan crude oil pipeline.[332]

Table 6-8
Oil-Related Joint Ventures in Uzbekistan

Foreign Partner	Local Partner	Project
Probadi (Malaysia)	Uzneftegazdobycha	Karaktai oil field
Gazprom (Russia)	Uzbekneftegaz	Develop 15 fields in the
Enron Oil & Gas (U.S)		Surhandarya and Bukhara regions
LUKoil (Russia)	Uzbekneftegaz	Develop 9 gas condensate fields in the Kashkadarin region
Stan Cornelius Consortium	Uzbekneftegaz	Develop the Mingbulak field
Sources: *Oil & Gas Journal,* February 13, 1995; Interfax, *Petroleum Report,* July 8-15, 1994.		

The Enron joint venture to develop gas reserves at 15 fields located in the Surhandarya and Bukhara regions is particularly promising. Reserves dedicated to the joint venture exceed 570 billion cubic meters, and estimates of recoverable liquids reserves exceed 600 million bbls. Enron is working with Gazprom on transporting future natural gas production to markets in Europe. Present plans call for steadily increasing extraction to a level of 6 bcm annually.[333]

The Karaktai is an old field and has been worked for some 20 years. The Malaysian-Uzbek joint venture was the first joint venture registered in the country and will seek to restore production at Karaktai and other fields as well.[334]

Natural Gas

Proven natural gas reserves are large enough to permit Uzbekistan to become a major exporter. However, Uzbekistan faces serious competition from Kazakstan and Turkmenistan, and the high tariffs imposed by transit countries reduce the competitiveness of Uzbek natural gas outside the country's borders.

Uzbekistan is a relatively large producer of natural gas (Table 6-9), trailing

332. *Platt's Oilgram News,* November 5, 1996
333. *FBIS-SOV,* April 11, 1996.
334. *Interfax,* Tashkent, July 10, 1995.

only Russia among the former Soviet republics, now that Turkmenistan has cut back because of a loss of markets. One field, Shurtanskoye, produces about 18 bcm/year. Gazli, discovered in 1962, is the largest of the gas fields in Uzbekistan, with recoverable gas of 0.74 trillion cubic meters, triple those of Shurtanskoye.[335]

A joint Uzbek-Ukrainian-Russian grouping is undertaking construction of a gas pipeline linking the Gazli gas fields with the city of Nukus in the remote northwest of the country. This pipeline was to have been completed in early 1996 but has been behind schedule.[336] To be built at a cost of $63 million, the new pipeline will have a carrying capacity of 6 bcm and will permit Uzbekistan to eliminate the annual import of 3.5 bcm of natural gas from Turkmenistan. Uzbekistan will pay for the construction by delivering to Russia 1.9 bcm of gas annually for a period of 5 years.

Table 6-9
Natural Gas Production in Uzbekistan

Year	Billion cubic meters
1980	34.8
1985	35.5
1990	40.8
1991	41.9
1992	42.8
1993	45
1994	47.2
1995 plan	48
1996 plan	50
2000 plan	60

Sources: Interfax, *Petroleum Report,* March 17-24, 1995 and June 16-23, 1995; FBIS-SOV, July 28, 1995; *IEA/NMC (92)*9, June 10, 1992; Interfax, *Petroleum Information Agency,* Tashkent, September 22, 1995; U.S. government, *Uzbekistan: An Economic Profile,* October 1993.

Natural gas production plans call for output to increase 20 percent over a five-year period, and this is not overly ambitious. Nor does it imply that gas exports will substantially increase in coming years. Most of the production over these coming years should stay at home, as it has in the past.

Some improvement in natural gas export levels will come about if the Uzbekistan proposal to deliver 6 bcm of natural gas to Ukraine during 1997 can be imple-

---

335.   Joseph P. Riva. Jr., *Petroleum in the Muslim Republics of the Commonwealth of Independent States: More Oil for OPEC?* (Library of Congress: Congressional Research Service, September 1, 1992).

336.   British Broadcasting Corporation, *Summary of World Broadcasts, Part 1, Former USSR,* September 8, 1995.

mented.[337] Whether this proposal is effected depends upon securing access to the Russian pipeline network. There are no other options. Transmission gas pipelines in Uzbekistan have a rated carrying capacity of 60 bcm, but the actual volumes that can be carried presently fall below that because of the poor operational conditions of the pipelines and compressor stations. Between 5 percent to 8 percent of the gas being moved by pipeline is lost through leakage.

Over the years, Uzbekistan has been a steady but unspectacular exporter of natural gas, with these exports limited to the nearby former republics of Central Asia. The volumes exported in 1994 exceeded 1985 exports by little more than 3 percent and were equivalent to just 10 percent of production (Table 6-10).

Table 6-10
Uzbekistan Exports of Natural Gas, 1994

Destination	Billion cubic meters
Kazakstan	2.9
Kyrgyzstan	0.856
Tajikistan	0.963
Turkmenistan	0.041
Total	4.760
Sources: Interfax, *Petroleum Report,* February 24-March 3, 1995 and March 17–24, 1995.	

Unocal and Delta Oil, partners in a project to pipe Turkmen natural gas to Pakistan, have shifted their interests eastward to Uzbekistan, where additional pipeline projects have been discussed.[338] Pakistan and India would be natural markets for Uzbek natural gas, as for Turkmen natural gas.

Household consumption of natural gas in Uzbekistan, in terms of available supply, is fairly high, although little more than one-third of households are provided with natural gas (Table 6-11). The high annual consumption rate reflects the heavily subsidized price to consumers. As of April 1, 1995, household consumers were paying just 30 sum (equivalent to $1) per 1,000 cubic meters. For comparison, the producer cost was placed at 345 sum ($11.20).[339]

Uzbekistan's officials understand that the household use of natural gas must be contained. They hope to accomplish this by requiring that all household consumers have gas meters installed by 2000. At present, few households are equipped with meters, and no more than 8 percent of the municipal sector is so equipped. Moreover, much of the natural gas consumed in Uzbekistan is burned at power stations that produce both electricity and heat for consumers.However, no more than 1 percent of the heat supplied passes through meters.[340]

---

337.   *Interfax-Ukraine*, Kiev, December 2, 1996.

338.   FBIS-SOV, May 6, 1996.

339.   Interfax, *Petroleum Report*, July 28 to August 4, 1995. Officials of Uzbekneftegaz proposed that the price of natural gas sold to households be raised by 2000 percent, if the price is to cover the costs of gas extraction and transportation, as well as providing a profit. See Interfax, *Petroleum Information Agency,* Tashkent, September 22, 1995.

Table 6-11
Natural Gas Supply and Demand, 1994 and 1995 Plan
(Billion cubic meters)

Supply	1994	1995 Plan
Production	47.18	48.0
Imports	2.34	-
Total	49.52	48.0
Demand		
Exports	4.01	7.15
Consumption	36.48	37.34
Of which: Households	9.02	10.56
Industry	23.13	22.78
Utilities/		
services	4.33	4.0
Subtotal	36.48	37.34

Note: No attempt has been made to force the data in this table to compare precisely with data presented in other tables.

Source: United Nations, Economic Commission For Europe, *Energy/WP.3/R.39/add 1,* November 23, 1995.

Much publicity has been given to a plan for the use of liquefied petroleum gas (LPG) as an automotive fuel. In that regard, the U.S. government has granted $250,000 to fund a feasibility study. Demand has been estimated at 80,000 b/d, but no LPG is produced in Uzbekistan at the present.[341] At present, Uzbekistan consumes about 10,000 b/d of LPG as household fuel, most of which is imported from Russia. An LPG facility is under construction in Surtan, which will draw on natural gas produced at the Surtan gas field. The first stage of this complex, with a production capacity of 1,500 b/d, was to have been completed by the end of 1995. Plans call for the eventual addition of two more stages.

Electric Power

The Uzbek electric power system presently includes 37 thermal and hydropower stations with a total generating capacity of 11 million kw (up to 52 billion kwh annually).[342] Some idle capacity is emerging because the demand for electric power has slackened. On the whole, electric power usage in Uzbekistan has fluctuated very little, as industrial output has not collapsed to the extent it has elsewhere in the former Soviet Union.[343]

---

340. *FBIS-SOV,* November 2, 94.
341. Interfax, *Petroleum Information Agency,* Tashkent, August 31, 1995.
342. *Interfax,* Moscow, March 6, 1995.

Table 6-12
Electric Power Generation in Uzbekistan

Year	Billion kwh
1980	33.9
1990	56.3
1991	54.2
1992	51
1993	49.1
1994	46.5

Sources: Interfax, Tashkent, July 20, 1995; Reuters, Vienna, March 24, 1994; Central Intelligence Agency (CIA), Handbook of International Economic Statistics (Washington, D. C.: CIA, September 1994); DEIK Bulletin, Uzbekistan, April 1993; U.S. government, Uzbekistan: An Economic Profile, October 1993.

The largest of the hydropower stations in the country—and in Central Asia as well—is the SyrDarya station, which has a generating capacity of 3,000 Mw. This station requires almost immediate renovation, if it is to continue to function.

In the past, Uzbekistan has engaged in substantial trade in electric power, although exports have always exceeded imports. Power transmission lines allow interchanges with Russia, Kyrgyzstan, Tajikistan, Turkmenistan, and Kazakstan. As a result of these exchanges, consumption of electric power in Uzbekistan has been slightly less than the electric power generated.

Table 6-13
Uzbekistan Trade in Electric Power

Year.	Billion kilowatt-hours			
	Production	Exports	Imports	Consumption
1985	47.9	15.4	14.1	46.6
1990	56.3	18.6	16.5	54.2

Source: International Monetary Fund, *Economic Review, Uzbekistan*, Washington, D. C., May 1992, Table A11.

---

343.   Two analysts at the World Bank argue that electric power consumption is a far better indicator of true economic activity in the former Soviet Union than any of the officially reported economic statistics that are widely used by the IMF, the World Bank, and the international community at large.

Interestingly for Uzbekistan, the official estimate of the decline in the Gross Domestic Product (GDP) for the country matches precisely the GDP decline as estimated by electric power consumption. Moreover, Uzbekistan is the only country of the former Soviet Union for which that is true. For all others, the GDP decline as estimated by electric power consumption is much, much less than official estimates. For the former Soviet Union as a whole, this analysis results in a threefold overstatement of the downturn in aggregate economic activity. See *Transition,* Vol. 6, Nos. 1-2.

Uranium and Gold

Uzbekistan had been an important supplier of uranium to the former Soviet Union, which it mines largely through *in situ* leaching, the lowest-cost method of extracting uranium. Annual production approaches 3,000 tons of uranium, or about 8 percent of the world total, a level that can be sustained. Uzbekistan's largest producer of nuclear fuel is completing negotiations with Nukem (a U.S. firm) for a joint venture to extract and process uranium.[344] A dispute has emerged, however, as to how large a share each partner would receive and how much Nukem was to invest.[345]

The mining of gold is also a key part of the country's industrial sector. Uzbekistan presently produces about 70 tons of gold annually, making it the eighth largest producer in the world. Uzbekistan holds 29 percent of the gold reserves of the CIS and accounts for 25 percent of the CIS output of this commodity, but it only accounts for 0.5 percent of the gold consumed by the CIS.[346] Stated another way, most of the gold mined in Uzbekistan is sold abroad.

One of the more successful investments in the CIS has been the Zarafshan-Newmont gold mining joint venture, which exported its first gold in October 1995.

344.   *Interfax,* Tashkent, May 16, 1996.
345.   *Interfax*, Tashkent, June 24, 1996.
346.   *FBIS-SOV,* November 30, 1994.

Source: States of the Former Soviet Union, CIA, 1992.

CHAPTER 7

Armenia

Table 7-1
Armenia at a Glance

Currency	The dram, introduced November 1993
Rate of Exchange	405.5/$1 (April 19, 1996)
Gross Domestic Product	Up 6.9 percent in 1995
Inflation	20 percent (1996 est.)
Population	3.5 million (mid-1994)
By Nationality	
Armenian	93 percent
Russian	2 percent
Kurds	2 percent
Others	3 percent
Note: The exchange rate (dram/$) has held between 405-406 drams/$1 for the past number of months. The inflation rate in 1994 was 1,884.5 percent.	
Sources: Central Intelligence Agency (CIA), *The World Factbook 1995* (Washington, D.C.: CIA, July 1995; *FBIS-SOV*, December 29, 1995; Interfax, *Financial Information Agency*, January 18, 1996; Open Media Research Institute, *Daily Report*, April 26, 1996.	

The six-year-old conflict over the Christian-Armenian enclave of Nagorno-Karabakh in neighboring Muslim-Turkic Azerbaijan continues to dominate Armenia's political and economic landscape. In 1988, as the Soviet Union was disintegrating, Nagorno-Karabakh demanded union with Armenia, with the hope of eventual independence. Armenia responded positively to that request, and civil unrest ensued in both Armenia and Azerbaijan. Russia stepped in to take over direct control of the enclave in January 1989. Azerbaijan blockaded Armenia, and Moscow returned Nagorno-Karabakh control to Azerbaijan. The issue of Nagorno-Karabakh is not likely to be resolved anytime soon. The governments of Armenia and Azerbaijan are not themselves strong enough to bring about a settlement. If there is to be a solution, then outside forces will have to intervene.

The presidential election held in late September 1996 was marred by vote fraud and by the arrest or exiling (some went underground) of the opposition. The American media generally offered a negative assessment of that election process, which incumbent president Levon Ter-Petrossian won with less than 52 percent of the votes cast. The media noted that Armenia receives more U.S. aid per capita than any other country besides Israel, and noted also its treatment of Armenia at the expense of Azerbaijan.

The Organization for Security and Cooperation in Europe monitored the election and concluded that "very serious breaches in the election law" caused "concern for the overall integrity of the election process."The riots which broke out following the election however, represented more a deep-seated dissatisfaction with the reform process and less a dislike of the president.[347]

Armenian forces now occupy about 20–25 percent of Azeri territory. An informal cease-fire agreement, struck in May 1994, has been holding, but embargoes imposed against Armenia by both Azerbaijan and Turkey as a result of this conflict remain in place. These embargoes, among other things, have led to a severe energy crisis for Armenia, which was compounded by the mothballing of the Medsamor nuclear power plant following a very severe earthquake of December 1988. Because Armenia lacks an indigenous energy base, the combined impact of the embargo and the closure of Medsamor had been especially severe.

The considerable hydropower potential of the country is being only partially utilized, but much of the unexploited potential would support only small or mini-hydropower stations. Moreover, there is little or no local capital to develop these sites; funds would have to come from abroad.

The conflict between Chechnya and Russia has also had a negative impact on Armenia, because the road used to bring fuel in from Russia, which passes through Grozny, has been closed. Furthermore, instability in neighboring Georgia has had some negative implications for Armenia.

The combined effect of these events and conflicts was the devastation of Armenian economy between 1990 and 1994 (Table 7-2). Many of the country's manufacturing facilities now stand idle, an energy shortage has nearly paralyzed the country, and perhaps as much as 90 percent of the labor force remains either idle or unemployed.[348] A major turnaround occurred in the economy in 1994, with Gross Domestic Product (GDP) rising by 5 percent, in real terms. GDP continued to rise in 1995, growing at an annual rate of 6.9 percent.[349] and growth may have reached 5 percent in 1996. The *dram*, the national currency, has held steady at 400/$1. Inflation during 1996 probably averaged about 20 percent. But wages in Armenia are among the lowest in the former Soviet Union, averaging just $20/month, and unemployment stands around 20 percent.[350]

---

347.   *Financial Times*, October 5, 1996.

348.   U.S. Department of Commerce/Bisnis, *Armenia, Economic and Trade Overview*, June 28, 1995. The U.S. Department of State, in its report *Armenia Human Rights Practices, 1994*, dated February 1995, notes that as a result of the economic dislocations caused by the breakup of the Soviet Union, the 1988 earthquake, the conflict in Nagorno-Karabakh, and the resultant disruption in Armenia's trade, the overwhelming majority of Armenians live below the officially recognized poverty line.

349.   In the judgment of the U.S. Embassy in Armenia, remarkable progress has been made in adjusting business legislation to international standards. A significant increase in U.S. business interest in Armenia was recorded in 1995 and in early 1996. It is noteworthy that 50 percent of U.S. firms in Armenia were founded by Diaspora Armenians. See *BISNIS Search for Partners*, June 1996, published by the U.S. Department of Commerce.

Table 7-2
Collapse of the Armenian Economy, 1990–1994

	1994 indicators, as percent of 1990 level
Gross domestic product (GDP)*	74.2
Real GDP growth	37.4
Per capita real income	2.6
Index of consumer goods prices	
and service rates (1990=1)	4,054
*GDP at constant prices.	
Source: EIU, *Country Report 1st Quarter, 1995.*	

As with other republics of the former Soviet Union, Armenia's economy is comparatively energy-intensive, fostered by the availability in the past of cheap fuels. Therefore, the drop in electricity requirements that accompanied the decline in economic activity after 1990 has not been as great proportionally.

Coal, Crude Oil, and Natural Gas

As a member of the Soviet Union, Armenia depended on suppliers outside its borders for 96 percent of the natural gas and petroleum products needed to keep its economy going.[351] This dependency has remained since the Soviet breakup. Indeed, the conflicts noted above—which were spawned at least in part by political independence—have disrupted the flow of oil and natural gas to Armenian consumers.

Coal deposits in Armenia are mostly too small to be commercially exploited. There is a very small coal extraction industry, but the annual output is quite insignificant in terms of the country's energy requirements.[352] Armenia also lacks a crude oil and natural gas resource base, and all need for these fuels must be met through imports. Energy imports from all sources cost Armenia almost $350 million in 1994. [353]

The conflict with Azerbaijan has interrupted and at times halted normal import flows. Russia wants to be seen as being neutral in this conflict and has therefore continued to provide Armenia with oil, albeit in limited amounts. Armenia's oil imports from Russia have averaged little more than 5,000 b/d (Table 7-3), a level that does little for the economic health of the country.

---

350.   *Financial Times*, October 11, 1996.

351.   *FBIS-SOV*, March 27, 1995.

352.   The U.S. Agency for International Development (USAID) is to provide $3 million in technical assistance to improve the effectiveness of prospecting for coal in Armenia. Another $1 million had earlier been allocated to develop a coal field at Dzhadzhur, with the aim of producing an extra 50,000 tons of coal a year. See *Interfax*, Yerevan, December 28, 1995.

Table 7-3
Oil Imports from Russia, 1994
(Thousand b/d)

Petroleum products	2.34
Crude oil	2.7
Source: Interfax, *Petroleum Report*, July 28 to August 4, 1995.	

The interruption of normal surface transport routes has spurred development of other routes, but these are considerably more expensive. Most of the petroleum products destined for Armenia are now landed at the Georgian port of Poti and trucked over 360 km to the border town of Airum, and then an additional 130 km to Yerevan. All this adds about $2 to the delivered cost per barrel. An alternate route, through the Georgian port of Batumi, is even more expensive.[354] Under this alternative route, Armenia buys imports from Russia, which are processed at the Batumi refinery in Georgia (Armenia has no refining capacity); the refined petroleum products are then shipped from Batumi by rail.

Russia of course is not the only supplier of petroleum products to Armenia. Some small amounts of fuel oil also are trucked from Iran to Armenia,[355] and very small amounts arrive by air cargo. To help Armenia make it through the winter of 1995–1996, the United States arranged to purchase about 500,000 bbl of fuel oil, to be delivered by tanker, during September-October 1995 for use by Armenian power stations.[356]

The United States also arranged to supply about 180,000 barrels of kerosine

---

353.   There is some dispute over the presence of oil and natural gas in Armenia. A British-Portuguese consortium (Simon Petroleum Technology-Partex) has surveyed Armenia and has concluded there are no commercial reserves of oil and gas in the country. See Interfax, *Petroleum Information Agency*, Yerevan, August 23, 1995. Another report on the findings of this group (see Interfax, *Petroleum Report*, July 28 to August 4, 1995) stated that Armenia may have some small reserves of oil and gas, but that any further exploration should be undertaken only by foreign investors. The work of SPT-Partex was financed by the European Commission as part of its TACIS—Technical Aid to Commonwealth of Independent States—program. A Swiss geologist (Philippe Bodmer) has written that Armenia's natural gas reserves are "colossal" but little is known as to just how he arrived at this finding.

Soon after gaining independence in 1991, Armenia turned to the U.S. Trade and Development Agency for assistance in determining whether the country possessed commercial reserves of crude oil and/or natural gas. A consulting arm of Mariposa Petroleum Company won a contract to evaluate the potential for hydrocarbons in Armenia and to recommend how the country could organize its oil and gas efforts. Two reports were issued. Much of the team's findings had to be based on assumptions and extrapolations, given that information was scarce and, when available, was not completely reliable. Oil in place was estimated at 6.37 billion bbl, and recoverable natural gas was estimated at 6.193 trillion cubic feet. No effort was made to ascertain realistic rates of recovery. See *Oil & Gas Journal*, May 22, 1995.

354.   *East Bloc Energy*, November 1994. The United States, through its humanitarian assistance programs, agreed to pay for the shipment of up to 100,000 tons of fuel oil that Armenia would be importing in 1994 from Russia—by tanker from Novorosiisk to a Georgian port on the Black Sea and from there by road or rail to Armenia. See *Platt's Oilgram News*, August 26, 1994.

355.   *Platt's Oilgram News*, May 24, 1995.

for heating and cooking,[357] to be sold to the population at one-fourth of the market price. The proceeds were earmarked for social security programs. The United States began supplying kerosine to Armenia during the winter of 1993-94, as part of its humanitarian relief program. The U.S. government has set aside about 150,000 barrels of kerosine for delivery during the 1996-97 winter to Armenia under a humanitarian program called "Warm Winter." U.S. humanitarian aid to Armenia totalled $140 million during Fiscal Year 1996 but will be cut to $96 million during Fiscal Year 1997, in part reflecting improved electricity availability because of the return of Medsamor.[358]

Armenia has augmented its energy supply by importing comparatively large volumes of liquefied petroleum gases. Such imports totalled about 7,500 b/d during 1994, up from a bare 184 b/d during 1993.

Other events, unrelated to the conflicts described above, also have interrupted fuel supplies. For example, natural gas flows from Turkmenistan, which transit Uzbekistan, Kazakstan, and Russia enroute to consumers in Armenia, were cut off by a dispute between Russia and Turkmenistan over transit fees that shut the pipeline down temporarily. Also, the closure of the Medsamor nuclear power station virtually necessitated that the bulk of natural gas supplies be directed toward electricity generation (Table 7-4.)

Table 7-4
Natural Gas Supply and Disposition, 1994

Supply	Million cubic meters
Imports	868
Disposition	
Electric power generation	685
Industrial consumption	96
Domestic use	10
Losses, etc.	77
Total	868

Source: United Nations, Economic and Social Council, Economic Commission for Europe, *ENERGY/WP.3/R.39/Add.1,* November 23, 1995.

Before Azerbaijan imposed its embargo on Armenia, natural gas from Russia and Turkmenistan was delivered via a pipeline through Azerbaijan. Today's route

---

356.   USAID, in cooperation with the Fund for Democracy, was to buy 5 cargoes of fuel oil for delivery to both Armenia and Georgia for use in the generation of electric power. See *Petroleum Intelligence Weekly*, August 28, 1995.

357.   *Interfax*, Yerevan, November 13, 1995.

358.   *Interfax*, Yerevan, October 7, 1996 and November 1, 1996.

through Georgia was developed to subvert the Azeri blockade. But this bypass is subject to constant interruption by Azeri or Georgian factions that claimed they need the natural gas themselves.

Armenia has accused Georgia of siphoning off a large portion of natural gas shipments as it transits Georgia. Authorities claim that only 1.5 bcm of the 2.1 bcm of gas Armenia was to have received by 1 August 1995 were actually delivered.[359] Georgian officials were quick to deny this, and claimed that Armenia had an agreement with Turkmenistan to import 2.2 bcm of Turkmen natural gas per year, that Armenia had received 808 mcm from January to July 1995, and that Georgia had received 644 mcm, each under its own agreements. The shortfall in natural gas deliveries to Armenia totalled only 48 mcm—compared to the Armenian claim of 600 mcm—and was caused largely by bombings of the Russian and Georgian sectors that put the pipeline out of service for a number of days. In addition, the pipeline is not in very good shape, and losses through leakage are high.[360]

Armenia actually received only 1.6 bcm (out of the planned 2.2 bcm) of Turkmen gas during 1995.[361] During the latter part of 1995, imports of gas from Turkmenistan were averaging 6–7 mcm per day—roughly half the country's needs. A portion of this gas is stored as reserves to cover the frequent interruptions in imports. Natural gas imports from various sources should have totalled 1 bcm during 1996 and are to increase marginally during 1997, to 1.1 bcm. Of that volume, 692 mcm is for power generation, 170 mcm for industry use, and 170 mcm for other customers. Losses and gas industry use account for the remainder.[362]

One source of interruption in supplies stems from the fact that Turkmen natural gas transits Georgia and that Georgia owes Turkmenistan an estimated $400 million in unpaid gas bills. Turkmenistan periodically cuts off Georgia, which disrupts supplies to Armenia. Armenia itself had run up unpaid gas bills of $40 million, but in March 1996, $34 million of this was restructured into a five-year credit, with the remaining $6 million to be paid in kind with jewelry.[363]

The 1995-1999 plan for developing Armenia's economy includes commissioning an Iran-Armenia gas pipeline. An agreement signed in May 1995 between the National Iranian Gas Company and Armgazprom of Armenia called for construction to begin in the latter half of 1995 and completion in two years. The pipeline will be 24 inches in diameter and some 140 km in length (100 km in Iran and 40 km in Armenia), will cost $70 million to build, and will deliver about 1.5 bcm of gas to Armenia annually.[364] Given that Armenian gas requirements are estimated at 5 bcm annually, other suppliers will still be needed even after completion of the pipeline. This gas contract between Armenia and Iran is somewhat historic,

---

359.   *FBIS-SOV*, August 17, 1995.

360.   *FBIS-SOV*, August 21, 1995.

361.   *Interfax*, Moscow, March 19, 1996. An understanding was reached under which Turkmenistan would supply another 2.2 bcm of gas to Armenia in 1996. See Interfax, *Petroleum Information Agency*, Ashgabat, October 4, 1995.

362.   Interfax, *Petroleum Information Agency*, Yerevan, December 2, 1996.

363.   See *Interfax*, Yerevan, May 10, 1996.

364.   Interfax, *Petroleum Report*, May 12-19, 1995. The diameter of the gas pipeline was originally to be 20 inches for annual delivery of 1 bcm.

because it marks the first time since 1966 that Iran has concluded a gas sales contract with a foreign company. Moreover, it reportedly also marks the first time that a former Soviet republic has signed a long-term gas purchase contract with a supplier outside the FSU.[365] Nevertheless, financing this pipeline will be difficult, if not impossible, as long as the U.S. policy of containment toward Iran remains in place.

The five-year plan for 1995–1999 anticipates a very sharp improvement in natural gas supplies, coming wholly from an increases in imports from 2 bcm in 1995 to 6 bcm by 1999. The expected increase in imports is no doubt based on two assumptions—that the Iran–Armenia pipeline will be completed and that the conflict between Armenia and Azerbaijan will be resolved—but neither of these assumptions seems very likely to come about anytime soon. Such increased supply would allow the household/commercial use of natural gas to jump from just 0.3 bcm in 1995 to 1.4 bcm in 1999. Electricity generation nonetheless would continue to be the primary use for natural gas, with consumption for this use rising from 1.2 bcm in 1995 rising to 3.2 bcm in 1999.

Electric Power

Before the Soviet Union disintegrated, the Armenian power system had been an integrated part of the Transcaucasia power system. Although Armenia had to import oil and natural gas for fueling thermal power stations and nuclear fuel for the Medsamor nuclear power plant, Armenia was a net exporter of electricity. Several of the power stations constructed during the 1970s and 1980s, including Medsamor, had been designed to help satisfy regional electric power needs rather than just domestic requirements.[366]

The supply of electric power in Armenia has fallen rather substantially in recent years, in part because of the closure of Medsamor and in part because of the military conflict with Azerbaijan which cut off natural gas and oil imports (Table 7-5). The closure of Medsamor meant that the thermal power station at Hrazdan had to carry the burden of electricity generation for all of Armenia. But this station had run exclusively on natural gas imported from Azerbaijan, a vulnerability that ultimately was exploited by Azerbaijan, which cut off supplies.[367]

---

365. *Platt's Oilgram News*, May 22, 1995.
366. United Nations, Economic and Social Council, *ENERGY/R.111/Add.5*, July 19, 1995.

Table 7-5
Electric Power Generation in Armenia, 1985–2005

Year	Billion kwh
1985	14.9
1988	15.28
1990	10.4
1992	9
1993	6.2
1994	5.65
1995	5.56*
2000 plan**	10.7
2005 plan***	12.3
*The plan for 1995 was 7.9 billion kwh.	
**If the 1995-99 plan for the electric power sector is fulfilled.	
***As envisaged in the 1995-2005 comprehensive energy program.	
Sources: *FBIS-SOV*, August 18, 1995; *FBIS-SOV*, August 7, 1995; *FBIS-SOV*, May 22, 1996.	

During 1995, electricity was available just 1 hour a day during the winter and 2 hours a day otherwise. There had been no hot running water or natural gas for homes since 1992. Nonetheless, electricity generation basically held its own during 1995, declining just slightly from the 1994 level, thanks largely to the Medsamor nuclear power plant coming back on-line in November 1995.

The daily demand for electricity probably averages around 30 million kwh. Power generation (before the return of Medsamor) was providing around 12 million kwh. As in most countries in the Near Abroad, electricity tariffs in Armenia fall well short of covering costs. Electricity is sold first to the government, which in turn sells to domestic consumers at heavily subsidized prices. Given the financial state of affairs of most consumers in Armenia, raising tariffs at this time would be politically risky.

Electric power generating facilities have deteriorated rapidly during the past several years because maintenance and repairs have been performed at the bare minimum level due to a lack of funds. Transmission losses are extremely high, which helps explain the continued shortages. On average, a loss of 8 to 10 percent might be expected as electricity moved along the grid.[368] For CIS countries as a whole, losses reach 16 to 18 percent, but in Armenia they reached 40 percent in

367.   Ara Tatevosyan, "Living Dangerously With Nuclear Power in Armenia," *Transition*, May 3, 1996.

368.   In very general terms, losses would be calculated as the difference between measured electric power generation and metered consumption.

1995, with theft undoubtedly accounting for a considerable portion. Electricity is stolen by the simple means of rewiring to bypass the meter.[369]

The World Bank, through its International Development Association, in December 1994 approved a credit to Armenia of $13.7 million to help reverse capacity deterioration. These credits will be used to maintain power generation at:

❏ two existing 200-megawatt (Mw) thermal units at Hrazdan;

❏ a 150-Mw heat and power unit at Yerevan;

❏ a 199-Mw and a 44-Mw plant on the Sevan-Hrazdan hydropower cascade; and

❏ a 170-Mw plant on the Vorotan cascade.

An agreement has been concluded between Iran and Armenia on building a power transmission line from Skhara, in Iran, to Megri, in southern Armenia.[370] Assuming adequate financing can be secured, construction will take about a year and a half.[371]

Funds were received during 1994 from the EBRD for constructing a fifth block at the Hrazdan regional power plant. Completion had been scheduled for 1995. The capacity of this block will be 300 Mw, approaching that of Medsamor reactor no. 2. Moreover, the possibilities of financing the construction of a sixth block of the same capacity at Hrazdan are being reviewed. However, because Hrazdan burns residual fuel oil and natural gas, whether the fifth block could operate upon completion remains questionable.

In the past and excluding the provision of electricity from Medsamor, 90 percent of electric power was provided by fossil-fueled plants and just 10 percent by hydropower stations, although just half the country's generating capacity burned oil and natural gas (Table 7-6). That pattern has now been essentially reversed, with the disruption of oil and gas supplies due to the Azeri blockade.

---

369. *FBIS-SOV*, January 22, 1996.
370. *FBIS-SOV*, May 9, 1995.
371. *FBIS-SOV*, May 15, 1995.

Table 7-6
Armenia's Electric Power Generating Capacity

Facility	Type	Capacity (Mw)	Percent of Total
Hrazdan	Steam	1,100	30.96
Yerevan	Steam	550	15.48
Vanatzor	Steam	94	2.65
Sevan/Hrazdan	Hydro	554	15.59
Vorotan	Hydro	404	11.37
Gyumri	Hydro	3	
Tzoroget	Hydro	25	0.99
Yerevan	Hydro	7	
Medsamor	Nuclear	816	22.97
Total		3,553	100.00*

* Total does not add because of rounding.

Source: *Armenia & Karabakh Factbook* (Washington, D. C.: Office of Research and Analysis, Armenian Assembly of America, July 1996)

Of the thermal electric power stations listed above, only three—Vanadzor, Yerevan and Hrazdan—can be regarded as fully operating. Also, 60 percent of the hydropower is produced from the waters of Lake Sevan, where the water level has been lowered to such an extent that serious ecological problems are being encountered. Lake Sevan had previously fed a number of rivers that contained hydroelectric power plants. Overuse threatened to damage the lake beyond repair, and the hydroelectric plants were shut down in 1979. Following the closure of Medsamor and the conflict with Azerbaijan, the hydroelectric power plants were put back to work—the fate of Lake Sevan was subordinated to national interests. If Armenia moves to protect Lake Sevan once Medsamor is back on line and if hydropower generation is scaled back, total electricity supply might not change much from current levels.

Hydroelectric power stations now account for the bulk of the electric power generated in Armenia (63 percent in 1994), but are able to cover no more than 25–30 percent of the country's electricity needs. It is no surprise that Armenia turned to the idle Medsamor nuclear power plant to help meet electricity needs. However, authorities warn that returning Medsamor to operation will not by itself radically improve the electric power supply. Roughly half the electricity to be generated by Medsamor will be used to raise the electric power system of the country to 50 Hertz (it now operates at a frequency of 45-46 Hertz).

Some have suggested that there will be no shortage of generating capacity in Armenia for many years to come, because of the low demand for electricity. In fact, some suggest that the existing plant capacity, especially thermal, will need to be retired or mothballed.[372]

Medsamor and the Earthquake

The Armenian nuclear power plant situated near the village of Medsamor successfully withstood an earthquake that devastated much of northwestern Soviet Armenia on December 7, 1988.[373] The earthquake is said to have measured 6.9 on the Richter scale and to have lasted for 200 seconds. Medsamor is located just 16 miles west of Yerevan, the capital of Armenia, with a population well over 1.3 million. The nearby town of Hoktemberian, with a population of about 50,000, is just 5 miles to the southwest of the nuclear facility.

The Medsamor nuclear power facility consists of two VVER-440 Model V230 reactors. Reactor no. 1 was connected to the electric power grid in 1976; reactor no. 2 followed in late 1979. The VVER is a pressurized light-water reactor that, despite the fact that it shares certain basic features with Western reactors, does not meet Western safety standards. These reactors have just partial containment. If the larger coolant pipes rupture, radioactivity would be discharged directly into the atmosphere.

Apparently the two VVER-440\230 reactors at the facility, roughly 160 km from the quake's epicenter, were undamaged and remained on-line, if initial reports by Soviet authorities to the International Atomic Energy Agency (IAEA) were correct. The earthquake measured 5.5 on the 12-point Soviet scale in the vicinity of the nuclear plant; a reading of 6 would have shut the plant down automatically. Despite all the early attention given to the Armenian nuclear power plant in the aftermath of the earthquake, no photos of the plant appeared in the Soviet popular press.

Reactor no. 1 is of conventional design, with no specific seismic criteria reflected in its construction. But reactor no. 2 benefited from the lessons of the Vrancea, Romania, earthquake of 1977, and was designed to be earthquake-proof—that is, to withstand a magnitude 8 earthquake.[374] The main building also was redesigned toward the same goal.

The first information about the disaster was broadcast on Yerevan radio just 17 minutes after the quake and stressed that the Armenian nuclear power station had not been affected, in part to reassure the local population that they faced no health threat—a sensitive issue in the wake of the Chornobyl disaster. However, five days after the quake, Soviet Prime Minister Nikolai Ryzhkov announced that the plant would be shut down completely by 1990. This was most likely a conciliatory gesture toward the Armenian people, but the government had earlier promised to close

372.   United Nations, Economic and Social Council, *ENERGY/R.111/Add.5*, July 19, 1995.

373.   The town of Spitak, with a population of 30,000, was completely destroyed. Leninakin, population exceeding 20,000, and located 20 miles west of Spitak, was severely damaged. Reports place the loss of life as high as 50,000, with over 500,000 homeless.

374.   It appears that the reactors at Medsamor may be able to withstand an earthquake of the indicated intensity. However, reports have disclosed that the water system was built to withstand only weaker tremors, and disruptions in the water supply would mean that the reactor could not be cooled.

the plant by 1991 in response to highly vocal local opposition.

Subsequently, the Central Committee of the Communist Party decided to shut down reactor no. 1 on February 25, 1989, and reactor no. 2 on March 18, just after peak winter demand. Both reactors were shut down on schedule.

Reopening Medsamor. Public concerns over the safety of Medsamor disappeared with the onset of war with Azerbaijan and the severe deterioration of the standard of living, including the availability of electricity to households for only one or two hours a day. There was little public opposition when the government made public its plans to bring Medsamor back on-line.

Following that announcement, at the request of the Armenian government, the International Atomic Energy Agency (IAEA) established a technical cooperation program to assist in restarting Medsamor.[375] The location of Medsamor in an earthquake-prone region presented three concerns that had to be resolved.

☐ The site should be shown to be geologically safe.

☐ The seismic design basis for the site should be reevaluated.

☐ Seismic requalification of Medsamor's buildings and components to the new seismic design basis should be performed.

Additionally, the need for Armenia to strengthen its nuclear regulatory body has been recognized, and the IAEA is providing support to that end. Reactor no. 2 was in better condition than reactor no. 1, which was commissioned three years later. Therefore, reactor no. 2 was renovated first.

Part of the funding to cover the costs of demothballing has been provided by Russia, and part has come from Armenians living abroad. Russian technicians were on the site, and Russia also indicated that it would provide the nuclear fuel rods needed by the reactor. Lending funds to Armenia, in part for the restoration of Medsamor, was the subject of intense debate in the Russian parliament. The proposal was for a 110-billion ruble loan, of which 60 billion rubles would be used to reopen Medsamor. The loan agreement had been signed on July 4, 1994, but it took more than six months for ratification. The loan eventually was "sold" to a skeptical parliament on the basis that reopening Medsamor would be in Russia's national interests because:

☐ Improvements in the supply of electricity from reopening Medsamor would benefit those ethnic Russians living in Armenia.

☐ The loan, to be repaid over four years, would be secured by shares in Mesdamor and in a number of other Armenian enterprises.

---

375.   Specialists from the IAEA have made a number of visits to Medsamor. These experts recommended that a number of safety modifications be made at the plant; that comprehensive tests of safety systems be done before restarting the plant; that steps be taken to ensure sufficient numbers of qualified and licensed staff; that issues relating to the integrity of the unannealed reactor pressure vessel be resolved; that continuous efforts be made to assess and upgrade the seismic safety of the plant; and that additional steps be taken for emergency planning. See *IAEA Bulletin*, 2/1995.

❏ The funds would actually return to Russia to be used for the purchase of a variety of equipment, commodities, and raw materials, and to cover the wages of Russian specialists working in Armenia.

❏ Russia did not have many allies in the Caucasus, and cementing ties with Armenia would be one result of the loan.

The loan was approved, and Russia subsequently provided an additional 20 billion rubles in support of Medsamor.[376]

Original estimates had Medsamor generating power again as early as mid-1995.[377] These schedules turned out to be optimistic; Medsamor did not begin generating until early November 1995,[378] and its rated capacity of 9 million kwh per day was achieved only in early 1996.[379] The Armenian government has placed Medsamor in the trust of a joint stock company, ostensibly to improve plant operations.[380]

Medsamor reactor no. 1 is scheduled to be generating power sometime between 1996 and 1998.[381] More important, Armenia and Russia have agreed to replace the two Medsamor reactors with new VVER-640 nuclear reactors sometime after 2000.[382]

Western Opposition. There was Western opposition to the reopening of Medsamor. This opposition is based on a number of factors, with the key concerns centered on the following.

❏ The VVER-440 reactors at Medsamor are the earliest of the Soviet-designed PWR (pressurized water reactor) generation and are considered the least safe.

❏ Much-needed safety upgrades would not be completed before the restart of reactor no. 2.

---

376. France has agreed to provide a privileged loan equivalent to $4.99 million to Armenia for use in upgrading Medsamor. See Interfax, *Financial Information Agency*, Yerevan, December 27, 1995.

377. The dangers of reopening Medsamor have not been lost on Armenian authorities. The government reportedly has imported potassium iodide from Ukraine for the residents of Yerevan and a 30-kilometer zone surrounding Medsamor. The potassium iodide will be used to produce pills to be distributed free of charge and to be taken as protection against possible radiation exposure in the event of an accident at Medsamor. Residents of the exclusion zone around Medsamor will be the first to receive the pills. See *Interfax*, Yerevan, May 19, 1995.

378. *Interfax*, Yerevan, November 6, 1995.

379. *Interfax*, Yerevan, December 6, 1995. France has expressed its concern over the conditions of nuclear safety from the Medsamor reopening (*FBIS-SOV*, November 6, 1995). So has Turkey, which fears that any disaster at Medsamor would directly affect it. See Open Media Research Institute, Inc., *Daily Report*, November 10, 1995.

380. *Interfax*, Yerevan, March 29, 1996.

381. *Interfax*, Yerevan, August 11, 1995. Russian Minister of Atomic Energy Viktor Mikhailov, on the occasion of a visit to Medsamor in early November 1995, stated that reactor no. 1 would be returned to operation in 1996. See *Interfax*, Yerevan, November 8, 1995.

382. *Interfax*, Moscow, November 24, 1995.

Although recognizing the impact that continuing electricity shortages have on the Armenian economy and quality of life, the U.S. government nonetheless refused to help upgrade Medsamor and remained opposed to its reopening. The U.S. position is based largely on the fact that the first-generation VVER 440 V230 reactors at Medsamor have just partial reactor containment systems.

In a much broader sense, Western misgivings centered around design deficiencies, insufficient testing of materials, and hurried and substandard operator training. There is also the uncertainty of reopening a nuclear power plant that has been mothballed, the ever-present possibility of earthquakes, and the political instability in the Caucasus. These concerns combine to make catastrophe a real possibility, critics say.[383]

Moreover, the loss of experienced personnel from Medsamor has been cited as the most serious challenge. As of the end of 1993, up to 40 percent of staff members had departed, and that drain most likely continued thereafter.[384]

There have been some cracks in the Western opposition. The West has accepted that Medsamor will continue to operate, and the United States and the European Union indicated in late May 1996 that they were ready to earmark between $50 million and $100 million annually in grant money to increase the safety of Medsamor.[385] The head of the Nuclear Safety Department of the IAEA, Morris Rosen, told Armenian Prime Minister Hrant Bagratyan that the IAEA believed there were no reasons to prevent the recommissioning of Medsamor.[386] The then Deputy U.S. Secretary of Energy William White presumably misstated the U.S. position during his visit to Armenia in April 1995, when he was quoted as saying, "in the opinion of the United States the Armenian Republic has no other alternative (to the nuclear plant) in the years ahead to secure its energy needs."[387]

A New Nuclear Power Plant

The 1995–1999 plan for bolstering the economy includes preparatory work for the construction of a new nuclear power plant at an unidentified site. The present schedule calls for this new facility to go on-line before 2005–2007, as a replacement for Medsamor.[388] A contrary report indicated that Armenia plans to replace the two reactors at Medsamor, and that Armenia was soon to begin talks with France in the hope of hiring French firms to help with the design and construction of the reactors.[389]

---

383.   *Washington Post*, May 25, 1995. Although not stated as a specific concern, nonetheless, observers in the West must be cognizant of the fact that a total of 2,165,000 people live within a 30-kilometer radius of Medsamor. See *The Armenia Mirror-Spectator*, September 18, 1993.

384.   *The Armenia Mirror-Spectator*, October 9, 1993.

385.   See *Interfax*, Yerevan, June 4, 1996.

386.   *Interfax*, Yerevan, April 18, 1995.

387.   *FBIS-SOV*, April 21, 1995.

388.   *FBIS-SOV*, August 18,1995.

389.   British Broadcasting Corporation, *Summary of World Broadcasts, Part 1, Former USSR*, September 15, 1995.

Nonpayment

Armenia is not immune to the problem of nonpayment facing all former Soviet republics. Armenian Premier Bagratyan has defined nonpayment as the number one problem in the republic. In early 1995, nonpayment stood at 40 billion drams (roughly equivalent to $100 million). The country's energy complex alone was owed 9 billion drams ($22.5 million).

Consumers in Armenia are no different from those in other former Soviet republics: they are either unwilling or unable to pay for the various forms of energy the use. For example, just 23.5 percent of the electricity provided to Armenian consumers in July 1995 was paid for.[390] By the end of 1995, the debt to Turkmenistan for natural gas supplies had reached some $50 million.[391] Prime Minister Bagratyan, recognizing that the population simply was not in a position to pay, has recommended that individuals switch to bottled gas. Households may be supplied with pipeline gas in about seven years.[392]

The largest use of natural gas supplies is for power generation, but most of the natural gas-related arrears derive from consumer nonpayment. That leaves the government strapped for funds and unable to pay Turkmenistan for its natural gas. In effect, the mostly domestic debt is transformed into a foreign debt, which negatively affects Armenia's general solvency and thereby impedes its ability to obtain foreign loans.[393]

Access to Caspian Oil: The Importance of a Pipeline

The early crude oil to be produced offshore in the Caspian Sea by a western consortium will move to markets via two pipeline routings. One pipeline, the northern route, will transport the early oil through Grozny to the port of Novorossisk on the Black Sea. A second pipeline, the western route, will carry early oil westward through Georgia to the port of Supsa, also on the Black Sea.

The bulk of the crude oil to be produced, whether early oil or later oil,[394] will be directed to the export market. Exportable surpluses will be considerable after

---

390.   As of January 1, 1995 the total debt for electricity consumed but not paid for reached 8 billion drams, and at that time the population (probably meaning households) were paying for just 8 percent of the electric power used. One month later, the arrears had reached to 10 billion drams. See *FBIS-SOV*, February 8, 1995.

It has been suggested that perhaps as much as 50 percent of the electricity used in Armenia disappears through illegal connections to power lines. See *FBIS-SOV*, February 10. 1995.

On a broader scale, Prime Minister Hrant Bagratyan accused the directors of certain enterprises of illegally transferring revenues out of the country, and opening accounts in foreign banks. Because of this, budget revenues suffered greatly, in that taxes were not being paid on these illegal transfers. See Interfax, *Financial Information Agency*, Yerevan, August 16, 1995.

391.   To put this size of this debt in the proper perspective, the overall budget revenue for Armenia in 1995 was just $216 million. Of that, revenue from taxation totalled $134 million. See *FBIS-SOV*, December 19, 1995.

392.   *FBIS-SOV*, May 4, 1995.

393.   *Interfax*, Yerevan, November 16, 1995.

domestic requirements are satisfied. At the same time, the existing pipeline network is physically inadequate for the amount of oil to be moved, and it transits volatile Chechnya.

Armenia was never in the running as a transit country for the early oil. The issue now is selection of a route (or routes) to move the later crude oil to market. A pipeline routing that would take the crude oil to the Mediterranean Sea port of Ceyhan, in Turkey, is the leading option.

The government of Turkey is particularly supportive of this pipeline, in part for the transit fees and in part because the pipeline would help relieve heavy oil tanker traffic through the Bosphorus Straits.

Several variations of a Baku-Ceyhan routing have been tabled. One variation envisages a pipeline passing through Georgia and into Turkey; a second variation runs through Armenia, with a small segment transiting Iran; a third variation would transit Armenia but bypass Iran. Given the present U.S. policy, which is to oppose any actions that would materially benefit Iran, no American company could participate in construction of a pipeline transiting that country.

The matter of pipeline routings has become quite contentious. Much more than transit fees are at stake, although the income clearly would be welcome. Pipelines can become hostage in times of political dispute and therefore offer considerable leverage to a transit country—especially if the pipeline in question is the only access the producer has to export markets.

The U.S. government has not yet suggested any particular route that should be taken from Baku to the Turkish port of Ceyhan.[395] But whether Armenia will be given serious consideration depends to a large extent on the progress toward peace in Nagorno-Karabakh and the state of relations between Armenia and Turkey and between Azerbaijan and Turkey. If progress can be made in these areas, then Armenia could well find itself in a competitive position to serve as a transit country for large volumes of crude oil moving from Baku to the Mediterranean.

Selection of Armenia as a transit country for Azeri crude oil could be a tremendous political and economic boost. Equally important, if not more so, the steady and reliable flow of oil could well provide the opportunity to close Medsamor.[396] Nonetheless, the Nagorno-Karabakh conflict stands as a very real obstacle to any agreement, and Armenian officials are opposed to any linkage between the future of Nagorno-Karabakh and a possible oil pipeline routing through Armenia. Azeri officials are equally adamant that the later oil will not transit Armenia in the absence of a Nagorno-Karabakh settlement.

---

394.   Production of the "early" crude oil by the western consortium probably will begin in mid-1997 and build over the coming months to a peak on the order of 100,000 b/d, or perhaps even higher. Development of the "later" oil will then follow, and its output should peak at around 700,000 b/d.

395.   Armenian National Committee of America Press Release, *"U.S. Official States that Main Oil Pipeline For Caspian Sea Oil May Traverse Armenia,"* October 17, 1995.

396.   CSIS Panel Report, *Nuclear Energy Safety Challenges in the Former Soviet Union.* (Washington, D.C.: CSIS, 1995).

The Ten-Year Plan, 1995-2005

Armenia has worked out a comprehensive energy program for 1995–2005, of which the five-year plan 1995–1999 discussed above is an integral part. This program has been conceived with the ultimate aim of fully meeting the country's energy requirements by 2005. There are several key elements to the program (see Table 7-7):

❒ operation of Medsamor until the year 2005, after which new generation reactors are to come on-line

❒ substantial reduction of the role of hydroelectric power to 15 percent from the 63 percent share of electric power generation it comprised in 1994

❒ a role, though small, for electric power stations that burn alternative fuels in providing both heat and power, which will have a total capacity of 220 megawatts, of which some 140 megawatts will be located in rural areas and will be fueled by biogases

Table 7-7
Electric Power Generation in 2005, by Source

Form of Fuel	Percent of Power Generated
Thermal*	45
Nuclear	38
Hydropower	15
Alternative fuels	2
Total	100
*Note: Derived as a residual.	
Source: *FBIS-SOV*, August 7, 1995.	

CHAPTER 8

The Baltics

The three Baltic states of Estonia, Latvia, and Lithuania have long enjoyed the political and economic support of the United States. All three were independent nations between World Wars I and II but were annexed by the Soviet Union in August 1940. The United States did not recognize the legality of the Soviet annexation and was quick to back Baltic self-determination by adopting legislation providing direct U.S. assistance to the Baltics. The United States established formal diplomatic relations with the three newly independent Baltic states on September 2, 1991.

The Baltic states have something else in common: none has a competitive, indigenous fuel base. Estonia boasts of huge shale reserves, but extracting oil from this shale has never been economically feasible, and the Estonian shale industry has long been in a deep slump. The oil and gas consumed in these three states must be imported.

Politically, the three Baltic states share a common goal: to gain entry to the North Atlantic Treaty Organization (NATO), which they feel would offer a degree of security and stability not otherwise available to them. Russia, not surprisingly, has stated for the record that Baltic membership in NATO would not be tolerated.[397] The Baltic states are fearful of ending up in a political void, between NATO to the west and Russia to the east.

Moscow does not object to the Baltics seeking membership in the European Union (EU) because that would not represent a military threat. However, if they gained EU membership the next step would be full membership in the Western European Union (WEU), the defense arm of the EU. Recognizing the implications for Russia of Baltic membership in the WEU, the European Union has advised that membership for the Baltics would be conditional on no full membership for them in the WEU.

The Baltics lead the republics of the former Soviet Union in making the transition to a free market economy.[398] During 1995, the private sector accounted for 65 percent of GDP in Estonia and Lithuania and 60 percent in Latvia.[399] The average monthly wages earned in the three Baltic states were higher than in any other

---

397. *Financial Times*, September 22, 1995. In its semi-annual ranking (as of September 1996) of country credit worthiness, *Euromoney* placed the three Baltic states the highest of the republics of the former Soviet Union. See *Transition*, September-October 1996.

398. The economic performance of the Baltics generally has not been too divergent from that of the CIS as a whole, except for 1994. In that year the Baltics showed positive gains in real GDP, in contrast to the CIS, where the decline in real GDP was the greatest of the past five years. See *Financial Times*, March 7, 1995, quoting the European Bank for Reconstruction and Development.

399. *Finansovyye Izvestiya*, May 14, 1996.

former republic. All three countries also posted positive growth in GDP during 1995, with Estonia leading the way with 6 percent. In comparison, there were declines in GDP in 1995 in Azerbaijan (-17.2 percent), Kazakstan (-8.9 percent), and Russia (-4.4 percent).

Foreign investors have found Estonia the most attractive of the three Baltic states, in part because of its proximity to Finland and its wide-open economy. Throughout 1994 Estonia had per capita foreign investment of $314, compared with $145 for Latvia and just $83 for Lithuania.[400] Lithuania also brought up the rear in per capita GDP at just $1,088 in 1994, compared to $1,600 for Estonia.

The three Baltic nations separate Russia from commercial ports on the Baltic Sea, leaving Russia access only to the port of St. Petersburg (formerly Leningrad), which is icebound almost five months a year.[401] The only ice-free Russian port on the Baltic is Kaliningrad, but Lithuania and Belarus are between Kaliningrad and Russia, which complicates the transit of goods.[402] Lithuania and Latvia have pressed their geographic advantage over Russia, particularly by raising transit charges on Russian oil exports.

Despite these considerable commonalities, the Baltics find themselves separated by radically different cultural traditions, very sharp demographic differences, obvious geographic differences, and economic and political differences.[403] Because of these, Estonia, Latvia, and Lithuania solve questions of national interest in quite contrasting ways.[404] Moscow may already understand how to exploit these differences to its own benefit, but the West must be sensitive to what binds and separates the Baltic nations for them to secure true political and economic independence.

The Baltics as a Gateway to Russia

There are seven active ports serving the Baltics, three each in Estonia and Latvia and one in Lithuania (see Table 8-1). Of these ports, Klaipeda is the most active in terms of tonnage handled. Muuga handles considerable amounts of coal, while Ventspils is the main oil port, linked by pipeline to oilfields in Western Siberia. Klaipeda also handles oil exports, but in limited volumes.

---

400. *Central European Economic Review*, October 1995.

401. *Financial Times*, February 15, 1995. Additionally, the Morskoy Channel must be dredged on a regular basis. Shippers will also try to avoid St. Petersburg because of theft and cumbersome customs procedures.

402. Russia very much wants to reduce its reliance on Ventspils as an oil export port. Kaliningrad, although separated geographically from Russia, nevertheless is one of Russia's just three ice-free year-round warm water ports, the others being Novorossiisk and Tuapse on the Black Sea. An agreement reportedly has been reached between LUKoil and Tatneft to construct an export-oriented oil terminal at Kaliningrad. Crude oil and petroleum products destined for export would be delivered to Kaliningrad by a new pipeline. The routing of this new pipeline has not yet been made public. See *Oil & Gas Journal*, July 31, 1995.

403. Paul A. Goble, "The Baltics: Three States, Three Fates," *Current History*, October 1994.

Table 8-1
Major Baltic Ports

Country	Port
Estonia	Muuga
	Padilski
	Tallinn
Latvia	Riga
	Ventspils
	Liepaja
Lithuania	Klaipeda

Russian oil exports to buyers outside the former Soviet Union are delivered directly by pipeline or to ports of export. Pipeline exports are handled solely by the Druzhba (Friendship) crude oil pipeline, which is linked with refineries in the former Eastern Bloc countries. This pipeline presently is not utilized to its fullest because Eastern European requirements are down, but the lack of pipeline extensions into Western Europe prevents Druzhba's spare capacity from being utilized.

The pipeline/port patterns of 1994 are typical of those of the past several years. In 1994, some 64 percent of Russian oil exports to the Far Abroad moved through ports rather than pipelines. Although the key oil export port for Russia was Novorossiisk on the Black Sea, the two Baltic ports of Ventspils and Klaipeda facilitate deliveries to Northern Europe and Scandinavia (Table 8-2).

---

404.   *Ibid.* Paul Goble, Assistant Director, Radio Free Europe/Radio Liberty, relates an anecdote which illustrates how Estonia, Latvia, and Lithuania reacted so differently to a common problem.

> Shortly after the August 1991 coup that brought them independence, the three Baltic governments decided they should take down the statue of Lenin that had adorned their main squares in Soviet times. Naturally, each government decided to do it in its own way.
>
> In Lithuania, President Vytautas Landsbergis gave a passionate speech to a large audience before the parliament building denouncing Lenin, Moscow, and the entire Communist era. Fired up by his remarks, the crowd ran to where Lenin was standing, found some rope, and pulled Lenin down, smashing him in the street.
>
> In Latvia, the government also decided that Lenin had to go, but the Latvians did it their way. They formed a committee of their best engineering talent in order to determine just how large a crane and just how large a truck would be needed to lift Lenin off his pedestal and cart him off to the dump. That night, after the Riga rush hour, the engineers came with just the right size crane and just the right size truck and carried Lenin away.
>
> Meanwhile, in Estonia, the authorities also decided that Lenin had to go, but few in the government could remember just how big the statue of the Soviet leader actually was. After all, they had largely ignored it for years. Consequently, a group of officials walked down from the government offices on Toompea to where Lenin was standing, looked up, and were shocked at just how big the statue of the Soviet leader was. Shaking their heads, the officials returned to their offices and then did what any self-respecting Estonian would do—they picked up their cellular phones, called Helsinki, and contracted with a Finnish firm to take Lenin down.

182 Energy Choices in the Near Abroad

This pattern held relatively unchanged through 1996. In that year 60.1 percent of Russian crude oil sales to the Far Abroad moved by sea, with continuing heavy dependence on ports outside Russia. Reliance on foreign ports is even greater for petroleum product deliveries to the Far Abroad. In 1996 just 14.5 percent of the volumes exported transited the domestic ports of Tuapse and Novorossiisk.

Table 8-2
Russian Oil Exports by Pipeline and Port, 1994*

Mode	Thousand b/d
Druzhba pipeline	776
Port of Export	
Novorossiisk (Russia)	551
Ventspils (Latvia)	382
Tuapse (Russia)	131
Klaipeda (Lithuania)	91
Other**	240
Port Total	1,404
Total exports	2,180

*Both crude oil and petroleum products.
**Largely Odesa, Ukraine.

Source: Energy Information Agency, *Russian Oil and Gas Exports Fact Sheet, 1994 Update.*

Russia very much would like to end its dependence on the Baltic ports for exporting oil. One option now under serious study is construction of the pipeline from the Timan-Pechora oilfields to the Finnish port of Porvoo, but it is questionable whether this proposed pipeline would relieve that dependence unless its carrying capacity is substantially enlarged. At the same time, the foreign companies involved in developing Timan-Pechora oil also are considering building a pipeline to the nearby Barents Sea to avoid a long transit across Russian territory. Russia obviously favors the proposed pipeline to Porvoo. Route selection will be a test of wills between Moscow and these foreign oil companies.

For the Baltic nations, the prospects for future economic growth are tied to development of port facilities, first for importing goods and commodities from the West and thereby reducing their dependence on Russia, and second as a point of entry for Western goods destined for Russia and for other former Soviet republics.

Energy Prospects

The Baltics share a common energy supply problem, and so it is appropriate for them to seek a common solution. The energy systems of the individual Baltic countries are comparatively small and relatively unsophisticated. Moreover, none of the Baltic states have the financial capability to ensure an adequate and reliable energy supply at reasonable cost. Seeking to offset that liability and to counter the growing presence of foreign oil marketers in the Baltics, a joint stock venture was established to coordinate the activities of the three national oil companies and to supply fuel to Estonia, Latvia, and Lithuania, although its influence was never apparent.[405]

The longer-term energy strategy for the three Baltic nations is quite evident.

❏ Intensify the search for indigenous fuels.

❏ Make energy conservation an integral part of any forward-looking energy strategy.

❏ Gradually shift the purchase of fuels away from Russia and toward Western Europe.

Expanding Indigenous Energy Supply

Geology would seem to prevent indigenous energy production in meaningful quantities. The relative share of local fuels ranges from 8 percent in Lithuania to 67 percent in Estonia, with the latter reflecting the wide availability of oil shale.

Nonetheless, Latvia has turned offshore to the generally untested waters of the Baltic Sea.[406] Lacking any capability of its own, Latvia initiated contacts with two foreign oil companies, one Swedish (Oljeprospektering AB, or OPAB) and one American (Amoco).[407] Lithuania objected to the arrangement before any agreements could be reached and before exploration could be initiated, because the sea border of the area involved has been the subject of negotiations between Lithuania and Latvia. In a note to the Latvian foreign ministry, Lithuanian deputy foreign minister Rimantas Sidlauskas called Latvia's actions "unlawful."[408]

Latvian president Guntis Ulmanis, in responding, said that a compromise was being sought with Lithuania over maritime borders and offshore oil reserves and that if oil was discovered the oilfields would be jointly controlled. Importantly, he added, any deals between Latvia and Western companies would not be valid until the border dispute had been settled.[409]

---

405.   *FBIS-SOV*, August 25, 1995.

406.   According to data provided by Russian, Lithuanian, and Swedish oil companies, the Baltic Sea shelf contains considerable resources of high-grade crude oil, estimated at roughly 1.1 billion bbl. The Gulf of Bothnia and the western part of the Gulf of Finland, that is, the area between Finland and Estonia, are also considered prospective. Prospecting is underway in a joint venture between a German company (Feba Oel), Rosneft, and LUKoil on the shelf close to the northwest shore of Kaliningrad Oblast and close to its border with Lithuania. See *FBIS-SOV*, December 28, 1995.

Preliminary research has shown that the largest oil reserves might be found on the sea border between Latvia and Sweden. See Interfax, *Petroleum Report,* March 24–31, 1995, and March 31–April 7, 1995.

407.   *FBIS-SOV*, June 27, 1995.

408.   Moreover, Latvia found it impossible to continue discussing the draft agreement on the sea border between the two countries because "the spirit of negotiations has been disrupted." *FBIS-SOV*, January 28, 1995.

Nonetheless, an agreement was signed between Latvia, Amoco, and OPAB on prospecting and developing oil offshore in a section of the Baltic Sea claimed by both Latvia and Lithuania. The agreement rules out any action on drilling until an official borderline is drawn, but the Lithuanian reaction was immediate. Lithuania claimed that Latvia was prohibited from signing any agreement on offshore development in the disputed area until a treaty on the borderline issue could be resolved.[410]

Lithuania also has protested Russian oil exploration in the Baltic Sea on the grounds that such activities should be delayed until the offshore borders have been delineated.[411] There will likely be a certain measure of discord among all parties involved—Latvia, Estonia, Finland, Lithuania, and Russia—as long as the boundaries remain undefined.

The Baltics remain dependent on Russia for oil and gas (Table 8-3). The Baltics can easily realign their sources of oil from Russia to suppliers in the West. Doing so, however, requires port facilities to handle oil imports and the ability to pay for the oil upon delivery in hard currency.

Table 8-3
Russian Oil and Natural Gas Deliveries to the Baltics, 1996

Commodity	Amount
Crude oil	33,000 b/d
Petroleum products	16,500 b/d
Natural gas	4.1 bcm
Note: Estimated based on January-November 1996 deliveries.	
Source: Interfax, *Petroleum Information Agency*, Moscow, December 17, 18, 24, 1996.	

Reducing the current reliance upon Russia as a supplier of natural gas would be a much more difficult undertaking. An independent study by the PHARE program of the EU found that alternative sources of supply, such as gas piped from Norway or from Denmark, or liquefied natural gas imported from Algeria, are economically unfeasible and concluded that Russia therefore would remain the sole supplier of natural gas to the Baltic countries for the next 10 to 15 years.[412]

---

409.   *Journal of Commerce*, July 10, 1995. Talks with Amoco were put on hold for three months, in the hope that demarcation of its sea border with Lithuania would have been resolved by that time. See *Interfax*, Riga, May 31, 1995.

410.   *Platt's Oilgram News*, November 10, 1995.

411.   *FBIS-SOV*, June 29, 1995. The Russian company Kaliningradmorneftegaz (Kaliningrad Offshore Oil and Gas) continues prospecting the D-6 field, which is located in disputed territorial waters in the Baltic Sea. Production has not yet begun.

The Russian Interfax news agency has reported (*FBIS-SOV*, June 22, 1995) that the Russian state enterprise Rosneft, together with Kaliningradmorneftegaz and two oil companies from Germany—RWE-DEA and Feba Oil—have formed a consortium (referred to as KANT) for development of the D-6 oil field. Russia claims the oilfield lies within offshore boundaries belonging to Kaliningrad, while Lithuania holds that the oilfield is closer to Lithuania.

With dependence on Russian gas a fact of life for some time to come, the Baltic nations can only reduce their vulnerability to disruptions in supply by restraining demand—setting natural gas tariffs to reflect the full cost of the gas consumed; metering gas consumption; instituting customer billing, collection, and cutoff procedures; and enforcing these procedures.

The electric power systems of the Baltic countries were integrated following the breakup of the Soviet Union in 1991, and are controlled from the Baltija Dispatch Center in Riga, Latvia. In 1991, the Baltics produced 52 billion kilowatt-hours (kwh) of electricity, consumed just 37 billion kwh, and exported the surplus to Russia and Belarus.[413] The Baltic 330 kV grid is part of a high voltage network loop that runs from Estonia through St. Petersburg, Moscow, and Smolensk (all in Russia), and through Belarus into Lithuania and Latvia. The electric power needs of the Baltic states would better be served if their grids could be linked with the West European or Scandinavian grids. Representatives from the three Baltic states, and Finland, Sweden, Poland, Germany, Denmark, Norway, and Russia met in Tallinn, Lithuania in mid-March 1995 to discuss integration of the Baltic electric power grid into the EU grid, as well as construction of a so-called Baltic Circle—a network of power transmission lines around the Baltic Sea. Most of the countries around the Baltic Sea are already linked, and only an underwater cable between Estonia and Finland and a power line between Lithuania and Poland would have to be built. The project is scheduled for completion by the year 2000.[414]

The Nonpayment Issue

Sales of fuels and energy by Russia to the Baltics generally are made at world market prices, with settlement in hard or national currencies.[415] Nonetheless, the Baltic states compare favorably with other former Soviet republics in terms of energy-related indebtedness to Russia. At the end of November 1996, the Near Abroad owed Russia 8,300 billion rubles for fuels, but the Baltics' share was less than 1.5 percent, virtually all for natural gas. The Baltics' generally healthy financial position, their comparatively low energy intensity, and the gradual displacement of Russian supplies with those from the West combine to hold down arrears.

---

412. *Platt's Oilgram News,* June 6, 1995. PHARE is the acronym for the EU's assistance program for Eastern Europe: Pologne Hongrois Actions pour la Reconstruction Economique.

413. "New Energy Markets in the Baltics and Eastern Europe," a paper by Vidmantas Jankauskas, Lithuanian Energy Institute, presented at the 18th International Conference of the International Association for Energy Economics, Washington, D. C., July 5-8, 1995.

414. See *FBIS-SOV,* March 21, 1995.

415. *Petroleum Information Agency*, Moscow, April 10, 1995.

Estonia

Table 8-4
Estonia At a Glance

Currency	kroon, introduced June 20, 1992
Rate of Exchange	12.001 kroons/$1 (November 6, 1996)
Gross Domestic Product	$3.9 billion (1994)*
Inflation	28 percent (1995)
Population	1.62 million (mid-1994)
By nationality	
Estonian	61.5 percent
Russian	30.3 percent
Ukrainian	3.2 percent
Other	5.0 percent

Note: Estonia was the first of the former Soviet republics to abandon the ruble. The kroon is tied by law to German currency at 8 kroons to the deutsche mark.

Sources: *EIU Country Report*, 1st Quarter 1995; Central Intelligence Agency (CIA), *The World Factbook 1995* (Washington, D. C.: CIA, 1995); *Finansovyye Izvestiya*, December 22, 1995; Interfax, *Financial Information Agency*, Vilnius, January 9, 1996; Open Media Research Institute, *Daily Report*, April 26, 1996, World Bank data.

On February 24, 1918, Estonia proclaimed independence. Before that, it had been a part of the Russian Empire. In November 1918, Estonian Bolsheviks proclaimed their country to be a socialist republic, which led to a civil war that lasted until February 2, 1920, when the Tartu Peace Treaty was signed with Russia. Russia then recognized Estonia as an independent state. Nonetheless, Estonia was forcibly incorporated into the Soviet Union in 1940. Estonia's association with the Soviet Union continued until September 6, 1991, when Estonia again declared independence.

Estonia has fared comparatively well over the past several years. There was positive GDP growth (3.4 percent) in 1994 and again in 1995 (6.0 percent). In comparison, Russia's GDP declined by 12.6 percent in 1994 and by a further 4 percent in 1995. Equally important, the Estonian budget was in surplus in 1994 and 1995, albeit by relatively small percentages.[416] Per capita real income was up 47 percent in 1995 compared to 1992.

Estonia has certain advantages compared with the other Baltic states: a stable national currency, reasonably successful economic reform, and favorable trading conditions with most countries. Foreign investors have responded to these attractive conditions and had invested a reported $471 million in Estonia by the close of

---

416.   *Finansovyye Izvestiya*, December 22, 1995.

Source: States of the Former Soviet Union, CIA, 1992.

1994.[417] Finnish investors led the way, accounting for 53 percent of the total. The largest share of investment—36 percent—has been directed to trade and light industry.

Estonia is now in the process of drawing up an energy development program that would take the country to 2030. The centerpiece of that program will be a continuing reliance on natural gas supplies from Russia.[418] Looking for ways to reduce energy dependence on Russia, Estonia had investigated importing natural gas from other sources, including Norway, but Estonian natural gas requirements in the coming years were considered too limited to justify such projects.

Fuel shale and peat dominate as local fuels in Estonia; there is no coal, crude oil, or natural gas (Table 8-5). Forced development of fuel shale production in Estonia during the Soviet era left the country in an enviable position: Estonia can satisfy all its electricity needs—and 65 percent of its total energy requirements— from burning shale.[419] Indeed, Estonia is probably the only country in the world where shale is the major form of primary energy. Burning fuel shale is a major contributor to pollution because it has a very high sulfur content, but local availability has outweighed concerns for the environment.[420]

Table 8-5
Estonian Energy Production, Selected Years

	1993	**1992**	**1985**
Electric power (billion kwh)	9.1	11.8	17.6
Fuel shale (million tons)	14.9	18.8	26.4
Peat (thousand tons)	n.a.	n.a.	430

Sources: *FBIS-USR*, March 28, 1994. Department of Commerce, U.S. Bureau of the Census, Eurasia Branch, *Estonia: An Economic Profile*, July, 1992.

Peat is plentiful but not always competitive in terms of price and its use as a fuel is quite limited. Peat briquettes are used mostly by households, although some is used for electric power generation.[421]

Given the likelihood that Estonian oil and natural gas requirements will always be met through imports, attention must be focused on improving the efficiency of energy use and securing its supply. This is the position of the EBRD, and any forthcoming financial assistance will likely reflect that position.

---

417.   *FBIS-SOV*, July 27, 1995.

418.   Interfax, *Petroleum Information Agency*, Tallinn, January 10, 1996.

419.   *Financial Times*, April 19, 1994.

420.   Some shale is imported from the Leningradslanets joint stock company (Russia), which has been supplying the Baltic regional power plant (Estonia) with shale for years in exchange for electricity. See British Broadcasting Corporation, *Summary of World Broadcasts, Part 1, Former USSR*, December 13, 1995.

421.   International Energy Agency, *Electricity in European Economies in Transition* (OECD: Paris, 1994).

Oil

Estonia has no crude oil production and no crude oil refinery.[422] Requirements for petroleum products (Table 8-6) must therefore be met through imports. In the past, Russia was the dominant supplier of gasoline, for example, but today Western oil companies are becoming major suppliers of motor gasoline and lubricants, which are marketed through brand name filling stations.

Table 8-6
Estonian Oil Consumption, Selected Years

Year	Thousand b/d
1989	52.7
1992	14.0
1993	23.1
Source: *Petroleum Intelligence Weekly*, March 21, 1994.	

Fuel oil is the dominant petroleum product, accounting for roughly 60 percent of total consumption. Fuel oil requirements average about 14,500 b/d, of which some 70 percent is imported from Russia.[423] In relative terms, the demand for gasoline has declined most dramatically since independence, with 1993 demand accounting only about a third of the 1989 level. Demand for diesel fuel and fuel oil has declined by half.

The largest port in Estonia is Muuga, located in the suburbs of Tallinn. It is to be renovated through a joint venture involving Coscol Petroleum Corporation, a subsidiary of the Coastal Corporation (United States), Sadkora AB (Sweden), and Esoil Ltd. (Estonia). Renovation will include refurbishing the existing terminal, adding new storage tanks, and linking Maardu with the nearby port of Muuga by means of a 7.3 km pipeline. The renovated terminal will be used to import and export crude oil and petroleum products.[424] This new terminal was opened in September 1996. Muuga is a major terminal for product exports, handling an average of 80,000 b/d during 1995.[425]

Natural Gas

Estonia's consumption of natural gas has been steadily increasing, and that trend may continue as a number of large consumers shift to this fuel. The schedule for

422. Esoil Ltd., Estonia's state-owned oil company, wants to build a refinery at the port of Muuga. This proposed refinery would cost $500 million and would have a capacity of 40,000 to 60,000 b/d, quite small by world standards. Such an undertaking is well beyond the financial capability of Esoil. See *Platt's Oilgram News*, October 27, 1995.

423. *FBIS-SOV*, February 1, 1995; *Platt's Oilgram News*, December 10, 1995.

424. *Platt's Oilgram News*, November 23, 1995.

425. Interfax, *Petroleum Information Agency,* Tallinn, September 3, 1996.

1995 called for importation of 1 bcm of natural gas, all from Russia (Table 8-7), but natural gas consumption for 1995 was reported to be only 0.73 bcm.[426]

All of the increase in natural gas consumption during 1994 was taken by the firm "Nitrofert," a facility that uses natural gas as a raw material for making nitrogen fertilizer. When Nitrofert was recently privatized, all of the stock was purchased by Gazprom, Russia's gas monopoly, and virtually all of the output is sold in European markets, at European prices.[427]

Table 8-7
Estonian Natural Gas Imports, 1993–1995

Year	Million cubic meters (mcm)
1993	442
1994	644
1995 Plan	1,000
1995 Actual	730
Note: All from Russia.	
Source: *Finansovyye Izvestiya*, January 17, 1995 and June 1, 1995 and Interfax, *Petroleum Report*, July 14-21, 1995.	

Natural gas consumption in Estonia differs from that of other countries because no gas is burned for electric power generation. Instead, about 40 percent is burned as an industrial fuel or used as a chemical feedstock. The greater share, 48 percent, is consumed by district heating.

Near-term plans call for natural gas imports to reach 820 mcm by 1999, indicating a relatively slow growth pattern for the coming three years. Similarly, little if any change should be expected in the consumption pattern.

Natural gas is purchased for Estonia by Eesti Gaas, which was established in 1992 and has monopoly control over natural gas transportation in Estonia. In May 1995, a portion of the government's share was sold to Ruhrgas (Germany). Currently, Gazprom holds 30 percent, Ruhrgas 15 percent, and the Estonian government 39.9 percent; the remainder is in the hands of a number of Estonian legal entities and private individuals.[428] The state-owned shares are to be offered at an open auction. Estonia takes pride in noting that it is the only Baltic state with no debts to Gazprom.[429] As noted, Estonia's energy plan centers around continuing large supplies of natural gas from Russia, largely because projected import requirements will be insufficient to support development of alternative supplies, such as construction of a pipeline to link Estonia with Norwegian suppliers.

---

426.   Interfax, *Petroleum Information Agency*, Tallinn, January 10, 1996.
427.   *Finansovyye Izvestiya*, January 17, 1995.
428.   Interfax, *Petroleum Information Agency*, Tallinn, October 24, 1996.
429.   Interfax, Tallinn, February 3, 1995.

Electric Power

Estonia relies very heavily on burning shale to generate electric power. Fuel oil imported from Russia accounts for most of the remainder. Small amounts of peat are also burned, more as a backup fuel. Estonia has no hydroelectric potential and there is no nuclear power (Table 8-8).

Table 8-8
Estonian Electric Power Generating Capacity, 1994

Source	Megawatts
Thermal	3311
Of which:	
shale, shale products and peat	3,121
Fuel oil	190
Nuclear	0
Hydro	0
Total	3,311

Source: International Energy Agency, *Electricity in European Economies in Transition* (OECD: Paris, 1994).

There are two nuclear reactors at Padilski, but these reactors were used for training purposes (Padilski was a Soviet submarine base) and do not generate electricity. Withdrawal of Russian military from Estonia has meant closure of the base and will mean dismantling of the reactors and clean up of the surrounding environment.[430] A concrete sarcophagus 30 centimeters thick has been built around the reactors, and the facility has been turned over to Estonia.[431]

Just two electric power stations—the Baltic Power Station and the Estonian Power Station—account for roughly 90 percent of Estonia's electric power generating capacity. Both stations burn shale oil, and both are so outdated as to require reconstruction or upgrading.[432] At the same time, the reduction in electricity use may make it unnecessary to maintain generating capacity at current levels.

In the past, Estonia was a major exporter of electricity to Russia and Latvia. Estonia also imported electric power from the Leningrad nuclear power plant near St. Petersburg, which were passed on to Latvia. Exports have declined sharply in recent years, in part because of the decline in demand in Latvia's former export markets and in part because of the inability or unwillingness of foreign customers to pay for imports (Table 8-9).

430. The cost of cleaning up the radioactive pollution from the nuclear reactors has been placed at about 40 billion kroons, or approaching $4 billion. See Radio Free Europe/Radio Liberty, *Daily Report*, 22 August 1994.
431. *Interfax*, Tallinn, September 26, 1995.
432. *FBIS-SOV*, March 29, 1995.

Table 8-9
Estonian Electricity Exports, 1990–1995

Year	Billion kwh
1990	8.5
1992	3.5
1993	2.0
1994	1.2
1995	0.7

Sources: *FBIS-SOV*, March 29, 1995; The US Energy Association, quoting Eesti Energia, the state-owned energy company; OECD/IEA, *Electricity in European Economies in Transition* (Paris, 1994); British Broadcasting Corporation, *Summary of World Broadcasts, Part 1, Former USSR*, April 18, 1996; H, Kaar *et al*, "Prospectus of Natural Gas in Baltics: Efficiency of Consumption and Security of Supply," a paper presented to the 19th International Conference of the International Association for Energy Economics, Budapest, May 27-30, 1996.

The fall in exports, coupled with the decline in domestic requirements, have cut electric power generation roughly in half (Table 8-10).

Table 8-10
Estonian Electric Power Generation, 1980–1996

Year	Billion kwh
1980	18.9
1985	17.8
1990	17.2
1992	11.8
1993	9.1
1994	8.0
1996 est.	7-8

Sources: *FBIS-USR*, March 28, 1994; Eastern Bloc Research Ltd., *CIS and Eastern Europe Energy Databook*, 1992; H, Kaar *et al*, "Prospects of Natural Gas in Baltics: Efficiency of Consumption and Security of Supply," a paper presented at the 19th International Conference of the International Association For Energy Economics, Budapest, May 27-30, 1996.

Virtually all the electric power generation and distribution within Estonia comes under the authority of Eesti Energia, a state-owned monopoly. Estonia hopes eventually to link its electric power system with the integrated network of the EU by means of an underwater cable between Estonia and the Nordic countries.[433] Such a step would be very costly, and is currently beyond the country's capabilities and needs.

In the interim a U.S. company, NRG Energy Inc., (a subsidiary of Northern States Power Company), became co-owner of all the main power engineering enterprises in Estonia.[434] Under this arrangement, NRG is to manage, operate, and jointly own all of Estonia's major power generating interests. This is by far the largest American investment in the Baltics. The country's two largest plants are involved and together account for 96 percent of Estonian electricity generation.

Latvia

Table 8-11
Latvia at a Glance

Currency	Lat, introduced June 28, 1993
Rate of Exchange	0.5520 lati/$1 (November 19, 1996)
Gross domestic product	$5.8 billion (1994)
Inflation	13.1 percent (1996)
Population	2.56 million (midyear 1994)
By nationality	
Latvian	54.2 percent
Russian	33.1 percent
Others	12.7 percent

Sources: *EIU Country Report,* 1st Quarter 1995, select appendices; *Financial Times,* November 18, 1994, p. 30; International Energy Agency, *Electricity in European Economies in Transition* (Paris: OECD, 1994); *Finansovyye Izvestiya,* February 29, 1996; Open Media Research Institute, *Daily Report,* April 26, 1996; *Interfax,* Riga, January 8, 1997.

Latvia was an independent nation following World War I but was annexed by the Soviet Union in 1940, as were the other Baltic states. A strong movement toward political independence took hold during the latter half of the 1980s and quickly won popular support. Latvian formal declaration of independence from the Soviet Union on August 21, 1991 was quickly recognized by both the United States (September 2) and the Soviet Union (September 6).

Although Latvia has no coal, crude oil, or natural gas of its own, its hydroelectric, wood, and peat resources have been put to good use, particularly for generating electric power. Indeed, hydropower provides in excess of three-quarters of electricity production in the country, and peat is used as a backup fuel at one of the

---

433. *FBIS-SOV,* June 9, 1995.

434. British Broadcasting Corporation, *Summary of World Broadcasts, Part 1, Former USSR,* April 4, 1996.

Source: States of the Former Soviet Union, CIA, 1992.

thermal power plants. Nonetheless, Latvia must import about 90 percent of the energy it consumes[435] (Table 8-12). The high cost of these imports is a major contributing factor to the country's poor financial condition.

Although Latvia must look to Russia for its supplies of oil and gas, it is reasonably up-to-date on its payments for fuels delivered. Most of its debt is for natural gas that has been delivered but not paid for.[436]

Table 8-12
Latvian Energy Imports, 1993

Type of Fuel	Level
Crude oil	0 b/d
Pet. products	8,080 b/d
Natural gas	947 mcm
Coal	205,000 tons
Sources: see Table 8-9.	

Natural Gas

Latvia has been totally dependent on Russia for supplies of natural gas, placing the country in a somewhat uncomfortable position. In searching for alternative suppliers, Latvia looked westward, to Germany. Ruhrgas (Germany) has received a quota for natural gas deliveries. Privatization organs of Latvia have stated that they will carry out business exclusively with a German consortium that includes, in addition to Ruhrgas, the company Preisen Elektra, after this consortium had won a tender. Preisen Elektra has already signed cooperative agreements with all of the Baltics and with Russia.[437] (Table 8-13). Importantly, a very large underground natural gas storage facility has been created at Inchulkans, in the central part of Latvia, to meet peak wintertime demands and to cover breaks in gas deliveries. Inchulkans can store 4 bcm of natural gas, of which 2.3 bcm can actually be withdrawn.[438] It is the only underground storage facility in the Baltics, and Latvia, which has unique geological conditions for underground natural gas storage, envisages creating additional underground storage facilities.

---

435.   "Energy Conservation Policy in Latvia and Baltic Region for the Next Century," a paper presented by Viktor Zebergs, Nameys Zeltinsh, and Yu. Stripnieks, at the 18th International Conference of the International Association for Energy Economics, Washington, D. C., July 5-8, 1995.

436.   Interfax, *Petroleum Report*, April 7-14, 1995, 22. Nonetheless, Gazprom did not intend to raise prices for gas supplies to Latvia in 1996. The price would remain the same: $73.60 for 1,000 cubic meters. See *Interfax*, Riga, October 13, 1995.

437.   *Finansovyye Izvestiya*, August 6, 1996.

438.   The remaining 1.7 bcm provides good working conditions for the storage facility and would not be withdrawn.

Table 8-13
Latvian Natural Gas Imports, 1991–1996

Year	Billion cubic meters
1991	2.961
1993	0.950
1994	1.028
1995 plan	2.6
1995 actual	1.2
1996 plan	3.2

Note: All natural gas imports are from Russia. The gas is sold to Latvia at $73.6 per 1,000 cubic meters if payment is made on schedule. If not, the price will be increased by about 5.3 percent.

Sources: Interfax, *Petroleum Report*, June 10-17, 1994; December 16-30, 1994; and July 14-21, 1995; *Platt's Oilgram News*, January 11, 1996; United Nations, Economic and Social Council, Economic Commission for Europe, *ENERGY/WP.3/R.39/Add.1*, November 23, 1995.

Russian natural gas is delivered to Latvia via two pipeline systems, one entering the country from the northeast and transiting a very small segment of Estonia, and the second coming in from the south, transiting Lithuania.[439]

Natural gas transmission and distribution within Latvia is handled by Latvijas Gaze, the national gas company. Foreign investors are to be offered 32.5 percent of the shares of Latvijas Gaze as a way of raising capital. Gazprom will purchase half of these shares, or 16.25 percent of the total and 16.5 percent will be sold to the German team of Ruhrgas and Preisen Elektra.[440] The Latvian government will hold a controlling 65.5 percent. Latvia was scheduled to purchase 3.2 bcm of natural gas from Russia for delivery during 1996, indicating a growing energy dependence on that country.[441]

As in Estonia, comparatively little natural gas is burned in electricity generation. Industrial use has been reduced sharply, commensurate with the decline in economic activity in Latvia. Conversely, household consumption actually rose after 1991, although just slightly.

Steady increases in natural gas imports have been forecast. Household use of natural gas is scheduled to decline, giving way to much higher industrial consumption, presumably based on an anticipated upturn in the economy. The burning of natural gas in electricity generation is to hold constant at 160 mcm annually.

---

439.   Latvia wants to privatize the Latvijas Gaze enterprise and decided to sell 22 percent of the shares of Latvijas Gaz to foreign investors. Gazprom, in responding, insisted on purchasing no less than 50 percent of the shares in the company, thus giving it control. Latvia has resisted so far, but its stand is complicated by its debt to Gazprom for gas delivered but not paid for. See *Interfax*, Riga, September 22, 1995.

440.   Interfax, *Petroleum Information Agency*, Riga, December 21, 1995.

441.   Latvijas Gaze owed Gazprom $16 million for 1995 gas deliveries, plus late payment penalties of $5.2 million. Latvijas Gaze has agreed to repay this debt in full in the first quarter of 1996. See *Platt's Oilgram News*, August 7, 1996.

Oil

Latvia has no crude oil production nor any oil refineries. This means that oil is imported in the form of petroleum products, brought in by rail and pipeline from Russia, Belarus, and Lithuania.

There is a mutual dependence between Latvia and Russia in terms of oil. While Latvia looks to Russia to meet its oil requirements, Russia in turn depends on the Latvian port of Ventspils to move oil to Western markets (Table 8-14).

Table 8-14
Russian Oil Exports from Ventspils, Latvia, 1992–1996

Year	b/d
1992	280,000
1993	334,000
1994	370,000
1995	394,000
1996	505,000

Sources: *Interfax*, Moscow, July 24, 1995; Interfax, *Petroleum Information Agency*, Ventspils, January 4, 1996; British Broadcasting Corporation, *Summary of World Broadcasts, Part 1, Former USSR*, January 10. 1996; Interfax, *Petroleum Information Agency*, Riga, January 9, 1997.

There is growing demand in the Baltics for gasoline and diesel fuel. The Finnish firm of Neste has an expanding network of filling stations in the Baltics and has entered into an agreement with Norway's Statoil and four local Latvian firms to construct an oil import terminal at Riga. This terminal, with an initial capacity of 30,000 b/d, increasing to 50,000 b/d by 2000, will handle jet fuels as well as motor gasoline and diesel fuel.[442]

The Latvian government indicated its intention to privatize Ventspils Nafta (the import and distribution group), selling off between 30 and 49 percent of the shares during 1996.[443] LUKoil, the largest of the Russian vertically integrated oil companies, has demanded exclusive rights to all shares offered, to be acquired basically through a debt-equity swap. Latvia wants to involve investors from Western countries in the privatization process.

Russia's use of Ventspils as an oil export port has been substantially increasing, as noted above.[444] Oil exports through Ventspils in 1996 matched the port's effec-

---

442.   *Platt's Oilgram News*, December 1, 1995. If the situation warrants, some products may be reexported to Estonia and Lithuania.

443.   *Platt's Oilgram News*, May 13, 1996.

444.   Ventspils Nafta has responsibility for shipping crude oil and petroleum products from the port of Ventspils. The transportation of crude oil and petroleum products through Latvia is the responsibility of LaSam, Lavtia's participant in LatRosTrans, a Latvian-Russian joint venture. Proposals are being discussed to transform Ventspils Nafta and LaSam into a national oil company. See Interfax, *Petroleum Information Agency*, Riga, September 12, 1995.

tive capacity, which currently reaches about 500,000 b/d.[445] When reconstruction of a deepwater pier at Ventspils is completed in 1997, the port will then be able to handle 1.1 million b/d, allocated roughly equally between crude oil (560,000 b/d) and petroleum products (540,000 b/d).[446]

Crude oil is delivered to the port of Ventspils via the Samara-Polotsk-Ventspils leg of the Druzhba pipeline. A petroleum products pipeline links a Russian refinery center at Samara with Ventspils, transiting Belarus and Lithuania enroute.[447] But this 50,000 b/d pipeline was closed in October 1992 following a dispute between Russia and Latvia over transit fees and ownership.[448] It then remained closed for 21 months because the two countries could not reach agreement on ownership of the portion of the pipeline transiting Latvia.[449] The Latvian segment of this pipeline had been nationalized by Latvia in 1992, and management was to have been conducted through a joint venture (66 percent Latvia, 34 percent Russia).

This 20-inch pipeline, which carries diesel fuel, has been subject to constant thievery. In just one incident during 1994, between 700 to 1,400 bbl of fuel were siphoned off through a hole made in the line, and a further 1,000 bbl leaked out onto the ground before the damage was discovered.[450]

---

445.   The cost of moving crude oil from Tyumen in Western Siberia to the port of Ventspils is higher than to any of the other ports of export (Novorossiisk, Tuapse, and Odesa). See *Neft i Kapital*, September 1995.

Most of the work at the port involves dredging to deepen the ship channel and turning basin and expanding the oil piers. When completed, larger oil tankers will be able to dock. See *Oil & Gas Journal*, April 22, 1996.

The port of Ventspils, together with LatRosTrans and the English company Alberts, has begun looking into the feasibility of building a new crude oil pipeline parallel to the Samara- Polotsk-Ventspils pipeline.

446.   Interfax, *Petroleum Report*, July 21-28, 1995.

447.   The Ufa-Samara-Nikolskoye-Unecha-Gomel-Mozyr-Ventspils pipeline reportedly is a popular pipeline with exporters, running at 94 percent capacity up to and including the Belarus section, and up to 90 percent in the Latvian section. See *Russian Petroleum Investor*, October 1995.

448.   *Weekly Petroleum Argus*, August 15, 1994. The pipeline reopened in mid-June 1994 but was closed again after a few weeks. That closure was blamed on Lithuania, which demanded a share of the transit revenues. Prior to closure, the pipeline had been handling up to 120,000 b/d. *See Journal of Commerce*, June 9, 1994.

449.   *FBIS-SOV*, August 17, 1994. Latvia had nationalized the Latvian segment of the pipeline in 1992, which quite naturally angered the Russians, who retaliated by halting shipments. With the pipeline closed, shipments of Russian diesel fuel to the port of Ventspils for export had to be shifted to rail, a more expensive and much slower form of transport. See *Platt's Oilgram News*, August 10, 1994.

450.   *Platt's Oilgram News*, October 26, 1994. This was the fourteenth incident involving theft of oil from the pipeline between January and October, 1994. The stolen oil is then sold tax-free in Latvia, in a thriving black market, with profits of between 300 to 500 percent See *FBIS-SOV*, September 28, 1994.

In a more recent incident, thieves tapped into the pipeline, which was carrying diesel fuel. More than 730 barrels spilled onto the ground. Some of the spilled fuel contaminated a tributary of the Venta River. Considerable amounts of petroleum products are smuggled into Latvia by various means, for sale on the domestic market or abroad, with profits coming out of the avoidance of customs duties and/or transit fees. Latvia's losses resulting from these illegal shipments reportedly are on a scale comparable to the country's annual budget. See *FBIS-SOV*, June 28, 1994.

At the same time, Russia does not regard the port of Ventspils as playing any significant role in its future oil exports.[451] Rather, Russia is giving priority to construction of a new crude oil pipeline following the route Torzhok-Kirishi-Primorsk-Porvoo (in Finland, to the northeast of Helsinki).[452] This pipeline would be able to handle 200,000 b/d upon completion of its first stage, expanding subsequently to 800,000 b/d and would draw upon crude oil production in the Russian northwest, primarily in the Timan-Pechora region.

The Western consortium responsible for developing Timan-Pechora has indicated its preference for a crude oil pipeline running northward, to a port on the Barents Sea. The consortium considers its interests would best be protected if crude oil transit across Russian territory could be held to the absolute minimum.

As noted above, Latvia signed a contract with Amoco and OPAB (Sweden) for exploration and development of offshore oil in the Baltic Sea, under which crude oil production could begin within a decade.[453] Lithuania has denounced the agreement because the area is the subject of boundary negotiations between the two countries. Lithuania wants a share in developing any oil found offshore, but Latvia has not yet prepared to grant that. Latvian negotiators insist on no more than 2.5 nautical miles of the disputed territories for Lithuania, while Lithuanian representatives demand 25 miles—leaving Latvia with 400 nautical miles—and participation in the exploration and development of the continental shelf on an equal footing.[454]

Latvia stated that oil exploration in the Baltic Sea would not begin until a treaty on the maritime border between Latvia and Lithuania is signed.[455] Further, OPAB has agreed to help Lithuania with oil exploration on its part of the Baltic Sea shelf.[456]

Corruption has emerged in Latvia, as it has elsewhere in the Baltics, with diversion of petroleum products coming in by rail from Russia. As the tank cars cross into Latvian territory, ostensibly to be delivered to local consumers or to buyers in the region, the destination is readdressed and the products are sold either through Latvian commercial structures or in the West.[457] Prices offered by non-state enterprises are much higher; exports to the West are extremely profitable because the very high Russian export taxes can therefore be avoided.

---

451.   Nonetheless, the port of Ventspils is to be tested as a possible port of export for crude oil to be produced by Amoco/YUKOS at the PriObskoye oil deposit in Western Siberia. See *Petroleum Intelligence Weekly*, May 13, 1996.

452.   Crude oil would be delivered to Torzhok through the existing Usa-Ukhta-Torzhok crude oil pipeline, which would have to be modernized.

453.   *Financial Times*, November 2, 1995. A semisubmersible rig, operating in 120 meters of water, was to drill the first wildcat well, slated for the second half of 1996, but continuing jurisdictional disputes prevented that. See *Oil & Gas Journal*, November 13, 1995.

454.   *Interfax*, Riga, October 26, 1995.

455.   *Interfax*, Riga, November 1, 1995.

456.   British Broadcasting Corporation, *Summary of World Broadcasts, Part 1, Former USSR*, November 30, 1995.

457.   *Interfax*, Tallinn, December 7, 1995.

Electric Power

The demand for electric power in Latvia consistently has exceeded domestic generating capacity, which is comparatively small and centers on hydroelectric power (Table 8-15). Although demand has declined substantially in recent years because of the fall in industrial activity, a reluctance to raise tariffs in line with higher costs has kept electricity use at artificially high levels. However, electricity use in 1993 was less than 50 percent of the 1985 level, which means that a considerable portion of the country's electric power generating capacity stands idle. But it also means that environmental pollution has been reduced, as many of Latvia's thermal electric power plants are badly in need of renovation.

Table 8-15
Latvian Electric Power Generating Capacity, 1993

Source	Megawatts
Thermal	586
Hydro	1,436
Total	2,022
Source: U.S. Energy Association.	

The primary role of hydropower has both advantages and disadvantages. Although hydropower is comparatively cheap and is a renewable source of energy, actual generation very much depends upon the amount of rainfall, a factor beyond anyone's control. In a very good year—that is, when rainfall has been heavy—Latvian hydropower plants can generate as much as 4.7 billion kwh. Conversely, generation might fall to a third of that level in a dry year.[458]

The hydropower potential of Lavtia's main river—the Daugava—is today very heavily utilized. Growth in electric power supply in coming years therefore will have to be satisfied through a combination of new construction of thermal power plants, utilizing imported fuels, and increased imports of electricity itself.

Greater reliance on imports obviates high thermal power plant construction costs but raises the country's vulnerability to future supply cutoffs. Latvia, like all nations, would prefer to hold its reliance on imports to a minimum. In the end, the amounts imported from historical suppliers may be determined as much by availability as by Latvian policy.

There are no nuclear power reactors in Latvia, and none are foreseen in long-range plans covering the period until 2010. There is a nuclear reactor at Salasils that has been used for scientific research and that may be shut down in 1996, if current recommendations are followed. Whether it was shut down is not known.

The gap between electricity production and consumption has been filled by

---

458.   International Energy Agency, *Electricity in European Economies in Transition* (OECD: Paris, 1994). The installed capacity of Latvian hydropower plants corresponds to an average annual generation of 2.6 billion kwh.

imports from neighboring Estonia and Russia (Table 8-16). Latvia has been both a buyer and a seller of electricity, but it has always been a net importer. Indeed, of the three Baltic republics, only Latvia has had to turn to imports to balance electricity supply and demand.

Table 8-16
Latvian Electricity Production and Consumption, 1985–1995

Year	Production (billion kwh)	Consumption (billion kwh)
1985	5.0	9.5
1990	6.6	10.1
1992	3.8	7.9
1993	3.9	4.9
1995	4.4	6.4

Note: Includes transmission losses and own use by power plants.

Sources: International Energy Agency, *Electricity in European Economies in Transition* (Paris: OECD, 1994); Vidmantas Jankauskas, "*New Energy Markets in the Baltics and Eastern Europe*," a paper presented to the 18th international Conference of the International Association for Energy Economics (IAEE), Washington, D. C., July 5-8, 1995; and H. Kaar *et al*, "Prospects of Natural Gas in Baltics: Efficiency of Consumption and Security of Supply," a paper given at the 19th international conference of the IAEE, Budapest, May 27-30, 1996.

Net imports of electricity reached 4.5 billion kwh in 1985, declining slightly to 4.1 billion kwh by 1992, but rather substantially to just 1 billion kwh in 1993, when power generation actually increased and consumption fell by almost 40 percent. By 1994, Latvia had become increasingly dependent on electricity imports and generated only 50 percent of its local power consumption. Reliance on imports dropped in 1995 to roughly a third.

Plans have been developed to increase the percentage of in-country electricity generation to between 80 and 85 percent by 2005.[459] To accomplish that, however, the power industry must first place itself on sound financial footing, primarily by establishing tariffs that reflect the true economic cost of electricity, a difficult step for any developing nation.

Long-range plans foresee electricity demand reaching 10.75 billion kwh by the year 2000, and to 12.5 billion kwh by 2010. The goal for 2000 merely restores demand to the 1990 level. Beyond that, the projected demand increment of just 1.75 billion kwh for the following decade appears unduly modest and likely understates the growth potential of the economy.

---

459.   U.S. Energy Association *Report*, May 1994.

Lithuania

Table 8-17
Lithuania at a Glance

Currency	Litas (June-July 1993)
Rate of Exchange	1 lit=$US 0.25*
Gross Domestic Product	$5.61 billion (1995)
Inflation	13.1 percent (1996)
Population	3.79 million (1992)
By Nationality	
Lithuanian	80 percent
Russian	9 percent
Polish	7 percent
Other	4 percent
*Fixed rate introduced April 1, 1994.	
Sources: Interfax, *Financial Information Agency*, Vilnius, December 8, 1995; *Interfax*, Vilnius, January 8, 1996; *Interfax*, Vilnius, May 15, 1996.	

For most of the Near Abroad, separation from the former Soviet Union and declaration of independence elicited no resistance from Moscow. Not so for Lithuania. Lithuania had been early in declaring independence in March 1990. Mikhail Gorbachev, then president of the Soviet Union and trying to hold onto power, responded with a blockade, cutting off fuel supplies for 10 weeks. Lithuania's declaration of independence was suspended shortly thereafter. Nevertheless, the independence movement continued, and Soviet tanks arrived on the scene in January 1991. Confronted with strong, negative world opinion, the Russian military was quickly restrained. Lithuania persevered and was recognized as an independent state by Moscow on September 6, 1991.

The Lithuanian government has been able to stabilize its economic situation. The rate of inflation had been reduced from 1,160 percent in 1992 to 45.1 percent in 1994. The 35.7 percent rate for 1995 underscored a further improvement but exceeded the 25 percent inflation rate goal the government had set for the year. The government was far more successful during 1996 with its efforts to control inflation, as the rate for that year fell to just 13.1 percent, the same as Latvia.[460]

GDP rose by 0.6 percent in 1994, a sizeable turnaround compared to 1993, when it declined by 23.4 percent. The positive growth trend was reaffirmed in 1995, when GDP rose by 5 percent.[461]

Some $310 million has been invested in the Lithuanian economy since inde-

---

460.   *Interfax-BNS*, Vilnius, January 7, 1997.
461.   *Finansovyye Izvestiya*, May 14, 1996.

Source: States of the Former Soviet Union, CIA, 1992.

pendence, with the overwhelming share in the past two years. At the same time, foreign credits granted totalled $458 million, well in excess of investments. A reported 40 percent of these credits were used to purchase fuels, and oil and gas debts to Russia were settled to the extent possible.[462]

In April 1994, the Lithuanian government approved the *Program For Restructuring the National Energy Complex*.[463] Highlights include:

☐ A decision on the continued use of nuclear power will be made in about five years.

☐ The Kruonis hydropower plant will be expanded.

☐ Incentives will be provided for the utilization of renewable sources of energy (water, wind, and geothermal).

☐ Particular efforts will be made to reduce by half the energy intensity of the country.

Like its Baltic neighbors, Lithuania is in the unenviable position of having little or no local resources of coal, crude oil, or natural gas. Whatever volumes of these primary fuels the economy requires must be imported (Table 8-18). Before the breakup of the Soviet Union, the absence of local fuels did not matter; Russia provided what the economy needed, at prices well below those on world markets. Lithuania became hooked on the steady supply of cheap energy, as did the other Soviet republics, which were all protected from swings in world prices. Again like other former Soviet republics, Lithuania's cheap energy has disappeared but the thirst of its economy for energy has not.

Unlike its neighbors, Lithuania can look to the Ignalina nuclear power plant, the largest nuclear facility in the former Soviet Union and the only one in the Baltics. Ignalina provides a considerable degree of independence in terms of electricity supply, although nuclear fuel rods are still provided by Russia.

Moreover, Lithuania has the Baltic's only oil refinery. If crude oil suppliers other than Russia could be lined up, additional independence could be secured. (See Map 16.)

---

462.   *Interfax*, Vilnius, May 3, 1995. Who actually benefits from credits used to settle oil and gas arrears with Russia? Providing credits to Lithuania—and others—to help settle energy-related debts in reality is nothing more than thinly disguised financial assistance to Russia. After all, the credits are not for use as advance payments for future deliveries. The oil and natural gas have already been consumed.

463.   *FBIS-USR*, May 9, 1994.

M A P   1 6 .

Lithuanian energy facilities

)))))	Thermal power	——	Electric powerline
⚒	Nuclear power	··········	Crude oil pipeline
🏭	Refinery	─ ─ ─	Petroleum products pipeline
⚓	Maritime port	─·─·─	Natural gas pipeline

Riga

L a t v i a

Liepaja

Mazeikiai

Baltic

Sea

Birzai

Siauliai

Daugavpils

Panevezys

Klaipeda

L i t h u a n i a

Ignalina

Ukmerge

Kaunas

Kaisiadorys

Elektranei

Vilnius

R u s s i a

P o l a n d

Lida

B e l a r u s

© NWD 1997

Table 8-18
Lithuanian Energy Imports From Russia, 1994

Source	Amount
Crude oil	64,700 b/d
Petroleum products	6,500 b/d
Natural gas	2.1 bcm

With cheap fuels no longer available, Lithuania must now address its energy supply problems by increasing energy efficiency through price reforms[464] and demand-side management programs.[465] In the end, however, the Lithuanian government must address the vulnerability derived from almost total dependence on fuel imports from Russia and the safety of the two RBMK reactors at the Ignalina nuclear power plant. At the same time, the electricity generating sector is faced with a considerable overcapacity, as local demand and export requirements have been sharply reduced.

A number of scenarios have been laid out by several different organizations in an effort to determine what actions should be taken now, and in the coming years. The Lithuanian ministry of economy released its report at the end of 1994. A World Bank study had been completed in July 1994. Findings of these two reports were compared by representatives of the Lithuanian Energy Institute and presented in the *National Strategy Report*.[466]

Four energy-demand scenarios were worked out and linked to a large number of supply options. The resultant strategy embraced a free market economy, emphasis on energy conservation and efficiency, rehabilitation of selected infrastructure, and cooperation among the three Baltic states in ensuring long-term, stable energy supplies. Priority will continue to be given to Ignalina as the cheapest energy producer, and the bulk of fossil fuel consumption will be provided by natural gas imported from Russia.[467]

The government does recognize that increasing supply is not the only route to satisfying the country's energy needs. Demand management is just as important, and the government proposes to make greater use of alternative energy sources and to take steps, necessarily over the longer term, to dramatically improve energy effi-

---

464.   Electricity prices were increased midyear 1995 from 4c/kwh, to 5c/kwh. Electricity tariffs in Lithuania now compare with those of the United States, where the average real retail revenue per kilowatt-hour (for all sectors of the economy) averaged a bit less than 5c in 1992.

465.   A new government investment plan ignores demand side management and instead focuses on developing a more energy-dependent infrastructure over the next 3 years. The plan, covering the years 1995–1997 is to cost $2 billion and includes the Butinge terminal, port development, transportation, and environmental protection. See *Platt's Oilgram News*, June 1, 1995.

466.   Arvydas Galinis *et al*, "Least Cost Power Sector Development Programme for Lithuania," presented to the 19th International Conference, International Association For Energy Economics, Budapest, May 27–30, 1996. The Ministry of Economy report was titled, *Projections of the Lithuanian Economy Development for 1995–1997;* the World Bank report was *Lithuania: Public Expenditure Review*.

467.   *FBIS-SOV*, November 12, 1993.

ciency. Greater efficiency is to play a major role in Lithuania's energy future, and planners hope to cut the input of energy per unit of output in half in the coming two decades.

Oil

At present there are 19 oil fields in Lithuania, but most are very small. Extraction of crude oil in (Table 8-19) Lithuania is quite limited and prospects for any meaningful growth are quite poor. Any major reduction in import dependency would not be realistic. A modest joint venture, involving the Danish state company Dansk Oile & Naturagas and the Lithuanian joint stock company Geonafta, has been established to explore for oil on the Baltic sea coast south of Klaipeda.[468] A joint oil venture in Lithuania, Genciunafta, was set up in 1992 between Swenska Petroleum Company (Sweden) and Geonafta, the state exploration and production company.

Lithuania has the only oil refinery, Mazeikiai, in the Baltics, but with little crude oil of its own, Lithuania has been dependent upon Russia for supplies.[469] (Mazeikiai is the city where the refinery is located; the refinery itself is known as the Nafta refinery.[470]) The Mazeikiai refinery, with a capacity to handle 276,000 b/d, has operated considerably under that capacity the last several years, reflecting a drop in local demand plus failures of crude oil suppliers to live up to contract terms and a lack of working capital.[471]

Table 8-19
Lithuania Production of Crude Oil

Year	Barrels/day
1995	2,300
1996 plan	3,600
1997 plan	6,900
2003 plan	10,000
Sources: *Interfax*, Vilnius, July 12, 1996 and *Baltic Business Weekly*, June 17-23, 1996.	

The plan of 10,000 b/d for the year 2003, if achieved, likely would cover no more than 10 to 12 percent of anticipated requirements.

468.   Interfax, *Petroleum Information Agency*, Vilnius, September 19, 1995.

469.   A Danish company, Dansk Olie & Naturagas A/S, has been licensed to explore and develop oil fields in an area covering 1,000 square kilometers south of Klaipeda. A joint venture was to be established for the project. At present about 500 b/d of oil is produced in the region. See Interfax, *Petroleum Report*, March 24-31, 1995. Another report put local production at about 2,200 b/d, and that the joint venture hoped to raise output to around 10,000 b/d after several years. See *FBIS-SOV*, March 24, 1995.

470.   The Lithuanian government holds 90 percent of the shares of Nafta, with the remaining 10 percent held by the refinery employees. See Interfax, *Petroleum Information Agency*, Vilnius, April 14, 1995.

Nearby Kaliningrad Oblast in Russia produces about 20,000 b/d of crude oil, all of which moves by rail tank car to the Mazeikiai refinery. But less than one-half the refined product output is returned to Kaliningrad.[472]

Indeed, shortages of crude oil, brought about because there was no working capital to buy crude oil, forced the refinery to stand idle for 130 days during 1995.[473] For comparison, the refinery reported 94 idle days for all of 1994.[474] Downtime in 1994 and 1995 reflected shortages of funds for purchasing crude oil. As an offset, product imports from Russia averaged 4,000 b/d in 1995, compared to total daily requirements of about 24,000 b/d.[475] Only a slight improvement was noted during 1996.

Table 8-20
Crude Oil Refined at Mazeikiai, Lithuania, 1990–1996

Year	Thousand b/d
1990	192
1992	98
1993	102
1994	75
1995 plan	120
1995 actual	62
1996 est.	73

Sources: Interfax, *Petroleum Information Agency*, Vilnius, April 14, 1995; *FBIS-SOV*, January 9, 1995; United Nations, Economic and Social Council, *ENERGY/R.111/Add.3*, July 5, 1995; British Broadcasting Corporation, *Summary of World Broadcasts, Part 1, Former USSR*, February 1, 1996; Interfax, *Petroleum Information Agency,* Vilnius, November 13, 1996.

Unreliable Russian oil delivery schedules have encouraged Lithuania to seek other suppliers. Discussions have been held with Saudi Arabia, Shell, and Mobil, but no agreements have been reached. Yet if Lithuania has difficulty in paying for Russian crude oil, changing suppliers will not help. To the contrary, Western suppliers would not be as forgiving as Russia has been. Russia may see political advantage in maintaining commercial links with Lithuania, whereas a Western

---

471.   The yield of light products (gasoline, jet fuels, and diesel fuels) at Mazeikiai is reported to be 72 percent, making it one of the more advanced refineries in the former Soviet Union. The average light product yield for Russian refineries today stands at about 62 percent. A 28-month modernization program is under way at Mazeikiai and, when completed, light product yields are to improve to 94 percent. The modernization program, drawn up by Asea Brown Boveri, is to cost an estimated $85 million. See Interfax, *Petroleum Report*, December 9-16, 1994, December 30, 1994, and January 6, 1995.

472.   *Oil & Gas Journal*, September 11, 1995.

473.   Interfax, *Petroleum Information Agency*, Vilnius, April 3, 1996.

474.   *Platt's Oilgram News*, August 16, 1995.

475.   *Neft i Kapital*, March 1996.

supplier of crude oil will seek timely payment and nothing more.

A program of privatization is to begin in Lithuania in 1997. Most consultants have advised the government to privatize the Mazeikiai refinery and sell a portion of the stock to an oil producing company, so that the problem of crude oil supply can be resolved. Plans call for 51 percent of the shares to be held by the government and 39 percent to be made available to private investors, with the remaining 10 percent to be distributed to the refinery work force.[476]

Two parallel petroleum product pipelines transit Lithuania, carrying fuels from Russian oil refineries and the oil refinery in Belarus to the Latvian port of Ventspils.[477] Lithuania tries to make the most of its position as a transit country, and the Samara-Ventspils petroleum product pipeline was shut down in August 1994 because Lithuania demanded a share of the transit revenue.[478]

Marketing

Competition is keen in Lithuania between international oil companies (Shell, Statoil, and Neste, among others)—not in the search for oil and natural gas but rather to secure a position in the marketing of gasoline, lubricants, and services to the motoring public.

In an attempt to contain Western marketing inroads, the four companies in Lithuania that handled oil transportation, refining, and marketing agreed to combine their activities under one national company, Lietuvos Nafta.[479] Initially, this new company would be fully state-owned, with the goal of offering shares at a later date.

Gasoline marketing in Lithuania carries much more than the normal business risks. The Finnish oil firm Neste, which operates 12 filling stations in the country, halted all future investments for a time in response to an attack in late 1994 on its local representative in Klaipeda.[480] Neste subsequently renewed its investment but decided to arm all its blue- and white-collar workers and to place guards at its filling stations, its oil storage facilities, and its managers' homes.[481]

Western suppliers of petroleum products nonetheless have made considerable inroads into the domestic market. For example, of the country's more than 600 gasoline stations, only 125 belong to Lithuania. Lithuania's national fuel supply company (Lietuvos Kuras) has lost much of its position in the market, and its share is down to 25 percent.[482]

---

476.   *Neft i Kapital*, no. 9, September 1996.

477.   *Petroleum Information Agency*, Moscow, June 20, 1995.

478.   *Weekly Petroleum Argus*, August 15, 1994.

479.   Interfax, *Petroleum Information Agency*, Vilnius, June 26, 1996.

480.   Economist Intelligence Unit *Country Report*, 1st Quarter 1995.

481.   *Platt's Oilgram News*, December 27, 1994. Neste indicated it would pay for training managers in the use of fire arms and in self defense techniques.

482.   British Broadcasting Corporation, *Summary of World Broadcasts, Part 1, Former USSR*, May 23, 1996.

Oil Terminals

Lithuania has one aging oil export terminal at Klaipeda. Klaipeda can handle about 135,000 b/d of crude oil and products. Rebuilding Klaipeda is essential because of its age and the need to comply with environmental regulations.[483] Once rebuilt, its capacity will remain the same, but it will also be oriented toward the import of small amounts of petroleum products. Modernization will use a loan from the European Investment Bank and a grant from the European Union. Modernization is to cost about $39 million, and upon completion Klaipeda will be able to handle about 136,000 b/d.[484]

A new oil import/export terminal has been scheduled for construction at Butinge, on the Lithuanian coast, near the resort town of Palanga, and completion had been set for November 1997.[485] Butinge will have the capacity to handle 160,000 b/d of crude oil and 50,000 b/d of petroleum products.[486] Work on the project, which began in June 1995, has been hampered by periodic shortages of working capital, which have left many suppliers unpaid.[487] The cost of construction has been placed at some $247 million.[488] Attempts to secure commitment from foreign investors and financial institutions so far have proven difficult.[489] The most recent negotiations collapsed following rejection of the demand by one potential investor—LUKoil—for a controlling interest in the terminal. Rather, Lithuania has indicated that it must hold controlling interest, and not any foreign investor.

International lending institutions, for their part, are not prepared to provide financing for this project unless and until a 10-year agreement from a supplier to use the terminal is in hand. The terminal at Butinge would be linked to the Mazeikiai refinery by both crude and product pipelines. The terminal itself is to be able to handle 160,000 b/d of crude oil and 50,000 b/d of petroleum products.[490]

Thievery

To complicate matters for Lithuania, some of the Russian crude oil destined for the Mazeikiai oil refinery never quite makes it. The pipeline delivering the crude oil

---

483.   *Weekly Petroleum Argus*, October 17, 1994.

484.   Interfax, *Petroleum Report*, July 7-14, 1995.

485.   *FBIS-SOV*, November 30, 1995. The government of Latvia has suggested that Lithuania, instead of building a new oil terminal, should make joint use of the Latvian port of Ventspils. See *Interfax*, Vilnius, July 13, 1995.

486.   British Broadcasting Corporation, *Summary of World Broadcasts, Part 1, Former USSR*, November 30, 1995.

487.   *Platt's Oilgram News*, November 24, 1995.

488.   The Butinge oil import and export terminal is to consist of a land station and a buoy type platform. The land station will be located at a site near Sventoji, 1.5 kilometers from the Lithuanian border with Latvia. See *Platt's Oilgram News*, June 16, 1995.

489.   The U.S. Export-Import Bank is willing to lend Lithuania $150 million toward construction of the terminal, if Lithuania can provide a guarantee for the sources of the remaining $100 million. In the interim, Fluor Daniel Williams Brothers (United States), which is responsible for designing the terminal, is likely to suspend its activities in view of current financial problems. See Interfax, *Petroleum Information Agency*, Vilnius, April 29, 1996.

490.   *Interfax*, Vilnius, July 27, 1995.

passes through Latvia and so-called oil pirates have been tapping into the line, stealing the crude, and selling it abroad.[491] These thefts are quite profitable because Russian export taxes are avoided (products refined from the crude oil would have been returned to Russia).[492]

Petroleum products move by rail from Russia through Lithuania enroute to Kaliningrad. Because Kaliningrad is Russian territory, these shipments escape the payment of high export taxes. Whole trainloads of petroleum products reportedly are stolen and then exported to international markets, often in collusion with the designated recipient in Kaliningrad.[493]

To put a halt to the thievery, Lithuania now requires that exporters employ armed guards to protect the oil cargoes moving by train. Lithuania provides the guards and bills the exporters.

Natural Gas

Lithuania is fully dependent on Russia for natural gas supplies; it has no production of its own. Contracted deliveries from Russia during 1995 were to total 3.23 bcm, reportedly sufficient to cover all needs.[494] Nonetheless, actual imports from Russia during 1995 totalled just 2.5 bcm, although this still represented a considerable increase over recent years[495] (Table 8-21). Imports will continue to increase during 1996 and further in 1997 if the plan is met.

---

491.   *Platt's Oilgram News*, August 9, 1994.

492.   Mazeikiai refines some crude oil on behalf of LUKoil and the refined products are then delivered to Kaliningrad. For 1995, the volumes involved were to have averaged 24,000 b/d. See *FBIS-SOV*, December 21, 1994.

493.   *Journal of Commerce*, May 18, 1995. On occasion, rail tank cars containing gasoline or other petroleum products, transiting Lithuania enroute to Kaliningrad, are instead diverted to Latvia. A small amount of the diverted products may remain in Latvia, but the bulk is sold abroad. See *FBIS-SOV*, August 17, 1995.

494.   Interfax, *Petroleum Report*, June 23–30, 1995.

495.   British Broadcasting Corporation, *Summary of World Broadcasts, Part 1, Former USSR*, February 15, 1996.

Table 8-21
Lithuanian Natural Gas Imports, 1993–1996

Year	Million cubic meters
1993	1,572
1994	1,559
1995	
plan	3,230
actual	2,500
1996 plan	3,200
1996 est.	2,700
1997 plan	3,000

Source: United Nations, Economic and Social Council, Economic Commission for Europe, *ENERGY/WP.3/R.39/Add.1*, November 23, 1995; H. Kaar *et al*, "Prospects of Natural Gas in Baltics: Efficiency of Consumption and Security of Supply," a paper presented to the 19th International Conference of the International Association for Energy Economics, Budapest, May 27– 30, 1996; *Interfax*, Vilnius, December 20, 1996.

Lithuanian consumers, like consumers in other former Soviet republics, simply do not pay their bills, recognizing that there is neither the will nor the means to cut them off.[496] As of August 1, 1996, consumers owed the equivalent of $25 million in unpaid electricity bills and $44 million in unpaid central heating charges.[497]

Part of the cost of importing natural gas is offset through a barter arrangement. Lithuania supplies electricity to Kaliningrad, an oblast geographically separated from Russia by Lithuania. In payment, Russia provides Lithuania with 0.3 cubic meters of natural gas for each kilowatt of electricity delivered to Kaliningrad.

Despite the presence of the Ignalina nuclear power facility, Lithuania burns comparatively more natural gas in electricity generation than the other two Baltic countries. Almost 60 percent of the natural gas imported in 1994 was burned by thermal power stations.

Natural gas imports likely will increase through the remainder of the 1990s at a steady but unspectacular pace. The consumption pattern should hold unchanged.

---

496.   As the winter of 1994-95 came to a close, Russian gas deliveries dropped from about 9 mcm per day to 6.8 mcm. The reason offered was that Lithuania owed the equivalent of $56.6 million to Gazprom, the Russian gas supplier, for volumes consumed but not yet paid for. But the Lithuanian government could not pay Gazprom simply because its customers were so heavily in arrears. See *Interfax*, Vilnius, March 2, 1995.

Gazprom, the Russian gas monopoly, has advised Lithuania that it is planning to rebuild those gas pipelines transiting Lithuania enroute to neighboring Kaliningrad Oblast. Moreover, Lithuanian consumers should expect to pay more for Russian gas. The price was to increase by 6 percent as of January 1, 1996, and future increases will be based on costs of gas extraction and on the inflation rate in Russia. See British Broadcasting Corporation, *Summary of World Broadcasts, Part 1, former USSR*, November 30, 1995.

497.   British Broadcasting Corporation, *Summary of World Broadcasts, Part 1, Former USSR*, August 10, 1996.

Electric Power

Lithuania enjoys an electric power generating capacity exceeding 5,800 megawatts, which is quite substantial for a country with a population just under 3.8 million. Nuclear power is the core of the country's power generating capacity (Table 8-22).

Table 8-22
Lithuanian Electric Power Generating Capacity

Source	Megawatts
Thermal	2,609
Nuclear	2,500
Hydro	711
Total	5,820

Note: Ignalina has an installed capacity of 3,000 Mw which has been reduced to 2,500 Mw for safety reasons.

Source: U.S. Energy Association.

The Ignalina nuclear power plant was built to cover regional electricity demand, rather than just Lithuanian needs. Ignalina was part of the Soviet northwestern power system. That meant that Belarus, Latvia, and the Kaliningrad (Russia) region would look to Lithuania for power supplies.

The demand for electricity in Lithuania in the past had been dominated by a handful of energy-intensive enterprises. In response, and reflecting the easy availability of cheap fuels, considerable generating capacity had been established over the years, with the Ignalina nuclear electric power plant as the centerpiece. Most of the thermal generating capacity is concentrated at the Elektrenai power station, which burns natural gas as a primary fuel and fuel oil as backup.

Like its sister republics, Lithuania is searching for ways to reduce its reliance upon Russia for fuels. To that end, Lithuania has entered into a contract with Venezuela's Bitor Europe for the delivery until 2012 of Orimulsion, a fuel based on the very heavy crude oils of Venezuela.[498] Deliveries to the Elektrenai power plant will be raised step by step from 100,000 tons initially to 600,000 tons once its experimental use has been completed.[499] Special scrubbers will have to be installed because burning Orimulsion results in large discharges of sulfur.

There does not appear to be a shortage of electricity in Lithuania, if gauged by

---

498.   To be more specific, Orimulsion is an emulsion that is 70 percent bitumen and 30 percent water. Venezuela's strategy has been to market Orimulsion for electricity generation on a coal-competitive basis. It works best in this regard as a conversion option at existing underutilized, coastal-located, oil-fired generating facilities that might otherwise repower to coal or natural gas. For international trading purposes, Orimulsion is classified as a natural bitumen and not a conventional crude oil. See *Middle East Economic Summary*, January 8, 1996.

499.   *Interfax*, December 1, 1995.

the fact that a considerable portion of that amount generated in the country has been exported—although the amounts exported have dropped considerably over the last several years (Table 8-23). Exports to Belarus during 1995 totaled around 2 billion kwh, and barter with Russia of electricity for nuclear fuel rods were to have reached 4 billion kwh during the period from November 1995 to May 1996.[500] Exports to Russia for the whole of 1995 totalled 2.7 billion kwh, and were to be raised to 4 to 5 billion kwh in 1996.[501]

Table 8-23
Lithuanian Electricity Generation and Exports, Selected Years

Year	Generation (billion kwh)	Exports (billion kwh)
1990	28.4	12.0
1993	14.7	2.7
1994	10.0	1.1

Sources: United Nations Economic and Social Council, *ENERGY/R.111/add.3*, July 5, 1995; H. Kaar *et al*, "Prospects of Natural Gas in Baltics: Efficiency of Consumption and Security of Supply," a paper presented to the 19th International Conference of the International Association for Energy Economics, Budapest, May 27-30, 1996.

Requirements in Lithuania's traditional export markets—Belarus, Kaliningrad, and Latvia—have receded as industrial activity has slowed, to the extent that exports as a share of production had fallen to no more than 20 percent of production by 1993. In absolute terms, the export losses were even more pronounced, as the export of electricity declined from 16.5 billion kwh in 1991 to 1.1 billion kwh in 1994.

Lithuania continues to search for electricity markets to replace those lost. With exports to the East no longer plausible, sales to the West must be cultivated. In that regard, a high voltage power line to Poland has been proposed,[502] hopefully with the financial assistance of Sweden. Increased exports, among other things, would permit Ignalina to operate more efficiently (i.e., at a higher output level).

At the same time, the very sharp decline in industrial output in Lithuania, which began in 1991, has led to reduced domestic electricity requirements as well and in turn to reduced power generation (Table 8-24). The decline has been such that Ignalina by itself is now able to satisfy most of the country's demand for power. Not all of the electricity generated by Ignalina remains in the country. Belarus and Latvia import 10 percent and 13 percent of the plant's output respectively, while 4 percent is bartered for Russian nuclear fuel.[503]

---

500.   *FBIS-SOV*, October 3, 1995.
501.   *Interfax*, Vilnius, March 7, 1996.
502.   *FBIS-SOV*, July 17, 1995.

Table 8-24
Electricity Generation in Lithuania, 1990–1994

Year	Generation (billion kwh)
1990	28.4
1991	29.4*
1992	18.7
1993	14.7
1994	10.0

*Historic peak.

Sources: *FBIS-SOV*, November 28, 1994; H. Kaar *et al*, "Prospects of Natural Gas in Baltics: Efficiency of Consumption and Security of Supply," a paper presented at the 19th International Conference of the International Association for Energy Economics, Budapest, May 27-30, 1996.

The position of nuclear electric power in Lithuania is quite unique. With the Ignalina nuclear power station providing roughly 85 percent of the electricity generated in the country, Lithuania is more dependent on nuclear power than any country in the world (Table 8-24). This very high dependence on nuclear power is by omission rather than commission. As demand for electricity has declined in the country, and as costs have risen for fuels imported from Russia, fossil power capacity has been idled, adding to the relative importance of nuclear power. Indeed, as late as 1991, nuclear power supplied only 58 percent of total electric power in the country (Table 8-25). The contribution of Ignalina to Lithuania's supply of electricity far exceeds the relative importance—44 percent—of its generating capacity, a situation comparable to the role of nuclear electric power in Ukraine, but even more pronounced.

Table 8-25
The Importance of the Ignalina Nuclear Plant

Year	Share of Electricity Generated (percent)
1991	57.9
1992	78.1
1993	88.7
1995 est.	85

Source: *Nuclear Energy*, Fourth Quarter, 1993.

The nuclear facility at Ignalina incorporates two 1,500–megawatt reactors

503.   British Broadcasting Corporation, *Summary of World Broadcasts, Part 1, Former USSR*, December 20, 1996.

based on the Chornobyl design. Reactor no. 1 came on line in 1985, followed by reactor no. 2 in 1987. This facility was the largest of its kind in the former Soviet Union. A third RBMK 1500 reactor had been under construction at the time of the Chornobyl accident, but further work was stopped shortly thereafter. This uncompleted reactor is to be dismantled.

Lithuania is perhaps less worried about the state of affairs at Ignalina than it is about how to meet its oil and gas needs. Preserving Ignalina while cutting back on electricity generation at fossil-fuel plants has been an easy decision to make. Not only must these fuels—oil, natural gas, and coal—be imported, but their prices have risen substantially. Moreover, when comparing the costs of generating electricity at fossil-fuel and nuclear power stations, planners consider just the fuel costs. On that basis, nuclear fuel holds an advantage over coal, oil, and natural gas.

All of the electricity generated at Ignalina is purchased by the Lithuanian State Power Company. Because the customers of the Lithuanian State Power Company are not paying their bills, the Power Company in turn cannot pay Ignalina. Arrears reach $50 million,[504] which puts facility repairs and maintenance and worker salaries in jeopardy.

Lithuania buys the nuclear fuel for Ignalina from Russia—about $70 million worth each year—but it has had difficulty covering these expenses.[505] An agreement has been reached under which Russia will continue to supply the needed nuclear fuel and will take imports of electric power from Ignalina in payment.[506] These imports are directed to Kaliningrad.

Of all the energy-related issues facing Lithuania, none is more contentious than the future of Ignalina and efforts by the West to seek its closure. Although Lithuania may not be particularly concerned about the safety of Ignalina's operation, the West is. Western governments seek closure of Ignalina because of safety concerns relating to the operation of the RBMK reactors and because of Ignalina's close proximity to European population centers. Nearby Scandinavian countries would strongly prefer to see Ignalina shut down but have accepted that this will not happen soon. In the interim, Scandinavia has been contributing to safety upgrades at the facility.

The Lithuanian government had been arguing against closure, citing the plant's importance to electricity generation and the high cost of imported fossil fuels. Additionally, export revenues could be lost if generating capacities were just matched to indigenous demand. The Ministry of Energy unsurprisingly was quick

---

504.   *Nucleonics Week*, December 7, 1995.

505.   A scandal has emerged regarding Lithuanian payments for nuclear fuel. Russia's nuclear fuel supplier to Lithuania is Tekhsnabeksport. In July 1995 a letter from Tekhsnabeksport arrived in Vilnius, requesting that payment for the nuclear fuel be transferred to an account held by Solfira, a private company and a Tekhsnabeksport agent registered in Lithuania. Solfira was receiving 0.5 percent of the payments for nuclear fuel and 2 percent of the proceeds from the sale of Lithuanian electricity to Russia for its middleman services. It turned out that Solfira had no license to represent foreign companies in Lithuania, and further was in violation of a law prohibiting private companies from engaging in activities related to nuclear matters. It had also failed to pay any taxes. The losses to Lithuania have been estimated at about $22 million. See *Interfax*, Vilnius, April 3, 1996.

506.   *FBIS-SOV*, October 3, 1995.

to refute the judgment by Pacific Northwest Labs that Ignalina was one of four nuclear power plants in Eastern Europe that were even more dangerous than Chornobyl.[507]

A safety analysis of the Ignalina nuclear power plant was being prepared during 1996 under contract to the EBRD and was to have been completed by the end of the year. Any shutdown decision should be made solely on the basis of this report, according to a representative of the Lithuanian Energy Institute. An agreement with the EBRD stipulates that Lithuania must have sufficient replacement power to meet domestic needs for shutting Ignalina.[508] Nonetheless, following prolonged discussion, the Lithuanian government has reversed itself and is now planning to close Ignalina.

Both units at Ignalina were scheduled to continue operating until at least 2004-2007. Funds equivalent to $8.75 million have been made available from the EBRD Nuclear Safety Account to be used in a safety analysis of Ignalina. A further $41.25 million is intended for use in safety upgrades at this facility, but these come with certain conditions attached:

☐ Operation of the reactors will not extend beyond the time when the pressure tubes will have to be replaced (probably sometime between 1998 and 2004).

☐ The safety analysis must be completed by mid-1996.

☐ Operation of reactor no. 1 will depend upon the energy situation in Lithuania and upon the cost of further upgrades. If a decision is taken to operate reactor no. 1 beyond 1998, the Lithuanian safety authority (VATESI) must issue a new license for the unit.

Plans for the least-cost development of the Lithuanian power sector are now being prepared. Once the safety assessment of Ignalina has been completed, a more definitive development program for the power sector can be worked out.

The opposition to these plans had hoped that the government would agree instead to reconstruction and modernization of the reactors, thus prolonging their life cycle. Closure and dismantling of the two reactors reportedly will cost at least $600 million.[509] To cover these costs, the Lithuanian government is planning to establish a special fund into which part of the income earned from the sale of electricity will be paid.

What will happen to the city of Visaginas (previously Snechkus) and its population of 20,000 when Ignalina closes down? The overwhelming majority of the population is Russian-speaking. It is unclear whether they will remain in Visaginas or will leave Lithuania in search of employment elsewhere.

Still, a new nuclear power plant may be in the offing, given that Lithuania has

---

507.   A Swedish nuclear expert observed that the United States report did not accurately reflect the current situation at Ignalina, that the report, written in May 1993, did not take into account various measures to improve safety at this nuclear facility. This expert added that once all these measures had been taken, at a cost of $100 million, Ignalina would be just as safe as nuclear power plants in the West. See Open Media Research Institute, *Daily Report*, August 10, 1995.

508.   *Nucleonics Week*, August 22, 1996.

509.   Open Media Research Institute, *Daily Report*, September 22, 1995.

no indigenous fuel resources on which to rely. A decision about whether to build a new nuclear power plant is to be taken no later than 1998.[510]

Facility Security

On November 7, 1994, a letter from a Lithuanian citizen was received by the Swedish prime minister's office that contained a threat to blow up Ignalina on Tuesday, November 15, unless the terrorist was paid the equivalent of $1 million. The threat was made in the name of a terrorist group UNC-41 "W."

A separate threat on Ignalina claimed a bombing would be carried out if the individual's son were sentenced to death for masterminding the assassination of a prominent Lithuanian journalist. The terrorist was arrested and sentenced roughly a month later to a two-year jail term. The son was sentenced to death on November 10, 1994.

Lithuania took these threats seriously, and security around the facility was tightened. A specially trained bomb team from Sweden, together with bomb-sniffing dogs, inspected all of Ignalina. Operators at Ignalina first shut down reactor no. 1 and, subsequently, reactor no. 2 as well, as a means of facilitating the search. The no. 1 reactor was searched first, because it had recently been shut down for repairs and because, in the judgment of Ignalina officials, this reactor was built earlier and "always causes more doubt."

During the short time Ignalina was out of operation, substitute electric power was secured from Russia, Belarus, and Estonia, and output at fossil-fuel power plants was increased.

Security is to be heightened at Ignalina, thanks to support from Sweden. Control will be lightened through the introduction of TV cameras, metal detectors, special ID cards, and other devices.[511]

---

510. *Journal of Commerce*, September 27, 1995.
511. *FBIS-SOV*, December 20, 1995.

Source: States of the Former Soviet Union, CIA, 1992.

CHAPTER 9

Belarus

Table 9-1
Belarus at a Glance

Currency	Belarusian ruble (BR)
Rate of Exchange	12,100 BR/$1 (April 19, 1996)
Gross Domestic Product	$22.8 billion (1994)
Inflation	344 percent (1995)
Population	10.5 million (1995)
By Nationality	
Ethnic Belarus	77.9 percent
Russian	13.2 percent
Polish	4.1 percent
Ukrainian	2.9 percent
Other	1.9 percent

Note: The Belarusian ruble became the country's sole legal tender as of August 20, 1994. A currency corridor was introduced effective January 1996 which limits the BR's value to 11,300- 13,100/$1.

Sources: The Economist Intelligence Unit, *Country Report*, 1st Quarter 1995; *Interfax*, Minsk, January 28, 1996; Open Media Research Institute, *Daily Report*, April 26, 1996.

Belarus declared its independence from the Soviet Union on July 27, 1991. Following the breakup of the Soviet Union in December 1991, Belarus has gradually taken steps toward reintegration with Russia. Russian once again is the national language; the state seal and flag used since independence have been replaced by modifications of old Soviet ones; and the appetite for sovereignty has diminished.[512]

Belarus has perhaps changed the least of any of the former Soviet republics. President Alexander Lukashenko, elected to office as his country's first president in July 1994, has permitted little political opposition, his policies are erratic, and he is gradually gathering up all the reins of power.[513]

---

512. *Washington Post*, July 2, 1995.
513. *The Washington Post*, December 27, 1995.

Voters went to the polls on November 24, 1996 to support a presidential-proposed draft constitution giving even broader powers to the president and extending his term to 2001. Among other things, the new constitution grants the president life-long immunity from prosecution and gives him the authority to declare a state of emergency at will. The U.S. Department of State did not recognize the results, calling them a sham.

While other republics were integrated, sometimes forcefully, into the Soviet Union relatively recently, Russia and Belarus have lived together for the better part of the last three centuries, and that kind of relationship is not easily set aside. The deep dependency, moral and physical, which has grown out of this association clearly defines the mood in Belarus today.

Belarusian reunification with Russia would appear to be only a matter of time, although it may assume a somewhat different shape than in the past. In May 1995, the Russian Duma (the lower house of the Parliament) voted to prepare for a national referendum on uniting Russia with Belarus.[514] Plans called for the referendum to be submitted to a popular vote on December 12, 1995, the day of parliamentary elections in Russia, but this did not occur. Economic accords were reached near the end of February 1996, which, among other things, renounced all mutual debts, including Belarus's unpaid energy bills and its claims for compensation for nuclear weapons transferred to Russia.

Russia and Belarus signed a Union Treaty in early April 1996, but Russian President Boris Yeltsin quickly disavowed that reunification was in the making.[515] Russia would be foolish to take on responsibility for an economically deprived Belarus at this time. Nor are foreign investors likely to come to the rescue any time soon. The World Bank, in a recent report on the Belarusian investment climate, observed that "(t)he extremely tangled, cumbersome and unstable" taxation system was the main obstacle to attracting national and foreign investments."[516] The country's legal, economic, and political environment, in the judgment of the World Bank, is one of the weakest in the world.[517]

This is quite a change from the heady days of late 1991, when leaders of Russia, Ukraine, and Belarus met to dismember the former Soviet Union and to replace it with the CIS. Minsk, the capital of Belarus, became the capital of the new CIS. Now, Belarus is on its way to making history as the first of the former Soviet republics to give up its sovereignty for reunification with Russia.[518]

President Lukashenko opposes market-style reforms, and this has meant that the multilateral lending institutions have stayed away. For all practical purposes, there is no formal privatization program in place. Although almost 36 percent of

---

514.   Open Media Research Institute, *Daily Report*, May 25, 1995.

515.   There was a strong political flavor to the signing, as Russian President Boris Yeltsin undoubtedly viewed it as helping his reelection campaign, in that it played to those voters nostalgic for the old Soviet Union.

516.   Interfax, *Financial Information Agency*, Minsk, March 27, 1996.

517.   The International Monetary Fund would seem to concur with this assessment. It has given up any idea of resuming loans to Belarus in view of the poor state of that country's market reforms and economy. See *The New York Times*, March 31, 1996.

518.   *Wall Street Journal*, June 16, 1994.

the labor force works in the nongovernmental sector, that sector contributed just 15 percent of GDP in 1995.[519]

Belarus was one of the more prosperous republics of the former Soviet Union, drawing upon a well-educated work force, a reasonably diversified economy, and a comparatively high degree of industrialization. Belarus could depend on Russia and other republics for cheap energy and raw materials. Those items the industrial sector produced found a ready market within the Soviet Union.

The breakup of the Soviet Union changed all that. Guaranteed markets disappeared, cheap raw materials were no longer available, and oil, natural gas, and electricity were no longer provided at heavily subsidized prices and in the amounts desired.

Belarus, one of the Have-Nots in terms of the capacity to be energy-independent, has long been dependent on fuels and energy imports. Almost 90 percent of the fuel and energy consumed in 1994 was imported (Table 9-2). At the same time, consumption of fuels and energy in Belarus has been declining, although not quite commensurate with the decline in economic activity, which has added to the energy intensity of the economy.

Table 9-2
Fuel Consumption in Belarus, 1994

Type of Fuel	Consumption
Oil	258,000 b/d
Natural gas	14.6 bcm
Coal	8.2 million tons
Electricity	35.2 billion kwh

Source: Interfax, *Petroleum Information Agency*, Minsk, April 27, 1995.

Oil

Most of the crude oil and virtually all the natural gas required by Belarus is supplied by Russia. Domestic crude oil production hit its peak in the mid-1970s and then began a gradual decline (Table 9-3). In recent years, domestic crude oil has not been a significant contributor to the amounts of oil annually refined in Belarus. Production has been holding at or near 40,000 b/d and is expected to decline at a rate of about 1 percent per year. There is a very high water content (about 80 percent) in the crude oil. Stated another way, for every 100 barrels of liquids brought to the surface, just 20 barrels are crude oil. The oil-bearing strata are deep-seated, the geology is complex, and available equipment is obsolete.

---

519. *Finansovyye Izvestiya*, May 14, 1996.

Table 9-3
Crude Oil Production in Belarus, 1975–2010

Year	Thousand b/d
1975	160
1980	54
1989	40
1990	40
1991	40
1993	40
1994	40.4
1995	38.6
1996 plan	37.16
1996 est.	37.2
2010 est.	20.2

Sources: Interfax, *Petroleum Information Agency*, Minsk, August 17, 1995:
Interfax, *Petroleum Report*, January 27 to February 3, 1995; International
Monetary Fund (IMF), *Economic Review Belarus* (Washington, D. C.: IMF,
April 1992); Interfax, *Petroleum Information Agency*, Minsk, January 5, 1996:
British Broadcasting Corporation, *Summary of World Broadcasts, Part 1,
Former USSR*, June 13, 1996; Interfax, *Petroleum Information Agency*, Minsk,
June 12, 1996.

A lack of capital works against an meaningful increase in Belarusian crude oil production during the remainder of this decade at least.[520] Beyond then, if foreign
investment can be attracted, some incremental increases may be possible. If not,
output will shrink, albeit gradually, to an estimated average 26,000 b/d for the
period 2001-2010.[521]

Refining

Belarus had been a major refining center during the Soviet era. Two very large oil
refineries—Naftan (formerly the Novopolotsk refinery)[522] and Mozyr—were the
industrial centerpieces of the country (Table 9-4). By Western standards, these two
refineries are very much obsolete. The yield of light products (basically gasoline,
jet fuels, and diesel fuel) at the Naftan and Mozyr refineries averages less than 40-

---

520.   There were 60 oil fields in Belarus as of January 1, 1995, with recoverable crude oil
reserves in excess of 160 million tons. See Interfax, *Petroleum Report*, January 20-27, 1995.
521.   Interfax, *Petroleum Report*, April 1–8, 1994.
522.   Novopolotsk was constructed at the beginning of the 1960s for the basic purpose of
supplying motor fuels to consumers in the European USSR. In practice, however the military took
what Novopolotsk produced. By 1970 the capacity at Novopolotsk had been expanded to 500,000
b/d, making it the second largest refinery in the former Soviet Union, trailing only the Omsk refinery. See *Neft i Kapital*, June 1996.

45 percent of the charge to refining.[523] For comparison, the light product yield at a modern Western refinery would roughly double that.

Table 9-4
Crude Oil Refining in Belarus, Selected Years

Year	Thousand b/d
1989 total	788,000*
Mozyr	314,000
Naftan	474,000
1994 total	260,000*
1995 total	258,000
Mozyr	114,000
Naftan	144,000
1996 total (est.) Mozyr Naftan	247,000 138,000 109,000
*Product yield.	
Sources: Interfax, *Petroleum Report*, July 14-21, 1995; Interfax, *Petroleum Information Agency*, Minsk, January 18, 1995 and December 30, 1996.	

The oil refining industry still remains under central control and, along with crude oil production, is under the authority of Belnefteprodukt, established in April 1994.[524] Belnefteprodukt also has authority over oil storage facilities, filling stations, and oil industry service companies.

The Naftan and Mozyr oil refineries are badly underutilized.[525] Russian crude oil deliveries averaged 220,000 b/d during 1995, making Belarus by far the largest importer of Russian crude oil among the Near Abroad countries.[526] Adding in the domestic production of about 39,000 b/d, volumes of crude oil available for refining totalled just 258,000 b/d, or less than one-half the available refining capacity of 540,000 b/d.[527] At the same time, domestic oil requirements, including small amounts earmarked for export, reach to about 200,000 b/d.[528] Thus, underutilization of refining capacity cannot be taken to mean that consumers are being denied

---

523. Interfax, *Petroleum Report*, August 8, 1995.

524. *FBIS-SOV*, August 24, 1995.

525. Interfax, *Petroleum Information Agency*, August 17, 1995.

526. Interfax, *Petroleum Information Agency*, Moscow, January 10, 1996. An earlier source (Interfax, *Petroleum Information Agency*, Moscow, December 20, 1995) put Russian crude oil deliveries to Belarus at 201,000 b/d.

527. Refineries in Belarus processed more crude oil during the first 4 months of the year but the general financial situation did not improve. Large stocks of petroleum products were accumulated because of a shortage of buyers able to pay. See British Broadcasting Corporation, *Summary of World Broadcasts, Part 1, Former USSR*, May 30, 1996.

528. *Finansovyye Izvestiya*, March 7, 1996.

the oil they may need.

Russia was to supply 200,000 b/d of crude oil to Belarus in 1995,[529] down from the 220,000 b/d delivered in 1994. As noted, actual deliveries exceeded that estimate. These imports are to cover domestic requirements, and are separate from those volumes provided on a give-and-take basis.[530] Indeed, Russia can be the only source of crude oil. Alternative suppliers would have no way to move large amounts of crude oil to the Belarusian refineries.

The Naftan Oil Refinery

Naftan is one of the largest oil refineries of the former Soviet Union, and has a throughput capacity of 320,000 b/d.[531] Naftan had been scheduled to receive about 192,000 b/d of Russian crude oil in 1995, half of which was to be provided by Surgutneftegaz. The remaining 50 percent would be split equally between LUKoil and Rosneft.

LUKoil and YUKOS, the two largest Russian vertically integrated oil companies, have signed an agreement on cooperation in the supply of crude oil and reconstruction of Naftan in exchange for refining capacity.[532] The Russian contribution would be a steady, reliable flow of crude oil. LUKoil and YUKOS have additionally reached an agreement with Belarus for the acquisition of 74 percent of the shares of Naftan Production Amalgamation, which includes the Naftan oil refinery and certain petrochemical facilities.[533]

The Mozyr Oil Refinery

The Mozyr oil refinery can process 220,000 b/d.[534] Slavneft, the joint Russian-Belarusian oil company,[535] has been anxious to take over majority ownership of the Mozyr refinery. To bring this about, Slavneft has agreed to act as guarantor of

---

529.   *FBIS-SOV*, May 17, 1995. Belarus had expected to pay Russia $40 per ton for crude oil in 1995. But delays in introducing a customs union between the two countries caused Russia to charge $75 per ton during the first quarter of the year. The price was raised to $112 per ton in the second quarter. See Interfax, *Financial Information Agency*, Minsk, May 15, 1995.

530.   Russia has taken steps to ensure that customs duties are paid on those volumes of crude oil processed outside the country on a give-and-take basis, that is, with the refined products being returned wholly or in part to Russia. The duties paid will be returned to the payer within 1 month of application, but not earlier than the return of the petroleum products to Russia. The refined products in turn must be returned to Russia no later than 6 months from the date of customs registration of the exported crude oil.

531.   Interfax, *Petroleum Report*, June 23-30, 1995.

532.   Interfax, *Petroleum Information Agency*, Minsk, December 22, 1995.

533.   *FBIS-SOV*, January 26 1996.

534.   Interfax, *Petroleum Information Agency*, Minsk, October 11, 1995.

535.   Slavneft was formed in April 1994 and incorporated Megionneftegaz (a Russian oil and gas producer), Megionneftegazgeologiya (a geological survey organization), and the Belarus Mozyr refinery. As of September 1, 1995, Slavneft was expanded to include the Yaroslavnefteorgsintez petrochemical facility (located in Yaroslavl, Russia), the Mendeleyev oil refinery (also located in Yaroslavl), and three petroleum product distribution companies in Russia, at Yaroslavl, Kostroma, and Ivanovo. See British Broadcasting Corporation, *Summary of World Broadcasts, Part 1, Former USSR*, October 6, 1995.

Deutsche Bank's $300 million credit to finance the modernization of Mozyr, if Belarus agrees to exchange 51 percent of the refinery shares for shares in Slavneft.[536] In addition Slavneft seeks majority stakes in the Belarus oil producing associations and in certain oil supply bases and filling stations. If this came about, Slavneft would hold a commanding position in the oil product market in southern Belarus. But only up to 40 percent of the refined products produced by the Mozyr refinery will be marketed in Belarus.[537]

Under the arrangement with Slavneft, some 60 percent of the products refined from the 120,000 b/d supplied to Mozyr will be marketed elsewhere[538] (e.g., Moldova, Ukraine, and the Baltics), or returned to Russia, the crude oil having been refined on a give-and take basis.[539] Give-and-take crude oil totalled 163,600 b/d in 1994.[540]

Give-and-Take Arrangements

Supplying crude oil on a "give-and-take" basis is designed to take advantage of excess refining capacities. Very simply, crude oil is delivered to a refinery for processing. The owner of the crude oil pays for the cost of processing with an agreed-upon portion of the petroleum products. The remaining volumes are at the disposal of the owner of the crude oil.

Crude oil delivered by Russian producers to refineries outside Russia escape the oil export tax, but the products must be returned to Russia. In 1994, roughly 211,000 b/d of crude oil was exported by Russia to refineries in Ukraine, Lithuania, and Belarus on a give-and-take basis. Some 179,000 b/d of petroleum products were to have been returned to Russia. Actually, just a little more than 114,000 b/d of petroleum products were returned. The remaining 65,000 b/d was most likely illegally exported or sold on the local economy outside regular commercial channels. Profits were immense, because no export tax had been paid.

Oil Requirements

The Belarusian economy needs between 200,000 and 240,000 b/d of petroleum products, much less than half the apparent oil consumption just six years ago. Russia supplies relatively modest amounts of petroleum products to Belarus.[541] These imports averaged just slightly more than 11,000 b/d in 1994.[542] The pipeline delivering these products (mainly gasoline and diesel fuel) has become an attractive target for thieves. There were 43 incidents registered in 1994 involving the theft of

---

536.   *Ibid.*

537.   Interfax, *Petroleum Report*, April 28 to May 5, 1995.

538.   Interfax, *Financial Information Agency*, Minsk, April 24, 1995.

539.   The two Belarusian refineries produced 24,800 b/d of gasoline and 42,600 b/d of diesel fuel in 1994 on a give-and-take basis, to be returned to the crude oil supplier. See Interfax, *Petroleum Report*, January 27 to February 3, 1995.

540.   Interfax, *Petroleum Information Agency*, January 26, 1995.

541.   Petroleum product deliveries from Russia to Belarus during 1995 were to average just 6,000 b/d. See *Interfax*, Moscow, May 18, 1995.

542.   Interfax, *Financial Information Agency*, May 15, 1995.

diesel fuel and gasoline. Thieves simply drilled holes in pipelines,[543] collected the product in a variety of containers, and walked away.

The supply of petroleum products from the Naftan and Mozyr oil refineries, plus those amounts of products imported from Russia, has always exceeded local requirements. Prior to the breakup of the Soviet Union, Belarus had been a major supplier of petroleum products to surrounding areas. The oil supply and demand balance for 1989 was typical for Belarus in the years preceding the disintegration of the Soviet Union (Table 9-5).

Table 9-5
Belarus Oil Supply and Demand, 1989

Product	Amount (thousand b/d)
Crude Oil	
Production	40
Imports	812
Total Supply	852
Petroleum Products	
Yield from refining	788*
Imports	26
Total Supply	814
Exports	262
Apparent consumption	552

*Estimated, taking into account crude oil losses in the field, additions to storage, and refinery gas and loss.

Natural Gas

Natural gas extraction in Belarus has always been very marginal and has tracked crude oil production in relative terms (Table 9-6). Yet natural gas plays a more dominant role in energy consumption in Belarus than in any of the former Soviet republics. In 1980 gas provided in excess of 31 percent of energy consumption, rising rapidly to more than 51 percent by 1993.[544]

---

543.   *FBIS-SOV*, July 7, 1995. The value of the petroleum products stolen in this manner in 1994 was placed at a little over $80,000.

Table 9-6
Natural Gas Extraction in Belarus, 1975–1995

Year	Billion cubic meters
1975	0.6
1980	0.3
1990	0.3
1994	0.290
1995	0.265

Source: Interfax, *Petroleum Information Agency*, Minsk, January 5, 1996;

Russian supplies of natural gas to Belarus have been reasonably consistent over the past several years (Table 9-7). The state enterprise Beltransgaz is responsible for receiving, transporting, distributing, and marketing natural gas to consumers and gas suppliers in Belarus. Beltransgaz also handles the transit of gas through the country.[545] Preferential pricing continues, with the 1995 price set at about $57 per 1,000 cubic meters, compared with a world price of about $80.[546] Russian gas exports to Belarus totalled just 14.2 bcm in 1994, considerably less than the 16.4 bcm that had been agreed upon. This reflected Russia's frustration with Belarusian failure to meet payment schedules. As a result, supplies were cut off from time to time. A further drop of some 13 percent occurred in 1995, as Belarus again ran up a sizeable debt to Gazprom, Russia's gas monopoly. Nonetheless, deliveries were generally consistent with requirements.

544.   *East Bloc Energy*, April 1994.

545.   See Interfax, *Petroleum Report*, March 24-31, 1995.

546.   *Interfax*, Moscow, May 18, 1995. Natural gas is sold to household consumers at a price less than that paid to Russia. Near the end of April 1995, new prices were established for individuals and for enterprises. Under this new price, individuals (presumably households) were to pay less than $36 per 1,000 cubic meters. The price to enterprises was roughly double that. See *Petroleum Information Agency*, Minsk, April 27, 1995.

Table 9-7
Russian Natural Gas Deliveries to Belarus, 1994–2010

Year	Billion cubic meters
1994	14.2
1995 plan	16
1995 actual	13.7
1996 plan	14.7
1996 est.	14.0
1997 plan	16.6
2000 plan	26
2015 plan	33

Sources: *Interfax*, Moscow, August 4, 1995; Interfax, *Financial Information Agency*, Minsk, May 15, 1995; Interfax Petroleum Report, January 6-13, 1995; Interfax, *Petroleum Information Agency*, Moscow, January 10, 1996; British Broadcasting Corporation, *Summary of World Broadcasts, Part 1, Former USSR*, January 10, 1996; Interfax, *Petroleum Information Agency*, Minsk, December 30, 1996.

Russian natural gas deliveries fell off slightly during 1996, in partial response to accumulating arrears which had reached the equivalent of $438 million by early December 1996.[547] Nonetheless, Belarus is planning to substantially increase gas imports during 1997, to an unlikely 16.6 bcm.

In an attempt to control consumption and to keep arrears within reason, large numbers of enterprises have had their natural gas supplies cut off, while deliveries to others have been reduced to the level of payments actually received.[548] Despite these efforts, indebtedness for natural gas consumed but not paid for continued to rise.

In the aftermath of Chornobyl, natural gas had been embraced as a safer, cleaner form of energy and began to take on a larger role in meeting the energy needs of Belarus. With nuclear electric power expansion now on hold, and with the loss of generating capacity at Chornobyl, the larger share of natural gas supply has been directed toward the generation of electric power. Utilization of natural gas by the industry and construction sector follows closely, while municipal and household consumers account for most of the remainder.[549]

Natural gas availability in Belarus should improve dramatically in the coming years. A multiple-link gas pipeline network, designed to move natural gas from the Yamal Peninsula in Russia to buyers in Europe, is to transit Belarus.[550] The first

547.   Interfax, *Petroleum Information Agency*, Minsk, December 10, 1996.

548.   British Broadcasting Corporation, *Summary of World Broadcasts, Part 1, Former USSR*, May 2, 1996.

549.   In 1991 almost 41 percent of available natural gas was burned in the generation of electric power. The industry and construction sector used about 37 percent of supply that year, while municipal and household consumers accounted for slightly less than 18 percent.

dual pipeline section of the Yamal project is to be laid between the Belarusian town of Nesvizh and the border with Poland, a distance of 209 km. Construction, using 56-inch pipe, was to have begun in the fourth quarter 1995, with completion scheduled for the first quarter 1997.[551] However, Gazprom, pleading a shortage of funds, has delayed the start of building the Belarusian portion of the pipeline to December 1996, with completion now scheduled for the second quarter 1999.[552]

The transit across all of Belarus will require 570 km of pipe. When the Yamal-Europe natural gas pipeline system becomes fully operational, Belarusian offtake may exceed 30 bcm, more than double current imports from Russia.[553] A gas-fired power generating station is to be constructed near Minsk. This facility will be funded by Gazprom, the Russian gas monopoly.

Transit nations normally can look forward to substantial earnings derived from pipelines crossing their territory. Not Belarus. Because Belarus is not in a position financially to participate in construction of the Belarusian portion of the Yamal-Europe gas pipeline, it will not receive transit payments in full.

Electric Power

Belarus has a highly electricity-intensive economy, made so in large part by the easy availability of cheap electric power (Table 9-8). Belarus has no hydropower or nuclear power plants, but relies on thermal power plants fired by fuel oil and natural gas, with only very minor amounts of solid fuels burned in power generation. Natural gas is the dominant fuel, accounting for two-thirds of the fuels consumed in 1994.[554]

---

550.   A reported 33.4 bcm of Russian gas transited Belarus in 1994, including those volumes designated for Belarusian consumers. See Interfax, *Petroleum Report*, March 24-31, 1994. The Yamal-Europe gas pipeline will triple the transit flow. See *FBIS-SOV*, May 5, 1995.

551.   British Broadcasting Corporation, *Summary of World Broadcasts, Part 1, Former USSR*, August 11, 1995.

552.   British Broadcasting Corporation, *Summary of World Broadcasts, Part 1, Former USSR*, June 6, 1996.

553.   *FBIS-SOV*, May 5, 1995.

Table 9-8
Electric Power Consumption in Belarus, 1980–1996

Year	Consumption (billion kwh)	Amount Imported (billion kwh)
1980	31.97	3.9
1985	39.48	9.8
1990	48.96	14.2
1994	35.2	3.8
1995	32.0	7.2
1996 plan	32.7	7.2

Sources: *Interfax*, Minsk, April 26, 1995; OECD/IEA, *Electricity in European Economies in Transition* (Paris, 1994); British Broadcasting Corporation, *Summary of World Broadcasts, Part 1, Former USSR*, January 10, 1996; UN/Economic and Social Council, *ENERGY/R.123/Add.1*, August 22, 1996.

Existing capacity could generate up to 50 billion kwh annually if needed and if fuels were available (Table 9-9). Much of the generating capacity is old—the average age of the generating facilities exceeds 23 years—and should be replaced or reconstructed. However, the larger stations are comparatively younger, while the comparatively small stations, which account for just 6 percent of generating capacity, are older.

A considerable portion of the power generating capacity stands idle, and output of electricity during 1995 probably did not exceed 25 billion kwh.[555] Available electricity generating capacity at the 22 thermal power stations totals 7,033 Mw.[556]

Table 9-9
Installed Power Generating Capacity in Belarus, 1980–1995

Year	Megawatts
1980	5,910
1990	6,842
1992	7,010
1995	7,033

Sources: OECD/IEA, *Electricity in European Economies in Transition* (Paris, 1994); *Business Moskovskiye Novosti*, November 1, 1995.

Belarusian demand for electricity began to steadily increase leading into the

554.   United Nations. Economic Commission For Europe, *ENERGY/R.111/Add. 4*, July 5, 1995.

555.   Electricity output was down 20 percent during the first 10 months of the year, and totalled just 20.3 billion kwh. See British Broadcasting Corporation, *Summary of World Broadcasts, Part 1 Former USSR*, November 30, 1995.

1980s, and a conscious decision was made to cover these increments not through the construction of local generating capacity but rather through expanded imports. For example, nearby Lithuania had considerable excess electricity generating capacity which could be made available to Belarus. In 1980 Belarus was a net electricity exporter of 2.1 billion kwh. Ten years later, in 1990, it had become a net importer to the extent of some 9.5 billion kwh, reaching a maximum net import position of 10.4 billion kwh the following year. Subsequently, the breakup of the Soviet Union and the declines in demand that followed cut net imports in half by 1992.[557]

Estimates are that present generating capacity will be adequate to cover Belarusian needs up to 2001–2002, at which time additional capacity should be made available.

Energy-Related Indebtedness

A close political and economic relationship has supported a reasonably steady and reliable flow of Russian energy to Belarus but has not spared Belarus from becoming heavily indebted to Russia. Arrears totalled about 2.7 trillion rubles at the close of 1995.[558] Arrears for crude oil deliveries are minimal, perhaps due in part to the comparatively low delivered price—Belarus had been paying less than $75 per metric ton, while the price is more than $80 on the Russian domestic market.[559]

Virtually all of the 1995 debt was for natural gas consumed but not paid for. Under a 1995 bilateral agreement, Belarus was to repay its fuels and energy debts by deliveries of trucks, tractors, consumer items, and the like, but Russia has refused delivery, saying that it lacks the necessary marketing network.[560] Cash payments which were made by Belarus to Gazprom came from the International Monetary Fund Systematic Transformation Facility loan. In lieu of cash payments, Gazprom would prefer debt-equity swap arrangements.

In addition to the huge natural gas-related debt, Belarus also owes the Lithuanian State Power System about 24 billion rubles for electricity imports, but somewhat more—83 billion rubles—to Russia.[561] The debt for Russian fuel oil had reached 300 billion rubles. Belarus countered Russian payment demands by stating that Russia owes it $800 million in compensation for ecological damage caused by strategic missiles positioned on its soil and $114 million for stationing Russian troops on its territory.[562]

---

556.   *Business Moskovskiye Novosti*, November 1, 1995. Much of the generating capacity requires reconstruction. A pilot project is under way, funded by the European Bank for Reconstruction and Development at a cost of about $49 million, to rehabilitate the Orshansk thermal power plant.

557.   It is now considered more cost-effective for Belarus to buy electricity from Lithuania (from the Ignalina nuclear power plant) than from Russia, and the reliance on Lithuania is to increase. See *Interfax*, Minsk, November 13, 1995.

558.   Interfax, *Petroleum Information Agency*, Moscow, January 10, 1996.

559.   *Ibid.*

560.   Interfax, *Petroleum Information Agency*, April 27, 1995.

561.   British Broadcasting Corporation, *Summary of World Broadcasts, Part 1, Former USSR*, May 2, 1996.

Belarus and Chornobyl

Belarus has suffered immensely from the radioactive fallout caused by the accident at the Chornobyl nuclear power plant.[563] Reportedly, 70 percent of the radioactivity from the Chornobyl explosion fell on Belarus.[564] Nearly 25 percent of its territory and 22 percent of the population were affected by the Chornobyl fallout.[565] More than 6,000 square kilometers of land have been declared unsuitable for farming, and it has been disclosed that every fifth citizen of Belarus lives in an area exposed to radiation.[566] Some 130,000 people had been evacuated from contaminated zones by the spring of 1995.

Responding to the Chornobyl accident has placed a considerable drain on Belarusian finances (Table 9-10). A comparatively large, although declining, share of the annual state budget is directed toward mitigating the impact of the accident.[567]

Table 9-10
Belarus Budget Allocations for Chornobyl-Related Issues, 1992–1996

Year	Percent of State Budget
1992	12.6
1993	11.4
1994	7.4
1996	11

Sources: *FBIS-SOV*, March 2, 1995; *Journal of Commerce*, March 26, 1996.

Despite the damage inflicted by the Chornobyl accident, the possibility of constructing a nuclear power station in Belarus has not been rejected. To the contrary, nuclear power does have a future in Belarus, in the judgment of certain officials, especially if energy conservation efforts are not successful.

562.   Open Media Research Institute, *Daily Report*, February 27, 1996.

563.   Belarus was deeply disappointed that President Alyaksandr Lukashenko was not invited to attend the G-7 mini-summit in Moscow April 19-20, 1996, when nuclear safety issues were discussed. Belarus suffered most of all from the Chornobyl catastrophe, it was argued, and was the first among the CIS to declare its territory a non-nuclear area. See *FBIS-SOV*, May 9, 1996.

564.   *Washington Post*, June 24, 1995.

565.   U.S. Department of Commerce/BisNIS, *The Republic of Belarus, Commercial Overview*, April 17, 1995.

The Foreign Minister of Belarus, Uladzimir Syanko, in addressing the UN General Assembly, stated that his country's birth rate had fallen 50 percent as a result of the accident at Chornobyl. See Open Media Research Institute, *Daily Report*, September 26, 1995.

566.   *Interfax-West*, Minsk, March 18, 1996.

567.   Belarus is taking steps to ensure that it will receive an early warning should there be another nuclear power accident in the region. Measuring stations are to be erected within the 30-km exclusion zone surrounding the Ignalina nuclear power station in Lithuania. See *FBIS-SOV*, September 19, 1995.

Earlier plans to build a reactor had been scrapped in the aftermath of the Chornobyl accident but are now being revived. Three sites have been qualified as meeting IAEA standards. Two sites are in the Mogilev region, one of hardest hit by fallout from Chornobyl. If built here, the reactors would be placed underground. Construction of a 2,000 Mw facility, at a cost of $3.5 to 4 billion, would cover the difference between the amount of electricity currently consumed and the country's generating capacity.[568]

Two serious obstacles lie ahead: how to finance this costly project, and how to overcome the inevitable local opposition, which still holds vivid memories of April-May 1986 then the Chornobyl fallout reached Belarus.

---

568. *Interfax-West*, Minsk, December 26, 1996.

Source: States of the Former Soviet Union, CIA, 1992.

CHAPTER 10

Georgia

Table 10-1
Georgia at a Glance

Currency	Lari
Rate of Exchange	1.28 lari/$1 (December 1996)
Gross Domestic Product	$2.3 billion
Inflation	57.4 percent (1995)
Population	5.7 million (July 1995 est.)
By Nationality	
Georgian	70.1 percent
Armenian	8.1 percent
Russian	6.3 percent
Azeri	5.7 percent
Ossetian	3 percent
Abkhaz	1.8 percent
Other	5 percent

Sources: Central Intelligence Agency (CIA), *The World Factbook 1995*. (Washington, D.C.: CIA, 1995); *Interfax*, Tbilisi, October 4, 1995; Interfax, *Financial Information Agency*, Moscow, January 18, 1996; Open Media Research Institute, *Daily Report*, April 26, 1996; World Bank data.

Georgia voted for independence from the Soviet Union in a referendum held in October 1990. Independence subsequently was declared on April 9, 1991, but the internal political situation began to deteriorate soon thereafter. Zviad Gamsakhurdia was elected president in May 1991, but opposition to him gathered strength in the subsequent months. Fighting broke out in Georgia in December 1991, and Gamsakhurdia took refuge in southern Russia in early January 1992.

Eduard Shevardnadze returned to Georgia from Russia where he had been foreign minister, and he was designated chair of the Supreme Soviet of Georgia and head of state from 1992 to 1995.

In the interim, separatist conflicts in the Abkhazia and South Ossetia regions continued. A cease-fire was reached in South Ossetia in June 1992 and a peacekeeping force has been in place since. Fighting continued in the Abkhaz region, and Georgian forces left in September 1993.

Eduard Shevardnadze was elected president in November 1995, and the high percentage of votes he received was a welcome sign of confidence following an attempt on his life the preceding August.

Georgian domestic politics today revolve around separatist Abkhazia, which insists on forming a confederation. Russia's views on the matter are quite simple: Abkhazia must be an integral part of the Georgian federal state.[569] That position reinforces Georgia's stand.

Despite these internal political issues, the Georgian economy performed well during 1995. Indeed, Georgia was only one of two CIS countries to achieve positive GDP growth in 1995 (the other was Armenia).[570] Whether that performance can be sustained depends to a considerable degree on the willingness of Georgia's citizens to pay taxes. The 1995 tax collection rate was just 3 percent, clearly not enough for budget support.[571] Moreover, the average monthly salary, equivalent to just $5, is the lowest by far of any of the former Soviet republics.[572]

Some progress has been made on privatization, to the extent that the nongovernmental sector provided 30 percent of GDP in 1995,[573] while those working in the nongovernmental sector represented 36.3 percent of those actively employed.

Oil

Crude oil is produced in very limited amounts in Georgia (Table 10-2). Extraction averaged just 854 b/d during 1995, down from about 3,700 b/d in 1990 and far short of local requirements.[574] Georgian annual oil requirements under normal circumstances average 100,000 b/d. Surprisingly, the bulk of local production is exported rather than directed to the Batumi refinery.

---

569.   *Interfax*, Tbilisi, November 28, 1995.
570.   *Finansovyye Izvestiya*, May 14, 1996.
571.   *Financial Times*, May 22, 1996.
572.   *Finansovyye Izvestiya*, May 14, 1996.
573.   *Intercon's Daily*, May 7, 1996.
574.   Interfax, *Petroleum Information Agency*, Tbilisi, January 9, 1996, July 24, 1996, September 23, 1996, and December 4, 1996.

Table 10-2
Georgian Crude Oil Production, 1990–2000

Year	Thousand b/d
1990	3.7
1995	
Plan	2.4
Actual	0.854
1996 est.	1.7
1997 plan	2.0-3.0
2000 plan	6.0

Two joint ventures—he Georgian British Oil Company and Ioris Valley—account for all of the crude oil currently produced in Georgia, both having started up in 1995. The Georgian British Oil Company Ltd. was set up with JP Kenny Exploration and Production Ltd.(JKX) a British company. Gruzneft has a venture, Ioris Valley, with Switzerland's National Petroleum Corporation Ltd.[575]

JKX has restored the Ninotsminda oil field in eastern Georgia to production via a production sharing agreement, reaching about 1,400 b/d by mid-1996.[576] The well workover program is eventually expected to raise output to 3,000 b/d.[577] Two nearby oilfields—South Samgori and Samgori-Patardzeuli (known together as just Samgori)—will be the focus of subsequent development.[578]

There is one refinery in Georgia—Batumi, located in Adzhariya—which is capable of processing about 160,000 b/d. This refinery is technologically obsolete and will require considerable upgrading for it to be competitive. At present it is virtually idle, having processed an average of just 774 b/d during 1995.[579] Given limited domestic production, the refinery has had to rely heavily on imported crude oil from Russia. But crude oil imports have drastically declined in recent years, from 80,000 to 90,000 b/d during the latter half of the 1980s to no more than 4,000 b/d in 1994. The drop in crude oil imports originally had been offset by imports of petroleum products from Russia, which had jumped from 40,000 b/d in 1988 to 80,000 b/d during 1990–1991. But these fell off to less than 2,000 b/d by 1994[580] and further to about 490 b/d during 1995.

In marketing there is one joint venture of note. The state-owned Greek oil refining company EKO and the Georgian state oil company have established a joint venture to set up a network of gasoline stations in Georgia and as well to market EKO oil products.[581]

575. Interfax, *Petroleum information Agency*, Tbilisi, September 23 and December 4, 1996.
576. Interfax, *Petroleum Information Agency*, Tbilisi, June 11, 1996.
577. *Oil & Gas Journal*, April 8, 1996.
578. *Oil & Gas Journal*, May 27, 1996.
579. British Broadcasting Corporation, *Summary of World Broadcasts, Part 1, Former USSR*, February 8, 1996.
580. OECD/IEA, *Oil and Gas Flows in the Black Sea Area: Problems of Interconnections and Transit*, IEA/NMC(96)14, January 25, 1996.

Natural Gas

Georgia changed natural gas suppliers in 1991, switching from Russia to Turkmenistan and paying for the natural gas with tea, wine, and other commodities. But Georgia built up arrears that reached $450 million by the end of October 1995, accounting for nearly half Georgia's total foreign debt.[582] In the past, payment guarantees for the natural gas had been provided by the Georgian government, but those guarantees were withdrawn in July 1995. Turkmenistan stopped delivering natural gas to Georgia in September 1995 when the Georgian debt became unacceptably high.[583]

For Georgia, which has very little natural gas of its own, consumption essentially is equal to imports (Table 10-3). A reported 7 bcm of natural gas must be made available if normal needs are to be met.[584]

Table 10-3
Natural Gas Consumption, 1994–1995 (million cubic meters)

Year	Volume	Imported from Russia	Imported from Turkmenistan
1995	954.8	300	644
1994	2,800	500	2,000
Note: In one of the better years, 1990, natural gas extraction totalled 60 million cubic meters but most of that has now been lost. It is unclear then how consumption could have totalled 2.8 bcm in 1994.			
Source: Interfax, *Petroleum Information Agency*, Tbilisi, February 1, 1996.			

The volumes actually supplied by Turkmenistan during 1995 were a bare 40 percent of the 1.56 bcm that had been contracted.[585] It is the Tbilisi power plant which has suffered the most in terms of reduced supplies. This facility consumes about 70 percent of available natural gas supplies, with the remainder directed to the Rustavi steel mill. Reduced gas supplies translate into restricted supplies of electricity to the country.

Georgia has moved to establish a private company to import natural gas. This company is to operate on a commercial basis and without state guarantees. The capital will be formed out of contributions from the major natural gas and electricity consuming enterprises in the country, which are the company's founders.

Several of the major natural gas consumers in Georgia have entered into contracts with Turkmen gas producers, putting matters on a strictly commercial basis

---

581.   Open Media Research Institute, *Daily Digest*, September 21, 1995. This source also noted that at present the mafia has a virtual monopoly on gasoline distribution in Georgia.

582.   Interfax, *Petroleum Information Agency*, October 16, 1995.

583.   Unpaid bills reportedly totalled $417 million when Turkmenistan decided to cut off delivers in 1995. See *Reuters*, Tbilisi, May 5, 1996.

584.   Interfax, *Financial Information Agency*, Tbilisi, June 11, 1996.

585.   *FBIS-SOV*, February 2, 1996.

and bypassing the state altogether. Turkmen natural gas is also provided to Georgia in lieu of transit fees for those volumes crossing Georgia enroute to Armenia.

Coal

Coal mining in Georgia has suffered from a combination of depleted reserves, obsolescent equipment, and a severe shortage of working capital. Coal mines produced a reported 2.3 million tons in 1970, but have gradually declined since. By 1993 indigenous coal supply, less than 300,000 tons, was just a fraction of earlier levels.

Electric Power

Georgia's sole indigenous energy source of any significance is hydropower. Output at Inguri, the largest hydropower station in the country, has fallen to about 2.2 million kwh per day because of low water reserves.[586] The larger share of that output is directed to Abkhazia, much to the displeasure of the Georgian Energy Department.

Most of Georgia's hydropower potential remains untouched, in large part because Moscow saw to it that plentiful supplies of cheap natural gas were available and making it unnecessary to invest in building dams and accompanying infrastructure. Lacking the funds to expand hydroelectric power generation and with natural gas supplies sharply reduced because of heavy arrears, Georgians are now forced to do without electricity except for a few hours every day.

Georgia has ample electricity generating capacity, with 2,700 Mw of hydroelectric power and 1,700 Mw of thermal generating capacity.[587] As a Georgian government official has stated, "Georgia faces no electricity shortages, what it faces instead is a shortage of paying consumers."[588] Much of the thermal capacity stands idle for lack of fuels.[589]

Power generation hit its peak in Georgia in 1989 and has fallen steadily since then (Table 10-4). Heavy dependence on hydropower puts the country in a vulnerable position because of the vagaries of weather. Moreover, the hydropower generating facilities are worn out and require replacement. The World Bank is to loan Georgia $35 million for just that purpose.

---

586.   British Broadcasting Corporation, *Summary of World Broadcasts, Part 1, Former USSR*, February 1, 1996.

587.   *Interfax*, April 21, 1996.

588.   A comment by Shota Maisuradze, deputy chairman of the Georgian Power Production Department. See *Interfax*, Tbilisi, November 8, 1995. Georgia's electricity generating capacity would seem sufficient for most needs.

589.   The United States was to help improve power supplies for the 1995-96 winter by providing about 700,000 barrels of fuel oil for the Bardabani power station. See British Broadcasting Corporation, *Summary of World Broadcasts, Part 1, Former USSR*, November 20, 1995.

Table 10-4
Electricity Generation in Georgia, 1970–1995

Year	Billion kwh
1970	9.0
1975	11.6
1980	14.7
1985	14.4
1989	15.8
1990	15
1991	13.3
1993	9.1
1995	6.8

Sources: *Post-Soviet Geography*, April 1992; Central Intelligence Agency (CIA), *The World Factbook, 1995* (Washington, D.C.: CIA, 1995); *Interfax*, Tbilisi, April 21, 1996.

Electricity consumption has also fallen, from 18.1 billion kwh in 1990 to 7.7 billion kwh in 1995. Previously, substantial amounts of power were imported from Russia (3 to 4 billion kwh per year) to cover the gap between supply and demand. In 1995, however, Georgia imported just 0.6 billion kwh from Russia.

Georgia also found it necessary in the past to import electricity from Turkey and Azerbaijan. In lieu of cash payments, Georgia has begun to compensate electricity exports to both counties, but Georgia must supply 2 kwh for each 1 kwh that had been imported.[590] Georgia also in arrears to Russia for past electricity imports, but repayment has not yet begun.

A high voltage power line between Russia and Georgia is to be put back into service, to the benefit of consumers in the western part of the country.[591]

Georgia as a Pipeline Transit Country

The deterioration of the Georgian coal, crude oil, and natural gas base adds even greater value to Georgia as a transit country for crude oil from Azerbaijan and possibly from Kazakstan. Georgia will have the opportunity to tap into the transit pipelines. Equally important, foreign investors, attracted to Georgia by the proposed pipelines, may be encouraged to explore for oil and natural gas onshore and offshore in the Black Sea and to engage in a variety of other oil-related activities.[592]

---

590.   British Broadcasting Corporation, *Summary of World Broadcasts, Part 1, Former USSR*, June 13, 1996.

591.   *FBIS-SOV*, December 5, 1995.

592.   As an example, Howe Baker Development Company (United States) is to establish a joint venture in Georgia to build a series of small oil refineries. The first such facility is to be located 25 km east of Tbilisi and is to have a processing capacity of just 1,000 b/d. It will refine locally produced crude oil. See Interfax, *Petroleum Information Agency*, Tbilisi, June 28, 1996.

The AIOC made Georgia a winner when it decided to move its early oil to be produced offshore Baku in the Caspian Sea through both western and northern routes. The western route will follow the path of the Baku-Batumi pipeline,[593] and a new terminal will be constructed near Supsa. This pipeline unfortunately is in very poor condition and will require a major reconstruction effort to restore it to acceptable operating condition.

Georgia has created an International Oil Corporation that will be in charge of restoring the oil pipeline running through Georgia and building other means of transporting, refining, and selling oil.[594] An oil terminal with a storage capacity of 1.6 million bbl is to be constructed off Supsa.[595]

But the real gains lie ahead. In the coming months the AIOC will have to determine by what pipeline route its so-called later oil will be moved to market. The AIOC currently favors a pipeline from Baku through Tbilisi (Georgia) to the Turkish port of Ceyhan on the Mediterranean Sea. At its peak, the later oil may average as much as 700,000 b/d. Moving this much oil through Georgia would bring a financial windfall in terms of transit fees, job creation, and the building and operation of supporting infrastructure.

Georgia may also benefit as a transit country for Turkmen natural gas destined for Turkey.[596] Additional transit revenues would be welcome, as would access to a more regular and reliable supply of natural gas. Yet some observers consider that pipeline transit through Georgia may not be any more secure than pipeline transit through Chechnya (Russia). Abkhazia separatists are still active as Abkhazia has run itself as an independent state, when it routed government troops after a year-long war.

---

593.   The Baku-Batumi pipeline, closed down in 1988, had carried Azeri crude oil to the Batumi oil refinery, located in Adzhariya. This pipeline is 926 km in length, of which 446 km lies within Georgian boundaries. See *Neft i Kapital*, June 1996.

Rebuilding this pipeline will be a costly undertaking and readying it for operation will take from 15 to 18 months.

594.   Interfax, *Petroleum Information Agency*, Tbilisi, November 15, 1995.

595.   Open Media Research Institute, *Daily Report*, November 9, 1995.

596.   *FBIS-SOV*, May 13, 1996. There is a preliminary agreement between Turkey and Turkmenistan for the purchase of 15 billion cubic meters of natural gas.

Source: States of the Former Soviet Union, CIA, 1992.

CHAPTER 11

Kyrgyzstan

Table 11-1
Kyrgyzstan at a Glance

Currency	Som
Rate of Exchange	11.6/$1 (April 19, 1996)
Gross Domestic Product	$2.8 billion (1994)
Inflation	31.9 percent (1995 est.)
Population	6.5 million (July 1995 est.)
By Nationality	
Tajik	64.9 percent
Uzbek	25 percent
Russian	3.5 percent
Other	6.6 percent

Sources: Central Intelligence Agency (CIA), *The World Factbook 1995*. (Washington, D. C.: CIA, 1995); Interfax, *Financial Information Agency*, Moscow, December 20, 1995; Interfax, *Financial Information Agency*, Bishkek, January 17, 1996; *Finansovyye Izvestiya*, March 7, 1996; Open Media Research Institute, *Daily Report*, April 26, 1996; World Bank data.

Kyrgyzstan, one of the more isolated of the former Soviet republics, declared independence on August 31, 1991. The president of Kyrgyzstan is Askar Akayev, who was first elected to his post by the Supreme Soviet in October 1990, and was reelected by popular vote in October 1991. There were no other candidates. The president received a vote of confidence in a national referendum held in January 1994.

Kyrgyzstan's economy is based largely on agriculture; its industrial base is quite small. Kyrgyzstan had been a rather significant supplier of antimony, mercury, and uranium ores to the former Soviet Union. In the early 1990s at least, Kyrgyzstan ranked third in the world as a producer of mercury.

Kyrgyzstan has been rewarded by international lending institutions for having one of the more progressive economic policies. As a result, Kyrgyzstan has attracted more aid per capita than any other former Soviet republic.[597] The relatively low inflation rate in 1995 seems even more remarkable when compared with

---

597. *Financial Times*, June 1, 1995.

an inflation rate of 466 percent in 1993 and 87 percent in 1994.

Domestic Energy Supply

Kyrgyzstan is clearly among the Have-Nots of the Near Abroad in terms of domestic energy production.Unlike its Central Asian neighbors Kazakstan, Turkmenistan, and Uzbekistan, domestic production of primary energy in Kyrgyzstan has been, and likely always will be, extremely modest (Table 11-2). Imports will continue to be important in bridging the gap between supply and demand. The best hope is to continue to develop potential hydroelectric power, which is far from exhausted, and to utilize exports of electricity to balance imports of oil and natural gas.

Table 11-2
Primary Energy Production in Kyrgyzstan, 1970–1990

Form of Energy	Unit of Measure	1970	1975	1980	1985	1990
Crude oil	Million tons	0.3	0.2	0.2	0.2	0.2
Coal	Million tons	3.7	4.3	4.0	4.0	4.0
Natural gas	Billion cubic m.	0.4	0.3	0.1	0.1	0.1
Source: *Energeticheskaya Programma Kyrgyzstana*, Bishkek, 1992.						

The modest amounts of crude oil produced have been exported to Uzbekistan for refining. Kyrgyzstan has no refining capability of its own.[598] Thus, petroleum product imports play a key role in meeting domestic requirements. Throughout the 1970s and 1980s, the import of petroleum products ranged between a minimum of 48,000 b/d to a maximum of 64,000 b/d, reached at the beginning of the 1980s. Since then, petroleum product requirements have slowly declined.

In 1992 the Kyrgyz State Energy Company and the Ministry of Economy and Finance developed the long-range *Energy Program of Kyrgyzstan*. This program, unacceptably optimistic, envisaged very substantial increases in the domestic supply of coal and in electricity generation (Table 11-3). Crude oil and natural gas production had been held constant, for want of a better understanding of the future.

---

598.   A mini-refinery operating on natural gas condensate has been built at Orlovka. It was designed to produce about 500 b/d, sufficient to cover about one-quarter of Bishkek's daily needs. But financial difficulties plagued its operation from the very beginning, the biggest problem being securing refinery feedstock at a price that would allow this mini-refinery to show a profit. See *East Bloc Energy*, July 1995.

Table 11-3
Planned Development of Kyrgyz Fuel and Energy Supplies, 1995-2010

Form of Energy	Unit of Measure	1995	2000	2005	2010
Coal	Thousand tons	4,200	5,300	6,350	7,000
Crude oil	Thousand tons	135	135	135	135
Natural gas	Million cu. m.	30	30	30	30
Electric power	Billion kwh	14.9	19.2	25.6	34.3
Source: Energeticheskaya Programma Kyrgyzstana, Bishkek, 1992.					

These plans have been overtaken by events of the day. The lack of capital, above all, coupled with the decline in industrial output, has rearranged at least the near-term future for Kyrgyzstan.

Crime and Corruption

In a speech before Kyrgyz law enforcement officials, Kyrgyz President Askar Akayev underscored the pervasive economic role now played by crime and corruption. Among other things, he noted that:

☐ Criminal income was equivalent to almost 9 percent of the country's gross domestic product.

☐ Economic crime exceeded entire sectors of the economy, in terms of scale.

☐ More than half of all petroleum products imports are smuggled.[599]

Those activities outside the law sap the economic vitality of Kyrgyzstan and impede its democratic progress.

Despite these concerns, expressed by the president in 1995, corruption continued unabated during 1996. It is a painful problem for Kyrgyzstan, he admitted in a year-end speech. "It is eroding not only government structures but also society, and represent(s) a serious danger for society." He promised to "struggle against corruption until a victorious end, especially with regard to the return of loans spent on purposes other than (that) intended...."[600]

Oil

Production of crude oil fell to just 1,760 b/d in 1994, about 10 percent less than what had been planned but roughly matching 1993 output (Table 11-4).[601] Of that amount, 1,360 b/d was sent to the Fergana refinery (Uzbekistan) for processing, on

---

599.   *FBIS-SOV*, July 14, 1995.
600.   *Interfax*, Bishkek, December 29, 1996.
601.   Interfax, *Petroleum Report*, April 21-28, 1995.

the condition that the petroleum products be returned to Kyrgyzstan. A further decline, to 1,500 b/d was registered during 1996, far short of meeting domestic requirements placed at about 40,000 b/d. The gap between supply and demand continues to be met through imports by rail from Uzbekistan, Kazakstan, Russia, and Turkmenistan.[602]

LUKoil has taken a position in the oil sector of Kyrgyzstan by agreeing to supply petroleum products originating at the Shymkent refinery in Kazakstan. Shymkent in turn processes crude oil supplied by LUKoil. LUKoil has not been shy about extending its market reach outside Russia and does so in often a forceful and uncompromising way.

Table 11-4
Crude Oil Production in Kyrgyzstan, 1991–1996

Year	Barrels/day
1991	2,800
1992	2,500
1994	1,760
1996 est.	1,500
Sources: *Platt's Oilgram News*, July 20, 1994 and August 7, 1996.	

A 10,000 b/d topping plant at Jalalabad was completed for operations in October 1996. A 50-50 joint venture between Kyrgyzneft, the state oil company, and Kyrgoil Corporation (a subsidiary of French Hydrocarbons, Ltd. of Canada), its output will be just 20 percent gasoline, 10 percent jet fuel, and 38.5 percent diesel fuel, with fuel oil accounting for the remainder.[603] Not surprisingly, the gasoline yield falls short of meeting demand. It had been planned to build a series of these topping plants but that has been set aside. Instead, the refinery will be upgraded, with capacity boosted to 20,000 to 25,000 b/d to raise the gasoline and jet fuel output.

The Kyrgoil-Kyrgyz joint venture also has been granted the exclusive right to repair large numbers of old oil wells and to drill new wells in the Fergana Valley. As with many such new joint ventures, early promises of what will be accomplished can be misleading when reality later sets in. For example, the Kyrgoil-Kyrgyz joint venture stated that it hoped to boost Kyrgyz crude oil production to 25,000 b/d within three years, thus matching the future requirements of the Jalalabad refinery. Circumstances cloud the prospect of success.

---

602.   British Broadcasting Corporation, *Summary of World Broadcasts, Part 1, Former USSR*, October 11, 1996.

603.   British Broadcasting Corporation, *Summary of World Broadcasts, Part 1, Former USSR*, October 11, 1996. See also *Finansovyye Izvestiya*, October 8, 1996.

Natural Gas

Natural gas production in Kyrgyzstan is extremely small, and imports cover the bulk of requirements. Kyrgyzstan imports natural gas from Uzbekistan but has not been diligent in paying for it. Kyrgyzgas, the national gas company, has been selling natural gas at a loss, mainly because of nonpayment by electric power generating plants and heavy subsidization of the domestic sector. Residential consumption is not metered, and consumers are charged flat rates that are below full cost recovery.[604]

An agreement had been reached that Uzbekistan would supply about 1.3 bcm of natural gas during 1995, with payment to be made in barter. When arrears reached $8 million, Uzbekistan cut off natural gas deliveries until the debt was paid off. The debt has not been repaid, but in an agreement between the presidents of the two countries, gas deliveries were resumed in early December 1995. Accounts were to be settled in 1996.[605]

Table 11-5
Kyrgyz Natural Gas Production, 1991–1994

Year	Million cubic meters
1991	70
1992	68
1993	41
1994	39

Sources: Interfax, *Petroleum Report*, April 21-28, 1995; *Platt's Oilgram News*, July 20, 1994.

Kyrgyzstan blames the nonpayment issue on Kazakstan, which has been importing electricity from Kyrgyzstan but has run up a considerable debt. Had Kazakstan paid its bills, then Kyrgyzstan could settle its arrears with Uzbekistan, the argument goes.

Kyrgyzstan is simply unable to meet the payments schedule for natural gas and has agreed to settle its debts with Russia through debt-equity swaps.[606] Under this arrangement, the Russian government will have the right to select those facilities it is interested in. Undoubtedly, the most financially viable plants will be chosen. The Russian government in turn can sell its shares to Russian buyers.

Electric power generation accounts for the bulk of the natural gas consumed in Kyrgyzstan. Industry takes most of the remainder; households and so-called communal use is comparatively modest, at around 11 percent of the total.

---

604.   The flat rates are based on the size of the premises, the number of occupants, and artificially low gas consumption standards. See United Nations Economic and Social Council/Economic Commission for Europe/ *Energy/WP.3/GE.4/R.9*, May 14, 1996.

605.   British Broadcasting Corporation, *Summary of World Broadcasts, Part 1, Former USSR*, December 13, 1995.

606.   Open Media Research Institute, *Daily Report*, January 26, 1996.

Table 11-6
Kyrgyzstan Imports of Natural Gas, 1993–1996

Year	Billion cubic meters
1993	1.8
1994 plan	1.4
1995	0.9
1996 plan	1.0

Note: the 1993 volume includes gas originally destined for Kazakstan but illegally diverted to Kyrgyzstan.

Sources: *East Bloc Energy*, May 1994; Interfax, *Petroleum Report*, April 8-15, 1994; British Broadcasting Corporation, *Summary of World Broadcasts, Part 1, Former USSR*, February 15, 1996.

Electric Power

Although the energy supply in Kyrgyzstan is constrained by the very limited coal, natural gas, and crude oil base, the country does enjoy a respectable hydroelectric power potential. That potential has been put to reasonable use over the years and has been providing roughly two-thirds of the electricity generated.[607] Indeed, the generation of electricity in Kyrgyzstan (Table 11-7) for a number of years has exceeded domestic requirements, enabling considerable amounts to be exported. For example, electricity generation in 1995 exceeded domestic needs by 4 to 5 billion kwh.[608]

---

607.   Analysts suggest that only 8 percent of the country's hydropower potential has been developed. See *USEA Report*, June 1994.

Table 11-7
Electricity Generation in Kyrgyzstan, 1970–1996

Year	Billion kwh
1970	3.5
1975	4.4
1980	9.2
1985	10.5
1990	13.3
1991	14
1994 est.	12.715
1995 est.	12.283
1996 est.	13.2

Sources: British Broadcasting Corporation, *Summary of World Broadcasts, Part 1, Former USSR*, November 30, 1995; Interfax, Bishkek, November 1, 1996.

Domestic electricity tariffs continue to be heavily subsidized, yet consumers continue to incur heavy debt obligations to the Kyrgyz Energy Holding Company.[609] Kyrgyzstan is to deregulate electricity tariffs sometime between 1996 and 1998.

The absence of domestic fossil fuels and the concomitant availability of hydropower clearly reflected in Kyrgyzstan's installed electricity generating capacity. Hydropower makes up almost 81 percent of the total (Table 11-8).

---

608.   *FBIS-SOV*, February 21, 1996.

609.   Open Materials Research Institute, *Daily Report*, September 2, 1995.

Table 11-8
Installed Electricity Generating Capacity in Kyrgyzstan, 1993

Type	Thousand kilowatts
Thermal	661
Bishkek no. 1	611
Osh	50
Hydroelectric	2,755
Bystrov	9
Alamedin	31
At-Bashi	40
Toktogul	1,200
Kurpsay	800
Tash-Kumyr	450
Shamaldy-Say	45
Uch-Kurgan	180
Total	3,416

Source: *Energeticheskaya Programma Kyrgyzstana*, Bishkek, 1992.

Nonetheless, the vagaries of weather are quickly reflected in hydroelectric power generation. In years of drought, supply declines; in years of abundant rainfall, it increases. For Kyrgyzstan, fluctuations in hydropower have been almost directly reflected in electricity export levels. Fluctuations in hydropower supply also are reflected in coal import requirements, although generally Kyrgyzstan has been a net importer of coal, if only in relatively small amounts.

Electricity exports and exchanges will continue to play an important role. Kyrgyzstan has hopes of providing Pakistan with 3 to 6 billion kwh of electricity annually, as a means of generating much-needed hard currency. Financing the construction of a new power transmission line between Kyrgyzstan and Pakistan, however, has encountered difficulties.

Electricity is to be exchanged with Uzbekistan, in part to help pay for natural gas imports from that country. Under this agreement, Kyrgyzstan is to supply 1.1 billion kwh to Uzbekistan and in return will receive 675 million kwh of electricity and 400 mcm of natural gas for the Bishkek heat and power plant.[610]

Coal

The coal mining sector continues to struggle against deteriorating working condi-

---

610.   British Broadcasting Corporation, *Summary of World Broadcasts, Part 1, Former USSR*, February 1, 1996.

tions at the mines and deteriorating living conditions for the workers. With little investment capital available to create new coal mining capacities, coal extraction continues to decline (Table 11-9). The impact of this decline is heightened by rising prices for imported natural gas and petroleum products.

Table 11-9
Coal Mining in Kyrgyzstan, 1993–1995

Year	Million tons
1993	1.7
1994	0.8
1995 plan	0.5
Source: *FBIS-SOV*, June 12, 1995.	

The coal industry is also disadvantaged because of mine location. The coal mines are located in southern Osh Oblast but delivery to domestic consumers involves transit across Uzbekistan and Kazakstan, which in turn require dollar payments for rail cars and transit fees.[611]

Gold

Kyrgyzstan has another natural resource in addition to hydropower, and that is gold (Table 11-10). Although not now a major producer, Kyrgyzstan is to benefit from a joint venture with Cameco (Canada) to develop the Kumtor gold ore deposit.[612] A sharp jump in gold output by 1998 is based on the successful development of Kumtor, where gold output is to reach 15 to 20 tons by 1997. The first commercial production at Kumtor is now not expected until the first quarter 1997, which puts the hoped-for output in considerable jeopardy.[613]

---

611.   *FBIS-SOV*, July 6, 1994.

612.   The Kyrgyz government signed a contract with Cameco in December 1992 to develop the Kumtor gold deposit. A joint venture, the Kumtor Operating Company, was formed in May 1994, and construction of facilities began in July 1995. The first gold bars were to be produced in 1997. *See FBIS-SOV*, September 7, 1995.

In an unusual arrangement, the joint venture will produce and sell all the gold, with neither party having rights to this valuable commodity. The revenues will be placed in an offshore account and will be distributed in proportion to the participants' share in the joint venture—two-thirds to Kyrgyzstan and one-third to Cameco. The Kumtor joint venture is the largest private capital investment in Kyrgyzstan.

Table 11-10
Gold Mining in Kyrgyzstan, 1994–1998

Year	Tons
1994	2
1995 plan	4
1998 est.	25-30
Source: *Interfax*, Moscow, December 20, 1995	

Santa Fe Pacific Gold Corporation (United States) has concluded a joint venture (designated Solton Sary) with Kyrgyzaltyn, the state mining concern, to explore for gold in an area 320 km southeast of Bishkek.[614]

---

613.   *Interfax,* Bishkek, December 17, 1996.
614.   *Interfax*, Bishkek, June 18, 1996.

Source: States of the Former Soviet Union, CIA, 1992.

CHAPTER 12

Moldova

Table 12-1
Moldova at a Glance

Currency:	The leu (plural-lei), introduced November 29, 1993
Exchange Rate:	4.5405 lei/$1 (April 19, 1996)
Gross Domestic Product:	$3.7 billion (1994)
Inflation:	24 percent (1995)
Population:	4,473,000 (July, 1994 estimate)
By Nationality	
Moldavian/Romanian	64.5 percent
Ukrainian	13.8 percent
Russian	13 percent
Gagauz	3.5 percent
Jewish	1.5 percent
Bulgarian	2.0 percent
Other	1.7 percent

Sources: *FBIS-SOV*, December 26, 1995: *FBIS-SOV*, November 28, 1995; *The Washington Post*, April 14, 1996; Central Intelligence Agency (CIA), *The World Factbook 1995* (Washington, D. C.: CIA, 1995); U.S. Department of Commerce, International Trade Administration, *Moldova- Trade Figures*, April 1996; Open Media Research Institute, *Daily Report*, April 26, 1996; World Bank data, World Bank data.

The territory of present-day Moldova had constituted the eastern part of Romania until the Soviet Union annexed the region in 1940 under the secret Molotov-Ribbentrop pact.[615] During the late 1980s, there were calls for creation of a separate state and reunification with Romania—the language and culture of Moldova is almost identical to that of neighboring Romania. Ethnic Russian and Ukrainians in the Trans-Dniester region, a narrow slice of territory in eastern Moldova, bordering Ukraine, feared just such a reunification.

Declaration of an independent Trans-Dniestrian Moldavian Republic was made

---

615.   Albert Ciafre, "Moldova in Transition," *Surviving Together*, Summer 1995.

in September 1990. The Trans-Dniester, unlike the rest of Moldova, had never been part of Romania. Troops from the (then) Soviet 14th Army backed a 1992 rebellion by the Trans-Dniester's Communists, minority Russians, and Ukrainians, which preserved the region as a Russian-aligned enclave.[616] Since that time, Russian troops have helped keep the Trans-Dniester government in power, which is comprised of hard-line, former Soviet bureaucrats and military officers. There has been an uneasy truce between Moldova and Trans-Dniester since the 1992 rebellion.

Moldova declared its independence from the former Soviet Union on August 27, 1991, and on December 8, Mircea Snegur was elected president. Not long after that, the country became immersed in a brief but costly civil war, brought on by the fear that Moldova might reunite with Russia—a fear which has now very much eased. Some 700,000 mainly Russian-speaking population on the left bank of the Dnestr River took to the streets. Hundreds were killed in the ensuing clashes.

The Gagauz minority in the south of the country has also declared its autonomy from the rest of Moldova. The Moldavian government in response has made considerable concessions to the Turkic-speaking minority.

Despite these internal disruptions, Moldova has done well in its movement away from a command economy and has been hailed by the World Bank and the Council of Europe as a model of post-communist economic and political reform.[617] At the same time, Russian influence still bears heavily on Moldova. Indeed, Moldova is the only former Soviet republic where Moscow keeps its forces without a formal agreement on military bases or any other accord.[618] An agreement was reached in August 1994 under which the Russian 14th Army would be withdrawn within three years.

Industry in Moldova had been organized to supply markets in the former Soviet Union, as it had in the other republics. Moldova concentrated on the manufacture of consumer goods and defense-related products. Now it is trying, with only limited success, to reorient its trade toward the West. The limited consumer appeal of what it has to offer and the lack of capital to diversify and upgrade quality largely confines Moldova's markets to the former Soviet Union. Moreover, the absence of any political settlement in the breakaway regions of Trans-Dnestr, where there is still a large Russian army presence, and in Gagauz in the south continue to discourage any potential foreign investor.

Energy Supply

Moldova has no coal, crude oil, or natural gas of its own and must look to imports from Russia, Ukraine, and Romania to cover its needs. Despite unfavorable political and economic conditions, the import of fuel and energy has held up comparatively well the past several years (Table 12-2). In 1995 requirements were placed at 3 bcm for natural gas and 40,000 b/d for petroleum products.[619] Natural gas imports

---

616.   *Washington Post*, May 18, 1996.

617.   *Financial Times*, October 13, 1995.

618.   *Financial Times*, September 1, 1994.

were short of requirements but not by much. Petroleum product imports, however, were probably no more than half the level hoped for.

Moldova's heavy reliance on imported energy does not imply that consumers make the most efficient use of what they have. On the contrary, energy input per unit of output in Moldova is probably five to six times greater than in the West. For example, current fuel consumption in electricity generation is double to triple Soviet-era averages.[620]

Moldova-Gas holds a monopoly over natural gas imports, while three-quarters of the petroleum product imports are handled by the State Fuel Production Association. Both organizations are to be privatized.

Table 12-2
Moldavian Fuels and Energy Imports, 1993–1995

Commodity	Unit of Measure	1993	1994	1995
Fuel oil	Million metric tons	1.045	0.507	0.534*
Gasoline	Thousand metric tons	111	148	0.200 plan
Diesel fuel	Thousand metric tons	463	370	0.400 plan
Coal	Million metric tons	n.a.	2.11	1.9
Natural gas	Billion cubic meters	3.09	2.986	2.8
Electricity	Billion kwh	n.a.	0.615 1.7*	

*January-September 1995 only.

Sources: British Broadcasting Corporation, *Summary of World Broadcasts, Part 1, Former USSR*, November 16, 1995; Interfax, *Petroleum Information Agency*, Chisinau, October 30, 1995; Interfax, *Financial Information Agency*, Chisinau, August 17, 1995; *FBIS-SOV*, February 7, 1995 and February 2, 1995.

Moldova is heavily in debt for its energy imports. Two repayment variants are being considered: debt-equity swaps and turning the debt into a state credit. The latter option is opposed by the International Monetary Fund in that it would place an additional heavy burden on the state budget. At the same time, the country's natural gas debt was almost matched by domestic customer arrears.

Moldova perhaps surprisingly is the second largest energy-related debtor to Russia among the Near Abroad countries, surpassed only by Ukraine. At the beginning of December 1996 Moldova owed Russia 2.156 trillion rubles, all for natural gas.[621] Moldova was supplied with an estimated 3.16 bcm of Russian gas during 1996, an improvement over recent years, despite its heavy arrears.[622] As

---

619.   British Broadcasting Corporation, *Summary of World Broadcasts, Part 1, Former USSR*, November 9, 1995; *FBIS-SOV*, February 2, 1995.

620.   *FBIS-SOV*, January 29, 1996.

621.   British Broadcasting Corporation, *Summary of World Broadcasts, Part 1, Former USSR*, January 3, 1997.

noted elsewhere, Moldova is important to Gazprom as a transit country, and Russia could not cut off gas deliveries without jeopardizing foreign export markets and for that reason the gas continues to flow.

Natural Gas

All of the 3 bcm of gas that the economy requires must be imported, and Russia has been the sole source to date. Of the 3.1 bcm of gas marketed in Moldova in 1993, about 15.4 percent was consumed by the household/commercial sector and a comparable volume by industry. Power generation was by far the largest user, accounting for 50 percent of total natural gas marketed in 1993.

Russia delivers natural gas to Moldova via two export pipelines.[623] One of these pipelines transits north Moldova enroute to customers in Central Europe; a second transits Moldova enroute to southern Europe.[624] In 1994 Moldova received a total of 3 bcm of natural gas from these pipelines, but it was not able to pay for most of the gas consumed. In partial repayment, and in order to ensure a stable and reliable supply of Russian gas to Moldova and as well the transit of natural gas to Central and Eastern Europe through the Moldavian gas pipeline network, a joint stock company was set up involving Gazprom and Moldovagaz.[625] Gazprom holds a 50 percent share in this new company.

A repayment program worked out in October 1995 calls for various Moldavian enterprises to ship to Russia certain products having a total value of $49 million. In addition, about $52 million in unpaid debts will be written off as a result of services provided by the Moldavian-Russian joint venture Gazsnabtranzit.[626] In addition, Moldova's national gas company, Moldovagaz, is to build employee housing for Gazprom as partial repayment of Moldova's debt to Gazprom.

Moldovagaz is to be privatized by splitting it into 43 joint stock companies, 80 percent of which will remain state-owned and 20 percent will be sold to workers. Subsequently, Moldovagaz will be reorganized into a holding company.[627]

Oil

Moldova has no crude oil production of its own and no refining capacity. Oil requirements must be met through the import of petroleum products. Russia is the largest supplier, with small volumes provided by Ukraine and a variety of others.

---

622.   Interfax, *Petroleum Information Agency*, Moscow, December 17, 1996.

623.   The length of transmission gas pipelines transiting Moldova totals about 600 km. These pipelines carry Russian natural gas to markets in Romania, Bulgaria, Greece, Albania, and Turkey. About 18 bcm of natural gas transited Moldova in 1994, and this level was to increase to 21.5 bcm in 1995. By 2000, the volume of transit natural gas is to almost double, to 35 bcm. See Interfax, *Petroleum Report*, February 24-March 3, 1995; *FBIS-SOV*, February 2, 1995.

624.   *FBIS-SOV*, May 15, 1995.

625.   Open Media Research Institute, *Daily Digest*, May 22, 1995.

626.   *Finansovyye Izvestiya*, October 10, 1995.

627.   Interfax, *Petroleum Information Agency*, Chisinau, October 30, 1995.

Product imports have steadily declined, from about 98,000 b/d in 1990, to under 20,000 b/d in 1994. Product imports from Ukraine can be expected to increase at the expense of Russia because of lower transportation costs.

The State Production Amalgamation for Fuel imports 75 percent of the petroleum products consumed in Moldova. It too is to be reorganized, into the Kirex-Petrol SA joint stock company. The state will hold 80 percent of the shares, 8.27 percent will be sold at auction, and 11.73 percent will be distributed to workers in exchange for privatization vouchers.[628]

LUKoil, through a cooperative agreement signed in early December 1995, is to assist Moldova in refining, transportation, and marketing.[629] At the same time, Moldova is attempting to develop non-Russian sources of supply, and to that end it signed an agreement purchasing about 15 million barrels of crude oil from Iran for delivery between July 1995 and July 1996.[630] Under this arrangement, the crude oil will be refined in Romania and Greece, and the petroleum products will be made available to Moldova.

A joint venture has been established between Moldova and Resources Development Company (United States) to explore for and develop crude oil and natural gas in the southern portion of the country.[631] The US company was given a 20-year concession to drill in Moldova's southwestern Veleni oil field. Prospects are quite modest, as it is thought that production might average 2,400 b/d.

A Moldavian-Greek joint venture—Terminal S.A—is to build an oil terminal with an annual capacity of 24,000 b/d at Giurgiulesti, on southern Moldova's Danube coast.[632]

Electric Power

Virtually all of the electricity generated in Moldova is provided by conventional thermal power plants (Table 12-3). One station, the Dniester power station, itself produces 85 percent of the total.[633] Very little originates at hydroelectric power plants, and there are no nuclear power generating facilities in the country. All the coal, natural gas, and residual fuel oil burned in electric power generation must be imported.

The use of electricity continues to be stimulated by the very low tariffs charged. Households are charged at the rate of about 1 US cent per kwh consumed. Moldova's domestic demand for electricity is about 16 billion kwh. The Dniester power plant itself could produce 18 billion kwh, if sufficient fuel were available,[634] which it is not.

---

628.   Interfax, *Petroleum Information Agency*, Chisinau, October 30, 1995.

629.   Interfax, *Petroleum Information Agency*, Moscow, December 9, 1995.

630.   British Broadcasting Corporation, *Summary of World Broadcasts, Part 1, Former USSR*, November 30, 1995.

631.   *Neft i Kapital*, September 1995.

632.   *Reuters*, Moscow, January 12, 1996.

633.   *FBIS-SOV*, January 27, 1995.

634.   *FBIS-SOV*, April 9, 1996.

Table 12-3
Electricity Generation in Moldova, 1980–1995

Year	Billion kwh
1980	15.6
1985	16.3
1990	15.2
1991	13.0
1992	11.1
1995 est.	5.0

Source: OECD/IEA, *Electricity in European Economies in Transition* (Paris, 1994).

The electric power sector in Moldova is experiencing the same difficulties as in many other former Soviet republics: generating capacities are nearing the end of their design life, repairs and maintenance have to be delayed or not performed at all because of a shortage of funds, and consumers are running up sizeable arrears.

Electricity generation has been cut by two-thirds in the past five years. The impact of this decline in domestic supply has erased Moldova's capability to export. In 1980, for example, Moldova exported roughly half the power generated by its thermal stations. The country was still a net exporter as late as 1992. Major buyers were Ukraine, Romania, and Bulgaria.[635]

Domestic demand now exceeds domestic supply, and in 1995 Moldova turned to Russia and Ukraine for electricity imports.[636] These imports accounted for about 40 percent of available electricity.

---

635.   British Broadcasting Corporation, *Summary of World Broadcasts, Part 1, Former USSR*, November 16, 1995.

636.   During the months January-September 1995 Moldova imported 1.7 billion kwh of electric power, chiefly from Ukraine. See British Broadcasting Corporation, *Summary of World Broadcasts, Part 1, Former USSR*, November 16, 1995.

Electricity imports from Ukraine originate chiefly from the South Ukraine nuclear power plant.

Source: States of the Former Soviet Union, CIA, 1992.

CHAPTER 13

Tajikistan

Table 13-1
Tajikistan at a Glance

Currency	The Tajik ruble*
Rate of Exchange	280.0/$1 (April 19, 1996)
Gross Domestic Product	$2.3 billion (1994)
Inflation	2,200 percent (1995 est.)
Population	6.155 million (July 1995 est.)
By Nationality	
Tajik	64.9 percent
Uzbek	25 percent
Russian	3.5 percent
Other	6.6 percent
*Introduced May 10, 1994, replacing the Russian ruble.	
Sources: Central Intelligence Agency (CIA), *The World Factbook 1995* (Washington, D.C.: CIA, 1995); *Finansovyye Izvestiya*, February 20, 1996; Open Media Research Institute, *Daily Report*, April 26, 1996; World Bank data.	

Tajikistan was the poorest and one of the least economically developed of those republics of the former Soviet Union even before the country's civil war deepened its economic decline. Tajikistan has the greatest percentage of rural population, the lowest per capita income, the lowest education level, and the highest infant mortality rate of the former republics.[637] The country is mountainous (93 percent), and only a very small portion of the land is arable. There is just one cash crop, cotton, although the growing and selling of opium is a large contributor to the underground economy. Over the past five years, Tajikistan has experienced coups, new presidents and governments, and a civil war, which has been for the most part a conflict between warring clans and regions.[638] Ideology does not appear to be an issue. The civil war has caused thousands of deaths and forced hundreds of thousands to flee to safe havens.

Tajikistan has very little sense of national identity.[639] The mountainous terrain

---

637. U.S. Department of Commerce, *Tajikistan Economic & Trade Overview*, June 26, 1995.

638. *Moscow News*, no. 6, February 1996.

has made the intermingling of peoples very difficult. There were no common ideals and no common goals when the Soviet Union broke up and Tajikistan became an independent state. Opposition to the government emerged rather quickly.

Russia tried to stay neutral in the civil war but was unable to do so for long. Russian troops pushed the opposition across the border into Afghanistan, then stayed on. A military stalemate is in place, and the truce is monitored by UN observers.

A cease-fire was signed in December 1996 between the Tajik government and opposing forces but has had little effect. The president is viewed as weak, is power is tenuous, and he lacks the authority to bring the civil war to a real end.

Sporadic fighting still occurs along the Tajik-Afghan border.[640] With a relatively strong military presence in Tajikistan, Russia views its mission as preventing a civil war but tries to stay out of the Tajik government-opposition conflict.[641]

Unfortunately for Tajikistan, economic assistance has not followed Russia's military presence. Tajikistan began to denationalize its economy in 1992, earlier than any of the other former Soviet republics. In 1991, the state sector accounted for 70.2 percent of all employment, the private sector 29.2 percent, and 0.6 percent by other nongovernmental enterprises and organizations. By 1995 a dramatic shift had taken place: employment in the private sector was up to 61.1 percent and had fallen to 34.8 percent for the state sector.[642]

If Tajikistan is to have a more fulfilling future, national reconciliation is a must. Peace talks continue, although neither side can win by military force alone. The fighting continues in the eastern part of the country, with both sides looking for leverage.

Tajikistan has very little in the way of an industrial base upon which to build. The north has cotton and gold, and the latter has attracted foreign investment. The south has little to offer. This considerable economic disparity between the rich north and the poor south further fuels internal tensions.[643] In sum, not much can be accomplished against the background of continuing political unrest. Neither can the regional disparities, which feed the political unrest, be easily overcome.

Oil

Crude oil production in Tajikistan is of minimal importance. The crippling civil war and the economic crisis confronting Tajikistan have exacted a heavy toll on even these small volumes. In the early 1980s Tajikistan was producing about 9,000 b/d of crude oil, but by 1995 production had slumped to just 514 b/d.[644] Because Tajikistan has no refining capacity of its own, these small volumes have been

---

639.   *Financial Times*, November 27, 1995.

640.   The American embassy staff, including the ambassador, had to be evacuated in October 1992 as the war came to Dushanbe, the capital of Tajikistan. The U.S. ambassador, Stanley T. Escudero, described the evacuation in considerable detail in the April 1993 issue of *State*.

641.   *Interfax*, Dushanbe, January 27, 1996.

642.   *Ekonomika i zhizn*, no. 18, May 1996.

643.   *Financial Times*, May 16, 1996.

644.   Interfax, *Petroleum Information Agency*, Dushanbe, January 19, 1996.

shipped to the Fergana oil refinery in Uzbekistan.

Turkmenistan continues to supply Tajikistan with petroleum products, and arrears for these commodities totalled $16.5 million by October 1995.[645] A plan is being devised whereby Iranian oil would be supplied to the Chardzhou refinery in Turkmenistan. Although the crude oil is to be supplied on a give-and-take basis, some products will remain behind as payment, and a portion of these products would then be sent on to Tajikistan.[646]

Natural Gas

Natural gas extraction in Tajikistan was just 38.7 million cubic meters in 1995, far short of the 1 bcm the economy requires. Imports cover the difference, and Tajikistan presently buys all of its gas from Uzbekistan (Table 13-2).[647] Imports reached 983 mcm in 1994 and were roughly comparable during 1995,[648] falling short of an agreement under which Uzbekistan was to supply 1.7 bcm during the year.[649]

Tajikistan has not always kept current its payments for Uzbek natural gas[650] and, in frustration, Uzbekistan shuts off deliveries from time to time, but not long enough to measurably impact upon Tajikistan's economic health.[651] A number of large enterprises, which produce something of interest to Uzbekistan, have signed direct contracts with Uzbek exporters and pay by barter for the natural gas supplied.[652]

Unfortunately, the 297 km pipeline which delivers Uzbek natural gas to Dushanbe, the capital of Tajikistan, is in very poor operating condition. Although owned by Uzbekistan, most of the pipeline lies within Tajikistan.

---

645.   *FBIS-SOV*, October 10, 1995.

646.   Ibid.

647.   Turkmenistan is trying to displace Uzbekistan as a supplier of natural gas to Tajikistan, and indicated it was prepared to supply 1.9 bcm at a price of $30 per 1,000 cubic meters for 1996. Uzbekistan's offer was for $65 per 1,000 cubic meters.

648.   Interfax, *Petroleum Report*, September 8-15, 1995.

649.   Interfax, *Petroleum Information Agency*, Tashkent, October 10, 1995.

650.   Tajikistan reportedly owes about $150 million to Uzbekistan for natural gas supplies. See British Broadcasting Corporation, *Summary of World Broadcasts, Part 1, Former USSR*, January 3, 1996.

651.   Uzbek natural gas is no particular bargain for Tajikistan. Uzbekistan had charged $84 per 1,000 cubic meters, dropping to $65 per 1,000 cubic meters during the fourth quarter 1995. Tajikistan has hopes of working out a deal with Turkmenistan for gas supplies to be provided at $30 1,000 cubic meters, sharply undercutting Uzbekistan. But Tajikistan owes Uzbekistan about $150 million for gas. It is difficult to assume under the circumstances that Uzbekistan would agree to the transit of Turkmen gas to buyers in Tajikistan. See Interfax, *Petroleum Information Agency*, Dushanbe, December 27, 1995.

652.   Interfax, *Petroleum Information Agency*, Tashkent, October 10, 1995.

Table 13-2
Uzbek Natural Gas Exports to Tajikistan, 1994–1995

Year	Billion cubic meters
1994	0.983
1995 est.	1.0
Source: Interfax, *Petroleum Information Agency*, Tashkent, November 24, 1995.	

A small natural gas condensate field was discovered at Khodzha-Sartiz in 1987, but its sulfur content is quite high. When eventually placed into production, it will yield no more than 45 to 50 mcm per year.

Electric Power

Hydroelectric power today provides 75 percent of Tajikistan's electricity requirements. In an effort to utilize a portion of Tajikistan's hydroelectric potential and to make electricity available to certain of the more remote areas of the Pamir mountains, the Aga Khan Foundation signed an agreement with Sweden for delivery of equipment to construct small hydropower stations in Tajikistan's eastern region.[653]

Despite its hydropower potential, Tajikistan still must import electricity to cover domestic demand. About 1 billion kwh were to be imported from Turkmenistan during 1996.[654]

This dependence on imports apparently is of some concern. New electricity tariffs were introduced July 1, 1996 which represented a 3.4 fold drop compared with 1995 and first half 1996. To balance however, consumption norms were worked out for the population, with excess consumption tariffed at five times the established rate.[655]

Mineral Resources

Although Tajikistan may lack a fuels resource base, the country is comparatively rich in valuable minerals, including holding 14 percent of the world's uranium reserves. There are sizable deposits of gold and silver, which are being heavily promoted by the government.

Tajikistan's economic and political instability has heavily impacted on the gold mining sector. Gold output has fallen from 2,031 kilograms to just 352 kilograms in 1994. Much of the blame has been placed on the civil war, during which some of

---

653.   British Broadcasting Corporation, *Summary of World Broadcasts, Part 1, Former USSR*, October 13, 1995. The Foundation is also providing financial assistance for the construction of the Pamir-1 hydropower station on the Gunt River.

654.   British Broadcasting Corporation, *Summary of World Broadcasts, Part 1, Former USSR*, February 15, 1996.

655.   *FBIS-SOV*, August 29, 1996.

the gold fields were looted, bridges and communication lines destroyed, and workers left to seek other opportunities. In addition, officials have been charged with criminal activity, such as selling for export gold that had been carried on the books as state assets.[656] Nonetheless, Nelson Gold (a UK company) entered into a joint venture, holding a 49 percent stake, to mine gold in Tajikistan.[657]

Following a series of conflicts with the government, Nelson Gold shut down in gold mining venture, as did privately held Gold and Mineral Excavation (U.K.) Nelson was closed for one month, while Gold & Mineral Excavation ceased operations for five months.[658] In sum, complications had arisen regarding gold exports and the two ventures took the only option available to them.

Rare mineral elements are also present, including quantities of sulfur, lead, tungsten, zinc, and antimony. Under the Soviet central planning system, the bulk of these natural resources either were underdeveloped or totally undeveloped. Tajikistan instead was designated as a major producer of aluminum.[659] The task now is to interest foreign investors in the development of these resources. Potential investors, if the are to succeed, must be careful to detail all conditionalities in the joint venture agreement.

656. *FBIS-SOV*, October 5, 1995.
657. *Financial Times*, April 17, 1996.
658. *Financial Times*, November 30, 1996.
659. Tajikistan is home to what once was the fourth largest aluminum plant in the world. See U.S. Department of Commerce, *Tajikistan Economic & Trade Overview*, June 26, 1995.

Source: States of the Former Soviet Union, CIA, 1992.

Ukraine

Table 14-1
Ukraine at a Glance

Currency	Hryvna
Rate of Exchange	1.861/$1 (November 6, 1996)
Gross Domestic Product	$89.8 billion (1994)
Inflation	39.7 percent (1996)
Population	51.3 million (January 1, 1996)
By Nationality	
Ukrainian	73 percent
Russian	22 percent
Jewish	1 percent
Other	4 percent

Sources: *Financial Times*, January 9, 1996; *Finansovyye Izvestiya*, December 22, 1995; Central Intelligence Agency (CIA), *The World Factbook 1995* (Washington, D.C.: CIA, 1995); *Interfax-Ukraine*, Lvov, February 3, 1996; *The Washington Post*, February 21, 1996; Open Media Research Institute, *Daily Report*, April 26, 1996; World Bank data; *Interfax-Ukraine*, Kiev, January 4, 1997.

Many Western observers thought that an independent Ukraine was best positioned of all the 15 republics of the former Soviet Union to successfully make the transition from a centrally planned economy to a free market economy.[660] Geographically, Ukraine is located much closer to Europe than the other republics. It has a very good agricultural sector, an advanced industrial base, and a well-educated labor force. In sum, most agreed Ukraine was positioned for a rapid takeoff, to be fueled in large part by foreign investors and international lending institutions.

That has yet to happen. Continuing political and economic uncertainties have kept investors wary. The country's commitment to reform is not yet clear or firm. A deteriorating economy and the absence of a transparent legal and banking infrastructure have not been conducive to major financial commitments. A heavy reliance on imported oil and gas sharply limits Ukraine's financial and economic

---

660.   Portions of this chapter have been based on information contained in CSIS Panel Report *Nuclear Energy Safety Challenges in the Former Soviet Union* (Washington, D. C.: Center for Strategic and International Studies, 1995).

options. These constraints are to be viewed against the background of a country inexperienced in the ways of a market economy and unfamiliar with what motivates the Western private sector.

Disputes between Russia and Ukraine—over debts owed for oil and gas delivered but not paid for, over the ownership of the Black Sea fleet, over the Crimea, over former Soviet assets in Ukraine, and the like—have combined to produce an unsettled atmosphere.

Ukraine has lost years because of delays in introducing economic reforms. Ukraine has been criticized for a slow economic transformation but much of the blame can be directed towards the collapsed economic system which Ukraine inherited. Once there was a strong, sophisticated military-industrial complex in Ukraine, accounting for about 40 percent of the Soviet complex. But now, what to do with these facilities and the millions employed there?

Hennadiy I. Udovenko, foreign minister of Ukraine, spelled out in very pragmatic terms just what ailed his country.[661]

❒ Our coal and steel industries have languished in recent years because of the absence of new investment. No new coal mines have been opened up since 1958. Coal is now very high cost, above the world market, and is not profitable, which leads to worker unrest. The coal sector must be restructured and the workers retrained. This is a very painful problem for us.

❒ Steel output has collapsed; the technology is obsolete.

❒ We also inherited Chornobyl. Responding to the Chornobyl accident today takes 10-12 percent of our budget.

❒ The old system of agriculture cannot be changed at once; it will take time.

❒ The psychology of our people also is most difficult to change. How to change? In the past people were taken care of. The free market concept is not yet fully accepted, especially among the older citizens.

❒ Regarding privatization, ownership may have changed, but little else has.

But, on the more positive side, he added that Ukraine was now nuclear-free, that the last nuclear warheads had been delivered to Russia.

Ukraine's weaknesses are many, its strengths few. One of Ukraine's strengths is its considerable agriculture potential. Once recognized as the Soviet Union's breadbasket, agribusiness in Ukraine today is stymied in large part by laws which preclude privatization. With proper and adequate inputs, Ukrainian agribusiness could become a substantial exporter and thus help offset the drain on the economy imposed by continuing high energy imports.[662]

---

661.   Remarks delivered at a breakfast meeting sponsored by the Carnegie Endowment for International Peace, Washington, D. C., October 21, 1996.

662.   A number of U.S. companies are to form the Ukraine Agricultural Development Company which would help finance Ukraine's purchases and leasing of farm inputs, from seeds to factory production lines. U.S.-Ukraine agribusiness is promoted by the Washington-based Citizens Network for Foreign Affairs.

The Government

Leonid Kuchma, formerly managing director of Ukraine's major manufacturer of interballistic missiles, was elected president of his country in July 1994, winning by a 52 percent to 45 percent margin over Leonid Kravchuk, the first president of an independent Ukraine. The performance of President Kuchma has been a pleasant surprise, for few had regarded him as a reformer. One of his first major steps was to release his program, entitled *The Path of Radical Economic Reforms*. One of the tenets of this program was privatization of three-quarters of state property by 1997.

Ukraine now has a new constitution, ratified by the parliament at the close of June 1996, which should help speed up the country's political and economic transformation.[663] The new constitution considerably strengthens President Kuchma's hand, but not in all regards. Parliament cannot be dissolved nor can the president call a state of emergency without parliament's consent. Presidential decrees are permitted for the coming three years but then only on economic matters unaffected by current legislation.

The president of the parliament is Olexander O. Moroz, a socialist who has the support of a substantial leftist bloc in the Parliament. He views socialism, rather than a market economy, as the correct path for Ukraine, and thus he opposes privatization. Indeed, in the past he has argued that the state must assume control of certain key aspects of the economy, including operation of enterprises vital to the state and, above all, to external trade.

Moroz can probably count upon the support of enough members of Parliament that Kuchma, if he is to be successful with privatization and other programs, must build a majority out of the nationalists and centrists of that body, which is not an easy task. The Centrists themselves are divided roughly equally between supporters of President Kuchma and supporters of ex-president Kravchuk.

The Economy

The administration of President Kravchuk did little to improve economic conditions in Ukraine or to enhance the international perception of Ukraine as a place where foreign investors could do business. Corruption was tolerated, Kravchuk ruled like a Communist, and he himself was not a strong leader.

Kravchuk extended minimal effort to move Ukraine along the path of a market economy. In fact, by mid-1994—that is, at the time of the presidential election—administrative controls had returned to large parts of the economy. Price controls were pervasive, the exchange rate had been fixed at an artificially low level, and many export licenses had been reinstated.

Some privatization had occurred, but Prime Minister Yevhen Marchuk's skepticism had slowed the process noticeably. Marchuk was unceremoniously sacked in May 1996 by President Kuchma, who cited among other things slow progress on economic reform. Pavlo Lazarenko, who had been first deputy prime minister, was

---

663.   *The Economist*, July 6, 1996.

promoted to replace Marchuk.[664] Initial reaction was muted, as observers questioned Lazarenko's ability to move Ukraine toward a market economy.

The role of the state in the economy is still too high. However, a full reform team is in place, matters are becoming more positive, and there should be a better read of Ukraine's future in the future. The standard of living is not likely to decline further. There is little public debate on Ukraine's situation; the public seems to be acceptant of what has been taking place. Although many are unhappy with current economic conditions, most are supportive of economic reform. In the absence of established political parties and strong unions, it is unclear where pressure for change will originate.

Nonetheless, the pace of reform will remain sensitive to public concerns, and that can easily translate into a slowdown. The transition to a market economy has been painful for Ukraine and belies the theory that those who reform more quickly suffer relatively more. In reality, slow reform is proving to be more damaging.

There are encouraging signs. For one, the rate of inflation reached 10,200 percent in 1993, but fell to around 850 percent in 1994, and the government had been hoping for a further decline, to 210 percent, in 1995. The economy actually performed even better in 1996, with inflation falling to just under 40 percent. The decline in GDP, which was dramatic during 1991–1994, has slowed noticeably, and a further improvement had been indicated for 1996 (Table 14-2).

Small-scale privatization has been moving along satisfactorily, but medium and large-scale privatization is on a slow pace. In 1995 about 30 percent of the work force was employed in the private (nongovernmental) sector, with this sector contributing 50 percent of the GDP that year.

Ukraine introduced a new currency, the *hryvna*, at the beginning of September 1996, replacing the *karbovanets* which had been the national tender in Ukraine since the collapse of the Soviet Union. The hryvna is named after money used in Ukraine some 300 years ago. The exchange took place at the rate of 100,000 karbovantsi per 1 hryvna. [665]

---

664.   *Financial Times*, May 29, 1996.

Table 14-2
GDP Decline in Ukraine, 1989–1996

Year	GDP
1989	100
1990	97.4
1991	84.2
1992	70.1
1993	60.1
1994	46.3
1995	42.6
1996 est.	41.7

Source: OECD/IEA, *Energy Policies of Ukraine, 1996 Survey* (Paris: OECD/IEA, 1996).

Attempts to measure industrial output in Ukraine can yield misleading results. Many of the factories have been simply producing for inventory, making items that no one wanted. Closing these factories and others that are virtually bankrupt would seem to be the correct choice. Yet this will be a very difficult decision to make, because the factories provide not only employment but housing for workers and their family, schools for the children, social and medical facilities, and the like.

At the same time, official statistics measuring the performance of the economy can also be misleading, failing to portray the full extent of economy activity in the country. "Off-the-books" activity, according to the World Bank, represent almost 49 percent of the overall GDP.[666] The resident head of the World Bank mission in Ukraine noted that "(t)here's a direct correlation between the level of economic liberalization and the size of the unofficial economy."[667] In other words, the high tax rates, bureaucratic burdens, and a general reluctance to move toward a market-oriented economy encourage businesses to operate underground. Moving these businesses out into the open will take time, as the government continues to give conflicting signals about the direction in which the country is moving.

Ukraine is very much dependent on the timely and adequate supply of goods and raw materials from other countries of the former Soviet Union. That was the way centralized planning and the managed economy worked in the Soviet era. Uzbekistan grew cotton, Azerbaijan manufactured oilfield equipment, and Ukraine emphasized agriculture, iron ore, hard coal, manganese ore, and steel. Ukraine also emphasized the manufacture of armaments, including ballistic missiles, for the military. In that regard, the Ukrainian economy has been very much a victim of demilitarization as the Cold War ended.

---

665. *Finansovyye Izvestiya*, May 14, 1996.
666. *Wall Street Journal*, May 13, 1996.
667. *Ibid.*

U.S. Financial Support

During the 1992–1996 fiscal years, the United States gave Ukraine grants worth more than $1.3 billion and loans for more than $790 million, making it the third largest recipient of U.S. aid, after Israel and Egypt. During 1997 the United States may provide an additional $554 million in grants and loans. Of that, $45 million will be for the nuclear power sector and about $107 million will finance the destruction of strategic nuclear weapons under the Nunn-Lugar program.[668]

Growing Corruption

American officials have expressed concern to their Ukrainian counterparts that growing corruption, linked to the expanding influence of the Dnepropetrovsk "clan," represents a key obstacle to market reform and works against foreign investment. The murder in early November 1996 at the Donets airport of Yevhen Shcherban, a well-to-do Ukrainian businessman, is a case in point. Shcherban had attempted to break the near monopoly on the gas import market held by United Energy Systems and apparently paid for his efforts.

Just what is the Dnepropetrovsk "clan" and where does its power originate?

Before taking office, President Kuchma had served as director of Yuzhmash, the largest missile factory in the former Soviet Union. Yuzhmash is located in the city of Dnepropetrovsk and many of the old *nomenklatura* from that city have been brought to Kiev by President Kuchma and placed in key government positions (a procedure equally employed in the U.S.) as well as in industry, banking, and the media. There are other groupings in Ukraine, e.g., from Poltava, who seek their share as well. Struggles between these groups have stalled privatization and have generally slowed the shift to a market economy.

Foreign Investment

Foreign investors encounter a number of roadblocks in Ukraine but the most effective roadblock to date has been the entrenched bureaucracy, particularly holdovers from the previous communist regime, who may dislike foreign investors, who may be looking out for their business friends, or who may be in search of payments from the investors.[669] Because of these difficulties, foreign investment in Ukraine to date has been minimal, on the order of just $1 billion.[670] Still, the U.S. is the largest investor in Ukraine, followed by Germany and then Russia.

Experience has shown, to the regret of many investors, that promises alone are not enough. There must be contractual obligations and even then investments are not necessarily safe from changes in the rules. A more transparent, a more predictable business environment must be created, if Ukraine is to attract the foreign investment it so badly needs.

---

668. *Interfax-Ukraine*, Kiev, December 14, 1996.
669. *Wall Street Journal*, November 4, 1996.
670. *Financial Times*, November 1, 1996.

Privatization

A limited privatization effort had been made prior to the election of President Kuchma. A number of privatization laws were passed in July 1992, and on that basis some small state-owned businesses were privatized through auctions. These businesses were mainly in retail trade and in services such as food.

In 1993, the International Finance Corporation, a component of the World Bank, initiated a privatization program in Ukraine, through auctions. Although this program was considered to have been quite successful, nevertheless it was quite limited in scope. A state privatization program had been approved for 1994, as noted, but it was far too optimistic under the circumstances and was largely ineffectual.

Privatization seems to have had the support of most of the country, except for the Parliament. Although the Parliament is not as communistic in ideology as is often thought, many of its members are holdovers from the old Soviet bureaucracy, and there is an innate opposition to change. Opposition stems in part from a lack of understanding about reform. There are those who oppose privatization for personal reasons—they fear losing their positions of authority under a change in ownership. Others may resist simply because they are against change. Yet, despite its vocal opposition, when the time comes to vote, the Parliament generally gives President Kuchma the support he needs.

Interestingly, the eastern Ukraine is supportive of change and reform, although one might assume otherwise. Heavy industry is concentrated in the eastern Ukraine, in part to take advantage of nearby coal fields, and many of the hard-liners in Parliament came from eastern Ukraine. Yet these businessmen seemingly have recognized that if Ukraine is to remain independent, it must proceed with economic reform, and as quickly as circumstances will allow.

At the same time, those who voice their support of privatization also voice opposition to price liberalization. Market reform really cannot move forward without market liberalization, but price liberalization hits the consumer immediately, and consumers are quick to voice their displeasure.

The privatization process began near the end of January 1995, under a January 31 deadline set by the international lending institutions for auctioning to begin if financial support was to continue. The support of these institutions is vital to the success of reform.

Ukraine profited from the early mistakes Russia had made in its privatization efforts. Ukrainian certificates cannot be bought, sold, or traded. They can be used only to secure a share(s) in an enterprise being privatized. In Russia, the vouchers often were purchased on the cheap by individuals who were seeking to gain control of a particular enterprise. Or, they were traded for something of immediate value, like a bottle of vodka, by individuals who had no understanding of, or interest in, what was going on.

Ukraine as a Transit Country

One of Ukraine's hidden strengths is its role as a transit country for Russian crude oil and natural gas moving to markets in Europe.[671](See Map 17) About 95 percent of the Russian natural gas delivered to Western Europe moves to these markets via pipelines laid across Ukrainian soil. In 1996, a planned 121.84 bcm of Russian natural gas destined for buyers in Europe were to transit Ukraine.[672] Actual deliveries slightly exceeded that plan.

Despite the payments problems between Ukraine and Gazprom, the gas transit pipelines are not going to be abandoned. To the contrary, the gas transit system will be restructured under a $500 million project funded by the World Bank.[673] Upon completion, the transit pipelines will be able to handle 200 to 220 bcm of natural gas annually. Ukraine will benefit from a considerably enhanced transit income, which could reach as high as $2.8 billion annually. At present, transit fees earned help offset natural gas purchases and would continue to do so.

Ukraine is also a transit country for Russian crude oil exports. More than half—1.26 million b/d out of 2.364 million b/d—of Russian crude oil exports during 1995 transited Ukraine enroute to buyers abroad. Roughly two-thirds of that amount was directed to the port of Odesa. The remainder was sent via the leg of the Druzhba (Friendship) pipeline which carries Russian crude oil to refineries in Eastern Europe (Slovakia, the Czech Republic, and Hungary). This leg is an important oil artery and handled almost 360,000 b/d along its 715 km Ukrainian section in 1995. Exports along the southern leg was interrupted on January 1, 1996, because Ukraine unilaterally raised the transit tariff for oil moving along this leg by 15 percent.[674] Deliveries were resumed several days later following agreements between Ukraine and Russian oil producers.[675]

A transit fee of $1.75 per 1,000 cubic meters covering 100 km was finally accepted. The annual gas transit fee for 1996 came to nearly $2 billion, of which Gazprom would cover $800 million by providing 10 bcm of natural gas and the

---

671.   According to Dmytro Yeher, Deputy Chairman of the State Committee on Oil, Gas and Oil processing Industry, the total carrying capacity of Ukrainian natural gas pipelines provides for exports of 160 bcm per year and 80 bcm for domestic consumption. But the transit capacity is now limited because the pipelines and compressor stations are badly in need of reconstruction.

There are 4,000 km of trunk crude oil pipelines in Ukraine, which can handle 2.5 million b/d. Of that, the carrying capacity of the transit crude oil pipelines represents slightly more half or 1.3 million b/d. During 1995 Ukrainian oil pipelines carried an average of just 1.32 million b/d, well below capacity (320,000 b/d were sent to Ukrainian oil refineries, and 1 million b/d were exported).

See *FBIS-SOV*, March 18, 1996.

672.   *Interfax-Ukraine,* Kiev, January 20, 1996. Ukraine acts as a transit country for markets in the Near Abroad as well. In 1996 Ukraine was to transit 24.3 bcm of natural gas to the southern regions of Russia and 3 bcm to Moldova.

673.   British Broadcasting Corporation, *Summary of World Broadcasts, Part 1, Former USSR*, February 1, 1996.

674.   Interfax, *Petroleum Information Agency*, Moscow, January 18, 1996.

675.   Perhaps coincidentally, perhaps not, Russia cut crude oil deliveries to the Drogobych oil refinery on January 23. About 70 percent of the crude processed at Drogobych comes from Russia. See British Broadcasting Corporation, *Summary of World Broadcasts, Part 1, Former USSR*, January 25, 1996.

Map 17. Ukraine: oil, natural gas, and nuclear facilities

remaining $1.2 billion would be paid for with goods and materials.[676]

The northern leg of Druzhba delivers Russian crude oil to customers in Ukraine.[677] Tariffs on the northern leg were not changed.[678]

Russia cannot deny Ukraine the natural gas it needs nor cut off deliveries because of unpaid bills. Cutting off Ukraine would also mean cutting off European customers, and Gazprom cannot allow that to happen. More commonly, Ukraine has been accused of tapping into the natural gas transit pipelines when extra volumes are needed.

Keeping deliveries to Ukraine high is important for Gazprom also because any cut in exports to Ukraine would be reflected in reduced Russian natural gas production. That is, if sales to Ukraine were cut, say, by 20 bcm, then Russian natural gas production would have to be reduced by a comparable volume. The natural gas market in Russia is declining and could not absorb these displaced volumes. Similarly, the natural gas market in Europe is fairly fixed because of the nature of gas purchase contracts.

Import Dependency

Ukrainian domestic production is able to meet just 23.3 percent of its oil requirements, 19.1 percent of natural gas, and 80 percent of coal needs. Ukraine today must import from Russia at least 50 to 55 bcm of natural gas and 560,000 to 600,000 b/d of crude oil to cover domestic demand, plus 20 bcm or so of natural gas from Turkmenistan. Reducing its dependence on imported fuels is a key feature of Ukraine's long-term strategy.

Russia usually meets its commitments despite nonpayment, but Turkmenistan is not so willing to continue natural gas deliveries as debts mount. Cuts or stoppages in deliveries quickly follow.

Table 14-3
Russian Fuel Deliveries to Ukraine, 1994, 1995, and 1996

Type of Fuel	Measurement	1994	1995	1996
Crude oil	Thousand b/d	291.8	254.1	157
Petroleum products	Thousand b/d	37.2	15.8	6.2
Natural gas	Billion cubic meters	57.0*	51.2	48.5

*Natural gas imports from Turkmenistan totalled 13.56 bcm in 1994. See *FBIS-SOV*, June 14, 1995.

Note: 1996 deliveries based on January-November data.

Sources: British Broadcasting Corporation, *Summary of World Broadcasts, Part 1, Former Soviet Union*, January 19, 1996; Interfax, *Petroleum Information Agency*, January 10, 1996; Interfax, *Petroleum Information Agency*, December 16, 1996.

676.   *Eastern Economist*, July 15, 1996.

677.   The Druzhba crude oil pipeline (both legs) carried in excess of 1.8 million b/d during the first 10 months of 1995. See *Neft i Kapital*, December 1995.

678.   *Izvestiya*, January 6, 1996.

Ukrainian dependence on imported fuels extends to nuclear fuels as well. All Ukraine's nuclear fuel needs are met by imports from Russia. In 1996 Ukraine was to transfer to Russia 26 percent of its nuclear warheads in exchange for fuel for nuclear power plants.[679] This exchange was to be made under the START 1 strategic arms reduction treaty.

Ukraine wants to spend $1.2 billion to establish its own capability to supply fuel rods for its reactors, thus easing this dependence upon Russia. Concern TVEL, a Russian joint-stock company, has been tentatively named the winner of an international tender for establishing a joint venture with Ukrainian companies for production of nuclear fuel. The projected processing plant is to produce fuel rods for VVER-1000 reactors, 11 of which are operating in Ukraine today.[680] However, the Cabinet will have the final say.

Ukraine has substantial uranium deposits but has no need to build a full-cycle nuclear fuel enrichment plant. The fuel rods will be enriched in Russia.[681]

The Ukrainian dependence on Russia for fuels and energy translates into a political linkage as well. Ukraine could look westward but no Western supplier would be willing to substitute for Russia under those financial arrangements agreed upon between Ukraine and Russia. The steel umbilical cord which nourishes Ukraine with Russian oil and natural gas will not be severed soon.

To help relieve Ukraine of this dependence on Russia, which in its own way forces Ukraine to hold onto its nuclear power, the West can expand donor programs to expand the search for oil and gas onshore and offshore in the Black Sea, or to ascertain the feasibility of coalbed methane commercial extraction.

The coal reserves of Ukraine are world class and are far from exhausted. But the coal mining industry needs a complete technological workover if it is to compete successfully against oil and natural gas. Closure of old, inefficient mines must be speeded up. Clearly, Ukraine would benefit substantially on all fronts if the West were to allocate funds for the rejuvenation of the coal industry. The coal resource base of some 57.7 billion tons is more than adequate for any reasonable program promoting a resurgence in the mining of coal.

Ukraine has tended to approach its energy problems from the supply side of the equation. Equal time must be given to demand-side management. Loss-making enterprises, usually very inefficient consumers of energy, must be forced into bankruptcy. Domestic prices must be raised to levels that at least cover delivered costs. Ukraine understands that it must restructure its energy sector. Unfortunately, restructuring is a function of broad-scale market reforms, and market reform in Ukraine is proceeding slowly.

Ukraine holds no pretense of becoming self-sufficient in terms of indigenous production of crude oil and natural gas. The national program, entitled *Ukrainian Gas and Oil Until the Year 2010*, which was approved by the Cabinet of Ministers in February 1995, sets substantial but overly ambitious goals for the production of crude oil and natural gas by 2010 (Table 14-4). Domestic crude oil and natural gas

---

679.   *FBIS-SOV*, January 11, 1996.
680.   *Eastern Economist Daily*, February 7, 1996.
681.   *Financial Times*, January 30, 1996.

can be expected to fall well short of covering likely demand, even assuming very substantial improvement in the efficiency of energy usage. Interestingly, the relative share of nuclear power plants in total electricity generation is placed at around 40 percent, substantially unchanged from the present-day level.[682] At the same time, planners forecast that 10 percent of power generation would come from alternate sources of energy, with the remaining 50 percent provided by fossil-fueled plants.

A high import dependency threatens national security. Foreign and domestic policy formulation in the coming years will have to recognize this particular vulnerability and the limits it places on policymakers. Ukraine may seek to diversify its sources of supply away from the overwhelming dependence on Russia, but it cannot to any meaningful degree, for it simply could not meet the terms of Western sellers—that is, market prices with payment in a convertible currency. Both Ukraine and Russia understand that and policies are implemented accordingly.

Table 14-4
Ukrainian Oil and Gas Production Goals, 2000 and 2010

Type of Fuel	Measurement	2000	2010
Crude Oil	Thousand b/d	120	400
Natural gas	Billion cu. m.	22	40
Sources: *FBIS-SOV*, September 26 and November 30, 1995.			

Importing nations always include alternative energy sources in their long-range plans, forever hopeful that wind and solar energy, for example, might displace fossil fuels to a meaningful degree. Ukraine is no different. The government recently passed a resolution to boost the development of geothermal electricity involving the construction of 1,500 geothermal power stations over a 10-year period.[683] These stations would have an aggregate generating capacity of 6,000 Mw, equal, for example, to the capacity of the Zaporizhzhya nuclear power plant. Only one element is lacking to bring this resolution to life—money.

Ukraine's economy is very energy-intensive, initially made so by Moscow's readiness to supply crude oil and natural gas in every-increasing amounts, at heavily preferential prices and further encouraged by heavily subsidized retail rates and by consumer recognition that arrears can be incurred without fear of being cut off. Low costs, obsolescent energy consuming equipment, and an industrial base centered on industries which by nature consume large amounts of energy will combine to keep the economy energy-intensive unless and until major restructuring takes place.

Energy consumption per unit of output is probably 60 percent higher than what it should be.[684] The fact that indigenous energy supplies are far short of require-

---

682.   *FBIS-SOV*, May 17, 1996.
683.   British Broadcasting Corporation, *Summary of World Broadcasts, Part 1, Former USSR*, May 30, 1996.
684.   *FBIS-SOV*, September 15, 1995.

ments has never been a drawback. Russia and other major energy producers of the former Soviet Union could always be counted upon to provide whatever volumes of crude oil and natural gas might be required, at heavily subsidized prices. By 1990 the amount of energy consumed per unit of GDP was more than 10 times the amount used by France per unit of GDP.[685] Energy intensity has risen in subsequent years as the decline in economic activity has exceeded the drop in primary energy consumption.

Distinct from Russia, where production held through mid-1988, declines in Ukrainian energy production had set in much earlier. Little attention had been given to seeking out new oil and gas fields. The potential for additional oil and natural gas was there, but the formations are deep-seated and the former Soviet Union never developed the capability to drill deep wells (that is, below 10,000 feet) on a routine basis. It was easier and cheaper to explore untested territory in Western Siberia, which attracted the bulk of new capital. There was little interest—and little funding—for developing oil and gas outside Russia. Ukrainian crude oil, natural gas, and coal were left to wither away. Instead, Russia would provide the oil and natural gas needed, and emphasis would be given to constructing nuclear power stations.

Energy production in Ukraine continues to fall behind previous levels, although the declines are generally smaller, in relative terms, than those registered in Russia. Only the willingness of Russia to continue to supply natural gas and crude oil in amounts sufficient to cover the gap between demand and indigenous supply has kept Ukraine from facing an energy supply crisis of proportions that would threaten the viability of the country and could quickly translate into civil unrest that could easily spill over into Russia.

Ukraine is shifting toward greater reliance on nuclear electric power, as its ability to pay for oil and gas imports is further eroded. Nuclear electricity is regarded as the cheapest form of electricity—annual nuclear fuel costs average around $300 million—and consequently it is more acceptable to reduce electricity generation at fossil-fuel power plants. Thermal generating capacity stands idle while nuclear generating capacity is utilized to the fullest.

The Nonpayment Issue

By early February 1996, Ukraine owed Russia the equivalent of $922 million for natural gas delivered during 1995 and the early part of 1996.[686] The value of the natural gas delivered during 1995 was $2.5 billion. Of that amount, Ukraine had paid Gazprom $1.346 billion in a combination of hard currency, goods, and con-

---

685.   H. Quan Chu and Wafik Grais, *Macroeconomic Consequences of Energy Supply Shocks in Ukraine*, World Bank Studies of Economies in Transformation, No. 12, 1994.

In 1990 Ukraine imported about 1.08 million b/d of crude oil, 220,000 b/d of petroleum products, and 87 billion cubic meters of natural gas, as well as 21 million tons of coal.

686.   British Broadcasting Corporation, *Summary of World Broadcasts, Part 1, Former USSR*, February 26, 1996. An agreement had been reached in mid-May 1996, under which Russia would forgive $450 million of Ukrainian energy debts as compensation for the tactical weapons given up by Ukraine in 1991. See Open Media Research Institute, *Daily Report*, May 20, 1996.

struction services.[687]

At the same time, Ukrainian consumers owed Ukrhazprom the equivalent of about $1.42 billion. Earlier, Ukraine had agreed to a restructuring of $2.5 billion of its debt to Russia, which largely covered the debt owed for natural gas delivered but not paid for through 1994.

The inability or unwillingness of consumers to pay for natural gas delivered has had little impact on the consumption of natural gas. Absent meters and absent enforced bill collection and cut-off procedures, consumers have no reason to change their ways.[688] Ukraine managed to keep arrears to Russia reasonably close in hand during 1996, and at the beginning of November 1996 owed just $670 million, of which $554 million was owed to Gazprom.[689]

The nuclear power sector has been particularly affected by consumer nonpayment.[690] Nuclear power plants, short of cash, have been unable to purchase nuclear fuel from Russia to keep reactors operational. Reportedly, only 13 percent of the electric power produced at nuclear power stations was being paid for.[691] A sizeable portion of those payments received were in the form of barter. Little was received in the way of cash. In the past, the nuclear power stations had to sell all their output directly to the Ministry of Energy. That was changed in August 1995, when the government permitted the nuclear facilities to independently sell 26 percent of the electricity they produce.[692] By concluding direct sales contracts with hopefully solvent customers, cash flow positions can be improved.

Matters relating to oil are somewhat better, and the debt owed by Ukraine to Russia for oil delivered is comparatively minimal.

---

687.   *Interfax-Ukraine*, Kiev, January 11, 1996. Most of the currency payments to Gazprom were credits provided to Ukraine by the International Monetary Fund. It would appear that Gazprom, not Ukraine, has benefited more from the IMF credits to Ukraine. Had not these credits not been made available, indebtedness to Gazprom would have increased, but with little likelihood of early payment. At the same time, natural gas deliveries to Ukraine would not have stopped, for to do so would have stopped deliveries to European customers as well, resulting in breaches of contract, an unacceptable result.

688.   There is a financial incentive to install meters measuring the consumption of natural gas for so-called domestic (household) purposes. If the consumer has a gas meter, the charge then was 6,000 karbovantsi per cubic meter. If there is no gas meter, the charge rose to 11,500 karbovantsi. See British Broadcasting Corporation, *Summary of World Broadcasts, Part 1, Former USSR*, January 19, 1996.

689.   Interfax, *Petroleum Information Agency*, Moscow, December 17, 1996.

690.   At the beginning of May 1996, consumers owed electric power generating stations the equivalent of $1,135 million. Of that sum, $648 million was owed to nuclear power plants. See British Broadcasting Corporation, *Summary of World Broadcasts, Part 1, Former USSR*, May 9, 1996.

691.   British Broadcasting Corporation, *Summary of World Broadcasts, Part 1, Former USSR*, January 19, 1996.

692.   *Nucleonics Week*, December 21, 1995.

Oil

Crude oil production continues its long but slow and relatively painless decline (Table 14-5). These small annual losses are typical for a mature industry. Russia has always been prepared to meet the country's oil needs and to protect the economy against the workings of the international market. That crude oil production in 1995 was roughly half of the 1980 level was not of any particular concern; the absolute loss in output is minimal when compared with annual requirements.

Table 14-5
Crude Oil Production In Ukraine, Selected Years 1971–1996 and 2000 Plan

Year	Thousand b/d
1971	268
1980	150
1985	116
1990	106
1991	98
1992	90
1993	85
1994	84
1995	78.9
Crude oil	66.2
Natural gas liquids	12.7
1996 plan	84
1996 est.	83
2000 plan	98

Note: Crude oil production statistics for Ukraine include natural gas condensate as well. Both UkrNafta and UkrGazProm produce condensates. Care must be taken to ensure that condensates are included in the national crude oil total; *Reuter,* Kiev, December 18, 1996; *FBIS-SOV,* July 12, 1996.

Sources: British Broadcasting Corporation, *Summary of World Broadcasts, Part 1, Former USSR,* January 3, 1996 and December 20, 1995; *Ukraine, An Economic Profile,* November 1992; *FBIS-SOV,* June 26, 1995 and September 25, 1995; British Broadcasting Corporation, *Summary of World Broadcasts, Part 1, Former USSR,* April 11, 1996.

Unlike Azerbaijan, Kazakstan, or Turkmenistan, Ukraine has no large discovered but undeveloped crude oil or natural gas fields to offer to foreign investors. The Black Sea offshore may be promising, but little is know of its potential. Chernomorneftegaz will be the main Ukrainian developer of Black Sea natural gas deposits. Its Director-General, Nikolai Ilnitsky, stated that it is inexpedient to allow foreign companies to develop those sectors of the Black Sea and the Azov shelf where gas lies at a water depth of less than 80 meters.[693] Such sectors can be developed by Ukrainian companies.

Ukraine has been slow, deliberately slow it appears, in opening up its offshore areas for exploration. JKX, a British independent, came away with a dry hole on is Delphin prospect in the Black Sea.[694] JKX is also involved in a joint venture to process gas production from the Stormovoye gas condensate field, which lies north of the Delphin block.[695] The Karpattia Petroleum Corporation, a subsidiary of United Kyiv Resources (Canada) has begun drilling operations at the Butkiv oilfield.[696] Its Ukrainian partners are NadvirnaNaftoGaz and PoltavaNaftaGaz, both subsidiaries of UkrNafta.

Refineries

Ukraine inherited a very substantial crude oil refining capability upon independence. Unfortunately, the refineries in Ukraine are just as obsolete as the refineries in Russia. The primary distillation capacity is quite substantial, at about 1.18 million b/d, but secondary refining facilities for maximizing the yields of so-called light products are of very limited availability.

There are six oil refineries in Ukraine: Kremenchuknaftoorhsyntez (formerly known as just Kremenchug) is the largest, and its operational processing capacity is on the order of 380,000 b/d,[697] or about 32 percent of the national total (Table 14-6). It is also the most modern refinery in the country in terms of secondary refining facilities.[698]

693. *Interfax-Ukraine*, Simferopol, September 4, 1996.

694. *Oil & Gas Journal*, May 27, 1996.

695. The JKX joint venture partner is Chernomorneftegaz, organized in Crimea in 1978, to carry out activities ranging from prospecting to the marketing of crude oil and natural gas. Chernomorneftegaz is producing at three gas condensate deposits in the Black Sea and one gas deposit in the Azov Sea. See *FBIS-SOV*, June 5, 1996.

696. *Eastern Economist*, July 1, 1996.

697. *Eastern Economist*, April 16, 1996.

Table 14-6
Ukrainian Oil Refineries

Old Name	New Name	Refining Capacity (b/d)
Kremenchug	Kremenchuknaf-toorhsyntez	380,000
Lysychansk	Lysychansknaf-toorhsyntez	460,000
Galicia	Halychykna	80,000
Nadvirna	Naftokhimik	80,000
Kherson	Prykarpattia	120,000
Odessa	Odesa	60,000
Total		1,180,000

Source: *Interfax-Ukraine*, Kiev, November 1, 1996.

Domestic oil production supplies just a fraction of the refinery throughput and imports must fill the gap (Table 14-7). Although domestic supplies continue to decline, the volumes of crude oil refined have been falling at a more rapid rate. As a result, the relative importance of domestic oil has been slowly improving (Table 14-8).

---

698.   As a step toward securing a stable flow of crude oil, a joint stock company—UkrNafta—has been established between the Kremenchuknaftoorhsyntez (refinery) and a number of oil producing enterprises from Tatarstan (Russia). Kremenchuknaftoorhsyntez will hold 49.96 percent of the shares while 26 percent are held by the Russian joint stock company TatNafta.

This new joint stock company planned to process 160,000 b/d of crude oil in 1996 at Kremen-chuknaftoorhsyntez and hopes to achieve a maximum processing of 360,000 b/d. See *Eastern Economist*, January 29, 1996.

Table 14-7
Ukrainian Crude Oil Imports, 1989–1996

Year	Million b/d
1989	1.234
1990	1.17
1991	1.10
1992	0.60
1993	0.39
1994	0.32
1995	0.266
1996 est.	0.246

Source: *FBIS-SOV*, October 24, 1995 and December 18, 1996; *Reuters*, Kiev, May 23, 1996 and December 18, 1996.

Kazakstan is a minor supplier of crude oil to Ukraine, having delivered about 36.4 thousand b/d in 1995, but rising to an estimated 92,000 b/d in 1996.[699]

Table 14-8
Ukraine's Charge to Refining, 1990–1996

Year	Million b/d	Percent Provided by Domestic Production
1990	1.162	9.1
1991	0.198	
1992	0.69	
1993	0.475	
1994	0.384	
1995	0.332	19.9
1996 est.	0.329	20.3

Note: Because Ukraine does not export any crude oil, then charge to refining is simply production plus imports. For the purpose of this table, losses in the field, the burning of crude oil as a fuel, and changes in storage have been ignored.

Sources: *FBIS-SOV*, October 10, 1995; *East Bloc Energy*, July 1995; *Reuters*, Kiev, May 24, 1996.

An estimated 329,000 b/d of crude oil were refined during 1996. That meant

---

699.   *Finansovyye Izvestiya*, January 25, 1996.

851,000 b/d, or more than two-thirds of the country's refining capacity, was standing idle. A wasted asset, to be sure. Nonetheless, the refined product yield, plus product imports, was more than adequate to meet domestic demand as it was in 1995. That year imports of crude oil from Russia (218,000 b/d) and from Kazakstan (48,000 b/d), together with domestic crude oil production (66,200) and product imports of 356,000 b/d, provided Ukraine with a total oil supply of 684,000 b/d. It has been reported that a high percentage of the country's requirements for gasoline and other petroleum products is met through imports from Greece, Belarus, and the Baltics, while Ukrainian oil refineries stand idle.[700] However, sources indicate that the Greek and Turkish suppliers are really Russians. The products originally were destined for markets in the Far Abroad and thus were exempt from export taxes. The products were resold to Ukrainian traders while still at sea, and imported through the port of Odesa.

The weakness of the oil refining sector clearly is not in primary distillation capacity. That capacity far exceeds current requirements and will likely be in excess of needs for a number of years to come. Rather, these refineries are wholly incapable of meeting the needs of a modern-day economy. Their product yield emphasizes residual fuel oil, at the expense of more valuable light products (gasoline, jet fuel, diesel fuel, and lubricants). The combined output of the latter products is 53 percent of total refinery yield.[701] In sharp contrast, the yield at a modern-day refinery would fall within 85 to 90 percent.

Petroleum product prices were freed from state control in February 1995. As a result, prices in Ukraine now exceed European prices for the higher octane gasoline. The market is at work. Refineries simply have not been able to keep up with growing demand. A complete makeover of the Ukrainian refining sector is in order. Some refineries might not be worth saving because the costs of modernization could never be recovered.

Ukraine is very much aware that its dependence on oil from Russia threatens national security. To ensure at least a minimum economic independence, Ukraine seeks to have no more than 25 percent of its imported oil coming from one source. But foreign suppliers like to be paid, in hard currency, and Ukraine today can hardly turn away from Russia, as much as it would like to. It has been estimated[702] that Ukraine will need 820,000 b/d of oil in the year 2000 but that domestic production will reach to no more than 98,000 b/d. That implies an oil import requirement (crude oil plus petroleum products) of some 720,000 b/d.

The Odesa Oil Terminal

Years ago, nations seeking an economic revitalization sought to base their future on steel mills. The ability to produce steel was a measure of the country's strength. Today, it seems that a country's future is linked to a modern, high-capacity oil terminal.

Ukraine's Cabinet of Ministers adopted a decree on February 15, 1993, on con-

---

700. *Eastern Economist*, July 22, 1996.
701. *Interfax-Ukraine*, Kiev, November 1, 1996.
702. *FBIS-SOV*, July 12, 1996.

struction at Pivdennyy, near Odesa,[703] an oil terminal that could handle an average of 800,000 b/d. This decree also stipulated that the first section of the terminal, with a capacity of 240,000 b/d, was to be readied for operation in 1994.[704]

The proposal met with considerable domestic criticism, chiefly on ecological grounds, although some conjectured that interests involved in exporting through Odesa were the real opponents. It was pointed out to opponents that considerable volumes of Russian crude oil had been exported through Odesa for a number of years—an average of 260,000 b/d during 1994.

The terminal construction plans have been put in abeyance for a lack of funds. Some initial construction was carried out, but funds were quickly depleted and work came to a stop. Contractors removed their equipment in June 1995, as unpaid bills mounted.

Building an oil terminal is just the first step. The operating pipeline infrastructure in Ukraine runs in a East-West direction. To distribute the oil arriving at Odesa will require pipelines laid South to North. A proposed 40-inch, 660 km pipeline would run from the port of Odesa inland to Brody (in western Ukraine), where it would link up with the southern leg of the Druzhba crude oil pipeline. The pipeline proposal also called for a 300 km extension beyond Brody to Adamowa Zastawa in Poland. At this juncture, the pipeline would join with the northern leg of the Druzhba system. The Odesa-Brody-Adamowa Zastawa pipeline would have a carrying capacity of 800,000 b/d, of which about 240,000 b/d would be used to supply refineries in Ukraine.

Ukrainian authorities hope to attract crude oil arriving at the Russian Black Sea port of Novorossiisk from producing fields in Kazakstan and Azerbaijan.[705] Plans are even being developed which envisage construction of an oil pipeline from Ceyhan, a Turkish port on the Mediterranean, to Samsun, a Turkish port on the Black Sea. These plans are based on the presumption that the later AIOC oil from Azerbaijan will be moved to Ceyhan by a pipeline yet to be approved and built. From Samsun the crude oil would be shipped by tanker to Odesa from which some volumes would be delivered to Ukrainian refineries and the remainder to the Druzhba crude oil pipeline.

Natural Gas

The natural gas sector of Ukraine, once a major contributor to total Soviet production, has fallen on particularly hard times. Natural gas extraction in 1995 was barely 31 percent of the 1980 level and, in relative terms at least, has suffered the most of any of the forms of primary energy (Table 14-9). A very modest produc-

---

703.   Another source placed the terminal at Yuzhnyy, about 50 miles north of Odesa, but still on the Black Sea. Yuzhnyy is a bulk port. A single-mooring buoy will be located offshore to which the tankers would anchor and the oil would be moved to the mainland by pipeline. See *Journal of Commerce*, June 15, 1995.

704.   *FBIS-SOV*, November 28, 1995.

705.   British Broadcasting Corporation, *Summary of World Broadcasts, Part 1, Former USSR*, November 8, 1996.

tion increment has been planned for 1996. Even so, the prospect for fulfillment is questionable. Reliable and steady imports of natural gas are absolutely essential to the well-being of the economy.

Table 14-9
Natural Gas Extraction in Ukraine, Selected Years 1975–1997

Year	Billion cubic meters
1975	68.3
1980	56.7
1985	42.9
1990	30.8
1993	19.2
1994	18.3
1995	17.44
Ukrhazprom	14.59
Ukrnafta	2.85
1996 plan	26.44
1996 est.	18.2
1997 plan	18.0

Sources: British Broadcasting Corporation, *Summary of World Broadcasts, Part 1, Former Soviet Union*, January 3, 1996 and December 20, 1995; *FIS-SOV*, September 25, 1995; *FBIS-SOV*, June 26, 1995; *Post-Soviet Geography*, April 1992; British Broadcasting Corporation, *Summary of World Broadcasts, Part 1, Former USSR*, April 11, 1996; *Interfax-Ukraine*, Kiev, December 14, 1996.

Natural gas consumption in Ukraine appears to have held up remarkably well the past several years, despite the sharp decline in industrial output and an inability to pay for volumes imported (Table 14-10). However, Ukrainian officials do not know for certain how much gas is in fact consumed by the country as a whole, or how much natural gas is lost through leakage, simply because there are so few meters measuring consumption.

Table 14-10
Natural Gas Consumption in Ukraine, 1990–1995

Year	Billion cubic meters	as Percent of 1990
1990	115.1	100
1991	130.8	113.6
1992	131.3	114.1
1993	96.2	83.6
1994	92.4	80.3
1995 (est)	91.5	79.5

Note: Gas consumption represents imports plus domestic production plus net withdrawals from storage. In each of the 5 years 1990-1994 withdrawals from storage have exceeded additions. For example, in 1994 withdrawals exceeded additions by 5.1 bcm.

Sources: *Holos Ukrayiny*, October 17, 1995; *FBIS-SOV*, June 6, 1995.

Natural gas is an important energy source in Ukraine. Some 16 million people rely on this fuel for cooking and heating.[706] Of that, 9 million are connected to the gas pipeline network. The other 7 million users depend on bottled gas.

Natural gas consumption in 1995 was about 20 percent less than in 1990, mostly because of forced cuts in imports as unpaid bills continued to mount. Incentives for consumers to use natural gas more wisely simply have not been put into place. Consumers continue to be heavily subsidized. Consumer needs are also met by pirating Russian natural gas—that is, taking more natural gas out of the transit pipelines than called for by current contracts.[707]

But the story of natural gas consumption in Ukraine is basically that of old-style gas bill calculation. That is, a per capita use is derived by dividing the volume of natural gas consumed by a particular entity (e.g., a town or a city) district. There is no link between the amount of gas consumed and the monthly gas bill. Because of that, the need to conserve or to make a more efficient use of natural gas is of no concern.

The largest single consumer of natural gas in Ukraine in the past has been electricity generation. But in 1992 the residential and commercial sector took over the top spot, and in 1994, this sector was consuming as much natural gas as all of industry. This sector, which consumes more than 30 bcm per year, is virtually unrestricted in its use of natural gas.

Residential use of natural gas is heavily subsidized. To illustrate, the actual cost of acquiring 1,000 cubic meters of natural gas in 1996 was $83, but residential consumers paid just $49.80 per 1,000 cubic meters.[708]

---

706.   *Eastern Economist*, April 29, 1996.
707.   By the end of January 1996 a reported 1 bcm of Russian natural gas had been taken out of underground storage facilities in Ukraine, without Russian permission.
708.   *Eastern Economist*, April 29, 1996.

Gazprom, in searching for a way to put its natural gas sales to Ukraine on a more commercial basis, rather than on a Gazprom-government basis, organized a tender, with the following outcome. The four winners are to supply natural gas to designated regions of the country (Table 14-11). For example, Unified Energy Systems will supply gas to consumers in the Dnepropetrovsk, Donetsk, and Cherkass regions, while ITERA will supply gas to the Republic of Crimea and a number of other regions.[709]

The Azov and Mariupol steel mills negotiated directly with Gazprom for the purchase of natural gas. A similar arrangement was worked out with Turkmenistan.[710]

Table 14-11
Ukrainian Natural Gas Imports Scheduled for 1996

Importing Company	Billion cubic meters
From Russia	
Unified Energy Systems	25.1
Ukrhazprom	10
Interhaz	10
Ukrzakordonnanaftohaz	2.5
Azov and Mariupol	
steel mills	3
Subtotal, from Russia	50.6
From Turkmenistan	
ITERA	6
Trading House	6
Interpipe	6
Ukrresursy	6
Subtotal, from Turkmenistan	24
Total scheduled imports	74.6

Sources: British Broadcasting Corporation, *Summary of World Broadcasts, Part 1, Former USSR*, January 10, 1996; *Interfax-Ukraine*, Kiev, December 15, 1995.

---

709. *Interfax-Ukraine*, Kiev, January 29, 1996.

710. A unique trilateral arrangement has been worked out to pay for the natural gas imported from Turkmenistan. The Kiev-based Antonov Aircraft Company is to modernize the Iranian aircraft plant, Iran Aircraft Enterprises, in Esfahan, and the manufacture of a series of Ukrainian AN-140 aircraft is to be set up. The contract is worth a reported $4 billion. Iran will not make payment directly to the Antonov Aircraft Company but instead to exporters of Turkmen natural gas. See *Eastern Economist*, February 19, 1996.

To secure its financial position, Gazprom demanded that state guarantees be provided for gas deliveries.[711] If the commercial organizations fail to meet their financial obligations, then the government of Ukraine becomes liable. This demand has been rejected.

The 74.6 bcm of natural gas imports initially scheduled for 1996 should have been responsive to Ukrainian needs, if the imports arrived on schedule. Interestingly, these scheduled imports of 74.6 bcm compare favorably with the 87 bcm imported in 1990, when economic activity in Ukraine was at a much higher level than it is today. The continued high energy intensity of the economy strongly supports the contention that demand-side management in Ukraine would help the country drastically reduce its reliance on imported energy.

Deliveries from Turkmenistan are always subject to interruption if timely payments are not being made. The apportionment of 1996 imports between Russia and Turkmenistan is fairly representative of past arrangements. In 1993, for example, Ukraine imported 79.8 bcm of natural gas, of which 54.3 bcm originated with Russia and 25.5 bcm with Turkmenistan.[712] This apportionment, as much as anything, represents the maximum access to its pipeline network that Russia will allow Turkmenistan.

ITERA (International Trading of Energy Resources), a New Zealand company was to deliver 21.1 bcm of the natural gas to be imported from Turkmenistan.[713] The parent company is US-based ITERA Inc., which has Russian cofounders. ITERA also holds 5 percent in the recently established TurkmenRosGaz (51 percent is held by the Turkmen government, and 44 percent by Gazprom). Olessandr Shevchenko, president of ITERA Energy, the Ukrainian subsidiary of ITERA, was murdered outside his company's office on March 28, 1996.[714] He had been on the job just three weeks. This may have been an attempt to intimidate ITERA, to force it to give up at least a portion of its control over imports of Turkmen natural gas.

This parceling-out of import allocations was by direction of Prime Minister Pavlo Lazarenko when he was deputy prime minister in charge of energy. He had particularly favored United Energy Systems (UES), a company based in Dnepropetrovsk and run by a friend of his. In May 1996 Lazarenko ordered another shift, this time making UES one of only two companies nationwide marketing natural gas to industry. The State Oil and Gas Committee directed that UES would sell 25.2 bcm and ITERA would sell 18.46 bcm, the entire import of gas from Turkmenistan. Intergaz was cut from 7.8 bcm to just 3.82 bcm. Olgaz was given a quota of just 1.53 bcm, a cut in half. UkrGazProm would sell 3.7 bcm and others a total of 5.42 bcm.　Natural gas imports would then total 58.13 bcm.[715]

Subsequently, the Ukrainian cabinet moved in early November 1996 to open up the lucrative natural gas distribution business, hopefully eliminating the virtual

---

711.　British Broadcasting Corporation, *Summary of World Broadcasts, Part 1, Former USSR*, January 25, 1996.

712.　Ostekonomiska Institutet, *Ostekonomisk Rapport*, October 24, 1994.

713.　*Eastern Economist*, April 1, 1996.

714.　*Eastern Economist*, April 1, 1996.

715.　*Financial Times*, August 7, 1996, quoting statistics from the *Ukrainian Oil and Gas Report*.

monopoly held by UES and ITERA.

Gazprom plans to supply Ukraine with 53 bcm of natural gas during 1997, of which 30 bcm will be in payment for its services as a transit country. In addition, Gazprom will transport 25 bcm of natural gas to Ukraine from Central Asia—about 19 bcm from Turkmenistan and 6 bcm from Uzbekistan.[716]

Coal

The coal industry, once the pride of Ukraine, has failed miserably in recent years. The continued operation of obsolete equipment in old, low-productivity mines and the depletion of workable reserves have been a major cause for the drop in coal extraction from 192.2 million tons in 1988 to 115.7 million tons in 1993 and further to 70 million tons in 1996 (Table 14-12). The 1996 plan was wildly optimistic, and a further drop in extraction should be expected. There are profitable coal mines, but their revenues are employed to keep loss-making mines afloat.

Much of the coal mined today in Ukraine is of poor quality. In a number of cases, the coal has to be mixed with oil or natural gas before it can be burned at power generation plants.

A common yardstick for measuring a coal industry's performance is the amount of coal produced per worker. Miner productivity to a large degree mirrors the health of a coal industry in that it reflects the quality of the mines being worked and the level of technology embodied in the mining equipment. In that regard, the Ukrainian coal sector is in miserable shape. In Ukraine in 1990, output per worker averaged about 335 tons. Five years later, in 1995, output had dropped dramatically to 100 tons per worker. For comparison, miner productivity in the United States in 1995 was 40 times that of an Ukrainian miner.[717] Productivity in Poland was four times higher.

Unsatisfactory working conditions and a lack of safety equipment have been blamed for the high rate of mining-related accidents. During 1995 there were almost 41,000 accidents registered at Ukrainian coal mines, 345 miners lost their lives, and 6,763 miners were disabled because of job-related illnesses or injuries. This fatality rate of five lives lost for every one million tons extracted is the highest in the world. The death rate was even higher during the first seven months of 1996, as 227 miners were killed in work-related accidents.[718]

Miners' morale, a basic ingredient in worker productivity, is seriously impaired by unpaid wages and the haunting fear of becoming unemployed, as mines are closed. Unpaid wages are the more immediate concern. As of May 1, 1996, back wages in the coal industry exceeded 82 trillion karbovantsi. Beyond that, the financial condition of the coal sector as a whole is miserable. Accounts receivable (as of April 1) reached 338.7 trillion karbovantsi, exceeding accounts payable by 173 trillion karbovantsi.[719] Extraction costs are rising as miner productivity is declining.

---

716. *Interfax-Ukraine*, Kiev, December 6, 1996.
717. *Eastern Economist*, April 22, 1996.
718. *Interfax-Ukraine*, Donets, August 16, 1996.
719. *FBIS-SOV*, May 6, 1996.

Just 58 percent of the country's coal mining capacity is being utilized, and coal cleaning plants work at just 29 percent of capacity. That means consumers must burn a poorer quality coal, which contributes to increased air pollution.

There are 242 underground and open-pit mines operating in Ukraine. Of these, some 30 percent were commissioned before World War II, and almost 50—that is, slightly more than 25 percent—were commissioned before 1917. Mining coal at old mines with obsolete equipment results in a high-cost end product. Only at 57 out of the 242 mines does the price of the coal exceed its cost of production. Yet the government has been very reluctant to raise coal prices to cost-clearing levels, for fear of political repercussions. Survival under these conditions is highly questionable without heavy subsidies.

Table 14-12
Coal Production in Ukraine, Selected Years 1976–1996

Year	Million tons
1976	218.1
1988	192
1989	179.21
1990	164.8
1991	166.6
1993	115.7
1994	94.4
1995	83.9
1996 plan	128.9
estimated	70

Sources: *Interfax-Ukraine*, Donetsk, December 21, 1995; *Finansovyye Izvestiya*, February 2, 1996; British Broadcasting Corporation, *Summary of World Broadcasts, Part 1, USSR*, April 4, 1996; *Eastern Economist*, April 22, 1996.

Only a handful of the coal mines in Ukraine can operate without subsidies. The reluctance to shut down unprofitable mining enterprises (which stems largely from the social cost), the lack of funds to replace obsolete and worn-out equipment, and the depletion of workable coal reserves almost ensure that extraction will fall even further over time.

Closing unprofitable mines is a costly process. According to estimates prepared by the Ministry of the Coal Industry, the cost of closing one mine will reach $21 million, if social benefits, retraining and employing displaced workers, and constructing new water pumping stations are included.[720] The cost of closing a mine, just by itself, probably would fall within the range of $5 to $7 million.

---

720.   *Eastern Economist*, April 22, 1996.

The coal industry was restructured on February 7, 1996, by presidential decree. State-owned joint stock companies and state holding companies were to be created on the basis of profitable coal mines.[721] These new companies are to operate independently, and coal will be sold at prices negotiated with the buyer. As many as 70 unprofitable coal mines are to be closed. This decree, which ordered the coal sector transformation by September 1, in essence creates a free market for coal in Ukraine.

Ukraine is seeking $500 million in World Bank credits for modernizing a number of its fossil-fuel power plants and in conjunction is seeking technology that will permit the burning of poor-quality coals while minimizing atmospheric pollution. About 80 plants in all, with capacities ranging between 200 to 300 Mw, are to be modernized.

The yearly demand for coal is put at about 100 million tons. This means that, given current coal extraction levels, hard-earned income has to be spent to purchase coal abroad, to balance supply and demand. Coal imports from Poland and Russia totalled some 20 million tons in 1995.[722] Imported coal often is cheaper than domestic and is of better quality. Indeed, Ukraine had become a net importer of coal by 1993, and the contribution of imported coal to total coal consumed in the country has considerably strengthened since then, to almost 20 percent in 1995. As noted, the 1996 coal extraction plan of almost 129 million tons would have covered domestic needs and eliminated imports, but was vastly optimistic in terms of past performance. Implied is a continued need for imports if domestic demand is not constrained.

Restructuring the coal industry should center on raising productivity while reducing the number of operating mines. This approach has been successful in the United States and in the United Kingdom. But closing mines raises two sensitive political issues: which mines should be closed, and how will displaced miners and their families be taken care of. Nonetheless, 14 of the 38 mines slated for immediate closure had already ceased production by the end of April 1996. Another 40 mines are to be closed over the next several years.

Ukraine continues to export small amounts of coal, largely to Western markets. Coal exports totalled approximately 2 million tons in 1995 and were scheduled to increase to 3 million tons in 1996.[723]

Coalbed Methane

Ukrainian mines are very gassy, and coalbed methane gas would appear to offer an attractive approach to partially substitute for natural gas imports. Western experts have placed Ukraine coalbed methane resources at about 60 trillion cubic feet (about 1.7 trillion cubic meters).

Several pilot projects are being put together to drill wells at selected mines, bring the coalbed methane to the surface, and use this gas to power small turbines

---

721. British Broadcasting Corporation, *Summary of World Broadcasts, Part 1 Former USSR*, February 16, 1996.

722. *Interfax-Ukraine*, Donetsk, January 29, 1996.

723. *Finansovyye Izvestiya*, February 2, 1996.

for electricity generation.[724] If these pilot projects prove feasible, then coalbed methane will be utilized to fuel cogeneration plants. At present, however, none of the gas is tapped and marketed.

Electric Power

Ukraine by no means is short of electrical power generating capacity. Electricity generating capacity in 1995 was 55 billion kw, a slight improvement over the 1985 capacity of 51.1 billion kw.[725] Some modification of nuclear power generating capacity took place in late 1996. As promised, Ukraine closed Chornobyl reactor no. 1, for a loss of 925 Mw. But this loss may be offset if plans to restart reactor no. 2 in 1997 are carried out. Nonetheless, electricity generating capacity in Ukraine at the beginning of 1997 stood at 54.1 Mw. Reactor no. 1 closure is discussed in detail below.

A considerable share of thermal generating capacity stands idle, the direct result of falling demand and rising fuel costs. Hydroelectric generating capacity is unlikely to be shut in because its generating costs are low and imported fuels are not required.

As electricity generation has fallen, it has been the facilities burning high-cost imported oil and natural gas that have been shut down. These power generating facilities quite old. Only very limited funds have been available for repairs and maintenance in recent years.

The efforts by Ukrainian authorities to secure Western support in the construction of new nuclear generating capacities (reviewed in detail below) are not based on need per se, but rather upon the desire to reduce the country's dependence upon imported crude oil and natural gas, to keep the nuclear reactor construction industry alive, to provide a social safety net for displaced workers, to pay for the construction of compensating generating capacity, and to build a new sarcophagus around destroyed reactor no. 4 at Chornobyl.

Still, the electricity consumption/GDP ratio in Ukraine is unacceptably high, almost triple the world average and even slightly higher than Russia. Tariff rates for electricity are held artificially low, below the cost of generation, which quite naturally leads to artificially high rates of consumption. This energy intensity, though currently a weakness, also represents an opportunity to gain some relief from the country's high energy import burden.

Ukraine, in privatizing its electric power sector, has chosen to sell its fossil fuel stations in clusters of four, combining both weak and strong stations. Power distribution has been in the hands of private companies since the autumn of 1995.

A $175 million credit facility has been made available to Ukraine, in return for which Ukraine committed to restructure its power market. The state-owned power monopoly would be broken up into the following parts:[726]

---

724.   Gas de France, Charbonnages de France, and Hunosa (Spain) have started to investigate developing coalbed methane in a project funded by the European Union. See *Financial Times*, December 1, 1995.

725.   *Eastern Economist*, April 1, 1996.

❏ Four already established, competing electricity generating companies will be privatized.

❏ A national electricity transmission company will be created.

❏ Twenty-seven independent, joint stock local electric companies will be formed.

❏ There was to be a competitive market for power by the end of March 1996, in which the generation companies bid to supply the local distribution companies with electricity at the lowest price.

Table 14-13
Ukraine Electricity Generating Capacity by Source, 1995

Source	Percent of Total Capacity
Fossil fuel	68
Nuclear	25
Hydro	7
Total	100

Source: CSIS Panel Report, *Nuclear Energy Safety Challenges in the Former Soviet Union* (Washington, D. C.: CSIS, 1995).

Generating capacity at nuclear power plants in 1995 represented just 25 percent of available electricity generating capacity in Ukraine, but supplied close to 37 percent of total electricity (Table 14-13). That underscores that more than a third of the fossil-fuel generating capacity is standing idle because of the combined impact of the high cost of fossil fuels and the decline in electric power requirements.

Electricity generation in Ukraine dropped by an estimated 7.3 percent in 1995 and by a further 7.4 percent in 1996, extending the decline trend which can be traced back to 1990 (Table 14-14). Since that year, generation of electric power has declined by more than 40 percent, a pace less than the drop in industrial output. Heavily subsidized tariffs and an unwillingness to cut off delinquent consumers has helped maintain electricity consumption at artificially high levels.

726.   *Congressional Record*, March 19, 1996, p. E377-378.

Table 14-14
Electric Power Production in Ukraine, Selected Years 1980–1998

Year	Billion Kwh	Index
1980	236.0	
1985	272.0	
1990	298.5	100
1991	278.7	
1992	252.5	
1993	230.0	
1994	200.8	
1995		
Plan	210	
Actual	192.1	64.4
1996 est.	178	59.6
1997–1998 plan	200	

Sources: *FBIS-SOV*, January 18, 1996; *Ukraine, An Economic Profile*, November 1992; OECD/IEA,*Electricity in European Economies in Transition* (Paris: OECD/IEA, 1994).

Ukrainian officials had been overly optimistic about 1995. Modest increases both in total electricity supply and in the amounts provided by nuclear power plants had been anticipated. Nonetheless, the financial situation of the nuclear power sector was no better, and perhaps even worse than in 1994. There were no spare parts, no funds for scheduled repairs and maintenance, and fuel was in short supply and these constraints continued throughout 1996.

Russia, however, has strongly resisted any accusations that it has failed to meet its commitments to supply Ukrainian nuclear power plants with nuclear fuel cassettes, which Ukraine has acknowledged. Ukraine was to receive 620 nuclear fuel cassettes during 1995, and all but 16 were delivered. A total of 1,800 cassettes is to be supplied to Ukraine during 1994-97, in line with an accord signed by the presidents of the United States, Russia, and Ukraine. In turn, Ukraine is to withdraw its nuclear weapons to Russia, and the United States is to fund the refinement of the enriched uranium, contained in the warheads, for subsequent use as nuclear fuel.[727] Nonetheless, acquiring fuel for its nuclear reactors has been one of the more difficult problems for the nuclear power industry.

As noted, the decline in electric power generation has been accompanied by a shift in the source of electricity. The relative importance of nuclear power has been steadily rising at the expense of power stations burning natural gas, coal, and fuel oil (Table 14-15). The shift to nuclear power was even more pronounced during 1996, as its share averaged an estimated 43.3 percent. The loss of Chornobyl reac-

---

727.   *Interfax*, Kiev, February 21, 1996.

tor no. 1 at the end of November 1996 had only a very modest impact on nuclear power generation and on total electricity supply that year.

Table 14-15
Ukrainian Electric Power by Source, 1990, 1994, and 1995

Source	Percent of Total		
	1990	1994	1995
Nuclear	25.5	34.1	36.7
Fossil fuels*	70.9	59.7	58
Hydroelectric	3.6	6.1	4
Total**	100.0	99.9	98.7

*includes power generated by small industrial plants.
**The reason that the figures for 1994 and 1995 do not add to 100 is unknown.

Sources: *Interfax-Ukraine*, Kiev, October 16, 1995; British Broadcasting Corporation, *Summary of World Broadcasts, Part 1, Former USSR*, October 13, 1995; *FBIS-SOV*, August 14, 1995.

As with most countries, the demand for electric power in Ukraine is higher during the cold winter months, when demand ranges between 560 million to 580 million kwh per day.[728] Demand drops as average temperatures rise. Electricity demand in the spring, for example, decreases to 500 million kwh. The nuclear share is equally affected by weather. For example, in August 1995, nuclear stations provided just 28.9 percent of electricity output. As the weather turns colder, the nuclear share rises.

The pattern of electricity consumption has remained essentially unchanged. The industry, transport, and construction sector is the largest consumer by far and is not surprisingly favored by low tariffs (Table 14-16).

---

728. *FBIS-SOV*, December 6, 1995.

Table 14-16
Ukrainian Electric Power Consumption, 1990 and 1995

Consumer	Percent of Total Consumption	
	1990	1995
Industry	58.1	49.6
Households	15.0	19.2
Agriculture	11.5	9.1
Municipal	10.1	14.8
Transport	5.3	7.3
Total	100.0	100.0

Source: OECD/IEA, *Energy Policies of Ukraine, 1996 Survey* (Paris: OECD/IEA, 1996).

The demand for electricity in Ukraine declined by about 43 percent during the five-year period 1991–1995, from 248.6 billion kwh to 140.8 billion kwh. There were no unexpected or dramatic shifts in the electricity use pattern. The relative shares of the heavily subsidized household, municipal, and transport sectors gained in prominence, at the expense of industry and agriculture (Table 14-16). Current exports average about 3 percent of the power generated and are directed mainly to Poland and Hungary.

Nuclear Power

There were five nuclear electric power stations in Ukraine, incorporating a total of 15 reactors at the beginning of 1996, the first of which came on line in 1978. The performance of the nuclear power sector in 1994 interrupted the past pattern of constancy, as nuclear electric power generation fell by 8.5 percent. Other performance indices also were not encouraging. Out of a total of 133 accidents, 30 resulted in reactor shutdowns. There were 112 accidents at the zero level on the international scale, and 21 at the first level. There were no accidents rated at the second or third level.

Performance improved in 1995. Nuclear power generation rose slightly (Table 14-17). Unplanned stoppages were cut in half, although there were 10 accidents rated at level one. Six of these occurred at the South Ukrainian facility, three at Zaporizhzhya, and one at Chornobyl. In two cases, at South Ukraine and at Chornobyl, the accidents caused radioactive contamination on the plant premises.[729]

The drop in Ukrainian nuclear electricity generation in 1994 paralleled the drop in Russia, and for the same reasons: shortages of cash kept reactors down for repairs and maintenance longer than the scheduled norm; and Ukraine was unable to purchase all the fuel rods it needed, which meant reduced operating capacity for

729.   British Broadcasting Corporation, *Summary of World Broadcasts, Part 1, Former USSR,* January 19, 1996.

the reactors. Moreover, there were complaints that the fuel rods supplied by Russia were of poor quality, which further reduced output.

Reactors stood idle not only because of equipment failures and a lack of funds with which to carry out immediate repairs and maintenance, but also because the reactors did not meet certain safety requirements which had to be resolved before they could return to operation. Extended down time was the result. In 1993, for example, the equivalent of a 1,000 Mw reactor stood idle for almost six months because of shortcomings in safety provisions.

Table 14-17
Nuclear Power Generation in Ukraine, 1990–1998

Year	Billion Kwh	Percent of Total Electricity Generated
1990	76.5	25.5
1991	75.1	26.9
1992	73.7	29.2
1993	75.2	32.7
1994	68.8	34.3
1995 plan	72	
1995 actual	70.5	36.7
1996 plan	77.6	
1996 est.	77	43.3
1997-98 plan	80.4	

Sources: *Interfax-Ukraine*, Kiev, January 13, 1996 and October 11, 1995; *FBIS-SOV*, January 18, 1996.

The estimated 10 percent increase in nuclear power generation achieved in 1996 reflects the full capacity operation of reactor no. 6 at Zaporizhzhya, which did not come on-line until late 1995 (Table 14-18). Output at Rivne is to increase just marginally, but output is to decline at Chornobyl, Khmelnitskyy, and South Ukraine. If these projected generation schedules are kept, nuclear power generation will be restored to the 1990 level. Continued inconsistency of Zaporizhzhya's operation jeopardized the 1996 goal. That nuclear facility has been plagued by a growing number of unplanned shutdowns.

Zaporizhzhya is described as the third largest nuclear power plant in the world, with 6 pressurized water reactors of 1,000 Mw each built on a single site. Officials at the facility have noted that their greatest concern is the problem of labor discipline and labor safety practices. Auxiliary personnel change frequently and there is a high turnover of operator personnel because of low wages. Efforts are being made to reduce worker turnover. Wages have been increased, employees are provided with apartments, loans, housing payments, and goods on credit. The nuclear plant has its own farming enterprise, raising cattle, and a trade outlet where goods are much cheaper than on the regular market.

There is a very real problem related to acid rain. The gas emissions from a nearby thermal power plant mingle with steam produced by the nuclear plant water cooling system. This produces acid rain. When the wind blows in the direction of the city of Enerhodar, everyone is affected. Plants die, clothing is ruined, and vehicle exteriors are damaged.[730]

It is unlikely that any new nuclear reactors will be brought on line in the coming several years. Two reactors—no.4 at Rivne and no. 2 at Khmelnitskyy—stand unfinished. Group of Seven (G-7) member-countries, through a Memorandum of Understanding with Ukraine, are to assist in financing the completion of these two reactors, but they are not expected to go on-line until after 1998.

At the same time, the relative role of nuclear power will continue to increase. The greater the role that nuclear power plays, the more difficult it will be to satisfy all Ukrainian requirements for closing Chornobyl.

Table 14-18
Nuclear Power Generation, by Facility, 1995 and 1996

Facility	Billion kwh	
	1995	**1996 Plan**
South Ukraine	16.3	15.7
Chornobyl	11.5	11.0
Zaporizhzhya	24.9	33.3
Rivne	11.2	11.3
Khmelnitsky	6.6	6.1
Total	70.5	77.6

Note: Totals may not add because of rounding.

Sources: British Broadcasting Corporation, *Summary of World Broadcasts, Part 1, Former USSR,* January 10, 1996; *Interfax-Ukraine,* Kiev, January 13, 1996.

A number of key issues relating to Ukrainian nuclear power have been identified that will affect at least the near-term future of nuclear electric power in Ukraine (these issues are presented in no particular order of priority).

❑ Nuclear power safety in Ukraine is jeopardized, just as it is in Russia, by the absence of a nuclear regulatory agency embodied with sufficient resources and sufficient authority to independently oversee the nuclear power industry. President Kuchma has decreed the folding of the Ukrainian Committee for Nuclear and Radiation safety into a new Ministry of Environmental Protection. Whether this will improve or weaken oversight is not yet clear.

---

730.   *FBIS-SOV,* August 1, 1996.

☐ The West has continued to focus its efforts on securing the closure of Chornobyl, although some are convinced that the deterioration of the sarcophagus, which entombs the destroyed reactor no. 4 at Chornobyl, defines it as the most dangerous nuclear site in Ukraine.[731]

☐ The absence of adequate liability protection laws in effect has frozen Western private sector support of Ukrainian nuclear power industry. Little safety-enhancing equipment has been delivered, and a variety of cooperative projects remains on hold. Training of personnel continues, but that alone is not going to sufficiently relieve Western safety concerns.

☐ Ukrainian authorities interpret the desire of the West to close down Chornobyl as a means of keeping Ukraine a nuclear-free state. RBMK-1000 or Chornobyl-type reactors are dual- purpose in that these reactors may also be used for producing weapons-grade plutonium.

☐ Ukrainian authorities have difficulty understanding the apparent lack of concern by the West over the 11 Chornobyl-type reactors currently operating in Russia. Why seek closure just of Chornobyl, and not Kursk or Smolensk, they ask, both of which are located in the Dnieper Basin and both of which are equipped with RBMK-1000 (Chornobyl-type) reactors?

☐ There is a shortage of space for storing spent nuclear fuels, and there may be forced closure of certain reactors if Russia is not willing to accept the spent fuel.

☐ Ukraine fears that once Chornobyl has been shut down, international donors will turn their attention elsewhere, leaving Ukraine to cope with the deteriorating sarcophagus and with nuclear waste disposal.

☐ More than 8,500 of the best nuclear specialists have left for higher-paying positions in Russia during the past two years, according to complaints by Mikhail Umanets, Chairman, State Committee for Nuclear Power. Many of these operators were ethnic Russians and had been trained in Moscow. This dilution of experienced staff can only lead to a higher incidence of operator errors. Moreover, the high turnover rate, coupled with the much-discussed prospect of closing Chornobyl, affects worker morale and reduces safety awareness.

A new corporation, UkrEnerghoAtom, was formed in August 1996 to sell electric power generated by Ukrainian nuclear power plants. This new organization

---

731.   Chornobyl-type reactors lack a containment structure to act as a barrier against large releases of radiation in the event of an accident. To "shut down" a nuclear power facility means taking the reactor off line and placing it in a safe position. To "close down" a nuclear power facility means decommissioning, cleaning up, and restoring the site. By definition then, closure is far more expensive and far more time-consuming. Unfortunately, these two terms are often used interchangeably.

will have no responsibility for the stations themselves. Nuclear plants in turn expect that the new corporation will allow them to bypass the Energy Ministry, to sell their power directly, with payments coming back to them directly.[732] But it also allows the government to strengthen its monopoly on nuclear power generation, sales, and prices. Previously, these stations were financially separate. The new firm will also manage all foreign aid for shutting down Chornobyl.[733]

Yet this new company has shown little promise to date in rectifying consumer arrears.

Consumer arrears to nuclear power stations in Ukraine reached about 1.4 billion hryvnyas by the end of 1996. The backlog of payments has been building since 1992, and is still growing. A reported 30 percent of the nuclear power output went unpaid in 1996 and no more than 5 to 6 percent is paid in cash. As a result nuclear power stations can do no more than maintain existing safety standards; they cannot improve upon them. Moreover, workers are still owed by 38 million hryvnyas.[734]

Chornobyl

Discussion of nuclear power in Ukraine and often in the former Soviet Union usually begins and ends with reference to Chornobyl, the accident at reactor no. 4 in April 1986, and its lasting impact.[735] The official death toll from the accident stands at 31, but others have placed the loss in the tens of thousands. Nor has it been officially established just how much nuclear fuel still remains in the sarcophagus entombing reactor no. 4.

The West has taken the stand that Chornobyl, because of its inherent safety problems, must be shut down as soon as possible.[736] Ukraine replies that the continued operation of Chornobyl—one of the five operating nuclear power plants in the country (Table 14-19)—is essential to Ukraine's supply of electricity and that equivalent generating capacity would have to be in place before Chornobyl can be taken out of operation. Moreover, Ukrainian nuclear reactors are now perfectly safe, so the argument goes, after a reported $320 million has been spent on safety upgrades.[737]

Whether Ukraine needs any new electric power generating units is questionable. Recognized authorities say no, at least not before 2010. That is, current gen-

---

732.   *FBIS-SOV*, August 30, 1996.

733.   Open Media Research Institute, *Daily Report*, October 22, 1996.

734.   British Broadcasting Corporation, *Summary of World Broadcasts, Part 1, Former USSR*, January 3, 1997.

735.   For a review of the accident at Chornobyl, see Robert E. Ebel, *Chornobyl and Its Aftermath: A Chronology of Events* (CSIS: Washington, 1994).

736.   Interestingly, French and German officials now acknowledge that the intense political and media pressure applied after 1986 to shut Chornobyl may even have been detrimental to its safety. Adolf Birkhofer, director of Gesellschaft fuer Anlagen-und Reaktorsicherheit mbH (Germany), is quoted as saying that the "attempt to close the plant led to safety problems because it delayed implementation of technical improvements and international programs." See *Nucleonics Week*, January 16, 1996.

737.   *Eastern Economist*, March 4, 1996.

erating capacity will be sufficient if

❑   fossil fuels are readily available,

❑   operating thermal power plants are reconstructed to the extent required,

❑   nuclear power plants continue operations, and

❑   electricity tariffs are set free.

Reactor no. 4 at the Chornobyl nuclear power plant exploded at 0123 hours on April 26, 1986, causing the first recorded major release of radionuclides into the atmosphere from an operating nuclear power facility. The accident at reactor no. 4 was caused by a combination of design faults and human operating errors. The major part of the radionuclides release occurred over a period of about 10 days.

Boris Hudyma, Ukraine's deputy permanent representative at the United Nations, summed up the full impact of the Chornobyl accident by stating that "(i)n Ukraine, the health of more than 3.3 million people was affected by the radiation. In more than 2,000 populated areas on the territory affected by the aftermath, more than 2.5 million people, including 500,000 children, continue to reside."[738] A reported 13.7 percent of Ukraine's state budget expenditures in 1994 was directed to Chornobyl cleanup operations,[739] a level that fell off to 4.9 percent in 1995. Mr. Hudyma however did not reference in his reported remarks the number of deaths that could be attributed to the Chornobyl accident.

The radioactive fallout has been especially damaging to the land. Reportedly, 12 percent of Ukraine's agricultural land and 40 percent of its woodlands have been affected by various levels of radioactive contamination.[740]

Radioactivity levels around Chornobyl remain unacceptably high and the surrounding population must be resettled elsewhere. At least 5,500 families, including 1,100 families with children, still live within the area of mandatory resettlement.[741]

Ukraine, unable by itself to resolve those issues related to the accident at Chornobyl, has worked hard to "internationalize" the consequences. The message put forward has been that the accident was a lesson for the world as a whole, and therefore the world should share in clearing up its aftermath. "Don't forget," admonished Ukraine President Leonid Kuchma, "that the Ukraine is not to blame for Chornobyl. It was the fault of the Soviet Union."[742] Ukraine has held itself blameless and because of that can stand firm on its demands to the G-7.[743]

---

738.   A fund had been established to assist those who had suffered following the accident at Chornobyl. Assistance included varying levels of compensation, the granting of early pensions, and special medical care. The Ukrainian Chornobyl Fund, established in 1991, has claimed that the government has diverted the equivalent of $60 million away from this fund to help out cash- short government programs. See *Financial Times*, January 24, 1996.

739.   *Washington Post*, February 29, 1996.

740.   *FBIS-SOV*, August 29, 1995.

741.   *Interfax-Ukraine*, Kiev, December 8, 1995.

742.   *Reuters*, London, December 14, 1995.

Table 14-19
Nuclear Power Plants in Operation in Ukraine, End 1996

Site	No. of Reactors*	Capacity (Mw)**
Chornobyl	1	925
Khmelnitskyy	1	950
Rivne	3	1,695
South Ukraine	3	2,850
Zaporizhzhya	6	5,700
Total	15	12,120

*Only Chornobyl is equipped with RBMK-1000 reactors. Reactor no. 4 was destroyed by an explosion in April 1986. Reactor no. 2 has been shut down following a fire in 1991. Reactor no. 1 was shut down in November 1996. Khmelnitskyy, South Ukraine, and Zaporizhzhya are equipped with VVER-1000 reactors, while Rivne has two VVER 400 Model V213 reactors and one VVER 1000 reactor.

**Net.

Chornobyl is not the largest nuclear power plant in Ukraine. In terms of capacity it is outranked by Zaporizhzhya and South Ukraine. Zaporizhzhya reactor no. 6 came on line in October 1995,[744] further solidifying this station's no. 1 ranking.[745] Unfortunately, Zaporizhzhya also has the poorest safety record of Ukraine's five nuclear power stations.[746]

The Ukrainian government has played political hardball with the West in terms of negotiating conditions under which Chornobyl would be shut down. After all, Ukraine has very few points of leverage left. One is Chornobyl and the desire by the West to see this nuclear facility closed. It should be expected that this point of leverage will not be easily traded away.

There has been considerable Western interest in helping out the Ukrainian nuclear power industry in general, and Chornobyl in particular. Part of this interest reflects the search for new business by vendors; part of the interest reflects the conviction that another nuclear accident in Ukraine (or in the former Soviet Union) on the scale of Chornobyl would drastically curtail if not foreclose at least the near-term future for nuclear power worldwide.[747]

Ukraine is finding it difficult to cope with the financial impact of the Chornobyl accident, let alone the psychological implications. Another accident might well destabilize the country, and an unstable Ukraine serves the interests of no one. Nonetheless, funding made available by the West has not yet been proportionate to

743.   Members of the G-7 include the United States, the United Kingdom, Italy, Japan, Canada, Germany, and France.

744.   British Broadcasting Corporation, *Summary of World Broadcasts, Part 1, Former USSR*, October 26, 1995.

745.   Not only is Zaporizhzhya the largest nuclear power plant in Ukraine, it is the largest in Europe and the third largest in the world.

746.   Open Media Research Institute, *Daily Report*, December 6, 1995.

the degree of concern shown over the continued operation of Chornobyl or over the instability of the sarcophagus entombing reactor no. 4.

The G-7 Memorandum of Understanding

Ukraine initially had put a very high price tag on Chornobyl. When President Kuchma met with President Clinton in November 1994, he sought:

❑ $1.5 billion to decommission Chornobyl,

❑ $2 billion to complete three unfinished reactors, and

❑ $3 billion to build 2 new reactors near Chornobyl.

❑ Ukraine would cover up to $6 billion in other costs associated with closing Chornobyl, including construction of a second sarcophagus.

❑ Chornobyl closure would come only after the new reactors have gone on-line. Moreover, work on restoring the fire-damaged no. 2 reactor would continue.

President Kuchma's "complex" solution to Chornobyl was presented to a combined European Union and G-7 delegation in April 1995. As part of this solution, President Kuchma proposed shutting down Chornobyl by 2000, if three conditions were met:

❑ Compensating electric power generating capacity was provided.

❑ A new covering was built over the sarcophagus entombing the destroyed no. 4 reactor at Chornobyl.

❑ A social safety net was provided for displaced Chornobyl workers.

Kuchma placed the cost of this proposal at $4.5 billion, to be shared equitably between the European Union member-countries, three of the G-7 members, and Ukraine itself. The proposal in itself was little more than a basis for beginning negotiations. Far too many questions had been left unanswered.

Subsequently, Ukraine sent to the June 1995 Halifax meeting of the G-7 a document that contained a series of proposals for replacing the power generating capacities at Chornobyl.[748] Ukraine asked for a total of $4.5 billion from the West. Of that, $2 billion would cover constructing a gas-fired thermal power plant near Chornobyl. The remainder would be used to build a new sarcophagus, to decommission Chornobyl, and to provide a social safety net for displaced employees. The

---

747.   President Reagan had been much affected by what had happened at Chornobyl, so writes General Colin Powell. "If an accident in a Soviet nuclear power plant could spread radioactive poison over so much of the globe, what would nuclear weapons do? The president had learned that the name Chornobyl derived from a Russian word meaning "wormwood." Because of wormwood's harsh taste, the plant is mentioned in the Bible as a symbol for bitterness. The President's train of thought ran from Chornobyl, to rancor, to Armageddon. He told us that what had happened in that city was a biblical warning to mankind." See Colin Powell, *An American Journey* (New York: Random House, 1995).

748.   *FBIS-SOV*, July 28, 1995.

West would also have to compensate Ukraine over a 10-year period for the difference between the prices of Russian natural gas, to be burned by this new power plant, and Russian nuclear fuel.

Importantly, Ukraine wanted the West to commit to grants, not loans, to cover the costs of closing Chornobyl.

Letters sent by Ukrainian president Kuchma in August 1995 to leaders of the G-7 countries contained proposals leading to further cooperation in resolving the Chornobyl problem. Concern was also expressed over the absence on the part of the G-7 of specific steps connected with Chornobyl decommissioning.[749]

Following months of meetings and extended discussions, much of which was highly tendentious, the G-7 countries and the European Union signed on December 20, 1995, in Ottawa a Memorandum of Understanding (MOU) with Ukraine to implement a comprehensive program to support the closure of Chornobyl. The MOU built upon the statement of Ukrainian President Leonid Kuchma of April 13, 1995, and his letter to the G-7 of August 8, 1995.

The MOU defines four separate areas for action.[750]

❑ power sector reforms,

❑ least-cost power supply and efficiency investments to meet national power demand,

❑ nuclear safety issues associated with Chornobyl decommissioning, and

❑ the social impact of closing Chornobyl.

A financial package was also agreed, which includes $498 million in grants and $1,809 million in financing from the international community. But this package relates in large part to projected investments by international lending institutions and also includes about $490 million in EURATOM[751] loans, which had been offered at the 1994 G-7 summit in Naples. The $498 million in grants represents a firm commitment by the G-7.

At the same time, Ukrainian in-kind and financial contributions to the Chornobyl closure program are to be defined as individual projects are developed. This stipulation, along with the fact that the MOU does not make clear just what the G-7 expected from Ukraine, that it does not include any reference to the sarcophagus, and that the closure date is vague (perhaps deliberately), all detract from the value of the MOU.

The G-7 financial contribution subsequently was improved somewhat, to $2.6 billion in credit lines and $514 million in grants. When the G-7 met in Moscow on April 19-20, 1996, in a mini-summit to discuss nuclear safety, the G-7 financial

---

749.   *FBIS-SOV*, September 6, 1995.

750.   *Memorandum of Understanding Between the Governments of the G-7 Countries and the Commission of the European Communities and the Government of Ukraine on the Closure of the Chornobyl Nuclear Power Plant.* Signed in Ottawa, Canada on December 20, 1995. See also the accompanying *Fact Sheet on Chornobyl Closure*.

751.   European Union Atomic Energy Committee. Membership includes Belgium, Great Britain, Denmark, France, Germany, Greece, Ireland, Italy, Luxembourg, the Netherlands, Portugal, and Spain.

commitment to Ukraine regarding Chornobyl was reaffirmed. Equally important for Ukraine, the issue of the sarcophagus was included in a joint statement released by the G-7 and Russia.[752] A study funded by the European Union on the state of the sarcophagus is under way and is to be completed by the end of 1996. At that time, a decision will be taken as what should be done.[753]

Ukraine President Kuchma, present at those discussions dealing with Chornobyl, subsequently told French President Jacques Chirac during a private discussion that Chornobyl reactor no. 1 would be shut down by the end of 1996.[754]

The larger portion of the financial package—about $1.8 billion—is for the so-called energy investment program, that is, for the construction of compensating generating capacity. Compensating generating capacity is to be found in the completion of unfinished reactors at the Rivne and Khmelnitsky nuclear power plants (Table 14-20). Reactor no. 4 at Rivne and no. 2 at Khmelnitsky are in various stages of construction.[755] Construction had been stopped in 1991 following a moratorium announced by the Ukrainian parliament. This moratorium was lifted in autumn 1993, but a shortage of funds has prevented completion. Ukrainian specialists believe that completing the unfinished reactors at Rivne and Khmelnitskyy would cost between $840 to $850 million.

Ukraine is also resisting the G-7 requirement that it sign the Vienna Convention on Nuclear Liability.[756] Before the G-7 is willing to actually deliver the funds

---

752.   Following is the full text of the G-7 joint statement on Ukraine. See *FBIS-SOV*, April 23, 1996.

"On April 20, we had a meeting with Ukrainian President Leonid Kuchma and jointly reviewed a wide range of questions involved in raising the level of nuclear safety. We agreed to continue our bilateral and multilateral cooperation with Ukraine in this field.

"President Kuchma declared Ukraine's support for the Programme of Prevention and Combating Illegal Trade in Nuclear Material and expressed readiness to support the aims and actions set out in the Moscow summit's declaration on nuclear safety. President Kuchma also supported the declaration on a comprehensive nuclear test ban treaty.

"The summit recognized the importance of President Kuchma's decision to shut down the Chornobyl nuclear power plant by the year 2000 in accordance with the Memorandum of Understanding signed on December 20, 1995 in its entirety.

"The states that signed the memorandum confirmed their commitment to its complete implementation. They will cooperate closely with Ukraine and international development banks in drawing up measures to support Ukraine's decision. For his part, President Kuchma reiterated Ukraine's readiness to cooperate actively and effectively within the context of the memorandum.

"We also discussed current EU-funded research into work on the sarcophagus covering the no. 4 reactor at Chornobyl. This research needs to be completed as quickly as possible, before the end of the year. We agreed that once this research is complete, a decision must be taken so that a solution can be found to this problem."

753.   An international consortium has come forward with its own proposals for shutting down Chornobyl, decommissioning Chornobyl reactors nos. 1,2, and 3, sealing reactor no. 4, and dealing with the matter of radioactive waste. Members of the consortium include SGN/Eurisys (a French state-owned company), AEA Technology (UK), EWN (Germany), JGC (Japan), Canatom (Canada, and Fluor Daniel (United States). Funding is now being sought. See *Financial Times*, June 14, 1996.

754.   *FBIS-SOV*, April 22, 1996.

755.   *Interfax-Ukraine*, Kiev, October 31, 1995.

756.   *FBIS-SOV*, June 5, 1996.

needed to complete Rivne and Khmelnitsky, it must be convinced that these reactors will be sound in terms of technology and safety.[757] If so, funds could be made available by mid-1997.

Table 14-20
Uncompleted Nuclear Reactors in Ukraine

Site	No. of Reactors	Completion Status
Khmelnitskyy	1	88 percent
	2	Limited work done
Rivne	1	75 percent
Note: All are VVER 1000 reactors. A reactor stands unfinished at South Ukraine, but has been deleted from this listing because there is strong local opposition to its completion.		

The social implications of closing a nuclear power facility are enormous. The needs of the nearby worker towns are the responsibility of the employer, just as they are for any large industrial employer in the former Soviet Union. The closure of Chornobyl will affect 5,000 workers at the nuclear facility and the 30,000 inhabitants of Slavutich.[758]

Ukrainian officials continued to emphasize Chornobyl's contribution to national electricity supply. In 1995, Chornobyl provided 6 percent of total electricity generated and accounted for about one-sixth of the nuclear contribution. Hardliners emphasize that the stoppage of Chornobyl would mean the collapse of Ukraine's power grid—a questionable assertion. The Ukrainian "spin" on Chornobyl is to put the facility in the best possible light so as to extract the maximum possible price from the West for its closure.

The financing package, as noted, consists of grants (21.6 percent) and loans (78.4 percent). The grants will be utilized to finance "nonprofit" programs, including decommissioning of Chornobyl, the social consequences of closure, safety improvement at reactor no. 3, restructuring the energy sector, and addressing the problems of the deteriorating sarcophagus.

Profit-making projects relate to the completion of Rivne no. 4 and Khmelnitskyy no. 2 reactors, reconstructing thermal power plants, building the Dniester hydroelectric pumped storage power plant, and controlling consumption.

---

757. British Broadcasting Corporation, *Summary of World Broadcasts, Part 1, Former USSR,* June 13, 1996.

758. Workers at the Southern Ukraine nuclear power plant live in the town of Pivden-noukrayinsk, population 42,000. Everything within the town except for schools is provided by South Ukraine: housing, all children's institutions, roads, communications, and the like. Land is cultivated, cows provide milk, pigs are raised for meat, and hothouses are operated for year-around vegetable growing. If South Ukraine were to close, for whatever the reason, all this support would be lost. Who could step in and assume funding of these support activities? No one. See *FBIS-SOV,* August 4, 1995.

A precautionary note must be sounded.

❑ The MOU is not legally binding.[759]

❑ Closure of Chornobyl before 2000 is fully contingent upon the financial aid becoming available, an important point for Ukraine.

❑ A definite closure date was omitted,[760] at least in the judgment of Ukraine.[761]

❑ The matter of resolving the deteriorating sarcophagus was left rather vague.

❑ The measure of Ukrainian contribution to Chornobyl closure was left equally vague. The MOU says only that Ukraine is to contribute as much as its resources and economy allow.

From the Ukrainian perspective what to do with the radioactive waste in the Chornobyl zone requires immediate attention. Reportedly, about 95 percent of all Ukrainian radioactive waste is found in this zone, and that includes waste associated with destroyed reactor no. 4 and about 800 radioactive waste repositories or sepulchers.[762]

Finally, the MOU falls well short of providing the $4.5 billion that Ukraine had defined as the cost of Chornobyl closure. And that sum, to Ukrainian concern, does not compensate for the loss of profits when Chornobyl is shut down. Chornobyl today earns up to $300 million in profits annually, Ukrainian experts point out. Further, considering the expected operating life of the facility, the total lost profit could reach $4 to $5 billion.[763]

Ukraine has been quick to complain that the MOU has no provision for financing decommissioning, dismantling, waste management, and cleanup work, let alone addressing the deteriorating sarcophagus entombing destroyed reactor no. 4.[764] That complaint is echoed by a group of five major international engineering companies, which have proposed a plan to manage the shutdown and cleanup of Chornobyl.

Whatever Happened to Demand-Side Management?

When growth in energy demand threatens to outrun energy supply, nations instinctively look for ways to increase production or imports to cover the gap. Little atten-

759. This point was stressed by Minister of Environment and Nuclear Safety Yuri Kostenko. See *Interfax-Ukraine*, Kiev, December 15, 1995.

760. Yuri Kostenko, Minister of Environment and Nuclear Safety, described the year 2000 as not a Ukrainian commitment but rather a common goal for Ukraine and the G-7. See *Interfax-Ukraine*, Kiev, December 8, 1995.

761. To the contrary, the G-7 would point out that the MOU clearly states that, upon fulfillment of certain conditions by G-7 members, Chornobyl will be closed by the year 2000. See *Nucleonics Week*, February 15, 1996.

762. *FBIS-SOV*, January 11, 1996. These sepulchers or repositories are for temporary radioactive waste product storage.

763. *Izvestiya*, February 15, 1996.

764. The cost of a new sarcophagus has been estimated to be between $1.1 to 1.5 billion. See *Nucleonics Week*, March 21, 1996.

tion is given actions or programs which would improve the effectiveness of energy utilization. That usually means higher prices to consumers through a combination of reduced subsidies and higher taxes. Politically, it is much less risky to attempt to increase supply than it is to constrain demand.

None of the proposals put forward by Ukraine on the matter of Chornobyl closure involve demand management but instead focus on creating compensating capacity—that is, power generating capacity sufficient at least to offset the loss of the two operating Chornobyl reactors.

The EBRD understood that demand side management has a place, but was not successful in securing G-7 support. The G-7 proposals, while characterized as calling for a "reform of Ukrainian energy industry," had more to do with completing unfinished nuclear reactors and reconstructing existing thermal power plants and less to do with a true reform of the electric power sector.

Fuel use in Ukraine is very inefficient. The amounts of fuel consumed just to heat homes is double that of the United States, reflecting poor construction and inadequate insulation, as well as an absence of meters and no incentive to conserve. About 30 percent of the water supplied to homes and public buildings is either used inefficiently or simply wasted. Almost 40 percent of the heat generated at central heating stations is lost in transportation to the consumer.[765]

It is not that Ukraine ignores the benefits of a successful energy conservation policy. On the contrary, a three-stage program has been worked out for the years leading up to 2010. The first stage, to be completed by 1997, does not call for any new investment. Instead, a savings of 15 percent is to be secured by "reorganizing existing resources."[766]

The second stage, covering the period 1998–2000, is to focus on improving the efficiency of existing technology. An energy savings of 15 to 20 percent is projected.

The third and final stage is based on savings flowing from a restructuring of the economy. Such savings are projected to reach 30 percent in terms of demand for fuel. An investment on the order of $6 billion will be required to support this program, but financial investment in energy conservation is three to five times more effective than investing, for example, in additional electricity generating capacity.[767]

The Sarcophagus

Certain expert opinion holds that the sarcophagus entombing reactor no. 4 is the most dangerous nuclear point in Ukraine.[768] The main danger is that the radioactive

---

765.   *Eastern Economist*, April 15, 1996.

766.   Ibid.

767.   So said Mykhailo Kovalko, Chair, Energy Conservation Committee, Ukrainian Union of Industrialists and Entrepreneurs. See *Eastern Economist*, April 15, 1996.

768.   During the debate between Ukraine and the G-7 on closing Chornobyl, Ukrainian President Kuchma sought to expedite matters and to secure a more acceptable response from the G-7 by underscoring the danger of a deteriorating sarcophagus. "Each year the danger grows, the cracks in the sarcophagus widen and the ground water rises," he said. "It poses a grave danger not just for Ukraine but for Europe and the world." See *Financial Times*, November 25, 1995.

dust might escape from within the sarcophagus during storm winds or an earth-quake, from a spontaneous chain reaction, or from another such cataclysm.[769] Nei-ther should the possibility be ignored that solid or liquid phase radioactivity might escape into the groundwater or the catchment area of the Pripyat River. Worst of all, however, no one knows for certain where the fuel-containing masses are within the sarcophagus.[770]

A study undertaken two years ago by the All-Ukrainian Scientific Institute for Construction Materials concluded that there was a 70-80 percent chance the sar-cophagus would collapse within 10 years. But with donor nations limited in their desire or capacity to provide funds for Chornobyl, the more pragmatic approach has been to concentrate on improving safety at operating reactors.

A consortium of European companies (the Alliance) investigated the status of the sarcophagus. Their July 1995 study noted that leaking nuclear waste trapped inside was already polluting local ground water.[771] This consortium proposed replacing the sarcophagus, at a cost of $1.6 billion. The study, funded by the Euro-pean Union, appears to support construction of a second sarcophagus around the first, which would then be dismantled.

The prospect of a second disaster at Chornobyl is unacceptably high. The Alli-ance found that pillars supporting a building sited between reactors no. 3 and 4 are in imminent danger of collapsing, which could send debris through the sarcopha-gus or into operating reactor no. 3. In either event, radioactivity would again be released into the atmosphere.

As noted above, the G-7 has agreed to study the sarcophagus and to determine how the risks associated with its deteriorating condition might be eliminated. The truth is, as Ukrainian officials admit, how much nuclear fuel remains in the sar-cophagus is not known, nor is there agreement as to how long the present covering might last. However, large amounts of radioactive waste have accumulated around the sarcophagus and underneath it, which threaten to contaminate underground waters.[772]

Nuclear's Future

Despite those constraints identified above, the Ukrainian nuclear electric power

---

769.   So said Valentin Kukpnyy, deputy managing director of Chornobyl. See *FBIS-SOV*, December 1, 1995.

770.   Alexander Sich, then a doctoral candidate from M.I.T., spent 18 months in Ukraine studying the sarcophagus, and reached the following conclusions:

> 1) The accident at Chornobyl released more than 185 million curies into the atmo-sphere, an amount 4 to 5 times higher than the Soviet estimate.

> 2) Attempts to put out the reactor core fire by dumping lead, sand, and boron from helicopters were futile. Most pilots missed the reactor and may have been directed to the wrong target.

771.   *Financial Times*, October 18, 1995. Members of the Alliance consortium are Campe-non Bernard, Bouygues, and SGN (all of France), AEA Technology and Taywood Engineering (both UK) and Walter Bau (Germany).

772.   *FBIS-SOV*, April 24, 1996.

sector has laid out for itself a 10-year modernization program which is expected to start in 1997.[773] Under this program, the oldest reactors could be shut down after the year 2011, or they could remain in service longer if feasible. In other words, no options are being foreclosed.

☐ Khmelnitskyy no. 2 and Rivne no. 4 would begin operations by the year 2000, providing an additional 12 billion kwh per year. The G-7 has been applying pressure on the EBRD to play a lead role in financing the cost of completion of these two reactors, estimated at $1 billion. The EBRD in turn has said that it could fund completion but only if shown to be part of the least cost option of meeting Ukraine's energy needs. An analysis, funded by the European Union and the U.S., is to determine whether completing the two reactors to "internationally recognized safety standards" was "economically justified."[774]

☐ Reactors no. 3 and no. 4 at Khmelnitskyy are less than 20 percent finished, and a decision to complete them is being reviewed.

The National Energy Plan, confirmed in May 1996, calls for nuclear power to provide 40 percent of electricity generated in the year 2010. Total power generation is to remain stable, as conservation efforts are presumed to be successful in containing consumption. There would be 17 to 18 gigawatts of nuclear generating capacity available that year, as compared with the present day total of 12.1 gigawatts (a gigawatt is 1,000 Mw). However, much of the currently operating generating capacity will have been decommissioned by that time, so it is urgent to begin working now on replacement capacity.[775] An international tender, to select the type of reactor to be used in the next generation of nuclear power plants to be commissioned by 2010, is planned in about two years.

Ukrainian and G-7 experts have agreed that the first stage would be the structural stabilization of the sarcophagus. The second stage calls for the construction of facilities for processing and burying the nuclear fuel waste. The top priority at the present is the removal of the nuclear fuel remnants. Proposed construction of a second sarcophagus, covering the first, was rejected.[776] A $150 million grant from the Nuclear Safety Account of the EBRD is to largely be used to finance an interim spent fuel storage facility and another facility for treating liquid radioactive waste.

Minister for Environmental Protection and Nuclear Safety Yuri Kostenko has said that most experts agree that more than 100 tons of nuclear fuel is hidden under the sarcophagus and it is not absolutely clear where this fuel is concentrated.[777] He proposed that the question of nuclear fuel remaining in the reactor should be resolved first, in one way or another. All other programs proposed so far have only

---

773.   Comments by Viktor Chebrov, chairman of the State Committee for the Use of Nuclear Power.   See British Broadcasting Corporation, *Summary of World Broadcasts, Part 1, Former USSR*, January 3, 1997.

774.   *Financial Times*, September 5, 1996.

775.   *Nucleonics Week*, June 27, 1996.

776.   *Intel News*, October 17, 1996.

777.   *Interfax-Ukraine*, Kiev, September 24, 1996.

suggested fortifying the encasement.

In the interim Russian scientists have come up with a rather unique approach to the problem posed by the sarcophagus. Simply put, pump in hundreds of thousands of cubic meters of concrete, turning the sarcophagus into a giant "rock." This approach would take 3-4 months and would cost about $200 million. Russia repeatedly asserts that Western claims that the containment structure is unsafe are politically motivated. Western vendors, in its judgment, are just trying to discredit the technical characteristics of Russian nuclear reactors in a bid to promote their own products.

Closing Reactor No. 1, Restarting No. 2

Reactor no. 1 was stopped at 10 p.m., local time, on November 30, 1996. The prior month Chornobyl with three operating reactors had accounted for 6.2 percent of Ukrainian electric power output and one-sixth of the nuclear power total. Ukraine now has 14 operating reactors, totalling about 12,100 Mw. As a result of shutting down the no. 1 reactor, employment will have to be found elsewhere for 1,600 workers.[778]

Ukraine has indicated it would like to resume operation of the 1,000 Mw no. 2 reactor which was shut down after a fire in October 1991, in place of the no. 1 reactor now taken out of operation. Experts believe that the loss of reactor no. 1 will aggravate an already strained situation, that reactor no. 2 will be needed and could be restored within 10 months, at a cost of $65 million.[779] In late 1996 it was reported that the Ukrainian State Atomic Committee was preparing a directive to restart reactor no. 2 in late 1997.[780] Its use until the year 2000 would help finance maintenance of the shutdown first unit. But to restart no.2 would be expensive, the state does not have the necessary funds, and President Kuchma has said that there are no plans to reopen it.[781]

---

778. *FBIS-SOV*, November 30, 1996.
779. *Interfax-Ukraine*, Kiev, November 18, 1996.
780. *Interfax-Ukraine*, Kiev, November 27, 1996.
781. *The Energy Daily*, December 4, 1996.

CHAPTER 15

Conclusions and Policy Recommendations

The Soviet Union was dissolved in December 1991. In its place emerged 15 sovereign and independent nations, each with its own set of national interests, and each with its own hopes for the future but with conflicts which jeopardize that future.

One of the first steps taken by these newly independent states was to open the door to foreign investment. The investor was heavily courted for his financing capabilities and his technical know-how. There was resentment as the presence of foreign investors was taken by some as an admission of weakness. But capital was in very short supply, international lending institutions moved slowly, and loan conditions were often viewed as onerous. Tapping into private sector financing was quicker and, importantly, investment conditions in large part could defined by the host governments and not an outside authority.

Not since the early days of North Sea oil has the world oil industry experienced such a rush of excitement and anticipation as the opening of the former Soviet Union to foreign investment has engendered. The world demand for these crude oil and natural gas resources to be put into play is too great to be ignored. The West brings capital and technology to the table, the Caspian Sea and Central Asia have the reserves, but one advantage is worthless without the other.

Outside Russia, the other 14 republics of the former Soviet Union can be neatly divided into Haves and the Have-nots in terms of indigenous fuel supplies sufficient to meet local needs. The future of the Haves—Azerbaijan, Kazakstan, Turkmenistan, and Uzbekistan—centers around the common aspiration of becoming major exporters of oil and natural gas to world markets, using the income to transform their respective economies and hopefully to secure as much political freedom as circumstances permit.

The Have-nots today are dependent on Russia to supply the oil and natural gas needed to balance out supply and demand. The Have-nots must either develop their own resource base—and here geology is against them—or work out mutually advantageous trading relationships with the Haves. The financially constrained Have-nots cannot yet give any realistic consideration towards exchanging dependence on Russia for dependence on a Western supplier, who would demand world market prices and payment in dollars.

Foreign investors and host governments have been successful in identifying approaches to natural resource development that are mutually attractive and mutually beneficial. Disinterested observers may express impatience at the perceived slow pace, but in Azerbaijan and in Central Asia patience and progress go hand-in-hand. The commitments being undertaken are long-term, extending 30 years or so and the financial requirements run into the billions of dollars. No one's interests will be served by an unprepared rush to action. Nonetheless, major decisions are being made, pipelines will be built and sooner, rather than later.

The future is not far away.

In a strange turn of events, Moscow is largely responsible for a promising future for the Haves. Under centralized planning Moscow had emphasized the production of crude oil and natural gas in Western Siberia. Because Moscow had been unwilling to invest in oil and natural gas development in Azerbaijan, Kazakstan, and Turkmenistan, their resource base remains relatively untouched. It is now theirs to develop. Had this resource base been drained dry in support of a different policy, the road to economic and political independence would be much longer, and far more painful.

U.S. Policy Recommendations

As a great power the United States has interests almost everywhere. Once pipeline projects are completed and the oil begins to flow, the United States must take care not to set the Caspian Sea basin and Central Asia aside in favor of other, seemingly more urgent "issues of the moment." But even before that, a reformulation of U.S. policy is in order if these interests are to better reflect the realities of the day.

❑ *Corporate interests deserve continued support.* Ensure to the extent possible that the interests of the U.S. government and of U.S. companies in the Near Abroad continue to coincide and are mutually supportive. U.S. company interests are unlikely to change, but U.S. government interests may.

❑ *Refrain from legislating foreign policy.* Near-term gains are soon replaced by long-term disadvantage, especially for U.S. companies doing business abroad.

❑ *Revisit U.S. policy towards Iran.* Has the policy of containment been working—has it forced Iran to move away from supporting terrorism and a desire to develop a nuclear weapons capability? Has this policy resulted in a net gain for the United States? Has Russia used the political vacuum to its advantage? A frozen policy towards Iran presents the very real risk of a coming confrontation between legitimate U.S. commercial interests and U.S. foreign policy interests.

❑ *Do not downgrade the Middle East.* Tomorrow's Middle East policies will be just as important as today's. Caspian oil, even at full development, cannot act as a substitute for Persian Gulf oil. Policymakers must be persuaded of that fact. Caspian oil will add to the diversity of supply and should capture a portion of incremental world demand. Although the appearance of a new supplier is always welcome by consumers, Caspian oil may be no more politically secure than Persian Gulf oil.

❑ *Maintain the dual pipeline policy wherever possible.* Transportation diversity is important for both producer and consumer, as it supports security of supply.

❑ *Rethink U.S. policy towards Azerbaijan.* Azerbaijan suffers from the absence of an influential lobbying body in the United States. At the same time Azerbaijan stood by the United States when Iran was denied an equity position in the AIOC and when the United States pressed for two pipelines to carry AIOC early oil. Limiting U.S. assistance basically to humanitarian aid would seem to be unfair recompense.

❑ *Balance Azeri support with advocacy of construction of a crude oil pipeline through Armenia,* either as the main route for the later Azeri oil moving to the Turkish port of Ceyhan, or as a branch pipeline off a possible Baku-Georgia-Ceyhan link. Armenia, in exchange, should offer to close the Medsamor nuclear power plant. However, the unresolved dispute over Nagorno-Karabakh between Azerbaijan and Armenia effectively precludes any pipeline across Armenia.

The Role of Economic Intelligence

The Cold War has been replaced by an "economic war." In an economic war, the battle flags are carried not by armed forces but by the private sector. Should the U.S. private sector be given at least limited access to information gathered and processed by the several intelligence agencies of the government? After all, the Cold War was just that, there were no confrontations on the battlefield between the United States and the Soviet Union. Billions were spent on intelligence gathering and analysis, for strategists required the best possible assessment of the opponent's intentions, vulnerabilities, and capabilities.

Waging an economic war and waging it successfully is no different. Superior intelligence can well carry the day. Philosophically however, it is difficult for the U.S. to employ its intelligence gathering and analysis arms in the support of the private sector. Other countries certainly do, but that in itself appears not to be sufficient justification for the United States to follow suit.

The U.S. national interest is just as much at stake during an economic war as it was during the Cold War. The struggle is still for influence and power. When U.S. government interests coincide with private sector interests, justification for intelligence-sharing is easy to come by. Both parties benefit by working together. The difficult part comes when these interests do not coincide or when the interests of the U.S. government are not at stake. What then is the more prudent course of action?

Legislating Foreign Policy Is Counter-Productive

The Clinton administration cannot deliver material support to Azerbaijan because of the restraints imposed by Section 907 of the Freedom Support Act, as much as they would like to. Any meaningful changes in Section 907, in favor of Azerbaijan, are not now politically feasible. In politics as in other matters, what the United States does is far more important than what it says. At the moment, much of the U.S. support for Azerbaijan has to be verbal.

Section 907 illustrates the dangers of legislating foreign policy. Foreign policy goals may shift, sometimes imperceptibly, sometimes resulting in a sea change. But the law of the land is far less flexible. To bring about changes in legislation is a daunting task, and the Congress has a way of moving very slowly in that regard.

Mother Russia's Steel Umbilical Cord

For the energy Have-nots of the former Soviet Union, Mother Russia's steel umbilical cord has been and will continue to be the primary source of oil and natural gas supplies. There are few if any other options open to them at this time. Deliveries to the Have-nots have dramatically declined in recent years—crude oil declining by almost 80 percent since 1990 and natural gas less so, but still by 54 percent. At first glance the sharp reductions in the export of oil and natural gas may appear politically motivated, especially when noting that the sales of crude oil to the Far Abroad have roughly approximated those volumes taken away from the Near Abroad. In other words, should we presume that the reductions were deliberate in order to sustain the badly needed hard currency income earned from sales to the Far Abroad? This would be an easy assumption to make, but an assumption not supported by the available evidence.

For all practical purposes, reduced deliveries have reflected reduced requirements. Moreover, the importers today find themselves heavily in debt to Russia for oil and gas consumed, but not paid for. Had Russia been playing political hardball with these importers, exports would have been further reduced or even cut off some time ago. But Russia has found it politically prudent not to do so, for energy famines can translate very quickly into civil unrest and disturbances, occurrences which Russia very much would want to avoid at a time when its own house is not yet in full order.

Ukraine, Belarus, and Moldova are the leading importers, among the Near Abroad countries, of oil and natural gas from Russia. They also head the list in terms of arrears, with the bulk of their debts not surprisingly owed to Gazprom. All three Have-nots are key transit countries for Russian natural gas moving to markets in the Far Abroad and although Gazprom may reduce their supplies from time to time, long-term cutoffs are out of the question for that would jeopardize Gazprom's place in the valued European gas market.

Ukraine continues to be a focus of G-7 attention, but only because of the Chornobyl nuclear power plant. The G-7 wants the plant closed, and Ukraine has promised to so by the year 2000. But, complications have arisen in funding those actions promised by the G-7 in return for a Chornobyl closure. Ukraine is quite ready and willing to exploit Chornobyl to the extent it can; it has few other points of leverage in its dealings with the West.

The Baltics can be expected to benefit from their proximity to Scandinavia and energy dependency on Russia is not particularly worrisome, although all nations would prefer to be self-sufficient. A very large nuclear power station continues operating at Ignalina, in Lithuania. Operational safety is very much of concern to downwind Scandinavia which in turn has done what it can to improve plant safety.

Georgia's future, by any and all measures, will be tied to its role as a transit country—a part of the Transcaucasus corridor—for oil and perhaps natural gas from Azerbaijan and Central Asia. At the same time, nearby Armenia cannot be too hopeful about what lies ahead unless and until the Nagorno-Karabakh dispute with Azerbaijan can be settled in a mutually satisfactory way.

Of the Near Abroad countries, Kyrgyzstan and Tajikistan may face the bleakest future of all. Although each is not without some strengths—gold and other precious metals, hydropower potential, prospects for tourism—internal political and economic strife block the way.

Pipelines Or Pipedreams

The scent of oil is very intoxicating. The opening up of the former Soviet Union to foreign investment has caught the eye of the major international oil companies, for several reasons.

❑ There is nothing quite as attractive as something which in the past has been denied but which is now available.

❑ The producing potential of the energy Haves is world-class.

❑ This potential cannot be realized within an acceptable time frame without outside participation.

❑ Domestic requirements are comparatively small, and thus most of the oil to be produced will be for the export market.

But the energy Haves are all landlocked and pipeline routes must be chosen before any substantial oil and gas exploration and development can get under way. Unfortunately, most prospective routes face challenges from dissident or separatist movements. The competition for these routings is fierce, and contentious. Decisions which elsewhere would be based almost solely on commercial considerations now are fraught with political consequences, no matter the route ultimately selected.

The players in the game of pipeline politics must remind themselves from time to time that *peace can bring a pipeline but a pipeline cannot bring peace*. Some hopeful transit countries may publicly state otherwise—build a pipeline and peace will follow—but that is wishful thinking.

Because the Haves are surrounded by such divergent interests, it was accepted early on that some form of compromise would be in order if oil- and gas-related projects were to move forward. But unfortunately, at the beginning not all the interested parties fully understood what compromise really meant. Finally it was recognized that compromise really meant giving Russia a seat at the table. It was evident to all that there would be no game unless Russia was invited to play, whether in pipeline construction and operation or in resource development.

Pipeline Politics

Where can the importance of Caspian and Central Asian oil and gas be found? The answers are easily identified. Pipelines carry multiple values beyond the obvious, which is that without pipelines, development of producing capacity cannot proceed. Pipelines are a source of hard currency earnings for transit countries. Local industries benefit through the increased availability of raw materials and fuels. The need for supporting infrastructure stimulates job creation.

Caspian oil and natural gas will also offer diversity of supply to importing countries worldwide and the benefits of competition to consumers. Diversity of supply translates into security of supply, which value should not be underestimated particularly when dealing with oil, a highly politicized commodity.

Yet the dominant concern today is not economic, that is, how much crude oil and natural gas will be put into the market place, who are the likely buyers, and the impact these new supplies might have on prices. Rather, it centers on pipeline route selection.

The pursuit of influence and control has raised the stakes measurably and has overwhelmed economic arguments.

The selection of transit countries will define areas of political influence for considerable time to come and will help shape international relations as long as the pipelines remain operational. Yet a larger question remains. Is the Caspian Sea region, which by virtue of its resource potential may influence world oil at the margin in the next Century, going to be pro-Western or will it develop political attachments elsewhere?

The Game Is Just Beginning

Many liken pipeline geopolitics to a game, some even call it the "great game." Perhaps it is a game but, if so, it is a game without an end. Oil and gas flows will be enduring magnets, attracting individuals and nations alike. Operating pipelines will represent major financial and political commitments by all parties, accompanied by higher risks. There is much at stake here, and all the players know it.

Host governments will be severely tested when the oil-derived income begins to flow. U.S. national interests may be as much influenced by decisions about how best to put that income to work as by the pipeline routings and oil flows themselves. Hopefully these revenues will be employed to shore up political and economic freedom. Unfortunately, that is not always the case. Far too often this newly found wealth is followed by corruption, continued subsidies, unwise investments and massive acquisitions of military equipment.

More worrisome perhaps, oil and gas revenues make it possible for the incumbents to buy off potential internal challenges.

Building a nation's economy on the development of its natural resources may actually retard expansion just as much as it fosters it. Some think that disproportionately favored extractive industries divert a country's labor, capital, and technological resources away from other sectors that may offer the prospects of more balanced growth. Nations short of natural resources such as Japan and Korea, not lulled by easy oil income, were forced to look inward, to define those potentials which did exist, and to put those potentials to work.

Looking Ahead

In looking ahead, it is very likely that the issues of tomorrow will very much mirror those that confront us today: China, Iran, Iraq, "loose nukes," terrorism, and Cuba.

The Near Abroad requires and deserves a place on our "national interests" list, and we should take care lest other issues divert our attention for too long.

Whether the natural resource potential of the Caspian Sea Basin can effectively be brought to life remains uncertain, clouded by the continuing uncertainty of domestic and international politics. The path to follow may not always be of one's own choosing, for the actions of others often define one's destiny. The potential for greatness is a heavy burden for nations and for individuals alike. Some collapse under that burden, unable to live up to expectations, and a disappointment to themselves and to others as well. But some, for whatever reason, will rise to the occasion and make their mark in history.

Russia has not yet demonstrated that it has a viable and well-thought-out policy towards the Near Abroad. Attempting to respond to the diverse interests and diverse issues of 14 separate countries has stretched Russia's capabilities very thin, especially when so much of its time and energy has been devoted to addressing domestic problems. Little is left over for the Near Abroad.

The United States mirrors Russia in this regard, for it has had difficulty in developing a blanket policy toward the Near Abroad for many of the same reasons. Political, ethnic, economic, and geographic diversities are simply too great for any universally-applied approach, other than to support and defend their hopes for a politically independent and market-oriented future.

CHAPTER 16

Epilogue

Those countries that form the Near Abroad are in a state of transition, of change of monumental proportions. We do not know for certain how long this transition may last, nor is it clear what this transition eventually will lead to. Attempting to forecast what the future may hold for these countries, while necessary at times, would reflect our limited knowledge and understanding of the forces at work. We can, however, continue to monitor developments closely while attempting to isolate those trends which may permit a more accurate assessment at least of the past and present, and that in turn will focus our views of the future.[782]

Armenia

The United States was visibly disappointed with the conduct of the September 22, 1996 presidential election. Widespread violations and irregularities in the voting process and serious abuses and breaches of the law during the vote count were reported by neutral nongovernmental organizations monitoring the process.[783] Nonetheless, Armenia emerges as the largest per capita recipient of U.S. aid among all of the former Soviet republics.

☐ Fuel supplies continue to be constrained as the Azeri embargo remains in place. The Medsamor nuclear power plant underscored its importance to the economy as it provided 46 percent of total electric power generated in Armenia during 1996.[784]

☐ The possible construction of a pipeline carrying natural gas from Russia to Turkey, transiting Armenia, has emerged. Contemplated delivery volumes range from 3 bcm to 9 bcm annually. But Armenia's gas transport system—transmission and distribution—will have to be rebuilt, at a cost estimated at $100 million.[785]

☐ An Armenian-U.S. joint venture, the Armenian Exploration Company, plans to spend $10 million in 1997 exploring for and developing crude oil and natural gas reserves.[786]

---

782.   The preceding chapters have been based on information available through December 31, 1996. The epilogue summarizes key developments since then, to March 3, 1997.

783.   *Washington Post*, March 1, 1997.

784.   *Interfax*, Yerevan, January 8, 1997.

785.   Interfax, *Petroleum Information Agency*, Yerevan, February 20, 1997.

786.   *Interfax*, Yerevan, January 30, 1997.

Azerbaijan

The issue of the legal status of the Caspian Sea was brought to the forefront when Turkmenistan said that the Azeri oil field and part of the Chirag oil field, both under contract to the AIOC, belonged to Turkmenistan.[787] These claims were immediately rejected by Azerbaijan, who asked for a clarification. Azerbaijan then followed with a letter to the Turkmen foreign minister which said that in 1970 the former Soviet Union introduced the practice of dividing the Caspian Sea into republican sectors, including the Russian, Azerbaijani and Turkmen sectors.[788] It was subsequently reported that the Turkmen president apologized for those remarks attributed to him by the *Financial Times*.

Azeri authorities then turned the issue to their advantage by noting that the Turkmen claim was indirectly supporting Azerbaijan's view that the Caspian should be divided into national sectors.[789]

Russia then jumped in by criticizing the Turkmen claim, noting that the Caspian Sea is common property.[790] Clearly, the Turkmen claim of Azeri and part of Chirag puts it in the camp of Azerbaijan and Kazakstan in supporting national sectors and the median line principle.

❏ SOCAR rejected LUKoil's overture to participate in developing the Inam offshore oil field, replying that was capable of developing the structure by itself and that financing would come from its own resources.[791]

❏ However, there may have been other reasons for this rejection. Baku has been disappointed that LUKoil has not been successful in lobbying Moscow to ease its stand on the status of the Caspian Sea, and used this opportunity to voice their disappointment.

❏ A fifth production sharing agreement was signed on January 13, 1997 with Elf Acquitaine (France) as operator with 40 percent of the Lenkoran-Talish Deniz field. Total (France) took 10 percent, with the 25 percent balance held by SOCAR.[792] The remaining stake has not yet been allocated, but Deminex (Germany) and Daewoo (Japan) have expressed an interest.

❏ Construction of the Baku-Supsa pipeline should begin in March 1997 and is to be finished by December 1998. The AIOC has set a date for shipment of the first cargo of early oil for December 31, 1998.[793]

❏ Repairing that 150 km section of the Baku-Novorossiisk pipeline, the so-

---

787.   The *Financial Times* first broke the story in its January 23, 1997 edition when it quoted Turkmenistan president Saparmurad Niyazov as marking on a map that these fields were really theirs.

788.   *Interfax*, Baku, January 27, 1997.

789.   Interfax, *Petroleum Information Agency*, Baku, January 29, 1997.

790.   *Interfax*, Moscow, February 13, 1997.

791.   Interfax, *Petroleum Information Agency*, Baku, January 12, 1997.

792.   *Platt's Oilgram News*, January 14, 1997.

793.   *Platt's Oilgram News*, January 31, 1997.

called northern route, passing through Chechnya will cost an estimated $1.2 million. The AIOC has responsibility for shipping oil up to the Azeri-Russian border. Beyond that point and to Novorossiisk, the responsibility is Russia's.[794]

In the interim, and until the Chechnya portion is repaired, Azerbaijan will export its oil by rail via Georgia.[795] These export volumes do not originate from the AIOC fields.

Although production of crude oil by the AIOC may begin as early as August 1997, several months will be required to fill the northern pipeline, which means that exports from Novorossiisk may not be expected until near the end of the year.

The AIOC is under no particular pressure to select a route for its later oil and is considering expanding the carrying capacity of the Western route. Indeed, the Bosphorus bypass option is now being presented as cost-competitive with the proposed Baku-Georgia-Ceyhan route.[796] If true, then geopolitics will likely have the final say.

Belarus

The United States has revised its policy regarding Belarus. In particular, the Belarusian constitutional referendum of November 1996 is largely seen as invalid and undemocratic.[797] Contacts with independent media, with democratic forces and with non-governmental organizations will be stepped up.

Georgia

Georgia is now ready to move crude oil from the Tengiz oil field in Kazakstan to its Black Sea port of Batumi. Rail shipments had started in late 1996 but were halted while repairs were being made to the terminal at Dubendi. Georgian authorities have indicated that it is ready to handle an average of 20,000 b/d.[798]

Kazakstan

Chevron and LUKoil finally reached an agreement, in principle, in mid-January 1997 under which 10 percent of Chevron's 50 percent equity in the Tengizchevroil joint venture will be transferred to LUKoil.[799] No price was given and a definitive agreement is yet to be worked out. LUKoil is also negotiating with the government of Kazakstan to add to this holding. That 5 percent holding translates into a

---

794. *Interfax*, Moscow, February 18, 1997.
795. British Broadcasting Corporation, *Summary of World Broadcasts, Part 1, Former USSR*, February 21, 1997.
796. *Reuter*, Moscow, February 25, 1997, quoting AIOC spokesman Greg Rich.
797. *Interfax-West*, Minsk, February 28, 1997.
798. Interfax, *Petroleum Information Agency,* Tbilisi, January 22, 1997.
799. *Platt's Oilgram News*, January 17, 1997.

10 percent financial commitment, in as much as the private sector is responsible for funding the whole of the 50 percent government share.

The much-advertised oil swap between Kazakstan and Iran was finally getting under way in mid-January.[800] None of the crude oil involved belongs either to Chevron or Mobil, both partners in Tengizchevroil. The 10-year contract calls for 40,000 b/d the first two years, then rising in stages to 120,000 b/d.

Shipment of Kazak oil by rail through Azerbaijan and Georgia to the Black Sea port of Batumi is to be emphasized by Chevron. Use of Russian pipelines is not profitable, and if exports from Tengiz are to reach the hoped-for level of 140,000 b/d during 1997, then rail shipments will have to be stepped up, and Chevron is to spend about $200 million to that end.[801]   Yet, this route may be able to handle no more than about 12,000 b/d, considerably less than those volumes suggested by Georgia.[802] In the interim, hope is still held that the Tengiz-Novorossiisk export pipeline will be ready by late 1999 at least. By the end of 1996, Tengiz production had reached 160,000 b/d and exports during the year averaged 110,000 b/d.[803]

The anticipated access of Texaco (U.S.) to Karachaganak was announced on March 3, 1997. Texaco secured a 20 percent stake, picking up 10 percent each from British Gas and from Agip.[804] Gazprom still holds 15 percent but apparently arrangements are under way to transfer that share to LUKoil.

Turkmenistan

Despite the obvious U.S. displeasure, Turkmenistan is moving ahead to complete a natural gas pipeline to Iran by late 1997. This pipeline will supply natural gas from western Turkmenistan to Iran's gas distribution network in the northern part of the country.[805] First-year deliveries are to average 2 bcm, rising to 8 bcm in ten years' time.

Monument Oil and Gas (United Kingdom) and Mobil (U.S.) have won the exclusive right to negotiate a production sharing arrangement which would cover a 20,000 sq. km are stretching from the Cheleken Peninsula in the north to the southern border with Iran.[806]

❑ A new pipeline, to carry Turkmen natural gas through Iran to Turkey, is under discussion.[807] This pipeline purportedly would run separately from the Turkmen-Iran pipeline currently under construction.

---

800.   *Middle East Economic Survey*, January 20, 1997.
801.   *Platt's Oilgram News*, February 13, 1997.
802.   *Platt's Oilgram News*, March 3, 1997.
803.   *Journal of Commerce*, February 19, 1997.
804.   Interfax, *Petroleum Information Agency*, Almaty, March 3, 1997.
805.   *Financial Times*, January 21, 1997.
806.   Ibid.
807.   *Reuter*, Tehran, February 12, 1997.

Ukraine

General

Pervasive corruption still plagues Ukraine and deters investment, so much so that World Bank president James Wolfenson deemed it necessary to send a letter to Ukrainian president Leonid Kuchma criticizing corruption within the government.[808] In that same regard, the EBRD in mid-January 1997 delayed new private sector lending in Ukraine until the government does more to improve the investment climate.[809]

Nuclear Electric Power

Ukraine's nuclear power stations generated a total of 79.6 billion kwh during 1996, accounting for 44 percent of the country's total electricity generation, compared with 36.7 percent in 1995.[810] This increasing role for nuclear power plays to the bargaining strength of Ukraine with regard to the closure of Chornobyl and especially to the need to complete the unfinished reactors at Rivne and Khmelnitskyy.

Chornobyl

A report commissioned by the EBRD states that it would not be economic to fund the completion of two nuclear reactors at Rivne and Khmelnitskyy, that to do so would not meet the "least-cost" lending criteria of the EBRD.[811] Ukrainian reaction was immediate, as might be expected, and some western officials questioned the quality of this report. EBRD rules prohibit it from lending money to energy projects which do not meet the "least-cost" criteria. A final decision on granting funds to complete these reactors—about $1.2 billion will be needed—is to be taken by the EBRD in July 1997.[812]

808.   Open Media Research Institute, *Daily Report*, January 9, 1997.

809.   *Financial Times*, January 14, 1997.

810.   British Broadcasting Corporation, *Summary of World Broadcasts, Part 1, Former USSR*, January 24, 1997.

811.   *Financial Times*, February 10, 1997.

812.   *FBIS-SOV*, February 18, 1997.

List of Acronyms

AIOC	Azerbaijan International Operating Company
ATC	American Trade Consortium
CAOPP	Central Asian Oil Pipeline Project
CIOC	Caspian International Oil Company
CIS	Commonwealth of Independent States
CPC	Caspian Pipeline Consortium
CSC	Caspian Sea Consortium
EBRD	European Bank for Reconstruction and Development
ECU	European Currency Unit
EU	European Union
FBIS-SOV	Foreign Broadcast Information Service, Former Soviet Union
FSU	Former Soviet Union
GDP	Gross Domestic Product
IAEA	International Atomic Energy Agency
LPG	Liquefied petroleum gas
MOU	Memorandum of Understanding
NATO	North Atlantic Treaty Organization
OOC	Oman Oil Company
OPEC	Organization of Petroleum Exporting Countries
OPIC	Overseas Private Investment Corporation
PHARE	Pologne Hongrois Actions pour la Reconstruction Economique
RBMK	Reaktory Bolshoi Moshchnosti Kanalnye (high-power pressure-tube reactors)
SOCAR	State Oil Company of Azerbaijan
TCO	Tengizchevroil
TPC	Timan-Pechora Company
UN	United Nations
USSR	Union of Soviet Socialist Republics
VVER	Vodo-Vodnannoy Energeticheskiy Reactor (water-cooled, water-moderated reactor)
WEU	Western European Union

Index

Note: *m* refers to maps, *n* refers to notes, and *t* refers to tables.

A

C

H

I

J

J. P. Morgan, 117
Jalalabad refinery, 248
Japan
  economic experience of, 324–325
  and Turkmen natural gas, 137, 138*m*
Japan Petroleum Exploration Company Ltd., 99
JKX. *See* JP Kenny Exploration and Production Ltd.
Johnson & Johnson, 115
JP Kenny Exploration and Production Ltd. (JKX), 239, 286

K

Kaliningrad, port of, 180, 180*n*
  tax issues regarding, 211
Kaliningradmorneftegaz, 184*n*
KANT consortium, 184*n*
Kantor Group, 150*n*, 153*n*
Karabakh oil field, 57–58, 58*n*
Karachaganak field, 70, 79–80, 94–96
  Caspian Pipeline Consortium and, 105*n*, 108, 112*t*
  natural gas yields of, 81, 89, 95*t*
  privatization of, 84, 330
  problems of, 95–96
  production of, 94–95, 95*t*
Karachaganak-Atyrau pipeline, 87
Karadag structure, 59
Karaganda coal, 83
Karagandinskaya Two, 86
Karaktai oil field, 154
Karakuduk field, 99
Karaulbazar refinery, 152–153
Karazhanbas Oil Company, 98
Karazhanbas oil field, 98
Karazhanbasmunai, 73*t*
Karimov, Islam, 145–146
Karpattia Petroleum Corporation, 286
Kazakhgaz, 72*t*, 88
KazakhstanCaspiiShelf, 97*t*, 97–98
Kazakhstanmunaigaz, 72
Kazakmunaigaz, in Caspian Pipeline Consortium, 108, 108*t*
Kazakstan, 68*m*, 69–113. *See also* Haves
  advantages of, 2–3
  basic information on, 69*t*, 69–70
  in Caspian Pipeline Consortium, 105–107, 108*t*, 109

M

P

T